MAKING TROUBLE

SOCIAL PROBLEMS AND SOCIAL ISSUES
An Aldine de Gruyter Series of Texts and Monographs
SERIES EDITOR
Joel Best, *Southern Illinois University at Carbondale*

MAKING TROUBLE
Cultural Constructions of Crime, Deviance, and Control

Jeff Ferrell and Neil Websdale
Editors

ALDINE DE GRUYTER
New York

About the Authors

Jeff Ferrell is Professor of Criminal Justice at Northern Arizona University. He is the author of *Crimes of Style: Urban Graffiti and the Politics of Criminality,* and co-editor with Clinton R. Sanders of *Cultural Criminology* and with Mark S. Hamm of *Ethnography at the Edge: Crime, Deviance, and Field Research.* Dr. Ferrell is the recipient of the 1998 Critical Criminologist of the Year Award presented by the Critical Criminology Division of the American Society of Criminology.

Neil Websdale is Associate Professor of Criminal Justice at Northern Arizona University. He has published work on the history of policing, violence within families, the state response to domestic violence, and the media portrayal of intimate partner and stranger violence. He is the author of *Rural Woman Battering and the Justice System: An Ethnography,* which won the Academy of Criminal Justice Sciences Outstanding Book award for 1999, and *Understanding Domestic Homicide.* He is currently writing a book on child deaths.

ALDINE DE GRUYTER
A division of Walter de Gruyter, Inc.
200 Saw Mill River Road
Hawthorne, New York 10532

This publication is printed on acid free paper ∞

Library of Congress Cataloging-in-Publication Data
Making trouble : cultural constructions of crime, deviance and
    control / Jeff Ferrell and Neil Websdale, editors.
        p.   cm. — (Social problems and social issues)
    Includes bibliographical references and index.
    ISBN 0-202-30617-8 (alk. paper). — ISBN 0-202-30618-6 (pbk. :
alk. paper)
        1. Criminology.   2. Deviant behavior.   3. Criminal behavior.
    4. Crime in mass media.   5. Social control.   I. Ferrell, Jeff.
    II. Websdale, Neil.   III. Series.
    HV6001.M35   1999
    364—dc21   99-13732
                                                             CIP

Manufactured in the United States of America

10 9 8 7 6 5 4 3 2 1

To Karen: "Twenty thousand roads . . ."

JF

To Amy and the continuing tangle of matter and ghost.

NW

"There is no escape from the politics of representation"

Stuart Hall

Contents

Preface and Acknowledgments

Making Trouble reflects some interesting developments in criminology and related fields. Over the past decade or so, more and more scholars in criminology, sociology, and criminal justice have taken as their subject of study not simply the domains of crime, deviance, and social control, but instead the complex, mediated dynamics that construct the meaning of these domains. As this subtle but significant shift in subject matter has continued, a second analytic shift has also emerged: media and cultural analysis has begun to seep into the core concepts and practices of these disciplines. Thus, *Making Trouble* developed out of our work as program committee members for the 1997 meetings of the Academy of Criminal Justice Sciences, put in charge of organizing a series of sessions on "Media, Culture, and Crime." The enthusiastic response to these sessions, and to our broader invitation for submissions of research in this area, produced the fine works collected in *Making Trouble*.

We are especially pleased that these works confront critical issues in the cultural construction of crime, deviance, and control. By intention, the works that we have incorporated here address the mythic and often misleading manufacture of public images; the pervasive and differential construction of meaning along lines of gender, ethnicity, and age; the migration of imagery and meaning across real and imagined borders; the contested emergence of alternative or illicit media; and the parallel evolution of new forms of social and legal control. It is our hope that taken collectively, then, these works begin to expose the complex cultural processes and mediated politics involved in "making trouble."

Portions of Chapter 1, "Materials for Making Trouble," were adapted from Jeff Ferrell, "Cultural Criminology," *Annual Review of Sociology,* Vol. 25, 1999. We thank Annual Reviews.

In bringing this project to completion, we thank especially Chris Schubert, for her remarkable collegiality and consistently professional assistance; Joel Best, editor of Aldine de Gruyter's highly regarded Social Problems and Social Issues series; and Richard Koffler, executive editor, and the staff at Aldine de Gruyter.

I

Introduction

1

Materials for Making Trouble

JEFF FERRELL and NEIL WEBSDALE

INTRODUCTION

Making Trouble develops and expands an intellectual endeavor that can
be denoted by the shorthand term "cultural criminology"—shorthand for
a mode of analysis that embodies sensitivities to image, meaning, and representation in the study of deviance, crime, and control. This notion of
"cultural criminology" references both specific perspectives and broader
orientations that have emerged in criminology, sociology, and criminal justice over the past few years, and that inform this collection. Most specifically, "cultural criminology" represents a perspective developed by Ferrell
(1995c) and Ferrell and Sanders (1995), and likewise employed by Redhead
(1995) and others (Kane 1998a), which explores the convergence of cultural
and criminal processes in contemporary social life. More broadly, cultural
criminology references the increasing analytic attention that many criminologists now give to popular culture constructions, and especially mass
media constructions, of crime and crime control. It in turn highlights the
emergence of this general area of media and cultural inquiry as a relatively
distinct domain within criminology, as evidenced, for example, by the number of recently published collections undertaking explorations of media,
culture, and crime (Anderson and Howard 1998; Bailey and Hale 1998;
Barak 1994; Ferrell and Sanders 1995; Kidd-Hewitt and Osborne 1995;
Potter and Kappeler 1998). Most broadly, the existence of a concept such as
"cultural criminology" underscores the steady seepage in recent years of
cultural and media analysis into the traditional domains of criminological
inquiry, such that criminologists increasingly utilize this style of analysis to
explore any number of conventional criminological subjects. As this collection shows, these range across the substantive domain of criminology, from
drug use, interpersonal violence, and terrorism to policing, delinquency,
and predatory crime.

3

HISTORICAL AND THEORETICAL FRAMES

At its most basic, the sort of cultural criminology utilized in *Making Trouble* attempts to integrate the fields of criminology and cultural studies or, put differently, to import the insights of cultural studies into contemporary criminology. Given this, much contemporary scholarship in cultural criminology takes as its foundation perspectives that emerged out of the British/Birmingham school of cultural studies and the British "new criminology" (Taylor, Walton, and Young 1973) of the 1970s. The work of Hebdige (1979, 1988), Hall and Jefferson (1976), Clarke (1976), McRobbie (1980), Willis (1977, 1990), and others has attuned cultural criminologists to the subtle, situated dynamics of deviant and criminal subcultures, and to the importance of symbolism and style in shaping internal and external constructions of subcultural meaning and identity. Similarly, the work of Cohen ([1972] 1980), Cohen and Young (1973), Hall, Critcher, Jefferson, Clarke, and Roberts (1978), and others has influenced contemporary understandings of the mass media's role in constructing the reality of crime and deviance, and in generating new forms of social and legal control.

As a hybrid orientation, though, cultural criminology builds from more than a simple integration of 1970s British cultural studies into contemporary American criminology. Certainly, cultural criminologists continue to draw on the insights of contemporary cultural studies as a developing field, and on current cultural studies explorations of identity, sexuality, and social space (for example, During 1993; Grossberg, Nelson, and Treichler 1992). Moreover, with its focus on representation, image, and style, cultural criminology incorporates not only the insights of cultural studies, but the intellectual reorientation afforded by postmodernism. In place of the modernist duality of form and content and the modernist hierarchy, which proposes that form must be stripped away to get at the meaningful core of content, cultural criminology operates from the postmodern proposition that form is content, that style is substance, that meaning thus resides in presentation and re-presentation. From this view, the study of crime necessitates not simply the examination of individual criminals and criminal events, not even the straightforward examination of media "coverage" of criminals and criminal events, but rather a journey into the spectacle and carnival of crime, a walk down an infinite hall of mirrors where images created and consumed by criminals, criminal subcultures, control agents, media institutions, and audiences bounce endlessly one off the other. In this collection and elsewhere, then, cultural criminologists explore the "networks . . . of connections, contact, contiguity, feedback and generalized interface" (Baudrillard 1985:127) out of which crime and crime control are constructed, the intertextual "media loops" (Manning 1998) through which these constructions circulate, and the discursive interconnections that emerge between media institutions, crime control agents, and criminal subcultures (Kane 1998b). As part of this exploration, they in turn investigate criminal and deviant subcultures as sites of criminalization, criminal activity, and legal control, but also as "subaltern counterpublic[s] . . . where members . . . invent and circulate counterdiscourses [and] expand discursive space" (Fraser 1995:291).

Grounded as it is in the frameworks of cultural studies and postmodernism, cultural criminology is at the same time firmly rooted in sociological perspectives. Perhaps because of its emergence out of sociological criminology, though, cultural criminology has to this point drawn less on the sociology of culture than it has on other sociological orientations more closely aligned, historically, with criminology. Central among these is the interactionist tradition in the sociology of deviance and in criminology (for example, Becker 1963). In examining the mediated networks and discursive connections noted above, cultural criminologists also trace the manifold interactions through which criminals, control agents, media producers, and others collectively construct the meaning of crime. In so doing, cultural criminologists attempt to elaborate on the "symbolic" in "symbolic interaction" by highlighting the popular prevalence of mediated crime imagery, the interpersonal negotiation of style within criminal and deviant subcultures, and the emergence of larger symbolic universes within which crime takes on political meaning. These understandings of deviance, crime, and crime control as social and political constructions, and this endeavor to unravel the mediated processes through which these constructions occur, also build on more recent constructionist perspectives in sociology (for example, Best 1995). Yet while cultural criminology certainly draws on constructionist sociology, it also contributes to constructionist orientations. As many of the essays in this collection show, cultural criminological perspectives embody a sensitivity to mediated circuits of meaning other than those of the mass media. Further, they offer a spiraling postmodern sensibility, moving beyond the dualisms of crime event and media coverage, factual truth and distortion, which at times frame constructionist analyses, to a conception of multiple, interwoven constructions of crime, deviance, and control contested within a world of ceaseless intertextuality.

Finally, cultural criminology emerges in many ways out of critical traditions in sociology, criminology, and cultural studies, incorporating as it does a variety of critical perspectives on deviance, crime, and crime control. Utilizing these perspectives, cultural criminologists attempt to unravel the politics of crime as played out through mediated anticrime campaigns; through evocative cultural constructions of deviance, crime, and marginality; and through criminalized subcultures and their resistance to legal control. To the extent that it integrates interactionist, constructionist, and critical traditions in sociology, cultural criminology thus undertakes to develop what Cohen has called "a structurally and politically informed version of labeling theory" (1988:68), or what Melossi (1985) has described as a "grounded labeling theory"—that is, an analysis that accounts for the complex circuitry of mediated interaction through which the meaning of crime and deviance is constructed, attributed, and enforced. Put more simply, cultural criminology heeds Becker's classic injunction—that we "look at all the people involved in any episode of alleged deviance . . . all the parties to a situation, and their relationships" (1963:183, 199)—and includes in this collective examination those cultural relationships, those webs of contested meaning and perception, in which all parties are entangled.

In its mix of historical and theoretical foundations, cultural criminology can thus be seen to incorporate both more traditional sociological perspectives and more recently ascendant cultural studies and postmodern approaches. As such, cultural criminology likewise embodies the creative tension in which sociology and cultural studies/postmodernism often exist (for example, Becker and McCall 1990; Denzin 1992), a tension that at its best produces attentiveness to structures of power and nuances of meaning, to fixed symbolic universes and emergent codes of marginality, to the mediated expansion of legal control and the stylized undermining of legal authority—and to the inevitable confounding of these very categories in the everyday practice of deviance, crime, and control.

CONTEMPORARY AREAS OF INQUIRY

Framed by these historical and theoretical orientations, cultural criminological research and analysis, as utilized in *Making Trouble* and elsewhere, today operates within a number of overlapping areas. The first of these can be characterized by the notion of "crime and deviance as culture." A second broad area incorporates the variety of ways in which media dynamics construct the reality of deviance, crime, and crime control. A third explores the social politics of "making trouble" and the intellectual politics of cultural criminology. Finally, a fourth emerging area incorporates those substantive and analytic innovations that the essays collected in *Making Trouble* contribute to the development of cultural criminology.

Crime and Deviance as Culture

To speak of crime and deviance as culture is to acknowledge at a minimum that much of what we label criminal or deviant behavior is at the same time cultural and subcultural behavior, collectively organized around networks of symbol, ritual, and shared meaning. While this general insight is hardly a new one, cultural criminology develops it in a number of directions. Bringing a postmodern sensibility to their understanding of deviant and criminal subcultures, cultural criminologists argue that such subcultures incorporate—indeed, are defined by—elaborate conventions of argot, appearance, aesthetics, and stylized presentation of self, and thus operate as repositories of collective meaning and representation for their members. Taken into a mediated world of dislocated communication and dispersed meaning, this insight further implies that deviant and criminal subcultures may now be exploding into universes of symbolic communication that in many ways transcend time and space. For computer hackers, graffiti writers, drug runners, and others, a mix of widespread spatial dislocation and precise normative organization implies subcultures defined less by face-to-face interaction than by shared, if secondhand, symbolic codes (Gelder and Thornton 1997:473–550).

Understandably, then, much research in this area of cultural criminology has focused on the dispersed dynamics of subcultural style. Following from Hebdige's (1979) classic exploration of "subculture: the meaning of style," cultural criminologists have investigated style as shaping both the internal characteristics of deviant and criminal subcultures and external constructions of them. Miller (1995), for example, has documented the many ways in which gang symbolism and style exist as the medium of meaning for both street gang members and the probation officers who attempt to control them. Reading gang styles as emblematic of gang immersion and gang defiance, enforcing court orders prohibiting gang clothing, confiscating gang paraphernalia, and displaying their confiscated collections on their own office walls, the probation officers in Miller's study construct the meanings of gang style as surely as do the gang members themselves. Likewise, Ferrell (1995a, 1996) has shown how contemporary hip hop graffiti exists essentially as a "crime of style" for graffiti writers, who operate and evaluate one another within complex stylistic and symbolic conventions, but also as a crime of style for media institutions and legal and political authorities, who perceive graffiti as violating the "aesthetics of authority" essential to their ongoing power and control. More broadly, Ferrell has explored style as "that most delicate but resilient of connecting tissues between cultural and criminal practices" (1995b:169), and examined the ways in which subcultural style shapes not only aesthetic communities, but official and unofficial reactions to subcultural identity. Finally, Lyng and Bracey (1995) have documented the multiply ironic process by which the style of the outlaw biker subculture came first to signify class-based cultural resistance, next to elicit the sorts of media reactions and legal controls that in fact amplified and confirmed its meaning, and finally to be appropriated and commodified in such a way as to void its political potential. Significantly, these and other studies (for example, Cosgrove 1984) demonstrate that the importance of illicit style resides not simply within the dynamics of deviant or criminal subcultures, nor in media and political constructions of its meaning, but in the contested interplay of the two.

In *Making Trouble* this exploration of subculture, style, and mediated response continues. In her chapter, "Punky in the Middle," for example, Lauraine Leblanc documents the complex and often contradictory processes by which politicians, the police, and the media constructed the meaning of the 1996 punk uprisings in Montreal, partially in response to the "spectacular forms of subcultural deviance," "stylistic innovation," and "sartorial terrorism" that the punks put on display. Similarly, Karim Murji's chapter, "Wild Life: Constructions and Representations of Yardies," explores the ways in which the cultural and media construction of the Jamaican "yardie" criminal in Great Britain draws on and reproduces stylized, stereotypical images of ethnicity and ethnic subcultures. Alternatively, Jeff Ferrell's chapter, "Freight Train Graffiti: Subculture, Media, Dislocation," documents the U.S. hip hop graffiti underground's use of shared symbolic and stylistic codes in constructing its own media of long-distance communication.

Media Constructions of Deviance, Crime, and Control

Cultural criminology incorporates a wealth of research on mediated characterizations of deviance, crime, and crime control, ranging across historical and contemporary texts and investigating images generated in newspaper reporting, popular film, television news and entertainment programming, popular music, comic books, and the cyberspaces of the Internet. To this diverse body of scholarship *Making Trouble* contributes research on a variety of contemporary media forms—television news and entertainment, newspaper reporting, popular film, alternative media—and provides important historical perspective as well. Jon'a Meyer's chapter, "The Elders Were Our Textbooks," investigates an often overlooked medium: the telling of traditional stories as a means of constructing understandings of deviance, crime, and control. In their chapter "The Historical Roots of Tabloid TV Crime," Paul Kooistra and John Mahoney likewise document the often unnoticed historical antecedents of contemporary tabloid television and "reality-based" crime programming. Gray Cavender, in his chapter "Detecting Masculinity," in turn explores significant historical changes in ideologies of crime and masculinity, as circulated through past and present popular films.

Further, as Neil Websdale's chapter in this collection, "Police Homicide Files as Situated Media Substrates," suggests, cultural criminologists explore the complex institutional and informational interconnections between the criminal justice system and the mass media. Researchers like Chermak

(1995, 1997, 1998) and Sanders and Lyon (1995) have documented not only the mass media's heavy reliance on criminal justice sources for imagery and information on crime, but more importantly, the reciprocal relationship that undergirds this reliance. Working within organizational imperatives of efficiency and routinization, media institutions regularly rely on data selectively provided by policing and court agencies. In so doing, they highlight for the public those issues chosen by criminal justice institutions and framed by criminal justice imperatives, and they in turn contribute to the political agendas of the criminal justice system and to the generation of public support for these agendas. In a relatively nonconspiratorial but nonetheless powerful fashion, media and criminal justice organizations thus coordinate their day-to-day operations, and cooperate in constructing circumscribed understandings of crime and crime control.

A significant body of research examines the nature of these understandings and the mediated dynamics of their production. Much of this research (for example, Adler and Adler 1994; Goode and Ben-Yehuda 1994; Hollywood 1997; Jenkins 1992; Sparks 1995; Thornton 1994) builds on the classic analytic models of cultural studies and interactionist sociology, as embodied in concepts such as moral entrepreneurship and moral enterprise in the creation of crime and deviance (Becker 1963), and the invention of folk devils as a means of generating moral panic (Cohen [1972] 1980) around issues of crime and deviance. Exploring the epistemic frameworks surrounding everyday understandings of crime controversies, this research (for example, Acland 1995; Best 1995; Fishman 1978; Hamm and Ferrell 1994; Perrone and Chesney-Lind 1997; Reinarman 1994; Surette 1998; Tunnell 1998; Websdale and Alvarez 1998) problematizes and unpacks taken-for-granted assumptions regarding the prevalence of criminality and the particular characteristics of criminals, and traces these assumptions to the interrelated workings of interest groups, media institutions, and criminal justice organizations.

Thus, in *Making Trouble,* Craig Reinarman and Ceres Duskin's chapter, "Dominant Ideology and Drugs in the Media," exposes a remarkable case in which a fabricated report on childhood drug use, featured in a prominent daily newspaper in the United States, won widespread attention and, for its author, a Pulitzer Prize. Meda Chesney-Lind's chapter, "Media Misogyny: Demonizing 'Violent' Girls and Women," contrasts sensational and often simplistic media constructions of female violence with the day-to-day realities of women's aggression and women's survival. Similarly, Adrian Howe's chapter, "The War against Women," reveals the "shock-of-the-new" tone and warlike metaphors with which one Australian newspaper represented domestic violence and sexual assault; and Neil Websdale's chapter, "Predators," compares mediated representations of predatory "stranger-danger" with the far more common occurrence of male intrafamilial violence against women and children. In his chapter, "Jihad as Terrorism," Fida Mohammed likewise documents the broadly inappropriate construction of Islamic culture and politics as terroristic, as well as specific media misattributions of terroristic violence to Islamic sources.

Emerging scholarship in *Making Trouble* and elsewhere also refines the analytic models through which cultural criminologists explore media constructions of crime, deviance, and control. As McRobbie and Thornton (1995) argue, and as Leblanc's chapter in this collection demonstrates, the essential concepts of "moral panic" and "folk devils" merit reconsideration in multimediated societies; with the proliferation of media channels and the saturation of media markets, moral panics become both dangerous endeavors and marketable commodities, and folk devils find themselves both stigmatized and lionized in mainstream media and alternative media alike. Similarly, Philip Jenkins's chapter in this collection, "Fighting Terrorism As If Women Mattered," begins to refine understandings of crime and justice issues as social and cultural constructions. Building on his earlier, meticulous deconstructions of drug panics, serial homicide scares, and other constructed crime controversies (for example, Jenkins 1994a, 1994b), he argues that attention must be paid as well to the media and political dynamics underlying "unconstructed" crime. Jenkins explores the failure to frame an activity like antiabortion violence as criminal terrorism, situates this failure within active media and political processes, and thus questions the meaning of that for which no criminal meaning is provided.

Throughout these many mediated constructions (and nonconstructions) of crime and criminality, cultural criminologists explore a complex process of presentation and re-presentation unfolding in the realm of sound bites, shock images, news conferences, and newspaper headlines. This mediated spiral, in which yardies, punks, "violent" girls, followers of Islam, drug users, and others are publicly constructed as criminal, leads once again into a complex hall of mirrors. It generates not only images, but images of images—that is, attempts by lawyers, police officials, political and religious leaders, media workers, and others to craft criminalized images of those images previously crafted by subcultural participants, and by other politicians, police officers, and media workers. Given this, cultural criminologists have begun to widen the notion of "criminalization" to include more than the simple creation and application of criminal law. Increasingly, they investigate the larger process of "cultural criminalization" (Ferrell 1998:80–82), the mediated reconstruction of stigmatized meaning and perception around issues of deviance, crime, and control. In some cases, this cultural criminalization stands as an end in itself, successfully dehumanizing or delegitimating those targeted, though no formal legal charges are brought against them. In other cases, cultural criminalization helps construct a perceptual context in which direct criminal charges can more easily follow. In either scenario, though, media and political dynamics drive and define this process of cultural criminalization.

In this light it is less than surprising that contemporary cases of cultural criminalization are aimed time and again at marginal(ized) groups and subcultures—street punks, minority and immigrant populations, alternative artists and musicians, young inner-city women, "foreign" political movements—whose stylized celebration of and confrontation with their marginality threaten particular patterns of moral and legal control. Cultural criminalization in this sense exposes yet another set of linkages between subcultural styles and symbols, and mediated constructions and reconstructions of these as criminal or criminogenic. In addition, as a process conducted in the public realm, cultural criminalization contributes to popular perceptions and panics, and thus to the further marginalization of those who are its focus. If successful, it constructs a degree of popular threat and discomfort that eventually seeps into the practice and understanding of everyday life.

Cultural criminologists further emphasize that in the process of constructing crime and crime control as social and political concerns, the media construct them as entertainment. Revisiting the classic cultural studies/new criminology notion of "policing the crisis" (Hall et al. 1978), Sparks (1995; see 1992), for example, characterizes the production and perception of crime and policing imagery in television crime dramas as a process of "entertaining the crisis." Intertwined with mediated moral panic over crime and crime waves, amplified fear of street crime and stranger violence, and politically popular concern for the harm done to crime victims, then, is the pleasure found in consuming mediated crime imagery and crime drama. To the extent that the mass media constructs crime as entertainment, we are thus offered not only selective images and agendas, but the ironic mechanism for amusing ourselves to death (Postman 1986) by way of our own collective pain, misery, and fear. Given this, contemporary scholarship in cultural criminology focuses not only on the mediated manufacture of news and information, but on popular film (as with Cavender's chapter in this collection), popular music, and television entertainment programming, and investigates the collapsing boundaries between such categories. Recent work in this area targets especially the popularity of "reality" crime programs (Fishman and Cavender 1998) and, as Kooistra and Mahoney's chapter in this collection shows, the long-standing popularity of similarly lurid entertainment. With their mix of street footage, theatrical staging, and patrol-car sermonizing, reality crime programs such as "Cops," "L.A.P.D.," and "True Stories of the Highway Patrol" generate conventional, though at times contradictory, images of crime and policing. Along with talk shows devoted largely to crime and deviance topics, they in turn spin off secondary merchandising schemes, lawsuits over videotaped police chases and televised

invasions of privacy, and criminal activities allegedly induced by the programs themselves. Such dynamics demonstrate the entangled reality of crime,
crime news, and crime entertainment, and suggest that as mediated crime
constructions come to be defined as real, "they are real in their consequences" (Thomas 1966:301).

The Politics of Making Trouble

As must by now be obvious, a common thread connects the many case
studies in cultural criminology collected in Making Trouble and elsewhere:
the presence of contested power relations, and the emergence of social
control, at the intersections of culture, crime, and deviance. The stylistic
practices and symbolic codes of illicit subcultures and groups are made the
object of legal surveillance and control or, alternatively, are appropriated,
commodified, and sanitized within a vast machinery of consumption. Sophisticated media and criminal justice "culture wars" (Bolton 1992; Dubin
1992; Ferrell 1998) are launched against marginalized cultural groups, and
against allegedly "obscene" forms of art, music, and entertainment, thereby
criminalizing participants, further marginalizing them from idealized notions of decency and community and, at the extreme, silencing the political
critiques that they present. Ongoing media constructions of crime and crime
control emerge out of an alliance of convenience between media institutions and criminal justice agencies, serve to promote and legitimate broader
political agendas regarding crime control, and in turn function to both trivi-
alize and dramatize the meaning of crime. Increasingly, then, it is television
crime shows and big budget detective movies, nightly newscasts and morning newspaper headlines, recurrent campaigns against the real and imagined crimes of the disenfranchised that constitute Foucault's "hundreds of
tiny theatres of punishment" (cited in Cohen 1979:339)—theatres in which
young people, ethnic minorities, women, and others play villains deserving
of penalty and public outrage.

At the same time, cultural criminologists emphasize and explore the
various forms that resistance to this complex, mediated web of social control
may take. As Sparks (1992, 1995) and others argue, the audiences for media
constructions of crime and deviance are diverse in both their composition
and in their readings of these constructions; they recontextualize, remake,
and even reverse mass media meanings as they incorporate them into their
daily lives and interactions. Varieties of resistance also emerge among those
groups more specifically targeted within the practice of mediated criminalization and control. Artists and musicians criminalized as obscene or otherwise criminogenic within contemporary "culture wars" have refused governmental awards, resigned high-profile positions, won legal judgments,
organized alternative media outlets and performances, and otherwise pro-

duced public counterattacks (Ferrell 1998). Within other marginalized sub-cultures and groups, participants certainly encounter collective style as a stigma inviting outside surveillance and control, but at the same time value this style as a badge of honor and resistance made all the more meaningful by its enduring defiance of outside authority (Hebdige 1988; Ferrell 1995b). And, as the studies collected in *Making Trouble* show, media constructions of drug use, of male and female violence, of punks, yardies, and terrorists are not unidimensionally imposed, but are instead contested and contradicted in their production and dissemination. In investigating the intersections of culture and crime for power relations and emerging forms of social control, then, cultural criminologists carry on the tradition of cultural studies (Hall and Jefferson 1976) by examining the many forms of resistance that emerge there as well.

Moreover, cultural criminology itself operates as a sort of intellectual resistance, as a diverse counterreading and counterdiscourse on conventional constructions of deviance, crime, and crime control. In deconstructing moments of mediated panic over crime and deviance, cultural criminologists work to expose the political processes behind seemingly spontaneous social concerns, and as many of the studies in *Making Trouble* reveal, to dismantle the recurring and often essentialist metaphors of disease, invasion, and decay on which crime panics are built (see also Brownstein 1995, 1996; Reinarman 1994). Moreover, Barak (1988, 1994) argues for an activist "newsmaking criminology" in which criminologists integrate themselves into the ongoing mediated construction of crime, develop as part of their role in this process alternative images and understandings of crime issues, and in so doing produce what constitutive criminologists (Henry and Milovanovic 1991; Barak 1995) call a "replacement discourse" regarding crime and crime control.

Much of cultural criminology's scholarship regarding subcultural and group domains functions similarly, as a critical move away from the "official definitions of reality" (Hagedorn 1990:244) produced by the media and the criminal justice system and reproduced by a "courthouse criminology" (see Polsky 1969) that relies on these sources. By attentively documenting the lived realities of groups whom conventional crime constructions have marginalized, and in turn documenting the situated politics of this marginalization process, cultural criminologists attempt to deconstruct the demonization of various "outsiders" (Becker 1963)—from gay hustlers (Pettiway 1996), homeless heroin addicts (Bourgois et al. 1997), and battered women (Websdale 1998) to the graffiti writers and minority drug users, girls and women, punks and yardies found in *Making Trouble*—and to produce alternative understandings of them. Approaching this task from the other direction, Hamm (1993, 1995) and others likewise venture inside the worlds of particularly violent criminals to document dangerous nuances of meaning and style often left invisible in official reporting on such groups. In its politics as in its theory, then, cultural criminology endeavors to produce alternative images of deviance, crime, and social control. And like other cultural criminologists, the contributors to this collection mean not only to investigate the cultural and political dynamics of "making trouble"; they themselves mean to make trouble for conventional understandings and taken-for-granted perceptions regarding crime, deviance, and control.

Thematic Threads and Conceptual Innovations

Along with an analysis of politics and power, other common threads run through the studies collected in *Making Trouble*. Some of them elaborations on existing themes in cultural criminological scholarship, others relatively new conceptualizations, these threads can perhaps contribute to ongoing innovation and exploration within the developing project of cultural criminology.

To begin with, many of the studies in this collection suggest that the everyday, subcultural processes of deviance, crime, and crime control, and the mass media's construction and reconstruction of these processes, are intertwined in ways far more complex than the latter's simple "reporting on" the former. As demonstrated time and again in *Making Trouble,* the mass media and associated culture industries certainly produce an ongoing flood of crime images and crime texts; but media audiences, deviant and criminal subcultures, control agencies, and others subsequently appropriate these texts and images, and remake their meaning as they utilize them in particular social situations. Similarly, as the chapters by Meyer, Ferrell, Websdale, and others show, the many subcultures concerned with deviance, crime, and crime control themselves produce complex circuits of communication, and within this circuitry all manner of images and symbols. From storytellers and their mythic accounts, to graffiti writers and their illustrated trains, to police detectives and their homicide files, these situated media circulate within and between social worlds, generate competing symbolic references and public perceptions of crime, and regularly reappear as caricature within the realm of mass media entertainment and reporting on crime, deviance, and crime control. Thus, as before, it is not subcultures and situations that merit the attention of cultural criminologists, nor mediated constructions of deviance, crime, and control, but rather the ongoing confounding and confluence of these categories.

This world of spiraling symbolism and fluid meaning, this dynamic integration of situated crime constructions and media crime constructions, further implies that commonly accepted understandings of "media," and the usual study of "media and crime" linkages, must be expanded to include those media that take shape within and among the various cultures and subcultures of crime, deviance, and crime control. Fully investigating the linkages between media and crime means investigating the many situations in which these linkages emerge, and moreover the situated meaning of media and audience within deviant and criminal worlds. Ultimately, perhaps, this investigation suggests blurring the analytic boundary between producer and audience—recognizing, in other words, that a variety of groups both produce and consume contested images of deviance, crime, and control—and moving ahead to explore the many microcircuits of meaning that collectively construct this complex reality.

This expanded understanding of "media and crime" must include a close analysis of mediated policing as well; increasingly, the production and consumption of mediated meaning frames not only the practice of crime, but of crime control. Contemporary policing can in fact hardly be understood apart from its interpenetration with media at all levels. As "reality" crime and policing television programs shape public perceptions of policing, serve as controversial tools of officer recruitment and suspect apprehension, and engender lawsuits over their effects on street-level policing, citizens shoot video footage of police conduct and misconduct—some of which finds its way, full circle, onto news and "reality" programs. Meanwhile, within the police subculture itself, surveillance cameras and on-board patrol car cameras capture the practices of police officers and citizens alike; and, as Websdale's chapter on police homicide files documents, police crime files themselves take shape as "situated media substrates," which, like surveillance and patrol car footage, regularly become building blocks for subsequent mass media images of crime and policing. The policing of a postmodern world emerges as a complex set of visual and semiotic practices, an expanding spiral of mediated control (Manning 1998, 1999; Marx 1995); and, as Peter Manning's chapter, "Reflections: The Visual as a Mode of Social Control," shows, the broader policing of perception in a postmodern world likewise circulates through a bewildering network of visual media, reflected meaning, and disjointed self-images.

Threaded through all of this—through the many cultural constructions of crime, deviance, and control—are taut lines of identity and difference. Time and again, *Making Trouble* places issues of power, difference, and identity at the forefront of its investigations, and explores these issues systematically—that is, not as an analytic afterthought, but as the motor force driving the situations under study. Thus, it is not by accident that chapter after chapter deals directly with contested constructions of gender, ethnicity, nationality, and youth, and that in particular, this collection attempts to investigate carefully the gendered construction of crime, deviance, and control. As the accumulated scholarship of cultural criminology has begun to show, and as this collection affirms, these dimensions are central to any critical understanding of the issues involved. They consistently define the construction of deviance, crime, and control, and as consistently animate the conflicts that these constructions both reflect and reproduce.

There are of course other threads as well. By intention, this collection moves outside the myopia that sometimes afflicts U.S. scholarship, to explore the cultural construction of crime, deviance, and control in Canada, Great Britain, Australia, and the United States; among immigrant and "foreign" populations; and in both contemporary and historical circumstances. By intention, *Making Trouble* widens the notion of crime and deviance to include the contested construction of terrorism and other events often excluded from criminological analysis. And, as discussed more fully in the final chapter, *Making Trouble* attempts not only to investigate cultural constructions of crime, deviance, and control, but to investigate the cultural voids, to interrogate the silences, which these constructions leave behind.

NO ESCAPE

As developed in *Making Trouble* and elsewhere, the enterprise of cultural criminology builds from a wide range of intellectual orientations. Revisiting and perhaps reinventing existing paradigms in cultural studies, the "new" criminology, interactionist sociology, and critical theory; integrating insights from postmodern and constructionist thought; and incorporating aspects of newsmaking, constitutive, and other evolving criminologies, cultural criminology seeks less to synthesize or subsume these various perspectives than to engage them in a critical, multifaceted exploration of culture, deviance, and crime. Linking these diverse intellectual dimensions is an overarching concern with the meaning of deviance, crime, and control. Cohen (1988:68, 1971:19) has proposed "placing on the agenda" of a culturally informed criminology issues of "subjective meaning" and of deviance and crime as "meaningful action." Cultural criminology generally, and this collection specifically, embrace and expand this agenda by exploring the complex construction, attribution, and appropriation of meaning that occurs within and between media and political formations, illicit groups and subcultures, and audiences around matters of deviance, crime, and social control. In so doing, the works gathered here and elsewhere within the field of cultural criminology likewise highlight the inevitability of the image. Reading a newspaper crime report or perusing a police file, caught between the panic and pleasure of crime, making trouble or trying to make sense, "there is no escape from the politics of representation" (Hall 1993:111).

REFERENCES

Acland, Charles R. 1995. *Youth, Murder, Spectacle: The Cultural Politics of 'Youth in Crisis'.* Boulder, CO: Westview.

Adler, Patricia A. and Peter Adler, eds. 1994. *Constructions of Deviance: Social Power, Context, and Interaction.* Belmont, CA: Wadsworth.

Anderson, Sean E. and Gregory J. Howard, eds. 1998. *Interrogating Popular Culture: Deviance, Justice, and Social Order.* Guilderland, NY: Harrow and Heston.

Bailey, Frankie Y. and Donna C. Hale, eds. 1998. *Popular Culture, Crime, and Justice.* Belmont, CA: West/Wadsworth.

Barak, Gregg. 1988. "Newsmaking Criminology: Reflections on the Media, Intellectuals, and Crime." *Justice Quarterly* 5:565–87.

Barak, Gregg, ed. 1994. *Media, Process, and the Social Construction of Crime: Studies in Newsmaking Criminology.* New York: Garland.

Barak, Gregg. 1995. "Media, Crime, and Justice: A Case for Constitutive Criminology." Pp. 142–66 in *Cultural Criminology,* edited by J. Ferrell and C. R. Sanders. Boston: Northeastern University Press.

Baudrillard, Jean. 1985. "The Ecstasy of Communication." Pp. 126–34 in *Postmodern Culture,* edited by H. Foster. London: Pluto.

Becker, Howard S. 1963. *Outsiders: Studies in the Sociology of Deviance.* New York: Free Press.

Becker, Howard S. and Michal McCall, eds. 1990. *Symbolic Interaction and Cultural Studies.* Chicago: University of Chicago Press.

Best, Joel, ed. 1995. *Images of Issues: Typifying Contemporary Social Problems,* 2nd edition. Hawthorne, NY: Aldine de Gruyter.

Bolton, Richard, ed. 1992. *Culture Wars: Documents from the Recent Controversies in the Arts.* New York: New Press.

Bourgois, Philippe, Mark Lettiere, and James Quesada. 1997. "Social Misery and the Sanctions of Substance Abuse: Confronting HIV Risk among Homeless Heroin Addicts in San Francisco." *Social Problems* 44:155–73.

Brownstein, Henry H. 1995. "The Media and the Construction of Random Drug Violence." Pp. 45–65 in *Cultural Criminology,* edited by J. Ferrell and C. R. Sanders. Boston: Northeastern University Press.

Brownstein, Henry H. 1996. *The Rise and Fall of a Violent Crime Wave: Crack Cocaine and the Social Construction of a Crime Problem.* Guilderland, NY: Harrow and Heston.

Chermak, Steven M. 1995. *Victims in the News: Crime and the American News Media.* Boulder, CO: Westview.

Chermak, Steven M. 1997. "The Presentation of Drugs in the News Media: The News Sources Involved in the Construction of Social Problems." *Justice Quarterly* 14:687–718.

Chermak, Steven M. 1998. "Police, Courts, and Corrections in the Media." Pp. 87–99 in *Popular Culture, Crime, and Justice,* edited by F. Y. Bailey and D. C. Hale. Belmont, CA: West/Wadsworth.

Clarke, John. 1976. "Style." Pp. 175–91 in *Resistance Through Rituals,* edited by S. Hall and T. Jefferson. London: Hutchinson.

Cohen, Stanley, ed. 1971. *Images of Deviance*. Harmondsworth, UK: Penguin.

Cohen, Stanley. [1972] 1980. *Folk Devils and Moral Panics*. London: Macgibbon and Kee.

Cohen, Stanley. 1979. "The Punitive City: Notes on the Dispersal of Social Control." *Contemporary Crises* 3:339–63.

Cohen, Stanley. 1988. *Against Criminology*. New Brunswick, NJ: Transaction.

Cohen, Stanley and Jock Young, eds. 1973. *The Manufacture of News: Deviance, Social Problems, and the Mass Media*. London: Constable.

Cosgrove, Stuart. 1984. "The Zoot-Suit and Style Warfare." *Radical America* 18:38–51.

Denzin, Norman K. 1992. *Symbolic Interaction and Cultural Studies: The Politics of Interpretation*. Cambridge, MA: Blackwell.

Dubin, Steven. 1992. *Arresting Images: Impolitic Art and Uncivil Actions*. London: Routledge.

During, Simon, ed. 1993. *The Cultural Studies Reader*. London: Routledge.

Ferrell, Jeff. 1995a. "Urban Graffiti: Crime, Control, and Resistance." *Youth and Society* 27:73–92.

Ferrell, Jeff. 1995b. "Style Matters: Criminal Identity and Social Control." Pp. 169–89 in *Cultural Criminology*, edited by J. Ferrell and C. R. Sanders. Boston: Northeastern University Press.

Ferrell, Jeff. 1995c. "Culture, Crime, and Cultural Criminology." *Journal of Criminal Justice and Popular Culture* 3:25–42.

Ferrell, Jeff. 1996. *Crimes of Style: Urban Graffiti and the Politics of Criminality*. Boston: Northeastern University Press.

Ferrell, Jeff. 1998. "Criminalizing Popular Culture." Pp. 71–83 in *Popular Culture, Crime, and Justice*, edited by F. Y. Bailey and D. C. Hale. Belmont, CA: West/Wadsworth.

Ferrell, Jeff and Clinton R. Sanders, eds. 1995. *Cultural Criminology*. Boston: Northeastern University Press.

Fishman, Mark. 1978. "Crime Waves as Ideology." *Social Problems* 25:531–43.

Fishman, Mark and Gray Cavender, eds. 1998. *Entertaining Crime: Television Reality Programs*. Hawthorne, NY: Aldine de Gruyter.

Fraser, Nancy. 1995. "Politics, Culture, and the Public Sphere: Toward a Postmodern Conception." Pp. 287–312 in *Social Postmodernism: Beyond Identity Politics*, edited by L. Nicholson and S. Seidman. Cambridge, UK: Cambridge University Press.

Gelder, Ken and Sarah Thornton, eds. 1997. *The Subcultures Reader*. London: Routledge.

Goode, Erich and Nachman Ben-Yehuda. 1994. *Moral Panics*. Cambridge, MA: Blackwell.

Grossberg, Lawrence, Cary Nelson, and Paula A. Treichler, eds. 1992. *Cultural Studies*. New York: Routledge.

Hagedorn, John M. 1990. "Back in the Field Again: Gang Research in the Nineties." Pp. 240–59 in *Gangs in America*, edited by C. R. Huff. Newbury Park, CA: Sage.

Hall, Stuart. 1993. "What Is This 'Black' in Black Popular Culture?" *Social Justice* 20:104–14.

Hall, Stuart and Tony Jefferson, eds. 1976. *Resistance Through Rituals: Youth Subcultures in Post-War Britain.* London: Hutchinson.

Hall, Stuart, Chas Critcher, Tony Jefferson, John Clarke, and Brian Roberts. 1978. *Policing the Crisis: Mugging, the State, and Law and Order.* Houndmills, UK: MacMillan.

Hamm, Mark S. 1993. *American Skinheads: The Criminology and Control of Hate Crime.* Westport, CT: Praeger.

Hamm, Mark S. 1995. "Hammer of the Gods Revisited: Neo-Nazi Skinheads, Domestic Terrorism, and the Rise of the New Protest Music." Pp. 190–212 in *Cultural Criminology,* edited by J. Ferrell and C. R. Sanders. Boston: Northeastern University Press.

Hamm, Mark S. and Jeff Ferrell. 1994. "Rap, Cops, and Crime: Clarifying the 'Cop Killer' Controversy." *ACJS Today* 13:1.

Hebdige, Dick. 1979. *Subculture: The Meaning of Style.* London: Methuen.

Hebdige, Dick. 1988. *Hiding in the Light.* London: Routledge.

Henry, Stuart and Dragan Milovanovic. 1991. "Constitutive Criminology: The Maturation of Critical Theory." *Criminology* 29:293–315.

Hollywood, Brian. 1997. "Dancing in the Dark: Ecstasy, the Dance Culture, and Moral Panic in Post Ceasefire Northern Ireland." *Critical Criminology* 8:62–77.

Jenkins, Philip. 1992. *Intimate Enemies: Moral Panics in Contemporary Great Britain.* Hawthorne, NY: Aldine de Gruyter.

Jenkins, Philip. 1994a. *Using Murder: The Social Construction of Serial Homicide.* Hawthorne, NY: Aldine de Gruyter.

Jenkins, Philip. 1994b. "'The Ice Age': The Social Construction of a Drug Panic." *Justice Quarterly* 11:7–31.

Kane, Stephanie. 1998a. "Reversing the Ethnographic Gaze: Experiments in Cultural Criminology." Pp. 132–45 in *Ethnography at the Edge,* edited by J. Ferrell and M. S. Hamm. Boston: Northeastern University Press.

Kane, Stephanie. 1998b. *AIDS Alibis: Sex, Drugs and Crime in the Americas.* Philadelphia: Temple University Press.

Kidd-Hewitt, David and Richard Osborne, eds. 1995. *Crime and the Media: The Post-Modern Spectacle.* London: Pluto.

Lyng, Stephen and Mitchell L. Bracey. 1995. "Squaring the One Percent: Biker Style and the Selling of Cultural Resistance." Pp. 235–76 in *Cultural Criminology,* edited by J. Ferrell and C. R. Sanders. Boston: Northeastern University Press.

Manning, Peter K. 1998. "Media Loops." Pp. 25–39 in *Popular Culture, Crime, and Justice,* edited by F. Y. Bailey and D. C. Hale. Belmont, CA: West/Wadsworth.

Manning, Peter K. 1999. "Semiotics and Social Justice." Pp. 131–49 in *Social Justice/Criminal Justice,* edited by B. A. Arrigo. Belmont, CA: West/Wadsworth.

Marx, Gary T. 1995. "Electric Eye in the Sky: Some Reflections on the New Surveillance and Popular Culture." Pp. 106–41 in *Cultural Criminology,* edited by J. Ferrell and C. R. Sanders. Boston: Northeastern University Press.

McRobbie, Angela. 1980. "Settling Accounts with Subcultures: A Feminist Critique." *Screen Education* 34:37–49.

McRobbie, Angela and Sarah L. Thornton. 1995. "Rethinking 'Moral Panic' for Multi-Mediated Social Worlds." *British Journal of Sociology* 46:559–74.

Melossi, Dario. 1985. "Overcoming the Crisis in Critical Criminology: Toward a Grounded Labeling Theory." *Criminology* 23:193–208.

Miller, Jody A. 1995. "Struggles Over the Symbolic: Gang Style and the Meanings of Social Control." Pp. 213–34 in *Cultural Criminology,* edited by J. Ferrell and C. R. Sanders. Boston: Northeastern University Press.

Perrone, Paul A. and Meda Chesney-Lind. 1997. "Representations of Gangs and Delinquency: Wild in the Streets?" *Social Justice* 24:96–116.

Pettiway, Leon E. 1996. *Honey, Honey, Miss Thang: Being Black, Gay, and on the Streets.* Philadelphia: Temple University Press.

Polsky, Ned. 1969. *Hustlers, Beats, and Others.* Garden City, NY: Anchor.

Postman, Neil. 1986. *Amusing Ourselves to Death.* New York: Viking.

Potter, Gary W. and Victor E. Kappeler, eds. 1998. *Constructing Crime: Perspectives on Making News and Social Problems.* Prospect Heights, IL: Waveland.

Redhead, Steve. 1995. *Unpopular Cultures: The Birth of Law and Popular Culture.* Manchester, UK: Manchester University Press.

Reinarman, Craig. 1994. "The Social Construction of Drug Scares." Pp. 92–104 in *Constructions of Deviance,* edited by P. A. Adler and P. Adler. Belmont, CA: Wadsworth.

Sanders, Clinton R. and Eleanor Lyon. 1995. "Repetitive Retribution: Media Images and the Cultural Construction of Criminal Justice." Pp. 25–44 in *Cultural Criminology,* edited by J. Ferrell and C. R. Sanders. Boston: Northeastern University Press.

Sparks, Richard. 1992. *Television and the Drama of Crime: Moral Tales and the Place of Crime in Public Life.* Buckingham, UK: Open University Press.

Sparks, Richard. 1995. "Entertaining the Crisis: Television and Moral Enterprise." Pp. 49–66 in *Crime and the Media,* edited by D. Kidd-Hewitt and R. Osborne. London: Pluto.

Surette, Ray. 1998. *Media, Crime, and Criminal Justice: Images and Realities,* 2nd edition. Belmont, CA: West/Wadsworth.

Taylor, Ian, Paul Walton, and Jock Young. 1973. *The New Criminology: For a Social Theory of Deviance.* New York: Harper & Row.

Thomas, W. I. 1966. "The Relation of Research to the Social Process." Pp. 289–305 in *W. I. Thomas on Social Organization and Social Personality,* edited by M. Janowitz. Chicago: University of Chicago Press.

Thornton, Sarah. 1994. "Moral Panic, The Media, and British Rave Culture." Pp. 176–92 in *Microphone Fiends: Youth Music and Youth Culture,* edited by A. Ross and T. Rose. New York: Routledge.

Tunnell, Kenneth D. 1998. "Reflections on Crime, Criminals, and Control in News-magazine Television Programs." Pp. 111–22 in *Popular Culture, Crime, and Justice,* edited by F. Y. Bailey and D. C. Hale. Belmont, CA: West/Wadsworth.

Websdale, Neil. 1998. *Rural Woman Battering and the Justice System: An Ethnography.* Thousand Oaks, CA: Sage.

Websdale, Neil and Alexander Alvarez. 1998. "Forensic Journalism as Patriarchal Ideology: The Newspaper Construction of Homicide-Suicide." Pp. 123–41 in

Popular Culture, Crime, and Justice, edited by F. Y. Bailey and D. C. Hale. Belmont, CA: West/Wadsworth.

Willis, Paul. 1977. *Learning to Labor: How Working Class Kids Get Working Class Jobs.* New York: Columbia University Press.

Willis, Paul. 1990. *Common Culture: Symbolic Work at Play in the Everyday Cultures of the Young.* Milton Keynes, UK: Open University Press.

II

Constructions of History and Myth

2

The Elders Were Our Textbooks
The Importance of Traditional Stories in Social Control

JON'A F. MEYER with GLORIA BOGDAN

The storyteller jumped forward, gesturing wildly with his hand drum, as he told those gathered around him about that bad ol' mean trickster, Coyote. The audience of junior high school students and their mentors riveted their attention on the man as he rapidly struck his drum to accentuate each event in the story. Coyote had done what Coyote was best known for: causing trouble.

First, Coyote had convinced a medicine (magical) rabbit to teach him how to toss his eyes into the sky and retrieve them later. Armed with this new knowledge, Coyote headed off to show the trick to others, but not before being warned not to repeat the feat more than three times in a given day. Of course, Coyote ignored the sage's advice and could not retrieve his eyes on the fourth trial. To add insult to injury, a passing crow gobbled up his eyes as a tasty meal. Now blind, Coyote first persuaded granny mouse and brother buffalo to each give of themselves one eye so that Coyote could see. Disgusted by the vastly different sizes of the two eyes, Coyote disposed of them in favor of two daisies, but quickly learned that the flowers close up each night. He then moved on to his next prey, a woman whom he convinced would be able to see through mountains if she possessed Coyote's "magic flower eyes."[1] Once she traded her own eyes, evening set, the daisies closed, and she immediately knew that she had been deceived. When she angrily demanded that Coyote return her eyes, he turned her into a snail that would forever grope around as though always in the dark.

There was more than just entertainment happening in the room that day. The storyteller was Terry Tafoya, who had come to share his culture with his young listeners. As he later explained (personal interview with author, July 1991), Coyote violated several important rules. First, Coyote ignored the medicine rabbit's instructions simply because he wanted to do otherwise. Then, despite the extreme generosity of two fellow creatures, he threw the gifted eyes away because he felt they weren't good enough for him. Then, he fraudulently obtained the woman's eyes. All three acts were despicable, and

25

it is acts like these that remind us why we hate Coyote so much. The storyteller then told the audience that the woman also shared the blame for her loss because she had relinquished two perfectly good eyes to Coyote in exchange for the coveted flower eyes. Instead, she should have been content with her own eyes; her sentence into snaildom befit her envy well.

While the listeners may not have recognized it, they had been shown a small portion of a code of conduct that has been handed down for generations among members of the southwestern Taos Pueblo tribe to which Tafoya belongs. Later, a few would remark about the many stories they heard that day, using parts of them to explain or justify their own actions or the actions of friends. One group of listeners, for example, later compared to Coyote a friend who would not share his candy with them, saying "You're pretty greedy, just like that [cursed] Coyote."

This was a typical reaction to such tales, especially those that discuss acceptable and unacceptable behavior or characteristics. Some scholars have compared such stories to more formal codes of conduct that govern the lives of their constituents (Bierhorst 1985). According to one scholar:

> Traditional audiences understand that trickster tales are humorous, that they test taboos and mores and teach that one should countenance contradictory impulses to achieve spiritual balance. (Monaghan 1994:A8)

It is in this spirit that the current study was conducted. Our goals were to learn what importance traditional tales hold for contemporary individuals, the myriad of uses people have found for them, and the effects the stories have had on their lives. It appears from the results of the current study that Americans value traditional stories and feel that such tales serve to transmit morals, convey cultural lessons, teach heritage or history, and inspire imagination. The participants found traditional stories to be useful both in their own lives, and in their responsibilities as caregivers for children.

Over and over, the participants referenced social control, noting that as children, traditional stories had provided them with important moral lessons, and that they had utilized those teachings when confronted with situations similar to those presented in the stories (for example, lying or stealing). When they later desired to control children within their care, many turned to traditional stories to achieve that task. They found that the stories were a palatable form of social control appropriate for children. In addition to long-lasting moral lessons, the stories could also be used to achieve more immediate needs. One entire type of stories, for example, was used to convince children to be good lest one of the characters come and get them (the Big Bad Wolf) or fail to treat them well (Santa Claus). Traditional myths and stories about deviance, then, are an important form of social control that influence childhood socialization and everyday adult conduct.

BACKGROUND AND LITERATURE REVIEW

One would be hard-pressed to find a society that did not have its fair share of traditional stories, myths and legends.[2] Throughout history, societies have transmitted their social knowledge from generation to generation through a variety of traditional stories, ranging from fanciful fairy tales to more realistic narratives.

The precise origins of traditional folk tales are uncertain, but we do know that they have been passed down orally for thousands of years (Zipes 1975:129). While the stories have undergone some alterations along the way, their fundamental messages have most likely survived the social editing to which they have been exposed. Creation stories still document the birth of the world and her inhabitants, and trickster tales still delight listeners with their detailed accounts of individuals being taken advantage of and paying the price for their gullibility.

Beyond the most basic elements of traditional stories, however, there have been many changes. We know, for example, that Christian missionaries who gathered traditional stories from the first nations on the American continent "sanitized" them by removing or altering some details, especially references to sexuality (Monaghan 1994:A8). It is also known that Native American tribes modified European tales for their own purposes and borrowed stories from other tribes; Aesop's famed story "The Tortoise and the Hare," for example, has been adapted by the Colville Indian tribe of Washington to explain how turtle got his tail (Regier 1993:432). Over time, some story parts have certainly been lost, and may have been replaced with other details. Consider that the ducks in different renditions of the same traditional Sioux trickster tale are slaughtered in a variety of fashions: one version has the birds' necks wrung by the trickster, another details how they are clubbed to death, while a third involves their being suffocated in a leather bag. Such changes may represent individual storytellers' preferences, but may also be based in broader historical or cultural contexts. Due to these editing and adaptation processes, it is difficult to know the precise roots of any given story, but despite these changes, the gist of most stories has likely remained. In all three versions of the above-mentioned tale, for example, the ducks are killed after being duped into singing and dancing for the trickster while keeping their eyes closed. The story reflects the intense distaste the Sioux have for falling victim to the greed of others.

Like other popular tales, "The Three Little Pigs" has undergone quite a number of changes, demonstrating the adaptation of the story within broader cultural contexts. One author attributes the tale to settlers who took the tale from the New World to England around 1609 (Pleasants 1994:4). In the Native American version, Pleasants argues, the pigs who built their houses of straw and sticks survived, but the pig who insisted on building his of bricks was eaten because it took him so long to complete his home that he could not hide inside it when the wolf called on him. In fact, the first two pigs invited the wolf to dine on corn and potatoes with them after he was unable to blow down even the house of straw. Pleasants (1994:10, 19–21) claims that the fate of the third pig, who represented the settlers' desires to own property (an idea that was in conflict with the Native American belief that property cannot be owned), had to be substantially changed when the European view of Native Americans turned sour. The more common version that Bryant ([1905] 1996:29–32) includes in her turn-of-the-century story-telling compendium has both the first two pigs and the wolf eaten.[3] Current versions are far less violent, and have the first two pigs safely escaping to the third pig's home, with the wolf taking off for parts unknown after catching his tail on fire by slipping down the chimney into a full fireplace. Whatever the validity of Pleasants's unique argument, a number of important changes happened between the original tale and the one currently told to children around the world.

The purposes of traditional stories are many. Zipes (1975:123) argues that fairy tales were neither designed for children nor based in a magical context; instead, they were modified by storytellers to "relate to the social conditions of the time." Though now popular children's tales, stories like "Hansel and Gretel" concealed deeper ideas such as the ability to overcome a sinister adversary (ibid.:127). In this manner, fairy tales served to stir the listeners' imaginations, and represented their hopes for survival in a difficult world.

Other stories recount historical events. Stories about Jesus' trial by the Pharisees, the "discovery" of the New World by Christopher Columbus, and Abraham Lincoln's childhood provide listeners with a wealth of historical information in an easily digestible format. Some stories involve a bit of fact-switching in order to make them more attractive. George Washington's famous coin toss across the Delaware River and Pocahontas's undying love for Captain John Smith are but two examples of stories that include some historical truths, but are so exaggerated that they are untrue as a whole. Stories as actual representations of history, then, are often suspect.[4] Along these lines, the northwest coastal Tlingit people are careful to divide their traditional stories into two categories: *tlagu* (of the long ago) and *ch'kalnik* (it really happened), indicating that they recognize that not all legends are true representations of historical happenings (Bierhorst 1985:52–53).

Some stories serve legal purposes. The Burmese Juristic (law) tales, which survive to this day as quaint parables, were developed as a way to train judges in remote areas before the Burmese had a writing system. The popular law tales contained essential parts of Burmese law within them. Of interest, the tales could be cited in court as part of official law, although many of them contained obvious elements of stylized fancy. One tale, for example, dealt with Tiger's lawsuit against Cat for three years' wages, because Cat did not teach him how to swish his tail from side to side during his apprenticeship with Cat. Tiger won the suit when it was learned that the oversight was intentional on the part of Cat, who did not want Tiger to be a better hunter than himself. Historically, the Burmese recognized custom as their only source of law; until their nation fell under British rule, Burmese laws were not enacted by any form of legislature or monarch (Htin Aung 1962:2, 6–7, 39–40, 150–51).

These law tales did more than simply convey accepted legal principles to those who found them useful. They were consulted with great fervor by Burmese judges, who sincerely sought the appropriate ruling in each of the cases before them. The Burmese felt that judges who ruled incorrectly in a case (even if inadvertently) subjected themselves to a host of terrible "dangers," including being swallowed up by the earth or eaten by a crocodile (ibid.:22–23). Judges, then, were very careful to react correctly to the cases before them, relying heavily upon the principles contained within the law tales.

The Sacred Legends of the Maori described by Rout (1926:10, 11, 56, 71, 193) enjoy the same respect as the Burmese law tales, and pass down to future generations important knowledge about social ethics, history, laws, and other culturally valued dimensions of social life. Like their Burmese counterparts, the Sacred Legends were viewed as "irrefutable legal proof" and could be presented in court. The Sacred Legends documented crimes such as a man forcing a woman to live with him when she desired a more physically fit partner[5], and judges sought to impose sentences that were "in harmony" with the legends. The lessons of the Sacred Legends were taught to children and other members of the community through the use of songs and stories containing allegories.[6]

One grouping of stories exists as little more than entertainment, or to convey a respect for the art of storytelling. In fact, Bryant ([1905] 1996:14) argues that amusement is the primary purpose of storytelling. Depriving children of fairy tales also deprives them of the mental imagery that accompanies them, so that, as adults, they are less able to appreciate literature built upon those common images, such as modern works whose plots contain references to women waiting for their Prince Charming (ibid.:21). Humorous tales such as "The Old Woman Who Ate a Spider" serve to elicit from those who hear them a hearty laugh, if little more.[7] Recognizing the entertainment value in stories, the Eskimos used storytelling to pass the long winter nights (Bierhorst 1985:57). Other tales entertain listeners through the use of mystery or drama.

Many stories contain moral lessons. A large number of Aesop's fables, for example, conclude with an easily comprehended message, such as "slow but steady wins the race" (from "The Tortoise and the Hare"). Others, although they have no summarizing words of advice, still contain well-known ethical principles; the story of the lion and the shepherd, for example, shows how a shepherd's kindly action in removing a thorn from a lion's paw results in the lion's later refusal to attack him when he is ordered cast to the lions for an offense he did not commit. Traditional Native American stories, too, often hide moral lessons within the text; as such, they are available only to those who are capable of understanding them (Caylor 1992). In fact, elders often tell children that they'll understand the importance of a story and be able to remember it only when they're "ready" to accept the story's meaning.[8]

Many religious works also contain stories. After referring to the Christian Bible as the "most influential literary work ever recorded," one team of scholars noted that parts of it are basically compendia of stories and myths that contain "messages or codes" that may be interpreted by readers (Sagarin and Kelly 1986:186). The Koran, the volumes of Vedic literature, and other important religious documents are also filled with stories that are literally full of meanings to be discovered by their readers. People have, of course, been known to debate the meanings of individual passages contained within these many religious works, thus leading to the accusation that some have constructed their own meanings, based only loosely upon the original texts, and have used them to control others. The belief held by some advocates of slavery that blacks were the sons of Ham, and deserved to be enslaved for that reason alone, is but one illustration of this phenomenon.[9]

Related to moral lessons are what might be called rules of everyday life. In this role, stories help teach listeners the informal policies that govern their everyday lives, much as the Maori allegories revealed socially acceptable actions to their listeners (Rout 1926). One creation myth told by the Karok people of the northern California coast, for example, documents how Pithvava (Big Dentalium Shell) created man, then provided instructions for creating many useful objects (money, clothing, and baby cradles) in addition to ordering compensation to the families of homicide victims, saying that killing a man is wrong (Kroeber and Gifford 1980:74–81). Similarly, the Luiseno of Southern California tell myths of their deity, Chinigchinix, who provided painful penalties to those who violated his strict moral code (Moriarty 1969:20). Such myths not only teach the listeners their cultural roots, but also how to live.

Most traditional stories have some form of instruction contained in them. One scholar noted that some creation myths are "so crammed with descriptions of ceremonial rules and procedures that they become more charter than story" (Bierhorst 1985:20). Nestled within the text of even less critical myths are important procedural lessons including: directions for planting and storing corn (McLaughlin 1916:64, 103), guides for snowshoe manufacture for Caribou hunting (Teit 1919:250), courtship rules (McLaughlin 1916:86), burial procedures (Bierhorst 1985:101; McLaughlin 1916:140), hunting taboos (Bierhorst 1985:201, 214; Teit 1919:230–32), rules for conducting traditional ceremonies (Bierhorst 1985:179, 201), and home building instructions (ibid.:201). Similarly, descriptions of upstanding people and actions are presented to those who listen to traditional tales. The stories in McLaughlin's (1916:98, 133, 169) collection present several descriptions of honorable deeds, including dying in battle for love, refusing to kill an unarmed man, and being honest. The bad that comes to unprincipled individuals is also commonly discussed (Bierhorst 1985:218, 220; McLaughlin 1916:12, 34, 78; Pokagon 1898:620). Echoing the Protestant work ethic, many popular European tales tell of the value of hard work and delayed gratification, while others extol the virtues of people who are kind to those less fortunate than they, often simultaneously condemning the actions by lazy, greedy, or otherwise unsavory individuals. Taken as a whole, traditional stories present important rules of conduct and ways of life, and "express a part of the world view of a people, the unexpressed but implicit conceptions of their place in nature and of the limits and workings of their world" (Haviland 1996:394). And, in doing so, traditional tales fulfill an important function often attributed to law: showing people the socially acceptable paths and actions to take in life.

STORIES AS REINFORCING LAW-WAYS
AND OTHER SOCIAL CODES

The most important function of law is debatable. Some scholars feel its primary concern is to deter would-be offenders from committing crimes through threats of punishment (Beccaria [1764] 1963; Bentham [1823] 1948; Blumstein, Cohen, and Nagin 1977:19). Others argue that the function of law is to provide for punishment or incapacitation of offenders in order to protect the rest of society (Berns 1989; Hawkins 1944; von Hirsch, Wasik, and Greene 1989). Some would argue that law exists as a way to bring offenders into the treatment programs they need in order to end their criminality (MacNamara 1977; Menninger 1959). What all these viewpoints have in common is their emphasis on law as a way to prevent crime through relatively oppressive means.

Another important function of law is education of the public as to right and wrong. Islamic law, for example, seeks directly to establish "upright manners and goodness, for they help [in] purifying [the] personality so as to resist evil and the desire to commit crimes" (Findlay and Zvekic 1988:125). While Islamic law certainly prescribes penalties for transgressors, the primary function is considered to be education. In a sense, such an approach seeks to prevent crimes well before they are even imagined. Similarly, Hoffman (1986:112) notes that the second basic function of law is "guidance," the first being a "moral" dimension, which is represented by mandatory orders (e.g., "thou shalt . . . "). In its guiding role, law endeavors to show the proper and the proscribed ways of living.

This educative role of law can be fulfilled through the telling of traditional stories. As values and proper courses of action are relayed, they ease their way into the lives of listeners one idea at a time. Those ideals that are important to a given people become the stuff from which their stories are spun. In a sense, the stories become penal codes by proxy. Important events are immortalized through stories, and with each retelling, the listener reabsorbs the intended lessons of the incident. People need guidance in their lives so that they will know what is expected of them in terms of "roles, relationships, and expectations" (ibid.:115). This can reduce conflict as societal norms about even everyday activities such as courtship and business transactions are reinforced through the telling of select stories. The importance of laws transmitted through story are not to be discounted:

> Every society has its own customs and values which are reflected upon people's behavior and manners. Some of these customs are so deeply rooted that they become binding, like formal penal laws. (Findlay and Zvekic 1988:106)

Stories, then, constitute influential sources of legal and social standards and a charter for living as a responsible member of society. In the end, it may be that so-called "primitive" societies did not need written laws because their legal codes were concealed within their traditional tales. Such stories helped guide the listeners in their lives, and in establishing proper parameters for living.

TELLING OF STORIES

Throughout history, children have looked forward to the arrival of the storyteller (Bierhorst 1985:117; Bryant [1905] 1996:9; McLaughlin 1916:5). As one famous Sioux storyteller (Lame Deer and Erdoes 1972:20–21) wrote about his childhood appreciation of storytelling:

> After I was six years old it was very hard to make me behave. The only way one could get me to sit still was to tell me a story. . . . The stories I liked best had to do with Iktome, the evil spiderman, a smart-ass who played tricks on everybody.[10]

Storytelling was an important time for those who gathered around to hear the tales. In fact, the event was so respected by some Native American tribes that "preliminary prayers" were said before the tales could be shared (Bierhorst 1985:6). In addition, according to several tribes' traditions, stories are not to be told out of season (winter stories may not be told during summer nor may "night stories" be told during the day), lest something bad happen to the storyteller or the audience (Gifford 1937:116).

The popularity of storytelling has declined over the years, presumably due to the advent of television and other entertainment forms. The importance of stories is not forgotten, however, even among contemporary youth; one television show, PBS's "Reading Rainbow," depicts actual storybooks being read to the audience. Further, traditional storytelling is being revived in South Africa and elsewhere (Medlicott 1992). Educators are now calling for the revival of traditional storytelling in school; advocates cite the power of oratory and the ability to transmit cultural traditions to students (Caylor 1992). Cree children are taught their traditional stories in school, but only after the selected pieces pass a review board that ensures that each is authentic and has a "moral ending and a strong message" (Campbell 1972).

We maintain that traditional stories hold importance for current-day people, and that they have in fact learned from the stories they have heard. We also believe that adults pass traditional tales down to children in their lives, and that the stories are useful in reinforcing teachings initiated by adult caregivers. In this way, traditional stories continue to survive, even in an age when technological media are gaining popularity. To shed light on this topic, we conducted an exploratory study of traditional stories.

THE CURRENT STUDY: RESULTS, DISCUSSION, AND EXPLORATION

A convenience sample of 342 students and campus visitors at four public colleges in the southwest United States participated in this exploratory study. Each participant was either interviewed or asked to complete a short open-ended survey about traditional stories. Traditional stories were defined as myths, legends, fairy tales, fables, parables, and other stories that had been handed down for at least two generations.[11] The participants were asked the identity and source of their favorite traditional story, the reasons they chose that story, the importance they attached to traditional stories, whether they had heard stories that teach morals or rules to listeners, and the effects of those stories. The participants were also asked whether they told traditional stories to children and if the tales had assisted them in any way as parents or caregivers.

The sample was predominantly white (55%, $n = 189$); other participants were Asian (18%, $n = 63$), Hispanic/Mexican-American (16%, $n = 54$),

Native American (4%, $n = 15$), African-American (2%, $n = 6$), or other ethnicities (3%, $n = 6$).[12] The participants' average age was 24 and ranged from 18 to 77.

The participants' favorite tales varied considerably. In all, 125 unique stories (or story types) were discussed by the participants. The favorite tales ranged from classic European fairy tales ("Cinderella," "Snow White"), historical legends (Geronimo, the foundation of Mexico City), and explanatory stories ("How Turtle Got His Red Ears," "How Frog Lost His Tail," the creation of California from a string of turtles) to dramatic love stories ("Romeo and Juliet") and popular allegories (*Aesop's Fables,* "The Little Boy Who Cried Wolf," Coyote/trickster tales, religious stories that teach forgiveness and kindness).

The reasons the participants had for selecting their favorite stories fell into several primary categories: participants noted that their tale was a likeable (exciting) story ($n = 31$), was somehow reflective of reality (it reminded them of themselves, $n = 13$), was a sentimental love story ($n = 13$), or was about a beloved type of animal or place ($n = 9$). The largest category, however, included participants whose favorite tales discussed good personality characteristics or morals ($n = 44$). Those who enjoyed the morals discussed in the tales felt that their favorite stories promoted good characteristics (morals, hard work, honor) or spoke against deviant behaviors (greed, ignorance). A few felt their favorite stories could be used to modify behavior; for example, one participant felt that children who heard his favorite parable would be less likely to "stay out late at night," while another mentioned that his story "scares children into learning their prayers." For such participants, traditional stories constituted a useful medium for teaching morals and other socially adaptive behaviors. These participants recognized the value of the stories as agents of what they perceived to be positive social control.

IMPORTANCE OF TRADITIONAL STORIES

All of the participants were asked what they felt was the importance of traditional stories in today's modern world. Over and over, their responses tapped their beliefs in the morals or code of conduct contained in the stories. Most of the responses could be grouped under five headings: that such stories transmit morals, convey culture, teach heritage, provide history, or inspire imagination. The breakdown of responses appears in Table 2.1.

The first category, indicating that the stories serve to transmit morals to listeners, was the largest. Nearly one-third (31%, $n = 94$) of the participants felt that teaching messages or lessons was the primary function of traditional stories; some mentioned that such tales "explained" life's morals to people

Table 2.1.   Primary Importance of Stories in Today's Modern
World as Discussed by Participants

	Frequency	Percentage
Transmit morals	94	31
Convey culture	79	26
Teach heritage	35	11
Provide history	21	7
Inspire imagination	10	3
All other answers	67	22
Total	306	100

or made them "real" to the listeners. Others stressed that traditional stories "kept good morals alive," or brought people back to "family values." A related group of participants noted that traditional stories serve to counteract the lack of innocence or wholesomeness on television. A few participants noted that morals presented in traditional tales were "easier to take" or more easily digested than those from more formal sources, including organized religions. Others felt that traditional tales teach the importance of good qualities to their listeners (to be kind, forgiving, or virtuous). One participant said their value lay in their effects on the ability to survive—that young people today "need all the help they can get" from morals contained in traditional tales. Overall, the participants who emphasized the importance of morals felt that traditional stories were a good way to convey this difficult concept to children. These participants valued the socializing effects of traditional stories.

The second largest number of participants (26%, $n = 79$) felt that the primary importance of traditional stories lay in their ability to transmit cultural traditions from one generation to the next. While some of these participants may have included morals in their ideas of culture, their answers did not directly mention morals or related concepts. Instead, their answers tended to emphasize the "vital role" that traditional tales played in keeping culture or customs "alive," "going strong," or "real." Some agreed that stories helped keep people "in touch" with their traditions. A few mentioned that experiences themselves could be passed down to the younger generations, saving the "uniqueness" of a given culture. A few reported that storytelling could be used as a "gentle" form of cross-cultural awareness, as well as a medium for teaching members of a given culture about their own ancient and contemporary traditions. Some participants mentioned passing on the "values and beliefs" of their culture to listeners. Traditional stories, then, could provide guidance in conducting everyday tasks. In other words, some of these participants saw the value of traditional stories as teaching informal laws governing how people go about their daily lives. In this role, stories may provide for behavioral change by offering support for cultural norms, or by highlighting the sanctions that accompany behavior that is disapproved of by others in the society.

The third, and related category (11%, $n = 35$) of answers showed that a number of the participants felt that the primary importance of traditional stories was to remind individuals of "where they came from." Those in this category focused on the ability of traditional tales to teach, preserve, or "pass along" their heritage. These answers differed from those enumerated above (for cultural traditions) in that they focused on peoples' roots, whereas the "culture" responses centered on actual life-ways and other cultural knowledge. To illustrate, most stories about the Navajo could serve to re-mind people from that heritage about their identity as Navajo, much as "Hansel and Gretel" could remind Germans about their roots, but without providing much additional specific knowledge about Germans or their cul-ture. Some Navajo stories, on the other hand, involve teachings such as cultural explanations (why weavers leave a tiny flaw in each of their rugs) or applied information (which herbs are best when one's sheep become ill). Respondents in the third category, then, felt the primary importance of traditional stories was to remind people of their roots rather than to provide specific cultural information to the audience. This opinion may stem, at least in part, from the urban/contemporary nature of the respondents. The likeli-hood, for example, of even the Navajo respondents in our sample needing to apply healing herbs to their sheep is slight, but all could enjoy and benefit from the stories in a broader cultural context.

A related category contained all answers that mentioned the past, but failed to attach it to the goals of cultural preservation or heritage. Instead, these participants (7%, $n = 21$) highlighted the provision of history in gener-al or the demonstration of how life has changed over time. Participants in this category felt that traditional stories could be used to teach about a variety of peoples and their histories. One participant noted that traditional stories are more "interesting than a history class," while another mentioned that the stories may "tell us about" the people they reference. Others noted that historical tales "give a glimpse into the past." For these participants, traditional tales represent a lively, interactive way to remember and docu-ment the past.

The final category, including all other answers, is a true hodgepodge of information (22%, $n = 67$). Participants here mentioned the importance of "passing happiness" to future generations, reminding people of their con-nection to nature, giving people hope, providing an interesting way to teach children in general, and entertaining the listeners. One small cluster of participants (3%, $n = 10$) agreed with Zipes (1975:118), who stated that traditional stories serve to excite the listeners' imaginations.

The participants in this study thus agreed with anthropologists who note that myths are viewed as socially important by people; they "tell people where they have come from and where they are going and thus how they should live right now" (Schultz and Lavenda 1995:196). Some participants said they felt that each hearing of the tales strengthened their connection to their pasts, be it their human ancestors, their membership in a special cultural group (religion or ethnicity), or a geographical location (the "old country"). The repetition reinforced messages that are passed down from one generation to another. One participant, for example, stated that he valued traditional stories because he knew who he was through his father, who knew who he was from his own father, and that the participant's son will grow up understanding both his ancestry and himself because traditional myths make him part of something larger.

Of interest, some of the participants had heritages from cultures with large pantheons of gods and goddesses (for example, Greek, Mexican Aztec). Despite being active in Christian churches, they still held that their non-Christian traditional myths were valid. Such myths serve as "charters" for group behavior and explain societal institutions by tying current life meanings to their divine histories (Howard 1996:312). The importance of these myths should not be undervalued.

The imagery presented in traditional tales has taught many individuals that good children are in bed by eight o'clock, that lying makes spots on their souls, that people with manners don't just help themselves to other people's (or bears') porridge, that dishonest individuals always get their due, and that brothers don't strike one another. Further, those who work hard, are good-natured, are honest, and care about others will be rewarded for having those virtues. Traditional tales represent a utopian ideal where good triumphs over evil, and where one's inner characteristics are valued for what they reference and represent.

THE EFFECT OF STORIES THAT TRANSMIT MORALS OR CONVEY RULES

In his writing on Native American stories, Regier (1993:431) noted that Colville Indian children are still "urged to behave" through threats that Owl Woman (a tribal bogeywoman) will visit them if they don't. This underscores one of the major uses of traditional stories, to create a portrayal of how upstanding and moral people act and what happens when people violate those expected roles. Traditional stories contain images that are introduced to listeners, symbolic images of the socially acceptable contrasted with the impermissible. As such, they are a valuable socializing agent, similar to the

Coyote story mentioned at the beginning of this chapter. Such stories may also advance social control, especially to the extent that the audience does not question their meaning (Ericson 1991:221–22). Seemingly unassuming stories about the Big Bad Wolf and other characters contain powerful comparisons to modern-day evils and may help shape listeners' future conceptions of what constitutes deviance and the appropriate reactions to it. Our participants agreed that traditional stories influenced their attitudes, though none felt that the effects were insidious.

The vast majority (90%, $n = 309$) of the participants remembered hearing at least one traditional tale about morals. When those participants were asked whether they had been affected by such stories, 84% ($n = 260$) indicated that they had. Their answers could be divided into three categories: the stories inspired morality, made them think before acting, and served as a positive guide in the participants' lives.

The largest category (53%, $n = 137$) stated that the stories had inspired morality or helped give them some sense of right and wrong. Most answers in this category emphasized the ability of the stories to teach lessons, give listeners "new morals," or generally present morals "from another angle." Some indicated that the stories were an "excellent" or "fun" way to teach morals and that they help children learn difficult concepts; a few noted that the stories break morals down into "simple" terms or "obvious lessons." In a sense, the stories gave the participants concrete examples on which to pattern their behavior, so that they could learn from "others' mistakes." A few participants said that, even to this day, the stories help reinforce what their parents had taught them as children, or that they remember the stories whenever they go "in the wrong direction."

Another group of participants (15%, $n = 39$) noted that stories containing morals "made them think" about what they were doing and about their future actions. This group of individuals felt that such tales helped them make decisions (they "cautioned me to think through my actions before engaging in them," or made a person "think about what you would do in the situation" presented in the story). A subset of this group credited moralistic stories with keeping them from participating in some questionable behavior ("kept me from doing wrong," "always made me think before stealing"). For these participants, traditional stories caused them to alter at least some behavior and bring it more in line with ethical principles. While it would be unfair to suggest that merely hearing the stories could cause such a change in a person, the stories likely played a part in the participants' overall moral development as children. One scholar (Spero 1982:155) argues that traditional stories fulfill an important part in the moral lives of children, though their exact wording is outgrown at some point. It is not the morals that become outdated; adults merely focus on the underlying meanings rather than on the specific details in a given legend.[13]

A third, smaller, group (4%, *n* = 10) noted that the stories served as a positive guide for them ("teach me things that help me succeed"). This group is, in some ways, a combination of the first two. For these participants, the stories' morals themselves were found to be useful guides, not only because they made the participants rethink their lives, but also because they provided a model for the listeners to follow.

Two-thirds (65%, *n* = 222) of the participants remembered hearing at least one traditional story that discussed rules or laws, which is somewhat lower than the percentage who had heard stories that convey morals. Of these, 90% (*n* = 199) indicated that they had been affected by those tales, and their answers are categorized and discussed in regard to morals.

One-third (33%, *n* = 65) of those who had heard such tales felt that the stories helped "explain the rationale" behind the rules/laws, gave them "understanding by illustration," or got them to learn the rules/laws from "another perspective." This group of participants noted that traditional tales helped them "understand rules better" or how rules/laws "were formed." Some credited the stories with helping establish within them "respect for the law" or making them "think favorably" about rules and laws. A few mentioned the normative boundary-setting function of traditional stories ("showed how others suffer when rules are not followed"). Finally, some had their interest in rules and laws "piqued" by the tales, or noted that the stories "teach [laws and rules] on an easier level." The basic idea underlying these participants' beliefs was that traditional tales taught them how to act by providing concrete examples in a format effective for youths. Other participants felt that stories that discuss laws or rules made them think about their future actions or kept them from participating in deviant acts (17%, *n* = 33), while a smaller third group felt that stories about laws and rules serve to inspire morality (11%, *n* = 21).

It is important to acknowledge those participants who did not feel that traditional tales had much (or, in some cases, any) influence in their lives. Roughly a tenth of respondents to each question (morals = 8%, *n* = 23; laws/rules = 12%, *n* = 23) felt that stories were just that—stories. These participants found the tales interesting or entertaining, but not life-changing. Many felt that the effects of the stories were "very little" or that the stories "go in one ear and out the other." One summed up this category of participants quite well: "Morality is complex, 'stories' won't do."

It is clear that traditional stories had a variety of positive effects on the participants in this study. Most acknowledged that they recognized and contemplated the morals in the stories, and many attempted to change their ways based on the stories' messages. Stories that convey rules or laws gave the participants respect for and understanding of rules rather than simple lists devoid of rationale. Even those who perceived that traditional stories did not affect them did not feel the stories detracted from their lives in any way. In a time when rules are so easily dismissed as arbitrary, movements to educate people about the rationale behind rules and laws may be a good investment of time. Indeed, scholars as early as Beccaria ([1764] 1963) argued that the public needs to support a law before it will be followed.

USES IN PARENTING/CAREGIVING

There is little doubt as to the strong influence of family on an individual's moral development. Criminologists have recognized that parental supervision of children, in addition to physically preventing children from committing crimes, also contributes to the child's exercise of self-control in situations in which the parent is not present (Hirschi and Gottfredson 1990:99). Indeed, it may be that the parent's being "psychologically present when the temptation" of deviance occurs, rather than physically nearby, determines whether a deviant act comes to fruition (Hirschi 1969:88). In fact, a person's family has been labeled as "an informal mechanism of crime control" due to its role in establishing and policing rules and values (Findlay and Zvekic 1988:99). This is particularly true during the preschool years. A child's parents and other family members engender cultural values and religious orientation (ibid.:100), and instill reactions to authority (Milgram 1974:137–38). The use of traditional stories helps serve these functions.

The participants were asked if they had ever told traditional stories to children, and if the stories were useful to them as parents/caregivers. Two-fifths (40%, $n = 137$) of the participants had told them to children; most (72%, $n = 98$) told them to their own children or other younger relatives, 15 percent ($n = 21$) to friends' or other unrelated children, and 13 percent ($n = 17$) to children in a work-related setting (for example, babysitting or teaching). Only nine participants did not find the stories to be helpful to them in their caregiving role.

As caregivers, some of the participants liked that traditional tales allowed them to teach "complex ideas in a simple manner" or that one can "teach lessons in a nonpreaching manner" that is more appropriate for children ($n = 23$). Others had used stories to "explain" morals, "communicate rules in a fun setting," or otherwise teach morals to their young charges ($n = 12$). A third group ($n = 10$) liked the two-for-one mentality behind storytelling; as caregivers they could both entertain and bond with their young listeners while simultaneously teaching them important morals and life skills. Another grouping of participants noted that traditional stories could be used to teach in general, rather than arguing that they were particularly suited to teaching children or any particular subject ($n = 7$). A few participants were more pragmatic and recognized that the effects of storytelling might be short-lived, but still noted that those to whom they tell stories "behave" nicely during the session, or that they are kept "occupied" for a short time by the stories ($n = 6$). All of these benefits underscore the stories' usefulness as devices of social control.

Other, less common responses noted that the stories helped children with their imagination, gave caregivers "back up" on their own rules established in the home, were useful for teaching children important events in a format they could remember, or created actual changes in behavior (stopping a fight due to the impact of a well-chosen tale). Others focused on the stories' ability to please people, including themselves (three participants told stories simply because they enjoyed storytelling). Some participants felt that hearing traditional stories brings "joy to the children" or "a smile to their faces." A few caregivers liked the enjoyment they themselves derived from sharing traditional stories, especially when they used them to share quality time with their children.

In general, the participants in this study felt that traditional stories were valuable to them as caregivers, especially as a way to instill moral codes into the children around them. It was interesting to note that half of those who used stories as part of their caregiving routine were 22 years of age or younger. Further, traditional stories represented a pleasurable method of delivery as both child and storyteller enjoyed the procedure. Along these lines, one caregiver succinctly summarized the stories' value:

> Kids are interested and often absorb messages. Traditional stories are important in society today because they usually have a happy, positive outcome. They lay out morals, some values, and beliefs that usually benefit children.

CONCLUSIONS AND PROSPECTS

While the precise historical roots of traditional stories may be uncertain, they nonetheless continue to occupy a place in contemporary social life. The stories have been used to preserve culture, heritage, and history, as well as to transmit morals and law-ways to those who listen to them. The participants in this exploratory study noted many benefits to traditional stories, and found them useful in their duties as parents/caregivers.

Traditional stories are an interesting form of social control that appears to be aimed at children. Countless children have been reminded that the Bogeyman gets kids who don't behave and that Santa Claus knows when they're good or bad, so they should act appropriately or suffer the consequences. They are taught that hard work and selflessness will be rewarded, and that good people do not cause harm to those with whom they share the planet. In short, traditional stories represent a palatable way to teach children moral lessons, and lessons about the lives they are expected to lead. This use is evident in that traditional stories are often somehow changed to make them more accessible to children; Native American stories, for example, are often abbreviated when told to younger audiences (Regier 1993:430).

That the stories are changed for use with children indicates that adults also enjoy them. Among adults, traditional stories serve to reinforce cultural traditions learned as children. Even tales that focus on historical events serve to convey a sense of one's origins and connection to others. The appeal of traditional stories may lie in their image-provoking language, which communicates norms and law-ways in an entertaining fashion. The lessons they contain are perhaps somewhat subliminal, in that the individuals who receive their messages may not realize that they are internalizing a code of conduct. That they are effective in reducing deviance indicates their power in shaping attitudes toward right and wrong.

In no way do we suggest that future crusades will be fought with subconscious messages slipped into an unsuspecting public through the use of allegory and rhyme. Instead, we recognize the strong cultural value of traditional stories. Prior to print media, the elders were our textbooks. They taught us how to live through the stories they told in community circles. Despite our society's move away from that medium, traditional myths and stories about deviance remain important elements in childhood socialization. This is true regardless of the cultural group to which one belongs. Indeed, traditional stories may represent one of the few truly cross-cultural deviance control mechanisms. Similar stories are told by different social groupings (many societies have stories that document a massive flood that reorganized the world), and traditional stories have been borrowed and adapted from other cultures, indicating that the principles contained within them have some applicability in the society that has adopted the tale as well.

Traditional stories also represent a wealth of knowledge regarding the past. More than a century after their legal system was forcibly replaced with one that employed European justice principles, the Navajo Nation is currently reexamining its own legends and songs for hints of its common law, and has used such concepts to revamp its legal system into one that is more culturally appropriate (Meyer 1998). This is but one way the Navajo are coping with the lack of records on their customary law, and their project reflects a real use of traditional tales. It also represents an acknowledgment by the Navajo that their tales were and continue to be important elements of social control.

Future researchers might expand on our findings by learning which stories are most effective in teaching morals and conveying rules, and by discerning the duration of the stories' effects. Some researchers may consider determining whether children can identify distinct morals, and at what stage in their lives this becomes possible; to what extent do traditional stories affect actions in childhood? In addition, traditional stories from various cultures should be examined further for traces of law-ways and codes of conduct, possibly comparing them cross-culturally. Finally, the storytellers themselves should be studied to learn which stories they feel best transfer these important ideals. In the end, it may be that the concepts taught in traditional stories are important enough to warrant the return of storytelling as a valued method of teaching and of social control:

> Elemental truths of moral law and general types of human experience are presented in the fairy tale, in the poetry of their images, and although the child is aware only of the image at the time, the truth enters with it and becomes a part of his individual experience, to be recognized in its relations at a later stage. Every truth and type so given broadens and deepens the capacity of the child's inner life, and adds an element to the store from which he draws his moral inferences. (Bryant [1905] 1996:20)

ACKNOWLEDGMENTS

The authors would like to thank Michael Martinez and Kathy Schaffer-Mauro for their research assistance, Drew Humphries for her comments on an earlier draft, and the many respondents who took their time to participate in the study.

NOTES

1. The woman was eager to try the flower eyes because Coyote had told her that they enabled him to see her husband with another woman on the other side of the mountain. This side issue in the story indicates that infidelity and the desire to uncover it are by no means new social issues.

2. Following the custom employed by Sagarin and Kelly (1986:186), we use the term "myth" as a neutral term rather than as a way to indicate our credence in the story as fact or fancy. At no time do we intend to criticize any of the myths with respect to accuracy or value. We feel that all traditional stories are cherished by some community of people and we do not wish to infringe on the symbolic meaning attached to the myths.

3. The first two pigs were eaten by the wolf. The wolf was then eaten by the third pig, who boiled him and "ate him for supper" (Bryant [1905] 1996:32).

4. Of course, some scholars argue that any historical account, written or otherwise, is suspect because it may reflect the social and political biases of the time in which the event happened or the account was relayed (Ericson 1991:221). In addi-

tion, the literature on eyewitness testimony demonstrates that even simple accounts may be greatly distorted by those who observe an event (see Loftus 1979).

5.   The husband was murdered by the wife, but she was exonerated because she only wanted to improve the genetic qualities of her offspring. This idea—race improvement—is the most fundamental belief among the Maori and guides their traditional legal system.

6.   Maori children attended daily classes in order to teach them how to live in accordance with the Sacred Legends (Rout 1926:77–78).

7.   Of course, some stories may have had the "lessons" edited out of them over time, leaving only the most entertaining kernels for future listeners. It is also possible that the teachings contained in a given tale remain, but are unrecognizable to con-temporary audiences.

8.   Bryant ([1905] 1996:60) alludes to this when she notes that those who do not "possess" the message of a story cannot "give" it to others. She advises storytellers to "listen, humbly, for the message" before attempting to recount the story on their own.

9.   According to Genesis 9:18–27, the offspring of Ham's son Canaan were cast by God into slavery. Some have argued that black Africans, as those offspring, were destined to serve others (see Buhlmann 1977:151).

10.   Iktome (also spelled Iktomi, Inktomi, or Unktomi) is a trickster along the ilk of Coyote, whose often hilarious stories are sought after at storytelling events. Zitkala-Sa ([1921] 1993:212), best known for her compendia of Sioux legends, also de-scribed her childhood love of Iktome stories: "I patiently [listened to the elders talking around the community campfire] . . . wishing all the time that they would begin the stories I loved best. At last, when I could not wait any longer, I whispered in my mother's ear, 'Ask them to tell an Iktome story, mother.' Soothing my impatience, my mother said aloud, 'My little daughter is anxious to hear your legends.'"

11.   This definition did not exclude stories that had been handed down in only one family. A few participants mentioned stories about their own family members' histories or about their ancestors' childhoods in foreign countries. Also, while it is possible that the meaning of traditional stories varied across cultures, we considered all stories and their sources to be equal for the purposes of this research.

12.   Nine participants (3%) declined to provide ethnic identities.

13.   Of interest, this scholar (Spero 1982:152) noted that some adults attach too much meaning to traditional stories. As a therapist, he documented a marriage that was failing due to both the husband and wife continually employing legends to control each other (for example, biblical tales of women who were rewarded for serving their husbands). Spero (ibid.:156–57) also noted that cult devotees continue to focus on the details of stories rather than the underlying messages.

REFERENCES

Beccaria, Cesare. [1764] 1963. *An Essay on Crimes and Punishments*. Translated by
     H. Paolucci. New York: Macmillan
Bentham, Jeremy. [1823] 1948. *The Principles of Morals and Legislation*. New York:
     Hafner.

Berns, Walter. 1989. "Retribution as the Ground for Punishment." Pp. 1–14 in *Crime and Punishment: Issues in Criminal Justice,* edited by Fred E. Baumann and Kenneth M. Jensen. Charlottesville: University Press of Virginia.

Bierhorst, John. 1985. *The Mythology of North America.* New York: William Morrow.

Blumstein, Albert, Jacqueline Cohen, and Daniel Nagin, eds. 1977. *Deterrence and Incapacitation: Estimating the Effects of Criminal Sanctions on Crime Rates.* Washington, DC: National Academy of Sciences.

Bryant, Sarah Cone. 1905. *How to Tell Stories to Children and Some Stories to Tell.* New York: Houghton. Redistributed in 1996 by Project Gutenberg (Illinois Benedictine College) as Etext #474.

Buhlmann, Walter. 1977. *The Coming of the Third Church.* Maryknoll, NY: Orbis.

Campbell, Barbara. 1972. "Young Crees in Montana Educated From an Indian's Point of View." *New York Times,* January 1, p. 21.

Caylor, Patricia S. 1992. "Indian Literature, in the Oral Tradition, Belongs in Classrooms." *Dakota Times,* February 19, p. C1.

Ericson, Richard V. 1991. "Mass Media, Crime, Law, and Justice: An Institutional Approach." *British Journal of Criminology* 31:219–49.

Findlay, Mark and Ugljesa Zvekic. 1988. *(In)formal Mechanisms of Crime Control: A Cross Cultural Perspective.* Rome: United Nations Social Defense Research Institute.

Gifford, E. W. 1937. "Coast Yuki Myths." *Journal of American Folk-Lore* 50:115–72.

Haviland, William. 1996. *Cultural Anthropology,* 8th edition. Fort Worth: Harcourt Brace.

Hawkins, D. J. B. 1944. "Punishment and Moral Responsibility." *Modern Law Review* 7:205–8.

Hirschi, Travis. 1969. *Causes of Delinquency.* Berkeley: University of California Press.

Hirschi, Travis and Michael R. Gottfredson. 1990. *A General Theory of Crime.* Stanford, CA: Stanford University Press.

Hoffman, John C. 1986. *Law, Freedom, and Story: The Role of Narrative in Therapy, Society, and Faith.* Waterloo, Canada: Lauvier University Press.

Howard, Michael C. 1996. *Contemporary Cultural Anthropology.* 5th edition. New York: HarperCollins.

Htin Aung, Maung. 1962. *Burmese Law Tales: The Legal Element in Burmese Folk-Lore.* London: Oxford University Press.

Kroeber, Alfred L. and Edward W. Gifford. 1980. *Karok Myths.* Berkeley: University of California Press.

Lame Deer, John and Richard Erdoes. 1972. *Lame Deer Seeker of Visions.* New York: Washington Square.

Loftus, Elizabeth F. 1979. *Eyewitness Testimony.* Cambridge, MA: Harvard University Press.

MacNamara, Donal E. J. 1977. "The Medical Model in Corrections: Requiescat in Pace." *Criminology* 14:439–47.

McLaughlin, Marie L. 1916. *Myths and Legends of the Sioux.* Bismarck, ND: Bismarck Tribune Co.

Medlicott, Mary. 1992. "Untying the Mother Tongue." *London Times,* November 6, p. 9.

Menninger, Karl. 1959. "Verdict Guilty—Now What?" *Harpers Magazine* 219(1311):60–64.

Meyer, Jon'a. 1998. "History Repeats Itself: Restorative Justice in Native American Communities." *Journal of Contemporary Criminal Justice* 14:42–57.

Milgram, Stanley. 1974. *Obedience to Authority.* New York: Harper & Row.

Monaghan, Peter. 1994. "A Writer to Be Reckoned With." *Chronicle of Higher Education,* July 13, p. A8.

Moriarty, James R. 1969. *Chinigchinix.* Los Angeles: Southland.

Pleasants, Craig. 1994. *The Three Little Pigs.* Richmond, VA: Gates of Heck.

Pokagon, Simon. 1898. "Indian Superstitions and Legends." *Forum* 25(July):618–29.

Regier, Willis G. 1993. *Masterpieces of American Indian Literature.* New York: MJF.

Rout, Ettie A. 1926. *Maori Symbolism.* New York: Harcourt Brace World.

Sagarin, Edward and Robert Kelly. 1986. "The First Recorded Murder and the Jehovan System of Justice." *Legal Studies Forum* 10:185–202.

Schultz, Emily and Robert Lavenda. 1995. *Cultural Anthropology: A Perspective on the Human Condition,* 3rd edition. Mountain View, CA: Mayfield.

Spero, Moshe Halevi. 1982. "The Use of Folklore as a Developmental Phenomenon in Nouveau-Orthodox Religionists." *American Journal of Psychoanalysis* 42:149–58.

Teit, James. 1919. "Tahltan Tales." *Journal of American Folk-Lore* 32:198–50.

von Hirsch, Andrew, Martin Wasik, and Judith Greene. 1989 "Punishments in the Community and the Principles of Desert." *Rutgers Law Journal* 20:595–618.

Zipes, Jack. 1975. "Breaking the Magic Spell: Politics and the Fairy Tale." *New German Critique* (Fall):116–35.

Zitkala-Sa. [1921] 1993. *American Indian Stories.* Edited by Willis G. Regier. New York: MJF.

3

The Historical Roots of Tabloid TV Crime

PAUL G. KOOISTRA and JOHN S. MAHONEY, JR.

INTRODUCTION

In the past decade a new form of television programming has emerged, startled into existence primarily by Rupert Murdoch's Fox Broadcasting Company. Sex and violence in scandalous proportions were served up in an effort to launch a fourth TV network made up of independent stations. The heart of this format included video news magazines such as "A Current Affair" and crime shows such as "Cops" and "America's Most Wanted." These shows were quickly imitated by other networks because of their profitability and popularity. They were relatively inexpensive to produce and attracted reasonable audience interest at the time slots into which they were placed (Fennell 1992; Sauter 1992). Soon the airwaves were inundated with reality-based police shows such as "American Detective," "Top Cops," and "True Stories of the Highway Patrol." Other news magazines such as "Hard Copy" made frequent use of the same common themes utilized by "A Current Affair"—sordid sex crimes and bloody murders.

The scholarly reaction to these new types of shows, often called "tabloid TV," is generally quite critical. Rapping (1994:36) claims that such shows "are sleazy, crude, and often quite openly racist. They are meant for an audience for whom niceties of taste and gradations of moral nuance and subtlety are not important." Waters (1989) suggests that these shows exploit suffering for their own profit and contribute to the belief that everyone arrested of crime is guilty, even before a trial has occurred. Rapping even proposes that these shows present a world view that "flirts dangerously with certain aspects of fascist ideology" (1992:35). For example, certain fictional crime dramas are very insensitive about how African-Americans are portrayed (cf. Gitlin 1983; Montgomery 1989). Kooistra, Mahoney, and Westervelt (1998), in a content analysis of "Cops," conclude that on these "reality-based" shows, where racial images may have a greater influence on audiences' beliefs, an oversimplified and uncritical image of crime as predominantly

47

the activity of black males is common. Furthermore, since whites are disproportionately shown as the victims of serious crime, such shows may produce
an irrational fear of crime that leads to an increasingly punitive criminal
justice system with fewer constitutional restraints (cf. Barrile 1984; Heath
1984; Roberts and Doob 1990; Surette 1992). Crimes, these shows may
seem to imply, are desperate acts of irrational evil committed by dark-
skinned males and sexually depraved females. These deviants are a breed of
humans different from "us"; they reject many of "our" goals and values.

This chapter examines the historical roots of tabloid television. By tabloid
we mean a form of media that emphasizes highly emotional, exaggerated
stories—often visual in nature—typically about crime, sex, and violence.
The content of these tabloid media is presumably reality-based; that is, it
presents itself as news rather than fiction, though the emphasis appears to be
more on entertainment than information. Consequently, dime novels of the
1870s or television shows like "Melrose Place" in the 1990s are not tabloid
formats. We consider the Penny presses of the 1830s, yellow journalism of
the 1900s, and current television shows such as "Cops," "America's Most
Wanted," "Hard Copy," and "A Current Affair" as examples of tabloid media. We will trace the origins of these media formats and compare the recent
television tabloid shows with their print predecessors. Of particular interest
are the roles that technology, media ownership, and audience characteristics play in shaping the content of tabloid media. As Robert Escarpit observes, to maintain a sociological perspective when examining literary
products, one must recognize that "each and every literary fact presupposes
a writer, a book, and a reader; or in more general terms an author, a product,
and a public" (1972:1–2). The relationships between these may be complex,
but it is important to understand them to gain a full understanding of any
form of media, literary or televisual.

In tracing the roots of tabloid television, one difficulty we face is determining a starting point. From the very beginning we find four common
elements linked in ways that sometimes complement and sometimes compete: politics and profit, education and entertainment. Goldschmidt comments that even the production of Gutenberg's Bible was driven by profit
and ran afoul of local politics (cited in Eisenstein 1979:49). As soon as the
first copies of the Bible came off the press, a financier, John Fust, set off with
a dozen copies to Paris to find a market for his Bibles. He quickly found
himself in trouble with a well-organized local guild of the book trade, who
informed the Paris police "that such a store of valuable books could be in
one man's possession through the help of the devil himself, and Fust had to
run for his life or his first business trip would have ended in a nasty bonfire."

Stephens suggests that sordid tales of sex and violence so characteristic of
tabloid media seem to be embedded in the very nature of news, that "the
trail of sensationalism can even be followed back to a news organ that was

published (made public) more than thirteen hundred years before the invention of the printing press" (1988:2). In ancient Rome near the end of the first century A.D., news sheets posted for public viewing typically featured two popular topics of the day: crime and divorce.

Mathias Shaaber finds that by the 1500s the bulk of news concerned such topics as "murders and other crimes; monstrous births and strange beasts; witchcraft; the plague; acts of god such as flood and fire, and the weather; and sporting events" (1966:138). Tales of murders committed by ghosts, dragons terrorizing countrysides, terrible spells cast by hideous witches, and the births of freakish children were dramatized even beyond the standards of the *Weekly World News* and the *National Enquirer.* As Stephens observes: "Anyone who clings to the notion that sensationalism practiced by Rupert Murdoch or even the most shameless present-day journalist is unprecedented could be set straight by spending a few minutes with any number of sixteenth- or seventeenth-century news books" (1988:112).

We will choose as our starting point 1833, with the availability of a rotary press that made it possible for the first time to mass produce forms of print media at low cost. This new technology greatly reduced the cost of newspapers and made them available to large numbers of lower-income readers. These early tabloid media favored a number of topics. These included travel adventures, sex scandals, bizarre and unusual stories, sports figures, and the life and times of celebrities in general.

THE PENNY PRESS

The early newspapers in the United States were primarily controlled by elites and written for elites, a small segment of the population that had the income to spend on producing and purchasing daily newspapers, and the level of literacy needed to read them. Many of these papers were little more than public relations instruments for various political and economic interests. Newspapers in the colonial period and the decades that followed the establishment of the country were marked by outspoken political partisanship as different political interests started newspapers to attack ideological rivals and promote their own causes. As a consequence, Stoler notes that early American editors "needed to be as skilled with pistols as they were with pencils, for they were often called out and required to defend their honor and that of their papers in duels" (1986:28). Other editors were less fortunate. Periodically, angry mobs would destroy the presses and sometimes lynch the editor. It was a safer course to turn attention to business matters, and by 1820 more than half of all newspapers in major U.S. cities featured titles like *Advertiser, Commercial,* or *Mercantile* and became little more than a collection of advertisements and business news (Schudson 1978:17).

However, the industrial revolution ushered in technological and structural changes that would permit a new style of newspaper to emerge. By the 1830s New York City's population was about 200,000, and it would grow to over 800,000 by the onset of the Civil War in 1861. Much of this population growth was fueled by immigration of the working class into the developing factory systems. Consequently, a new market for nonelite "news" was forming. A major thrust of Jacksonian democracy was a push for educational opportunities for the growing working classes. In order to make democracy work, argued some conservatives and most liberals, an educated and enlightened public was needed; and in an increasingly complex market economy based more and more on advertising and skilled labor, literacy became essential (cf. Leps 1992:72–73; Pessen 1985:62–63; Schudson 1978:58–60; Tucher 1994:14–15). By the 1830s the United States was a "nation of readers" (Mott 1962:304). Furthermore, technological changes made printing much cheaper. More efficient ways of processing paper had been developed, and rotary presses allowed the printing of thousands of copies of large newspapers in an hour at relatively low cost.

On September 3, 1833, a printer named Benjamin Day began a daily newspaper called the *New York Sun*. Unlike previous papers of its day, its target audience was the urban masses who began filling New York and toiling at its factories. He priced his paper at a penny and filled his columns with stories of crimes and disasters. As Mott observes, "the *Sun* broke sharply with the traditional American news concept, and began to print whatever was interesting and readable regardless of its wide significance or recognized importance" (ibid.:224). In August 1835, for instance, the *Sun* ran a series of reports of new astronomical discoveries made by the eminent astronomer Sir John Herschel. A new telescope was said to have discovered the presence of life on the moon, including a "strange amphibious creature of a spherical form, which rolled with great velocity across the pebbly beach" and "man-bat" residents (*New York Sun,* 25 August 1835).

Numerous papers passed on the report unchallenged, the country was filled with excitement, and Yale University sent a delegation of scientists to verify the claims. Unfortunately, the *Sun* reported, this miraculous telescope was damaged in an accident, and no further reports could be made. Eventually the reporter of the series, Richard Locke, confided to a fellow reporter from a rival paper that the series had been fabricated. The deception was quickly exposed. Mott observes: "Locke's moon hoax was probably the greatest 'fake' of our journalistic history. While other papers turned on the *Sun* with criticism for falsehood, the public in general accepted it all in good nature" (ibid.:226). Within a few years the paper had a circulation approaching 30,000. With such a large readership, the *Sun* was very appealing to advertisers, who paid for space to push their products. As a consequence, Day was able to be independent of the political and large business interests that typically footed the bill for newspapers. The format quickly attracted imitators. By 1837 there were at least a dozen penny presses in New York, and they were proliferating in virtually every American city.

These papers also attracted opposition. As Mott observes in his history of American journalism: "Bad taste, coarseness which sometimes became indecency, overemphasis on crime and sex, and disreputable advertising were outstanding sins of these papers" (ibid.:243). In New York, the *Ladies' Morning Star* appeared in 1836, primarily as a protest against what its publisher considered "the immorality of the *Sun* and similar papers" (Stoler 1986:30). From 1841 the *New York Tribune* offered itself as an alternative to the "immoral Police Reports, Advertisements, and other matter which has been allowed to disgrace the columns of our leading Penny Papers." By the 1840s, virtually all the "elite" papers in New York were attacking the "penny presses" for their "immorality," and some of the leading clergy of the region led an effective boycott. Businesses that feared to offend the "moral experts" withdrew their advertisements. Emery claims that the real cause for this "moral war" was resentment over the amazing economic success of the penny papers (1972:172–73). Politicians and business leaders, who from time to time were attacked in these populist papers, also did not have favorable opinions of the penny press (Mott 1962:242).

Newspapers that sold in the tens of thousands to working class readers rather than elite audiences had serious political implications, at least to entrenched political and economic interests. Tucher notes that several of the new "penny editors" had been active in "the Working Men's movement, Jacksonian New York's first, confused, and abortive encounter with radical popular politics" (1994:12). James Bennett, editor of one of the more successful penny presses, the *New York Herald,* put forth his journalistic philosophy:

> An editor must always be with the people—think with them, feel with them—and he need fear nothing, he will always be right—always be strong—always popular—always free. The world has been humbugged enough by spouters and talkers, and conventioneers, and legislators. (*Courier and Enquirer,* 12 November 1831)

Abuses of power—whether in the pulpit, politics, or business—were commonly reported. However, politics was generally "an afterthought" or "hobby" to the editors of the penny presses. The mainstream presses were the political and economic mouthpieces. Papers like the Democratic *New York Post* took up the cause of the poor and downtrodden, and in the process suffered financially when they alienated the merchants upon whom they depended for advertising or repulsed the growing middle class (Mott 1962:257–58). The penny presses were more interested in making profits. Consequently, Tucher notes that overtly political discourse was "almost entirely replaced by the low babble of the street, the theater, and the police court. The reckless demands for equal rights had been elbowed aside by the piquancies of rampaging elephants and dissolute clergymen" (1994:14). Such stories were not only "cheap and easy"; they also avoided antagonizing potential advertisers and subscribers. According to Stephens, "the political comments the penny papers did insert between their police stories eventually drifted safely into the mainstream" (1988:205).

As the penny presses became economically successful, it also became more and more difficult for their editors to identify with the working-class audiences who bought their papers. Moreover, the newspapers would inevitably be purchased by monied interests. As the sociologist E. A. Ross noted: "When the shares of a newspaper lie in the safe deposit box cheek by jowl with gas, telephone, and pipe-line stocks, a tenderness for these collateral interests is likely to affect the news columns" (1910:305).

Furthermore, the big city papers increasingly began to hire college graduates as reporters, typically men who hoped to parlay their close brushes with "realism" into literary careers. Among the late nineteenth-century novelists and authors who began their careers as newspaper reporters were Jack London, Stephen Crane, Theodore Drieser, Jacob Riis, H. L. Mencken, Lincoln Steffens, Ambrose Bierce, and Willa Cather. These gatherers of news were typically not from working-class backgrounds and began to push for the careful gathering of facts rather than the weaving of colorful tales—or perhaps more accurately, for the careful gathering of facts from which colorful stories might be constructed (Schudson 1978:68–87; Shi 1995:188–94). Investigative reporting of corruption in high places was a major calling, and most of it was done by the mainstream papers. Such investigative reporting was particularly prominent during the depression years of the 1890s, when hostility toward "robber barons" and corrupt politicians was widespread. For example, in spite of their different laboring experiences, the urban middle class and some of the elites breathed the same air, traveled the same congested streets, and ate the same adulterated food as the working class.

However, not only the corporate nature of the penny press's ownership and the changing background of reporters affected the news. It was advertising, more than circulation, that ensured the profit of these early tabloid papers. Consequently, in response to a toast at a meeting of the New York Press Association, John Swinton replied that the idea of an independent press in pursuit of "truth" was little more than myth:

> The business of the New York journalist is to distort the truth, to lie outright, to pervert, to vilify, to fawn at the feet of Mammon, and sell his country and

race for his daily bread. . . . We are tools, and the vassals of rich men behind
the scenes. We are jumping jacks. They pull the strings and we dance. Our
time, our talents, our lives, our possibilities all are the property of other men.
We are intellectual prostitutes. (quoted in Smith 1984:378–79)

With so much at stake, newspapers became increasingly careful about
publishing anything that might alienate either their audience or their advertisers, at times putting the penny presses into what Tucher (1994:13) called a
"state of delicate schizophrenia" as they attempted to balance the interests
of monied advertisers and working-class readers. Eventually, advertisers in-
variably led the papers toward more "respectable, monied readership, when
newspaper prices crept higher and their pages grew more 'serious'" (Stephens 1988:208).

As the tabloid papers wavered toward respectability in the latter half of
the nineteenth century, some of the more "respectable" papers from the
cities of the East borrowed heavily from the successful formats used by their
tabloid counterparts. However, in the West, tabloid journalism could still be
found among the papers of smaller cities, where cheap afternoon papers met
with some success (Mott 1962:540). Competition for readers was fierce. The
population base was smaller and the literacy levels not quite so high. As
Gans suggests, these conditions lead to an emphasis on sensationalism and
tabloid formats in general (1980:83–84). Tales of crime in particular boosted
sales, and were quickly seized upon by papers from Missouri to California.
Of great interest were outlaws, who often came from respectable backgrounds and victimized social institutions such as banks, railroads, monopolies, or any institution that could be portrayed as an "enemy of the common
folk." During the depressions of the 1870s and 1890s, the western presses
were a veritable celebrity industry, transforming ordinary lawbreakers into
heroic criminals who would appeal to popular audiences (cf. Kooistra
1989).

John Newman Edwards, for example, routinely extolled the virtues of his
Confederate outlaw brethren, the James-Younger gang, in his editorials for
various Missouri newspapers. The robbery of the Kansas City Fair, during
which a small girl was wounded by the outlaws, was lauded in an essay
entitled "The Chivalry of Crime" (Kansas City Times, 27 September 1872).
The robbers were described as "men who might have sat with Arthur at the
Round Table, ridden at tourney with Sir Lancelot or won the colors of
Guinevere. . . . It was as though three bandits had come to us from storied
Odenwald, with halo of medieval chivalry upon their garments and shown
us how the things were done that poets sing of."

Even the nonpartisan press found cause to extol the virtues of criminals
from time to time. After the James-Younger gang botched a bank robbery in
Northfield, Minnesota, in which several townspeople and bank officials

were killed by the gang, the *St. Paul (MN) Pioneer Press* (20 September 1876) commented:

> Truth is stranger than fiction, and no novel writer would dare invent such situations for his characters as these six men have passed through. The feats of Turpin, Shepherd, and the more recent Joaquin, and even the bloodcurdling and enormous achievement of the dime novels pale before the accomplishments of these desperate outlaws. . . . Such determination, daring and perseverance was worthy of a better cause, and cannot but evoke admiration even of those who desire their extermination. Probably no men were ever more desperately set upon, nor more intrepid daring ever displayed by mortal.

The *Pioneer Press* interviewed captured members of the gang at length and presented them to its readers as noble and virtuous Christian men, despite the death and destruction they caused!

The James-Younger gang was just one of many lawbreakers who achieved notoriety thanks to the western press. Billy the Kid, Butch Cassidy and the Sundance Kid, Sam Bass, John Wesley Hardin, the Daltons, Bill Doolin, Tom Horn, Belle Starr, and "Wild Bill" Hickock also were shaped into folk heroes during this time period, almost always beginning this journey in newspaper stories and then being transformed into larger-than-life heroes in books and magazines marketed to youth and working-class audiences (Jones 1978; Denning 1987).

THE RISE OF YELLOW JOURNALISM

Although the tabloid papers in the establishment East went through something of a lull following the Civil War, they were revived in all their splendor by the late 1890s primarily through the efforts of two men: Joseph Pulitzer and Randolph Hearst. Pulitzer came from Hungary at the age of seventeen to fight in the American Civil War. After the war he moved to St. Louis, where he studied law and worked as a reporter for a German-language newspaper. In 1878 he bought the *St. Louis Post-Dispatch* and turned it into the city's leading newspaper. His immigrant background made him sensitive to issues of corruption and exploitation, and a prominent feature of the *Post-Dispatch* was its crusading nature.

Pulitzer then decided to purchase the *New York World* in 1883 and to apply the same approach that had proved so successful in St. Louis. He was going to publish a paper for the working class:

> There is room in this great and growing city for a journal that is not only cheap but bright, not only bright but large, not only large but truly

democratic—dedicated to the cause of the people rather than that of the purse potentates—devoted more to news of the New than the Old world—that will expose all fraud and sham, fight all public evils and abuses—that will battle for the people with earnest sincerity. (*New York World,* 11 May 1883, p. 4)

He dropped the price of the paper in an attempt to attract wide readership, especially among the working-class and immigrant population in New York. And the immigrant population in New York was significant. By 1890 about 40 percent of New York's population was foreign-born, hence the reason for a newspaper that emphasized pictures and told simple but sensational stories to the working class struggling to master a new language (Juergens 1966:234–62). It also pursued women readers, particularly through its columns on etiquette and fashion featured in Sunday issues (ibid.:132–74).

The basic formula used by Pulitzer has been summarized as a six-point program (Mott 1962:436–39). First, there was a staff of reporters who hunted the city for incidents or gossip that could be dramatized and made interesting. These would be presented colorfully and marked with large and bold headlines. Among the types of stories played up by the *World* in its early years were accounts of human sacrifice by religious sects in the United States, a description of unusual types of weapons used to commit murder, a story of cannibalism at sea, and numerous accounts of sensational crimes (Juergens 1966:55). There was also a plethora of human interest stories and local gossip. An important feature of this "gossip" was that it often featured short biographies of ordinary working people and not just lifestyles of the rich and famous. In this regard, the *World* was truly a paper that addressed the situations of the ordinary citizen.

Second, the newspaper helped "create" news through crusades and publicity stunts. Populist crusades against various monopolies, and well-publicized acts of charity to the poor were well received. However, the most spectacular stunt involved a female reporter named Elizabeth Cochran, who was sent on an "around the world" voyage under the name of "Nellie Bly." She followed the path of Jules Verne's fictional hero, Phileas Fogg, and attempted to break his record of making it "Around the World in Eighty Days." She filed reports from various exotic locations, detailing her adventures. A contest was established in which the person who came closest to guessing the time "Bly" would complete her journey would receive a free trip to Europe.

A third important characteristic included a strong editorial page, where various causes and issues supporting working-class policies were discussed and promoted. While sensational headlines would lure readers to purchase the *World,* the editorial pages would be where they would be educated. Frequent attacks were made on political corruption and economic chicanery by the monied interests on Wall Street. And while rival newspapers attributed the poverty that existed in parts of Manhattan to "the moral degeneracy of the people who live there," Pulitzer publicized the plight of the poor and the sorry living conditions they faced. During the hot summer of 1883, sensational headlines such as "LINES OF LITTLE HEARSES" and "HOW BABIES ARE BAKED" dramatized the infant mortality the heat brought to low-income sections of New York (*World,* 3 July 1883, 6 July 1883). Such efforts, along with organized labor protests, helped lead to various reforms in housing, food processing, fire protection, police conduct, and labor laws.

These efforts contributed to increasing circulation, as Pulitzer turned sensationalism to what he considered to be the service of the public good. But success brought its own hazards, of which Pulitzer was quite aware:

> A newspaper conductor with an income of a quarter or half a million a year or more, with yachts, townhouses and country houses to keep up, with an intimate circle of millionaire friends to entertain and be entertained by—above all, with a surplus income which must be invested and which naturally goes into bonds and stocks and other securities of corporations and monopolies— which side would he be apt to drift into? Is he likely to be eager and zealous and earnest in resisting the encroachments of monopoly and the money power, in defending the rights of the common people? (*New York World,* 9 September 1883, p. 4)

But so long as there was widespread dissatisfaction among the "common people" with big business, the *World* continued to give voice to these types of social issues.

Points four to six of Pulitzer's six-point program included long stories, often running eight to twelve pages; innovative and extensive use of illustrations; and shameless self-promotion through contests and self-advertising. According to Schudson the *World* became the circulation giant of New York journalism, growing from 20,000 to 250,000 subscribers in the space of a few years, "because of its vigorous and unembarrassed use of illustrations and other techniques of self-advertisement" (1978:97). Obviously, the tremendous surge in the city's population and the ability to appeal to middle-class and female readers also helped.

Pulitzer's formula was ideal for reaching the growing working-class and immigrant population of New York. There was the appeal to working-class politics on the editorial page, the use of sensational stories and pictures for a semiliterate population, crusades against corrupt businesses and politicians who were exploiting the "common man," and the successful creation of news by a paper headed by a former immigrant who had made good. The astounding success of the *New York World* no doubt resulted primarily from being able to resonate with the goals and aspirations of the immigrants and working class that comprised the great bulk of its readers. But it also appealed to female readership. Heroic tales of women capturing criminals were common. So, too, were accounts of unmarried women successfully suing dishonest suitors for "fraud" or married women suing mistresses for "alienation of affection." And even the returns of "prodigal sons" from prison were presented as situations for rejoicing ("New Year's Gift of Pardon for Baldwin After Twenty-Two Years in Sing Sing," *New York World,* 1 January 1900, p. 2; "Goldstein Rejoins Brave Wife Who Got Him Out of Prison," *New York World,* 3 September 1900, p. 12) rather than as causes for community alarm.

Pulitzer's astonishing success in New York quickly attracted imitators, including one of the "purse potentates" against whom he often railed. In 1895 William Randolph Hearst bought the *New York Journal* and followed Pulitzer's formula to even greater success. Money was no object, for Hearst was independently wealthy. He quickly hired the best writers and illustrators away from Pulitzer's *World.* Among Hearst's greatest "steals" was the popular *World* cartoonist Richard Outcault, who drew a strip featuring the life and time of the "Yellow Kid," an adventurous working-class youth. "The figure of this silly fellow, with his toothless, vacant grin and his flaring yellow dress, struck some critics of the new sensationalism represented by the *Journal* and the *World* as symbolical of that type of journalism" and led to the term "yellow journalism" (Mott 1962:526).

Like Pulitzer, Hearst embarked upon colorful crusades and large-scale self-promotion of his paper. Hearst was also not above using sensationalism in the pursuit of circulation, and even creating news himself. According to legend, Hearst sent an illustrator to Havana to document atrocities and cover the possibility of war. When atrocities proved hard to find, the illustrator cabled: "EVERYTHING IS QUIET. THERE IS NO TROUBLE HERE. THERE WILL BE NO WAR. WISH TO RETURN." To which Hearst is said to have replied: "PLEASE REMAIN. YOU FURNISH THE PICTURES AND I'LL FURNISH THE WAR." The story is probably untrue, but it is commonly held that the Hearst and Pulitzer papers, in their desire to outdo each other and see who could most sensationalize Spanish injustices in Cuba, played a significant part in bringing about the Spanish-American war (cf. Mott 1962:527–33; Swanberg 1961:130–49).

Not content with helping to start a war, however, Pulitzer and Hearst wanted to be participants and help create news, turning the whole military situation into a public relations adventure. Pulitzer attempted to organize a salvage operation to determine what had sunk the *Maine.* Hearst attempted to organize a military regiment but was rebuffed. The Hearst yacht, anchored off Cuban waters, was pressed into service, however. Hearst's little navy of a couple dozen writers, artists, and photographers even managed to "capture" an unarmed band of Spanish sailors. *Journal* correspondents participated in a few minor military skirmishes. One correspondent, James Creelman, was wounded in action. In his autobiography years later, he described the scene:

> Someone knelt in the grass beside me and put his hand on my fevered head. Opening my eyes, I saw Mr. Hearst, . . . a straw hat with a bright ribbon on his head, a revolver at his belt, and a pencil and notebook in his hand. The man who had provoked the war had come to see the result with his own eyes, and, finding one of his correspondents prostrate, was doing the work himself. (Creelman 1901:211–12)

Needless to say, Hearst's paper took full advantage of the situation, with blaring headlines: "THE HEROIC CAPTURE OF CANEY TOLD BY THE JOURNAL'S EDITOR-IN-CHIEF" (*New York Journal* of June 30, 1898).

The success of the yellow presses led to numerous imitators both within and outside New York. Even the more traditional papers began emphasizing illustrations and "tasteful" human interest stories in attempts to hold onto readers. Other papers also participated in pushing for the war against Cuba and sent correspondents in order to report exciting victories in glorious detail. Not all the papers viewed the activities of the *World* or *Journal* favorably, however. An editorial in the *New York Evening Post* (19 February 1898) proclaimed:

> Nothing so disgraceful as the behavior of these newspapers [the *Journal* and the *World*] this week has been known in the history of American journalism. Gross misrepresentation of facts, deliberate invention of tales calculated to excite the public, and wanton recklessness in the construction of headlines . . . have combined to make the issues of the most widely circulated newspapers firebrands scattered broadcast throughout the country.

It was a common perception that the promotion of American intervention in Cuba by these two newspapers, particularly after the sinking of the *Maine,* was inspired by the thought that such a great story helps build profits (cf. Mott 1962:539).

In the process of promoting war and generating profit, Hearst and Pulitzer increased the animosity of the other New York papers toward them. Increases in circulation came at a cost: a steady decline in respect from their peers both within and outside the newspaper business. It was the assassination of President McKinley, however, that perhaps helped diminish yellow journalism more than anything else. McKinley had been the subject of ruthless editorial attacks by the *Journal*. Shortly after the assassination of the governor of Kentucky, Hearst's paper suggested that the same approach be tried with McKinley: "If bad institutions and bad men can be got rid of only by killing, then the killing must be done" (*New York Journal,* 10 April

1901). Several months later self-proclaimed anarchist Leon Czolgosz shot McKinley because he was "the enemy of the good people—the good working people" and expressed no remorse for his crime (cited in Clarke 1982:39). According to Mott: "Rage flamed against Hearst and his paper as the President lay dying. Czolgosz was reported to have a copy of the *Journal* containing the attack on McKinley in his pocket when he fired the fatal shot. The newspaper was boycotted by patriotic and business organizations and by libraries and clubs" (1962:541). Worst of all, circulation declined.

One other important factor hastened the demise of yellow journalism at this time. The *New York Times,* that bastion of higher-class civility, dropped the price of its paper to that of its tabloid competitor. Huge surges in circulation resulted. This also convinced the captains of yellow journalism that success was possible without the tawdry sensationalism so characteristic of the yellow papers. While obviously never quite mirroring the standards set by the *New York Times,* many of the yellow presses toned down a bit and became more moderate in their coverage. In doing so, they avoided the possible public reactions to excess and gained respect and status among their peers, while still holding on to a fair share of the market.

The Twentieth Century Tabloid

On January 1, 1901, Joseph Pulitzer conducted a small experiment. He turned the day's issue of the *New York World* over to Alfred Harmsworth, a London newspaper editor who had already made a fortune in the newspaper business. The paper that emerged was dubbed a "tabloid." It contained copious illustrations and short condensed stories, and each page was about half the size of a typical newspaper page. It sold well enough to require extra press runs, and generated much comment, but the next day the *World* went back to its old format. Harmsworth, however, started his own London tabloid a few years later, and eventually was selling a million copies per day.

The possibility that such a paper might prosper in New York City seemed evident. However, it was not until 1919, near the close of World War I, that an entrepreneur decided to try to imitate the successful London model. Joseph Patterson was a Yale graduate and managed the *Chicago Tribune.* He also happened to be an acquaintance of Alfred Harmsworth, and at Harmsworth's urging decided New York City was ready for a "new" kind of newspaper. For years, traditional papers like the *New York Times* had led in circulation. In order to break into the competitive New York market, Patterson borrowed from the tradition of the "yellow press" of the 1890s the format that was doing extremely well in London. Also significant was the improvement in the ability to print visual imagery in newspapers, a format that was used successfully during the Great War, with photos from the front presenting arresting images to readers. Patterson's *Illustrated Daily News* (later the *New York Daily News*) combined a yellow press format with a strong emphasis on photography. On some days, the entire front page consisted of little more than an eye-catching photo and bold headline. One of the more spectacular pictures was the execution of Ruth Snyder in the electric chair, a photo taken with a camera secretly attached to the leg of a reporter. Crime was a major topic in the *Daily News* and other tabloids that came into existence at the time.

This format caught the attention of New Yorkers, many of whom were not daily newspaper readers. It was a style of paper that was ideally suited to the countless New Yorkers now commuting by bus, train, or subway to work. It was a quick and easy read. It was simple to hold and turn pages on a crowded commute. While the circulation of most city papers remained steady, the *Daily News* became, for many years, the best-selling daily paper in America.

Like earlier papers that emphasized sensationalism to attract viewers, it also attracted imitators. Within a few years there were several tabloid papers in New York, each attempting to outdo the others in generating bizarre and sensational stories, most of them centered on sordid crimes. Stories of murdered ministers, eccentric female killers, and fatal seductions of youth followed one after another. Patterson's was the kind of publication that seemed to typify the jazz age of the 1920s, and the style became known as "jazz journalism."

Like the penny and yellow presses that preceded it, this tabloid format also quickly attracted opposition. As Mott observes, other New York papers had been protesting against the "excesses of tabloidism" for years, and in the late 1920s a moral crusade "led by educational and church agencies, developed against what was now commonly called the Daily Pornographic" (1962:671). Letters such as that below, following the publishing of Ruth Snyder's execution photo, were common:

> A small boy found a tabloid last week. He is a healthy boy, but of sensitive fiber. . . . He was a little hysterical at supper that night. . . . He screamed out in his sleep. . . . He was feverish and he babbled considerably about chairs. . . . Even the pleasant familiar chairs in his own little bedroom filled him with delirious horror. Off with their heads! commands the growing tabloid. The more children who can be put off their heads, the more borderline cases and psychoses and paranoiacs we'll have, and by the same token, the more murders—more and better murders—we'll have for stirring up circulation. Stir up the imagination of the incipient paranoiac and he'll make us news. (*New York Tribune,* January 1928; cited in Bessie 1938:19–20)

It is estimated, though, that the Snyder photo to which this letter alludes helped sell an additional 500,000 copies of the paper (ibid.:117). Moral fervor was easily eclipsed by the spiritual joy that resulted from soaring profits.

Despite the criticisms leveled against "jazz journalism," many of its innovations were adopted widely by the mainstream press. As one early admirer noted: "Pictures, fiction, columns of gossip, advice and consolation all proved their validity by becoming popular parts of all American dailies. In 1920 they were to be found almost exclusively in the tabloid and that is probably why people flocked to the *Daily News*" (ibid.:95). By the time Lindbergh flew alone across the Atlantic in 1927, virtually all newspapers in America were eager participants in the making and marketing of celebrities. Photos of exploding airships were considered more a form of art than of pornographic violence. Layout was thus a factor in the spectacular success of the *Daily News*. Since that time, all newspapers have become more aware of the importance of graphics and pictures in directing and holding the reader's attention.

As the *Daily News* became more successful, it began to downplay sensationalism a bit. Criticisms raised against it by moral entrepreneurs, and the effects of various boycotts, were not proving good for business. The depression years of the 1930s seemed to call for a more subdued tone that focused on serious matters. Crime news declined in coverage, and more attention was given to foreign events and political issues of the day. In part, the paper may have also been influenced in this regard by advertisers, for the *Daily News* was the only New York paper to steadily increase its advertisers throughout the depression. By 1935 it had the largest amount of retail and department store advertising in the city. In a slap at those who considered tabloid readers " 'the great unwashed,' the *News* announced that it had the largest annual total of soap advertising of any paper in New York" (Bessie 1938:130). Like the penny presses and yellow papers before them, the tabloid paper drifted slowly toward the mainstream.

Later, other related newspapers reinjected lurid news of social deviance. For example, in 1952, an entrepreneur named Gene Pope purchased a less successful "cousin" of the *Daily News,* called the *New York Enquirer.* He immediately began filling the paper with stories of crime, sex, and violence. In 1958 he renamed it the *National Enquirer* and began selling it in supermarkets, near the cash registers. He toned down the explicit sex and violence to appeal to a broader audience and began emphasizing celebrity gossip, the supernatural, Elvis and UFO sightings, government waste, diet successes, medical "information," and any other bizarre or unusual matter that might catch the eye of someone waiting in a grocery line. It quickly became the largest-circulating newspaper in the United States, selling over 4 million copies weekly. Soon imitators such as the *Globe,* the *Sun,* and the *Weekly World News* appeared alongside it. Headlines such as "NEW STAR OVER BETHLEHEM SIGNALS END OF WORLD" and stories about "waterproof tribes in the Amazon" were readily available to the inquiring shopper (*Weekly World News,* 26 December 1995).

THE RISE OF TABLOID TELEVISION

If it can be said that tabloid television was born of the Fox Television Network—home of such shows as "Cops," "A Current Affair," "America's Most Wanted," and "Wildest Police Videos"—it can also be said that the roots of its "sleazy" and sensational format lie in the efforts of Rupert Murdoch's father, Keith Murdoch, to increase the circulation of Australia's *Melbourne Herald* in the early 1920s. Within a year of taking over, the elder Murdoch had increased this "solid but boring" paper's circulation from 100,000 to 140,000. His methods were almost identical to Pulitzer's formula for the *World* discussed above. Journalists and reporters were considered critical to the paper's success, and Murdoch gave them daily feedback on what he wanted from them. He ran serials, introduced publicity stunts and competitions, ran sensational news stories, started a women's page, and shortened the editorials (Shawcross 1997:41).

Keith Murdoch was to use this formula over and over again, and although his competitors leveled charges of "yellow journalism," many found themselves scrambling to imitate his style to protect their own papers' circulations. Appointed to the board of the *Herald* group in 1925, Murdoch increased the number of its publications dramatically. The elder Murdoch was a farsighted and talented innovator—implementing high-speed printing presses and wire photo services. Under his direction, the *Herald* group became the first newspaper publisher to own a radio station in Australia. It also bought large tracts of forest land, moving into the newsprint industry (Shawcross 1997:42).

Rupert Murdoch followed in his father's footsteps. His climb to success began when he inherited a small Australian newspaper group from his father. He employed the same techniques that Keith Murdoch had thirty years earlier (the "Pulitzer formula") to increase circulation while at the same time looking for other newspapers and magazines to acquire. Rupert Murdoch's own style of journalism developed at this time: to create stories that would be as sensational as possible without offending the political or moral sensibilities of the "common man".

> Thus was born in the mid-1950s what has since come to be known the world over as Murdochian journalism—the exaggerated story filled with invented quotes; the rewriting of cryptic laconic news-service wire copy into lavishly sensationalized yarns; the eye-shattering unusually ungrammatical, irrelevant, and gratuitously blood-curdling headline ("Leper Rapes Virgin,

Gives Birth to Monster Baby," read a typical early front page); endless pages of pap disguised as service and entertainment features ("Your Horoscope," "Your Favorite Psychic's Predictions," "How to Keep UFOs out of Your Garden"); brisk, snappy, self-congratulatory editorials larded with bold face and under-linings, as though the reader had to be guided through the forest of verbiage . . . all wrapped in cheap, smudgy tabloid form and promoted with the apoca-lyptic fervor and energy of Bible Belt evangelism. (Kiernan 1986:51–52)

All that Rupert Murdoch needed to bring this format to television was a network. This occurred first in Australia in 1959 when he acquired the rights to open one of two television stations licensed for Adelaide. His station became an immediate success—beating the competition by being the first to transmit its programming, which consisted largely of "stunts and person-alities, . . . live breakfast television, and live children's programs" (Shaw-cross 1997:79). He then moved into Sydney in 1962, and was immensely successful due largely to vast amounts of American programming that he had managed to purchase from ABC ahead of his competitors.

In the United States, the world of tabloid journalism did not fully merge with network television until Rupert Murdoch's creation of the Fox televi-sion network on May 6, 1985. However, there were a number of important trend-setting forerunners. Even in the 1950s, crime shows like "Dragnet" emphasized "real-life" crimes redone in a fictional format. "The Verdict Is Yours" offered highly emotional courtroom dramas. Popular quiz shows, later rocked with scandal, transformed ordinary people into affluent celeb-rities using formulas not unlike those in the tabloid presses (Anderson 1978; MacDonald 1990). There were shows like "Queen for a Day" and "Strike it Rich," where a parade of contestants relayed their woes to a studio audi-ence, which through the use of an "applause meter" decided who was most deserving of sudden wealth. These shows were truly sensational in the de-piction of the miseries suffered by their contestants. Much of this was pack-aged in the sentimentality of public service and human kindness when the prizes were presented at the end of each show, but many less fortunate people came to New York City, the location of these shows, in hopes of being chosen. Social service agencies criticized these shows as "heartless exploitation of human misery" (ibid.:117).

Talk television moved the industry to new frontiers. Phil Donahue was a founding figure, beginning with a small show on a Dayton, Ohio, affiliate in 1967. In its first week on the air, the "Donahue" show established new boundaries and set the stage for "shock" television:

On Monday of his very first week, he interviewed the nationally known atheist, Madalyn Murray O'Hair. Tuesday, his show featured single men talk-ing about what they looked for in women. Wednesday, he showed a film of a baby being born, from the obstetrician's point of view. On Thursday, Phil sat in a coffin and interviewed a funeral director. And by the end of the week he had held up "Little Brother"—an anatomically correct doll without a diaper. (Heaton and Wilson 1995:16)

"Donahue" would remain the preeminent national television talk show from 1969 until the "Oprah Winfrey Show" was nationally syndicated in 1986. (Others, even more outrageous in content, soon followed: Sally Jessy Raphael and Geraldo in 1987; Morton Downey, Jr., in 1988; Maury Povich in 1991; Ricki Lake in 1993; and Jerry Springer in 1994.) By the 1990s, talk television had taken the nation by storm and the subjects it covered were more shocking and bizarre than ever before as "often in an exploitive and tawdry manner, long-standing video taboos against sexual frankness were broken" (MacDonald 1990:246).

In 1985, though, sensational and titillating talk television was still a very small segment of each of the three networks' programming. Fox television would be different. According to Barry Diller, "We had to do shows that demanded your attention, that yanked you by the throat to get you to change the channel" (quoted in Shawcross 1997:327). These shows included sitcoms—"Married with Children" (1986), "The Simpsons"—as well as "news magazines"—"A Current Affair" (1986), "America's Most Wanted" (1989), and "Cops" (1989). But it was the latter two crime shows that set the network on its feet and established its profitability. In the words of Murdoch biographer, William Shawcross:

> Diller and Murdoch realized that they had hit a gold mine, a string of raunchy, "realistic" programs that the image-conscious networks with their phalanx of censors and tastemakers had never dared attempt. As well as finding new, younger viewers, and the advertisers who pursued them, Fox was constantly pushing back the frontiers of what was acceptable to a living-room audience. (1997:331)

As a result, tabloid television became synonymous with the Fox network.

Television, by its very nature, is a tabloid medium emphasizing imagery and emotion. From its infancy in the early 1950s, critics deplored the content of this household appliance that brought beliefs and values into millions of households. By 1952 a congressional committee was investigating television for signs of immorality. The Catholic church was decrying its blatant use of sex. Educators were lamenting that the excessive and repeated violence found on television throughout the 1950s was promoting antisocial values (cf. MacDonald 1990:100–3). By 1962, FCC Chairman Newton Minnow was describing television as a "vast wasteland."

It was not until the 1980s, however, that what we call tabloid television surfaced as a major format, with the emergence of the Fox network. This was a natural outcome given the backgrounds of those operating the Fox network. The original pioneers of television, men like William Paley and David Sarnoff, entered the field from backgrounds in radio. Consequently much of early television borrowed, in some cases stole, from radio formats (Barnouw 1990; MacDonald 1990). The moving forces behind the Fox network, on the other hand, came from backgrounds in print tabloids. Murdoch could simply move people like Steve Dunleavy, who had worked for him overseeing tabloid papers—first in Australia, then London, and finally in New York—to translate tabloid formats like "A Current Affair" and "America's Most Wanted" into the language of television.

But the reasons for extensive development of tabloid television in the 1980s, and not before, may be explained by two interlocking factors. The first had to do with the social and political context in which television is embedded. The second concerned the changes in the organizational structure of television, namely the advent of cable and the Fox network intruding on the monopoly enjoyed by the three television networks.

In its infancy, major issues surrounded the content of television: Who owned the molecules upon which signals were broadcast? Were the airwaves the property of the government, the people, or private enterprise? What was the primary function of television? Was it to be a powerful educative tool, one that was in the words of Mortimer Leowi, director of the fledgling Dumont television network in the 1940s, "the greatest instrument of mass dissemination of information and knowledge since the days of Gutenberg" (quoted in MacDonald 1990:58)? Or would it simply become a "vast wasteland" of situation comedy, cheap drama, formulaic westerns, and other forms of mass entertainment? Ultimately, the airwaves were given to a handful of large corporations, which then leased time on them to other large corporations in order to sell products to a mass audience.

Amidst the commercialism and sensationalism stood television news and documentaries as forums for educating the public about a variety of social issues. The line between entertainment and information was not crossed. News sets were simple and stories were reported in a straightforward manner. It was in this arena that television justified its independence from government overseers and public pressure, while also claiming to be free from corporate censorship. Early television made a clear distinction between entertainment and information formats such as the news (Exoo 1994:45–131; MacDonald 1990:47–48; 163–64).

By the 1980s television had firmly established itself as a commercial enterprise relatively free from government interference. It was taken for granted that the airwaves were controlled by major corporations and used to market products to the general public. A major characteristic of the 1980s was a political philosophy emphasizing minimal governmental meddling in private enterprise. While social critics lamented what they perceived to be a failure on the part of mass media to fulfill their role as educators of the public, there was little pressure from regulatory agencies (cf. MacDonald 1990:231–40; Postman 1985). FCC Chairman Mark Fowler described television as just another household appliance, "a toaster with pictures" (Nossiter 1985:402). Documentaries began to disappear from the networks. News became more and more a forum for entertainment and human interest stories, as these proved easier and more profitable (Auletta 1991; Bennett 1995; MacDonald 1990:239–41).

The second factor was a change in the organizational structure of television. For most of television's history, three major networks blanketed the country and controlled most of the content. While competition between the networks could be fierce, they essentially copied each other. There was little incentive for changing content or taking risks. Consequently, television became highly formulaic, and the types of shows varied insignificantly from network to network.

By the 1980s, the advent of cable opened up competition and allowed for some experimentation with formats. The rise of issue-oriented talk shows starting out in local markets was one such experiment. These were relatively inexpensive video versions of the supermarket tabloids. The major networks then snatched some of the more promising of these and exposed their content to a national audience. Finally, with the emergence of the Fox network in 1985, the monopoly held by the "big three" networks—CBS, NBC, and ABC—was broken. Fox, as a fledgling network, was open to new programming ideas; looking for a demographic base from which to build an audience; and searching for inexpensive (cheap) shows to fill its schedule. One consequence was the development of glitzy news magazines and "crime and justice" shows; in short, tabloid television.

CONCLUSION

In our examination of the historical antecedents of tabloid television, we note the following pattern. Mass media news formats seem to emphasize one of two possible styles. One style places heavy emphasis on accuracy and information. It employs a language of "civility" and downplays sensationalism. It is aimed primarily at middle and higher classes (cf. Mott 1962; Tucher 1994). This audience has the income level that makes it attractive to advertisers. It is also an approach that over time, fits with the class backgrounds of reporters and editors who are media gatekeepers. A second format is tabloid in style. It emphasizes entertainment and sensationalism, uses dramatic images and hyperbole. Its target audience is typically lower and working-class. This audience may not have much disposable income, but has appeal to certain advertisers and is quite large in number. It is important to note that "mainstream media" are also interested in stories that are entertaining and somewhat sensational; and "tabloid" media do not necessarily eschew facts and accuracy. It is often simply a matter of emphasis given to one format or the other.

Tabloid media emerge when competition in a market is great and an appeal to sensationalism is utilized to broaden the market. More commonly, the resort to sensationalism occurs when a new media organization (newspaper, magazine, or television network) attempts to break into an established market. These new media organizations are usually helped by new developments in technology—rotary presses, an ability to print high-quality pictures in a newspaper format, or inexpensive hand-held cameras—that allow for innovative presentations that existing media are not using.

Typically, tabloid media are met with derision by established media organizations and moral entrepreneurs in the community. The gatekeepers of established media perhaps dislike tabloid formats because they are often successful in attracting audiences and eroding the market share of established media. It is also possible that moral entrepreneurs at the established media outlets resent the cultural capital of the tabloid media.

At the same time that they are derided by mainstream media, they are also imitated. Because tabloid media are often successful, selective elements are "borrowed" by the established media. A greater emphasis on crime, sexual misconduct, and "other forms of entertainment" emerges. The tabloid media, however, once they are established, begin to become less sensational and more like mainstream media. This may in part result from harsh reactions to some of their judged excesses in attempting to be sensational. It also is a result of advertiser influence, both direct and indirect, to appeal to a more affluent audience (cf. Tucher 1994:202). To some extent it is also linked to a desire for acceptance and respect from their peers in the media business.

If history were to repeat itself, then, one would expect that the major television networks will become more tabloid in their formats—utilizing news magazines and "true-life" crime shows. This has already happened with the emergence of shows such as "Hard Copy" (CBS), "Inside Edition" (NBC), "Unsolved Mysteries" (NBC), and "True Stories of the Highway Patrol" (CBS). The Fox Network would strive for respectability by developing critically acclaimed innovative programming (e.g., "The Simpsons," "X Files") or capturing respected media figures or programs from the major networks, such as NFL football and major league baseball.

Although this pattern already seems to be in evidence, there is one significant way in which more recent tabloid media have differed from their predecessors: in their portrayal of crime and deviance. Murder and mayhem have long been profitable for mass media, and a healthy market for such tales has long existed. Stories *from the streets* have also always offered certain advantages to media organizations. They are easily found. A quick trip to routine news sources such as the police station or the mayor's office is all that is required. Flashing lights, grieving loved ones, grim-faced law officers, and blood all make for compelling drama, whether in print or video formats. Those entrenched in positions of power have always had a decided edge in getting their versions of social reality told. More complex forms of deviance, which demand lengthy investigation and time to explain, typically are less likely to find their way into mass media (cf. Bennett 1988; Ericson, Banarek and Chan 1989; Fishman 1980; Kooistra 1989).

Yet early tabloids, written for and from a working-class perspective, were at times marked by a content that seemed intent on "comforting the afflicted and afflicting the comfortable." Tales of corruption in high places and sympathetic portrayals of the poor and unfortunate were common. Criminals such as Jesse James or "Pretty Boy" Floyd were politicized and glorified for their predations against powerful institutions such as banks, which were widely seen as unjust at the time (Kooistra 1989). Even criminals being released from prison were welcomed back "into the fold."

Recent tabloid formats, on the other hand, seem to mock the afflicted rather than "comfort" them. The disadvantaged are cast as freaks on talk shows or dangerous or pathetic criminals on true crime shows (Kooistra et al. 1998:141–58). As Rapping notes about modern tabloid television:

> The language, the brutality, the tackiness of the social scene, the bad hair, the untidy lawns, dirty sidewalks are a turnoff. We would not wish to have any of the participants . . . over for dinner. These are not our neighbors; they are the people we see on subways and sidewalks, begging or dozing. (1994: 37–38)

There is no one simple answer for why current tabloid media differ from their predecessors. In part this may be the result of the professionalizing of journalism. Even those reporters working at the lower levels of media organizations are now typically college educated and from upper-middle-class or more affluent backgrounds. There has been a growing concern among conservative media critics that the major media gatekeepers have lost touch with mainstream America (Stein 1979; Medved 1992). However true that may be, the media certainly have been disconnected from concerns and views of the white working class and minorities (Exoo 1994; MacDonald 1983; Parenti 1991). William Greider notes:

> Newspapers do still take up for the underdog, of course, and investigate public abuses, but very few surviving papers will consciously assume a working-class voice and political perspective. The newspapers that have endured and flourished, often as monopolies, were mostly morning papers and they moved further upscale, both in their readership and their content, re-

sponding to the demographics of the market. Their reporters all went to college. (1992:292)

This change in how tabloid media portray crime and poverty is also a reflection of the political climate of the 1980s and 1990s. Cavender and Fishman observe that "crime policy, ideological notions about crime, and television crime shows are interrelated; they occur within a particular social context" (1998:5). The types of themes and images shown on tabloid crime programs reflect and reconfirm public concern for crime. The past few decades have featured a "war on drugs" (Reinerman and Levine 1989), a "missing children" panic (Best 1990), a Satanism scare (Richardson, Best, and Bromley 1991), and an incessant "war on crime," where criminals were often demonized and conservatives who pushed for increased police powers and harsher sentences became a dominant voice (Kappeler, Blumberg, and Potter 1993; Surette 1992; Walker 1989).

Today's tabloid media—whether on television, on radio, in magazines, or in newspapers—have become more conservative both politically and economically. They are owned by vast corporate structures, rather than individual gadflies such as a Benjamin Day or Joseph Pulitzer (cf. Bagdikian 1987). Their main source of revenue comes from large multinational corporations rather than individual subscribers. They are staffed by members of the higher social classes, more at home at cocktail parties than the neighborhood bar. They often attempt to catch the eye of wealthier audiences than did their predecessors; they can no longer just target the working- or middle-class citizen. While tabloid media may once have been a potential voice for working-class dreams and fears, they end up today reflecting the dream world of middle America . . . and its fears and hopes.

REFERENCES

Anderson, Kent. 1978. *Television Fraud: The History and Implications of the Quiz Show Scandals.* Westport, CT: Greenwood.

Auletta, Ken. 1991. *Three Blind Mice.* New York: Random House.

Bagdikian, Ben. 1987. *Media Monopoly,* 2nd edition. Boston: Beacon.

Barnouw, Eric. 1990. *Tube of Plenty: The Evolution of American Television,* 2nd rev. edition. New York: Oxford University Press.

Barrile, Leo. 1984. "Television and Attitudes about Crime. Do Heavy Viewers Distort Criminality and Support Retributive Justice?" Pp. 141–58 in *Justice and the Media,* edited by R. Surette. Springfield, IL: Charles C. Thomas.

Bennett, W. Lance. 1995. *News: The Politics of Illusion,* 3rd edition. New York: Longman.

Bessie, Simon. 1938. *Jazz Journalism: The Story of the Tabloid Newspapers.* New York: E. P. Dutton.

Best, Joel. 1990. *Threatened Children.* Chicago: University of Chicago Press.

Cavender, Gray and Mark Fishman. 1998. "Introduction: Television Reality Crime Programs: Context and History." Pp. 1–17 in *Entertaining Crime: Reality Television Programs,* edited by M. Fishman and G. Cavender. Hawthorne, NY: Aldine de Gruyter.

Clarke, James. 1982. *American Assassins: The Darker Side of Politics.* Princeton, NJ: Princeton University Press.

Creelman, James. 1901. *On the Great Highway.* Boston: Harper.

Denning, Michael. 1987. *Mechanic Accents.* New York: Verso.

Eisenstein, Elizabeth. 1979. *The Printing Press as an Agent of Change.* New York: Cambridge University Press.

Emery, Edwin. 1972. *The Press and America,* 3rd edition. New York: Prentice-Hall.

Ericson, Richard, Patricia Banarek and Janet Chan. 1989. *Negotiating Control: A Study of News Sources.* Toronto: University of Toronto Press.

Escarpit, Robert. 1972. *The Sociology of Literature.* Painesville, OH: Lake Erie College Studies.

Exoo, Calvin. 1994. *The Politics of Mass Media.* New York: West.

Fennell, Tom. 1992. " TV." *Mclean's,* 105(December 7):48.

Fishman, Mark. 1980. *Manufacturing the News.* Austin: University of Texas Press.

Gans, Herbert. 1980. *Deciding What's News.* New York: Vintage.

Gitlin, Todd. 1983. *Inside Prime Time.* New York: Pantheon.

Greider, William. 1992. *Who Will Tell the People?* New York: Simon and Schuster.

Heath, L. 1984. "Impact of Newspaper Crime Reports on Fear of Crime." *Journal of Personality and Social Psychology* 47:263–76.

Heaton, Jeanne A. and Nona L. Wilson. 1995. *Tuning in Trouble: Talk TV's Destructive Impact on Mental Health.* San Francisco: Jossey-Bass.

Jones, Daryl. 1978. *The Dime Novel Western.* Bowling Green, OH: Bowling Green University Popular Press.

Juergens, George. 1966. *Joseph Pulitzer and the New York World.* Princeton, NJ: Princeton University Press.

Kappeler, Victor, Mark Blumberg, and Gary Potter. 1993. *The Mythology of Crime and Criminal Justice.* Prospect Heights, IL: Waveland.

Kiernan, Thomas. 1986. *Citizen Murdoch.* New York: Dodd, Mead.

Kooistra, Paul. 1989. *Criminals as Heroes: Structure, Power, and Identity.* Bowling Green, OH: Bowling Green University Popular Press.

Kooistra, Paul G., John S. Mahoney, and Saundra Westervelt. 1998. "The World of Crime According to 'Cops'." Pp. 141–58 in *Entertaining Crime: Television Reality Programs,* edited by Mark Fishman and Gray Cavendar. Hawthorne, NY: Aldine de Gruyter.

Leps, Marie-Christine. 1992. *Apprehending the Criminal: The Production of Deviance in Nineteenth-Century Discourse.* Durham, NC: Duke University Press.

MacDonald, J. Fred. 1983. *Blacks and White TV.* Chicago: Nelson.

MacDonald, J. Fred. 1990. *One Nation Under Television.* New York: Pantheon.

Medved, Michael. 1992. *Hollywood vs. America.* New York: Harper.

Montgomery, Kathryn. 1989. *Target: Prime Time.* New York: Oxford.

Mott, Frank L. 1962. *American Journalism,* 3rd edition. New York: MacMillan.

Nossiter, Bernard. 1985. "The FCC's Big Giveaway Show." *Nation,* October 26, pp. 402–5.

Parenti, Michael. 1991. *Make Believe Media: The Politics of Entertainment.* New York: St. Martin's.

Pessen, Edward. 1985. *Jacksonian America: Society, Personality, and Politics.* Urbana: University of Illinois Press.

Postman, Neil. 1985. *Amusing Ourselves to Death.* New York: Viking.

Rapping, Elayne. 1992. "Tabloid TV and Social Reality." *Progressive* 56(August):35–37.

Rapping, Elayne. 1994. "Cops, Crime, and TV." *Progressive* 58(April):36–39.

Reinerman, Craig and Harry Levine. 1989. "The Crack Attack: Politics and Media in America's Latest Drug Scare." Pp. 115–38 in *Images of Issues,* edited by Joel Best. Hawthorne, NY: Aldine de Gruyter.

Richardson, James, Joel Best, and David Bromley, eds. 1991. *The Satanism Scare.* Hawthorne, NY: Aldine de Gruyter.

Roberts, J. and A. Doob. 1990. "News Media Influences on Public Views on Sentencing." *Law and Human Behavior* 14(5):451–68.

Ross, E. A. 1910. "The Suppression of Important News." *Atlantic Monthly* 105(March):303–11.

Sauter, Van Gordon. 1992. "Rating the Reality Shows—and Keeping Tabs on the Tabloids." *TV Guide,* May 2–8, 18–21.

Schudson, Michael. 1978. *Discovering the News.* New York: Basic Books.

Shaaber, M. 1966. *Some Forerunners of the Newspaper in England, 1476–1622.* New York: Octagon.

Shawcross, William. 1997. *Murdoch: The Making of a Media Empire.* New York: Simon and Schuster.

Shi, David. 1995. *Facing Facts.* New York: Oxford University Press.

Smith, Page. 1984. *The Rise of Industrial America.* New York: Penguin.

Stein, Ben. 1979. *The View from Sunset Boulevard.* New York: Basic Books.

Stephens, Mitchell. 1988. *A History of News.* New York: Penguin.

Stoler, Peter. 1986. *The War Against the Press.* New York: Dodd Mead.

Surette, Ray. 1992. *Media, Crime and Criminal Justice.* Pacific Grove, CA: Brooks/Cole.

Swanberg, W. A. 1961. *Citizen Hearst.* New York: Charles Scribner's Sons.

Tucher, Andie. 1994. *Froth & Scum: Truth, Beauty, Goodness, and the Ax Murder in America's First Mass Medium.* Chapel Hill: University of North Carolina Press.

Walker, Samuel. 1989. *Sense and Nonsense About Crime,* 2nd edition. Pacific Grove, CA: Brooks/Cole.

Waters, Harry. 1989. "TV's Crime Wave Gets Real." *Newsweek,* May 15, 72.

4

Dominant Ideology and Drugs in the Media*

CRAIG REINARMAN and CERES DUSKIN

Jimmy is 8 years-old and a third-generation heroin addict, a precocious little boy with sandy hair, velvety brown eyes and needle marks freckling the baby-smooth skin of his thin brown arms.

So began a front-page feature in the *Washington Post* on Sunday, September 28, 1980. The reporter, Janet Cooke, claimed that Jimmy had "been an addict since the age of 5." She told of how Jimmy "doesn't usually go to school, preferring instead to hang with older boys." When he did go, Cooke wrote, it was "to learn more about his favorite subject—math," which he planned to use in his drug-dealing career. She noted the "cherubic expression" on Jimmy's face when he spoke about "hard drugs, fast money and the good life he believes both can bring." He sported "fancy running shoes" and an "Izod shirt." "Bad, ain't it, I got me six of these," the child reportedly told Cooke.

She described Jimmy's house in detail. There were addicts "casually" buying heroin everyday from Ron, Jimmy's mother's "live-in lover," cooking it, and then firing up in the bedrooms. "People of all shapes and sizes," a "human collage" including teenagers, "drift into the dwelling . . . some jittery, uptight and anxious for a fix, others calm and serene after they finally 'get off.'" These things were, Cooke wrote, "normal occurrences in Jimmy's world."

"And every day, Ron or someone else fires up Jimmy, plunging a needle into his bony arm, sending the fourth grader into a hypnotic nod." Cooke then quoted Ron on how he first "turned Jimmy on": "He'd been buggin' me all the time about what the shots were and what people was doin' and one day he said, 'When can I get off?'" She described Ron as "leaning against a wall in a narcotic haze, his eyes half-closed, yet piercing," and quoted him as answering Jimmy, "'Well, s——, you can have some now.' I let him snort a little and, damn, the little dude really did get off."

"Six months later," Cooke wrote, the five year old "was hooked." She quoted the boy as saying, "I felt like I was part of what was goin' down . . . . It [heroin] be real different from herb [marijuana]. That's baby s__."

Cooke also quoted Jimmy's mother: "I don't really like to see him fire up. But, you know, I think he would have got into it one day, anyway. Everybody does. When you live in the ghetto, it's all a matter of survival. . . . Drugs and black folk been together for a very long time."

The mother had been routinely raped, Cooke wrote, by her mother's boyfriend, one such instance leading to Jimmy's birth and then to heroin use to blot out her growing pain. When her drug sources dried up after a bust, she turned to prostitution to support further heroin use. Cooke quoted the mother as saying that she wasn't alarmed by her son's dealing ambitions "because drugs are as much a part of her world as they are of her son's."

Cooke made the more general point that heroin use had "become part of life" among people in poor neighborhoods—people who "feel cut off from the world around them"—often "filtering down to untold numbers of children like Jimmy who are bored with school and battered by life." Many kids "no older than 10," Cooke claimed, could "relate with uncanny accuracy" dealer names and drug nomenclature.

Cooke's story then offered a familiar litany of quotes to bolster and contextualize her story. Drug Enforcement Agency officials noted the influx of "Golden Crescent heroin." Local medical experts spoke of the "epidemic" of heroin deaths in Washington. Social workers observed how the lack of "male authority figures" and peer pressure combine to make such childhood tragedies common.

"At the end of an evening of strange questions about his life," Cooke concluded, "the calm and self-assured little man recedes" to reveal a "jittery and ill-behaved boy" who was "going into withdrawal." Ron then left the room, according to Cooke, and returned with "syringe in hand, and calls the little boy over to his chair." He grabbed Jimmy's "left arm just above the elbow, his massive hand tightly encircling the child's small limb. The needle slides into the boy's soft skin like a straw pushed into the center of a freshly baked cake. Liquid ebbs out of the syringe, replaced by bright red blood. The blood is then re-injected into the child." The final scene in Cooke's drama depicted little Jimmy "looking quickly around the room" and climbing into a rocking chair, "his head dipping and snapping upright again in what addicts call 'the nod.'"

THE STORY BECOMES THE STORY

Two days after Cooke's story appeared, the *Washington Post* ran a fascinating follow-up article entitled, "D.C. Authorities Seek Identity of Heroin

Addict, 8" (*Washington Post,* 30 September 1980) Such a tragic tale of a young life lost to drugs, so compellingly conveyed by Cooke and so prominently published by the *Post,* had led to hundreds of outraged calls and letters to the paper and to local officials.

The then-mayor Marion Barry was "incensed" by the story and assigned a task force of hundreds of police and social workers to find Jimmy. It was later learned that the police intensively combed the city for nearly three weeks. Teachers throughout Washington checked the arms of thousands of young students for needle marks. Citizens from housing projects called in offering to help. A $10,000 reward was offered. The police, supported by the mayor and the U.S. attorney, threatened to subpoena Cooke in an effort to find and "save" the boy. The *Post* refused to identify Jimmy, citing First Amendment rights to protect confidential sources (*New York Times,* 16 April 1981).

The *Post* assigned an eleven-member reporting team to cover all this, six of whom were told to search for another Jimmy, "on the theory that if there is one, there must be others" (Green 1981). Cooke and one of her editors searched for Jimmy's house for seven hours. For some unexplained reason, they never found it. Neither the police nor anyone else found Jimmy either. And, neither the other *Post* reporters nor anyone else ever found any other child addict.

Meanwhile, *Post* publisher Donald Graham congratulated Cooke. Bob Woodward, a senior editor who eight years earlier had broken the Watergate scandal, promoted her. The *Post* went on with its normal coverage of drug issues.

Six months later, on April 13, 1981, "Jimmy's World" resurfaced in a ceremony at Columbia University in New York, where it was announced that Janet Cooke had won the Pulitzer Prize in Feature Writing for her story. The next day, the *Post* published a piece proudly announcing Cooke's Prize and reprinted "Jimmy's World" in honor of the occasion (*Washington Post,* 14 April 1981). The story noted that "Jimmy's World" had first met with shock and disbelief. But despite the fact that none of the massive follow-up efforts had ever turned up Jimmy or anyone like him, the *Post* asserted that experts had confirmed the fact that heroin addicts of Jimmy's age were common.

For any American reporter, winning a Pulitzer—the journalist's equivalent of a Nobel Prize—is as good as it gets. Such prizes make careers, catapult people out of the grind of routine reportage into prestigious positions, often to fame and fortune. Journalism students fantasize about such feats. Competitive cub reporters across the country covet chances for front-page stories that might get noticed and nominated. Janet Cooke should have been ecstatic. As the world would soon learn, she wasn't.

Two days later, on April 16, the *Washington Post* published another front-page piece on "Jimmy's World": "The Pulitzer Prize Committee withdrew its feature-writing prize from Washington Post reporter Janet Cooke yesterday after she admitted that her award-winning story was a fabrication. . . . It was said to be based on interviews with the boy, his mother and his mother's boyfriend. Cooke now acknowledges that she never met or interviewed any of those people and that she made up the story of Jimmy" (*Washington Post,* 16 April 1981).

The *Post*'s lead editorial that day, "The End of the 'Jimmy' Story," began with an unusual phrase for papers of the *Post*'s stature: "We apologize." It went on to say, "This newspaper, which printed Janet Cooke's false account of a meeting with an 8-year-old heroin addict and his family, was itself the victim of a hoax—which we then passed along in a prominent page-one story, taking in the readers as we ourselves had been taken in. How could this have happened?"

To find out, Executive Editor Ben Bradlee invited the *Post*'s ombudsman, Bill Green, to conduct an independent, "full disclosure" investigation. Green learned that the *Post* had been running many more routine stories about drug problems in Washington, and that Cooke had been researching the local heroin problem for some time. She took extensive notes to City Editor Milton Coleman. In describing her material she mentioned in passing an eight-year-old addict. Recognizing the print media equivalent of "dramatic footage," Coleman stopped her right there and said, "That's the story. Go after it. It's a front-page story."

Green discovered that when Cooke followed Coleman's instructions she was unable to come up with the young addict. Coleman sent her back out to find him. Again she could not. A week later Cooke told him that she had found *another* eight-year-old addict, "Jimmy," by going to elementary school playgrounds and passing out her cards. She told her editor that one of her cards found its way to a mother, who called and angrily asked, "Why are you looking for my boy?"

Cooke said she then extracted promises of confidentiality for "Jimmy's" mother and told her editors that she had visited the child's home, according to Green's report. She soon turned in a thirteen-page draft of the story. She rendered the furnishings and other aspects of the home and "Jimmy's" life in such delicious detail, Green found, that no editor had ever asked for "Jimmy's" or his mother's identity. Editor Coleman later told Green that he went over the story carefully: "I wanted it to read like John Coltrane's music. Strong. It was a great story, and it never occurred to me that she could make it up. There was too much distance between Janet and the streets."[1]

Green came to feel that the *Post* had been blinded by its ambition for a dramatic feature and by the fine prose of a reporter who was African-American and thus assumed trustworthy on such matters. Editors dismissed doubts and decided to run "Jimmy's World." It was not until Cooke was awarded the Pulitzer that the story started to unravel. Even then, questions centered on her background, not her story.

The first clue emerged when Cooke's earlier employer, the *Toledo Blade,* wanted to run the prize-winning story. In setting up a sidebar on Cooke's Toledo roots, *Blade* editors discovered that the biographical information they had received over the Associated Press wire "did not jibe" with what they knew of Cooke's background. Her "official" resume—sent in by the *Post,* released by the Pulitzer Committee, and carried with the AP story—had Cooke graduating from Vassar magna cum laude, studying at the Sorbonne, earning a masters degree from the University of Toledo, speaking four languages, and winning half a dozen Ohio newspaper awards.[2] When the editors at the *Blade* called AP to check on the discrepancies, AP editors began to ask questions of their own. They discovered other discrepancies. No Sorbonne. No masters degree. They called Cooke. She asserted that her official resume was correct. AP knew at this point that "something was wrong."

Prompted by the AP inquiry, Green discovered, the *Post*'s editors compared her personnel file and the Pulitzer biography form she filled out. After discovering that the two did not match in several respects, Bradlee told Coleman to "take her to the woodshed." Coleman took Cooke for a walk and grilled her. Cooke eventually admitted she had not graduated from Vassar, but continued to insist that everything else, especially the Jimmy story, was true.

Coleman phoned his superiors with these answers, according to Green's report. Bradlee told him to bring Cooke back to the *Post* via a side entrance "to avoid being conspicuous" and to sequester her in a vacant office three stories above the newsroom. Bradlee came up and grilled her. He asked about the foreign language skills she had listed on her resume: "Say two words to me in Portuguese," Green quoted Bradlee as saying. She couldn't. Her French wasn't much better. He asked about her journalism prizes. Her answers were inconclusive. Bradlee said, "You're like Richard Nixon, you're trying to cover up."

In another office, Assistant Managing Editor Bob Woodward joined Deputy Metro Editor David Maraniss and another editor to go over the 145 pages of Cooke's notes and two hours of tape-recorded interviews. According to Green's report, they found "echoes" of the "Jimmy" story, but no evidence that she had actually spoken with a child addict.

Meanwhile, under pressure of intense questioning, Cooke gave Coleman what she claimed were the real names of Jimmy, his mother, and her boyfriend, as well as their address. Coleman and Cooke went there, but, as had been the case six months before, she somehow could not find the house. (Forgotten at this point in the investigation was the fact that in the immediate aftermath of her story, Cooke had been unable to find the house, returning the next day claiming to have found it but that the family had moved.)

It was nearly midnight when they got back to the *Post*. By this point, according to Green, each of the editors who had bought the story all along had become convinced that she was lying. Woodward then confronted Cooke: "It's all over. You've gotta come clean. The notes show us the story is wrong. We know it. We can show you point by point how you concocted it." Cooke continued to deny it. The more Woodward yelled, the more stubbornly she stuck to her story.

Exhausted from failed interrogations, they left Cooke in the room with only her closest colleague, Maraniss. Cooke knew that he knew, according to Green. They talked quietly for an hour about how tough it was to succeed at a national newspaper (Bradlee called it "major-league journalism" or "hardball") and how far they had come. After she had tiptoed all around a confession, Maraniss gently pushed Cooke by asking her what he should tell the others.

She broke down. "Jimmy's World" was, she finally admitted, "a fabrication." "There was no Jimmy and no family. . . . I want to give the prize back," Green quoted her as saying. Maraniss told the others. Bradlee asked him to get a written admission and a resignation. Cooke complied.

THE LESSONS LEARNED

The ombudsman's report (Green 1981) was the second longest article ever published in the *Post.* Its conclusions were that warning signals were ignored, that senior editors were uninformed, that competition for prizes had pushed an ambitious young reporter too hard, and that the result was "a temporary lapse." The majority of the *Post* editors and reporters interviewed agreed, interpreting this lapse in terms of ambition and competition.

The *Post* editorial accompanying the first admission of the fraud framed the whole affair in terms of the breakdown of normal journalistic editing procedures—"quality control," Green later dubbed it. The writers thus implied that this was the ultimate cause of fraud and expressed the hope that it would be seen as the aberration it was, thereby leaving intact the *Post's* "prized credibility" (*Washington Post,* 16 April 1981).

Other newspapers, of course, closely covered the scandal and offered similar interpretations. The *San Francisco Chronicle* (19 April 1981) blamed the *Post* editors for trusting their reporters too much. The *Los Angeles Times* (19 April 1981) blamed the fraud on the growing use of unnamed sources, a practice it claimed arose during the Vietnam and Watergate debacles. A few days later a *Los Angeles Times* columnist went further to opine that the lesson of the Cooke fraud was that the Watergate-era spirit of "gung-ho press investigators" needed to be reversed (23 April 1981).

According to the *New York Times* (23 April 1981), the six hundred editors who attended the annual convention of the American Society of Newspaper

Editors a week after the scandal broke talked of little else. They expressed a variety of concerns about the "loss of credibility for all newspapers." But almost all supported the ombudsman's principal conclusions that the scandal stemmed from "internal pressures" to "produce sensational articles and to win prizes" and from the failure to use the editing and checking "system that should have detected the fraud." Some editors added that the scandal had "forced them to re-examine" the procedures for checking the background of new reporters and the use of unidentified sources.

The *Post* itself (18 April 1981) published a summary of what other papers said about the Cooke affair. The core themes were the same: failure to check confidential sources and the risks of putting sensationalism above editorial judgment. The *Post* story also quoted a *Wall Street Journal* piece, which asked whether in all of these investigations "the hard questions" would be raised, but did not say what those questions were. The *Post*'s summary closed with a *Chicago Tribune* editor's rotten apple theory—like many others, he blamed the whole affair on "one highly unethical person."

Strangely, none of these accounts mentioned anything about the media's general assumptions and beliefs about drugs and drug users, which ultimately allowed Cooke's concoction to slip into print. For us, this is the hardest question, and it was neither asked nor answered in any of the press postmortems.

What of the Pulitzer Prize jury? Surely if the *Post*'s editors could suffer a "temporary lapse," at least one of the esteemed editors and journalists selected to serve on the prestigious Pulitzer jury should have detected some flaw in Cooke's story. As it turns out, a few of the jurors were concerned. One questioned Cooke's guarantee of confidentiality when a child's life seemed at stake. A second was troubled by the lack of attribution, but accepted Cooke's piece "on faith" because "it had gone through the editing process on a reputable newspaper." A third overcame her doubts because she felt the article "spoke to a very compelling problem of our time. We did not suspect that it was not what it seemed to be. *We had no reason to.*" (*Los Angeles Times* 1981a; emphasis added).

Still other jurors expressed doubts after the fact, but these centered largely on the unusual procedure by which Cooke's article had won. The *Post* had submitted it in the "general local reporting" category. The local reporting jury picked "Jimmy's World" second. The Pulitzer Board agreed with the jury, awarding that prize to another reporter. However, several board members felt that the Cooke piece belonged in the feature category. After discussion, board member Joseph Pulitzer suggested that it be reconsidered later in that category (Green 1981).

Meanwhile, the jury for the feature-writing prize had selected three finalists and submitted them to the board. None had ever seen the Cooke article. When the board discussed overruling the jury in favor of "Jimmy's World," some members raised the familiar questions about the article. Their opposition "evaporated," however, when one member, distinguished African-American journalist Roger Wilkins, "eloquently" argued "that he could easily find child addicts within 10 blocks" of where the board was meeting at Columbia University (*Los Angeles Times* 1981a). Just as no one at the *Post* had challenged an articulate African-American reporter six months earlier, no juror challenged Wilkins's assertions about addiction in the inner city. Whatever questions they may have had about "Jimmy's World" were quickly dropped. The board overruled the jury and unanimously awarded Janet Cooke the Pulitzer Prize in Feature Writing.[3]

THE LESSONS NOT LEARNED

In all of this, no one ever turned up any concrete evidence that a child addict such as "Jimmy" existed. It is, or course, statistically possible that American's inner cities may somewhere contain a few eight-year-old addicts whose mothers' boyfriends shoot them full of heroin every day. But it is a virtual certainty that if such child addicts exist at all they are exceedingly rare. So for us, the most curious part of the Cooke scandal is that in the ensuing decade and throughout the dozens of press accounts we analyzed, no one has yet critically examined the ideology that allowed her bizarre claim that such child addicts are common to pass unnoticed into publication and on to a Pulitzer.

No one doubts that Janet Cooke was a talented writer. No one disputes that the "Jimmy" story was compelling. And certainly no one questions that tragic drug problems persist across the United States, particularly in inner cities. Was it not reasonable, then, for the *Post*'s editors to have been "taken in," and for even the prestigious Pulitzer jury to have become "victims of a hoax?" Who could have seen through a fraud perpetrated by an otherwise fine reporter whose pathological ambition led her to such thorough deceit?

We wish to suggest that the "Jimmy" story was, in fact, rather unreasonable on its face, and that the media would not have been "taken in" by it had they not been blinded by bias. We think that the *Post* editors and Pulitzer jurors—and virtually all the others in the news business who interpreted the scandal—*missed the point.*

The "hoax" to which the American media became "victim" was one they played a central role in making. Drug scares have been a recurring feature of American history. From the early nineteenth century until Prohibition passed in 1919, many in the press were willing handmaidens to the zealous moral entrepreneurs in the Temperance crusade. Newspapers and magazines often uncritically repeated wild claims that alcohol was the primary cause of crime, insanity, poverty, divorce, "illegitimacy," business failure, and virtually all other social problem afflicting America at the time of its industrialization (Levine 1984).

Throughout the twentieth century the media helped foment a series of drug scares, each magnifying drug menaces well beyond their objective dimensions. From the turn of the century into the 1920s, the yellow journalism of the Hearst newspapers, for example, offered a steady stream of ruin and redemption melodramas. These depicted one or another chemical villain, typically in the hands of a "dangerous class" or racial minority, as responsible for the end of Western civilization (see Musto 1973; Mark 1975; Morgan 1978). In the 1930s, newspapers repeated unsubstantiated claims that marijuana, "the killer weed," led users, Mexicans in particular, to violence (Becker 1963). In the 1950s, the media spread a story of two teenagers in Colorado who had gotten high accidentally by inhaling model airplane glue. This led to nationwide hysteria, which in turn spread the practice of glue-sniffing (Brecher 1972).

In the 1960s, the press somehow remade "killer weed" into "the drop-out drug" (Himmelstein 1983), and spread other misleading reports that LSD broke chromosomes and yielded two-headed babies (Weil 1972; Becker 1967). The media that might have served as a source of credible warnings about the risks of drug abuse were dismissed with derision by the very users they needed to reach. In the 1970s, the press again falsely reported that "angel dust" or PCP gave users such superhuman strength that the police needed new stun guns to subdue them (Feldman, Agar, and Beschner 1979). In 1986, the press and politicians once again joined forces on crack use among the black underclass. The drug was unknown outside a few neighborhoods in three cities until newspapers, magazines, and TV networks blanketed the nation with horror stories that described the crack high (Reinarman and Levine 1989).

In each of these drug scares the media has consistently erred on the side of the sensational and dutifully repeated the self-serving scare stories of politicians in search of safe issues on which to take strong stands. And in each scare, including the current "war on drugs," reporters and editors have engaged in the *routinization of caricature*—rhetorically recrafting worst cases into typical cases, and profoundly distorting the nature of drug problems in the interest of dramatic stories.

A century from now historians may ponder this construction of drug demons just as they now ponder the burning of witches and heretics.[4] But what is already clear is that a century's worth of scapegoating chemical bogeymen left even the best journalists quite prepared to believe the very worst about drug users, especially inner-city addicts. Given the deep structure of bias prevailing within media institutions, it is little wonder that Janet Cooke's story elicited so little of the press's vaunted skepticism.

Thus, her immediate editor Milton Coleman told the *Post*'s investigating ombudsman that he "had no doubts" about "Jimmy's World" and that "it never occurred to me that she could make it up." Assistant managing editor and former Pulitzer winner Bob Woodward admitted similarly that "my skepticism left me," that his "alarm bells simply did not go off," and that "we never really debated whether or not it was true." The few doubts of the distinguished Pulitzer jury were washed away when one African-American voice asserted that "Jimmys" were everywhere in the ghetto. Even after the scandal broke wide open, ombudsman Green's thoroughly detailed report never really asked *why*, as he put it, "None of the *Post*'s senior editors subjected Cooke's story to close questioning."

These things were possible, we contend, precisely because America's guardians of truth had no touchstone of truth on drug problems apart from their own scare stories. In this the *Washington Post* was no worse than most media institutions in the United States. When seen as part of the historical pattern of news "coverage" of drug issues, the Pulitzer Prize–winning fraud was less a "lapse" than part of a long tradition. On almost any other subject, editors' "crap detectors" would have signaled that something was amiss.

The evidence for this contention oozed from every pore of Cooke's tale and was bolstered at every turn in the follow-up investigations. First, there were the shaky assumptions about addiction. Cooke alleged that "Jimmy" was "addicted" to heroin at age five and that he smoked marijuana before that. Children are curious creatures, so it is theoretically possible that a four- or five-year-old might push himself to learn to inhale foul-tasting smoke and hold it deep in his lungs repeatedly. It is even possible, although even less likely, that a five-year-old could learn to enjoy snorting heroin powder into his nostrils day after day. What is hardly possible and highly unlikely is that a five-year-old would ask to have a needle stuck in his "thin brown arms" more than once a day for the weeks it would take him to become addicted. One needn't be a drug expert for such claims to set off "alarm bells"; one need only have seen a doctor try to vaccinate a child.

All this aside, if any journalists had checked, they would have found that most heroin users experience serious nausea the first few times they use. In addition to the difficulties posed by needles and nausea, a mildly skeptical editor easily could have discovered that drug effects are rarely unambiguously pleasurable early on. Drug "highs" are in many important respects acquired tastes that are learned over time through processes that five- or eight-year-olds are exceedingly unlikely to endure (Becker 1953; Zinberg 1984). Yet, after all of journalism had put this story-scandal under its microscopes, no one had even asked about such things.

Cooke's fiction contained a second set of "red flags" having to do with assumptions about addicts. How moronic would addicts have to be (even crass "junkie" stereotypes depict them as shrewd) to allow a reporter from a top newspaper to witness them "firing up"? Even if paranoia were not an occupational hazard, there is no evidence that addicts are proud of their habits. And in a home Cooke herself described as a dealing den and shooting gallery full of other addicts, no known drug is capable of inducing the magnitude of stupidity necessary for adult addicts to show a reporter how they inject heroin into their small child.

Let us leave this aside, too, and examine a third set of "red flags." Neither *Post* editors nor Pulitzer jurors nor any of the other editors who both reprinted Cooke's article and later dissected the scandal ever seemed to question Cooke's claims that "Ron" routinely injected "Jimmy" and that his "mother" tacitly approved of this. Not even the tallest tales of Temperance crusaders gave us such villainous villains. What sort of people would knowingly and repeatedly inject heroin into a child that they clothed, fed, and bathed?

There is nothing in the scientific literature to suggest that addicts recommend addiction to anyone, much less their own kids. The media apparently knew so little about heroin that they could simply assume it induced depravity and transformed users into the sort of vile subhumans who think nothing of doing such things. Thus the media smuggled into their stories a simplistic sort of pharmacological determinism. Clearly heroin can be powerfully addicting, but even if it were capable of morally lobotomizing all addicts, why would such addicts *give away* the very expensive stuff for which they reputedly lie, cheat, and steal?[5]

Almost any street junkie could have served as an expert informant (a "Deep Throat," if you will) and saved the *Post* from scandal. If the editors had picked ten addicts at random and asked them if a junkie would give away precious junk to a child, nine would have thought it absurd, moral qualms aside. Asked to read the Cooke story, most addicts could have told the *Post* immediately that it was concocted. Even if one accepted all of the other demonstrably dubious assumptions upon which the story rested, it made no sense even according to the perverse logic attributed to addicts.

A final set of red flags shot up immediately after "Jimmy's World" was published. According to the *Post*'s own follow-up stories, hundreds of police officers and social workers scoured the city looking for "Jimmy." Elementary school teachers inspected thousands of small student arms. Aroused citizens from housing projects in neighborhoods like "Jimmy's" all over Washington hunted for him. As Green's (1981) report put it, "The intense police search continued for 17 days. The city had been finely combed. Nothing." Half a dozen *Post* reporters also searched in vain for any other child addict. Our point here is not merely that none of these myriad searchers turned up so much as a clue as to "Jimmy's" specific whereabouts. More significant is that with everyone so certain that "untold numbers of children like Jimmy" existed, no one found *any* child addict—not an eight-year-old, not a ten-year old, not a twelve-year-old.

For some reason these journalistic findings were not considered news-worthy. Presented with the choice of publishing the recalcitrant facts uncov-ered by their reporters or what they wanted to believe, the *Post* editors and their print brethren chose to print the more ideologically compliant assertion that eight-year-old heroin addicts are "common" in America's inner cities. The Cooke affair thus suggests that the *Post* had more in common with President Reagan than it likes to believe. Reagan was, for example, fond of attacking "welfare chiselers" for buying vodka with their food stamps. No matter how many times his own experts told him this was untrue due to food stamp redemption rules, he continued to tell the tale because it suited his ideological purposes. Lies uttered as political demagogy are one thing, but we expect more from the great newspapers on which we rely to expose such lies. In continuing to insist that "Jimmys" were everywhere in the face of their own evidence to the contrary, the *Post* seemed to be saying that if "Jimmy's World" doesn't exist in reality, then it can be made to exist in ideology.

Unfortunately, the nonfictional lives of African-Americans in our inner cities and of growing numbers of other poor Americans are sufficiently harsh that some of them seek solace, comfort, and meaning in drugs. But editors seem to believe that readers don't like to be reminded that there is some-thing fundamentally wrong with the social system from which most of them benefit. Editors and readers alike, it seems, feel more comfortable believing that the worsening horrors of our inner cities are caused by evil individuals from a different gene pool—"addicts." Thus, a story about how crushing poverty and racism give rise to despair that sometimes leads to drug use, abuse, or addiction is not considered "newsworthy." Stories that simply depict addicts as complicated, troubled human beings would be neither comforting enough for readers nor dramatic enough for prizes. To us, this sin of omission is more the real pity of this story than Janet Cooke's sin of commission.

About a week after the story first appeared and months before the scandal broke, *Post* publisher Donald Graham sent Cooke a congratulatory note on her "very fine story" (Green 1981). It said, in part, that "The *Post* has no more important and tougher job than explaining life in the black community in Washington." Here he was as close to the ideal of journalism as Cooke's tale was distant from it.

Graham went on to praise the struggle of "black reporters who try to see life through their own eyes instead of seeing it the way they're told they should." In calling attention to the importance of independent reporting, Graham again articulated an important ideal. Ironically, Cooke had so inter-nalized the way reporters in general "are told they should" see drug users that she gave a whole new meaning to the idea of seeing things through her "own eyes."

Finally, Graham wrote of how Cooke's article displayed the "gift" of "explaining" how the world works. "If there's any long-term justification for what we do," he wrote, it is that "people will act a bit differently and think a bit differently if we help them understand the world even slightly better. Much of what we write fails that first test because we don't understand what we're writing about ourselves." Here Graham displayed unintended prescience. For what he took to be an exception turned out to be a glaring example of his rule.

Cooke's concoction led readers to misunderstand the lives of addicts "in the black community." But hers was only an egregious case of the press's cultivated incapacity for understanding drug problems. If the *Post* scandal has value, it inheres in the accidental glimpse it affords into the normally hidden process by which media institutions force the untidy facts of social life through the sieve of dominant ideology (Molotch and Lester 1974). We submit that it is this process that allowed Cooke's tale to sail undetected past *Post* editors, Pulitzer jurors, and the hundreds of other journalists who analyzed the fraud. And we suggest that this process continues to camouflage the ways our world produces drug problems in the first place, and thereby helps to forge a public prepared to swallow the next junkie stereotype and to enlist in the next drug war.

ACKNOWLEDGMENTS

The authors are indebted to Harry Gene Levine and Peter Cohen for helpful suggestions on early drafts, to Pat O'Hare for encouraging us to write this chapter in the first place, and to Alan Matthews, Andrew Bennett, and Peter McDermott of the *International Journal on Drug Policy* for their help and hospitality in the course of revisions.

NOTES

1. By all accounts in Ombudsman Green's investigation, Janet Cooke was not streetwise. She was middle-class and upwardly mobile. Her immediate supervisor told Green that Cooke "was not really street-savvy—She was Gucci and Cardin and Yves St. Laurent—She didn't know the kinds of people she was dealing with, but she was tenacious and talented" (Green 1981).

2. The Vassar degree had caught Editor-in-Chief Ben Bradlee's eye, causing him to sift Cooke's resume from the hundreds he receives each week and to set in motion the hiring process that brought her to the *Post* (Green 1981).

3. The Pulitzer Board drew its own lesson from the Cooke scandal. Seven

months later it adopted new procedures to guard against such problems. Pulitzer juries would henceforth deliberate for two days instead of one (*New York Times,* 22 November 1981).

4.   The authors are indebted to Dr. Peter Cohen for the analogy to witches and heretics (personal communication, 1991).

5.   To be fair, we did find one article (*New York Times,* 16 April 1981) that mentioned the idea that addicts might not want to give away their heroin, but this lead was not pursued. Also, Mayor Marion Barry told the *Post* after the citywide search that he doubted "the mother or the pusher would allow a reporter to see them shoot up" (Green 1981).

REFERENCES

Becker, Howard S. 1953. "Becoming a Marijuana User." *American Journal of Sociology* 59:235–43.

Becker, Howard S. 1963. *Outsiders: Studies in the Sociology of Deviance.* New York: Free Press.

Becker, Howard S. 1967. "History, Culture, and Subjective Experience: An Exploration of the Social Bases of Drug-Induced Experiences." *Journal of Health and Social Behavior* 8:162–76.

Brecher, Edward M. 1972. *Licit and Illicit Drugs.* Boston: Little, Brown.

Cooke, Janet. 1980. "Jimmy's World—8-Year-Old Heroin Addict Lives for a Fix." *Washington Post,* 28 September, p. A1.

Feldman, Harvey, Michael Agar, and George Beschner. 1979. *Angel Dust.* Lexington, MA: D.C. Heath.

Green, Bill. 1981. "Janet's World—The Story of a Child Who Never Existed—How and Why It Came to Be Published." *Washington Post,* 19 April, p. A1.

Himmelstein, Jerome. 1983. *The Strange Career of Marihuana.* Westport, CT: Greenwood.

Levine, Harry Gene. 1984. "The Alcohol Problem in America: From Temperance to Prohibition." *British Journal of Addiction* 79:109–19.

Los Angeles Times. 1981a. "Story That Was Fabricated Found a Friend on Pulitzer Board." 17 April, Section I, p. 9.

Los Angeles Times. 1981b. "A Matter of Confidence." 19 April, p. IV5.

Los Angeles Times. 1981c. "Finally, the Watergate Spirit Is Dead in America." 23 April, Section II, p. 11.

Mark, Gregory. 1975. "Racial, Economic, and Political Factors in the Development of America's First Drug Laws." *Issues in Criminology* 10:56–75.

Molotch, Harvey and Marilyn Lester. 1974. "News as Purposive Behavior: On the Strategic Uses of Routine Events, Accidents, and Scandals." *American Sociological Review* 39:101–12.

Morgan, Patricia. 1978. "The Legislation of Drug Law." *Journal of Drug Issues* 8:53–62.

Musto, David. 1973. *The American Disease: Origins of Narcotic Control.* Oxford: Oxford University Press.

New York Times. 1981a. "Washington Post Gives Up Pulitzer, Calling Article on Addict, 8, Fiction." 16 April, p. A1.

New York Times. 1981b. "Paper's False Article Is a Major Topic at Convention of Newspaper Editors." 23 April, p. A16.

New York Times. 1981c. "Pulitzer Prize Board Adopts New Procedures." 22 November, p. A38.

Reinarman, Craig and Harry G. Levine. 1989. "Crack in Context: Politics and Media in the Making of a Drug Scare." *Contemporary Drug Problems* 16:535–77.

San Francisco Chronicle. 1981. "Washington Post Blames Its Editors for Pulitzer Fiasco." 19 April, p. A6.

Washington Post. 1980. "D.C. Authorities Seek Identity of Heroin Addict, 8." 30 September, p. A11.

Washington Post. 1981a. "Post Writer Wins Pulitzer for Story on Child Addict." 14 April, p. A1.

Washington Post. 1981b. "The End of the 'Jimmy' Story." 16 April, p. A18.

Washington Post. 1981c. "Post Reporter's Pulitzer Prize Is Withdrawn." 16 April, p. A1.

Washington Post. 1981d. "'Jimmy' Episode Evokes Outrage, Sadness." 17 April, p. C13.

Washington Post. 1981e. "The District Line—The Problem Is All Too Real." 17 April, p. C13.

Washington Post. 1981f. "Nation's Editors Plumb 'Jimmy's World.'" 18 April, p. A3.

Washington Post. 1981g. "Putting the Creator of 'Jimmy's World' in Context." 19 April, p. D1.

Weil, Andrew. 1972. *The Natural Mind: An Investigation of Drugs and the Higher Consciousness.* Boston, MA: Houghton Mifflin.

Zinberg, Norman. 1984. *Drug, Set, and Setting: The Basis for Controlled Intoxicant Use.* New Haven, CT: Yale University Press.

III

Constructions of Gender and Crime

5

Predators
The Social Construction of "Stranger-Danger"
in Washington State as a Form
*of Patriarchal Ideology**

NEIL WEBSDALE

INTRODUCTION: SEXUAL PSYCHOPATHY, HEINOUS ACTS, AND DRACONIAN LEGISLATION

Sexual Psychopathy

Edwin Sutherland (1950) argued that the emergence of sexual psychopathy laws from the late 1930s was heavily influenced by the media and the psychiatric community. The media manipulated public opinion and sensationalized sex offenses. This manipulation created an overreaction on the part of the public, which was further seized upon by the media and whipped into hysteria. The psychiatric community sought to colonize the problem of sex offenses and thereby bolster its own professional standing and influence. For Sutherland, the sexual psychopathy laws represented a shift from punishment to medical treatment of sex offenders. In 1937, Michigan became the first state to enact a sexual psychopathy law. By the mid-1980s over half of the states had followed suit. However, these statutes fell into disuse with the growing realization that sex offenders did not suffer from any mental illness and were not therefore amenable to treatment. This left treatment programs open to the possibility of legal attack. According to Brakel, Perry, and Weiner, this possibility was one of the reasons states shied away from using these laws (1985:739–43). By 1990, only a handful of states had sexual psychopathy laws on their books and few made regular use of them.

* Reprinted with permission of Haworth Press © 1996. Originally published in *Women and Criminal Justice* vol. 7(2) 1996, pp. 43–68.

Heinous Acts

Prior to 1990, the State of Washington incarcerated all its sex offenders with the general prison population. However, after a spate of heinous sex crimes, there were increasing calls for a more drastic solution to the threat posed by serious recidivist sex offenders. There were two main triggering offenses. First, Gene Raymond Kane, a work release prisoner who had two previous convictions for sexual assault, raped and murdered Diane Balasiotes in Seattle in September 1988. Second and most significantly, Earl Shriner was found guilty of raping, assaulting, and attempting to kill a seven-year-old boy. Prior to these offenses the infamous serial killer Ted Bundy murdered a number of women in Washington State during the 1970s and early 1980s. The Green River Killer, one of the most infamous of all modern-day American serial killers, performed most of his fifty or more killings in Washington State. More recently, the predatory acts of murderer Wesley Alan Dodd made national headlines and did much to publicize the phenomenon of sexually violent predation in Washington State. Dodd, who was executed in January 1993 for the murder of three children, admitted molesting more than one hundred children over a period of fifteen years.

Draconian Legislation

On July 1, 1990, Washington State's Community Protection Act went into effect (hereafter referred to as CPA; Washington Laws 1990:Chapter 3). This law, commonly known as the Predator Law, was passed in order to better manage the state's sexual offenders. The constitutionality of this law was upheld in August 1993 by a vote of six to three by the Washington State Supreme Court in the case of State of Washington v. Andre Brigham Young. Under the terms of the act, sex offenders were to receive longer sentences than they had previously and stricter monitoring both in and out of prison. Three strategies stand out. The first, and by far the most controversial strategy was the indefinite civil commitment clause (CPA, Part X, Civil Commitment, Washington Laws 1990:97–102). Upon committing the necessary heinous sex crimes or after serving a full prison term for such an offense, the sex offender could be subject to indefinite civil commitment to a mental health facility for control, care, and treatment. This neatly sidesteps the problem posed by offenders such as Shriner, who authorities "knew" would reoffend, but whom authorities could no longer detain. The predator law was primarily designed to cope with those offenders who had served their full term and who still posed a threat, while the CPA also sought longer prison terms for new sex offenders (CPA, Part VII, Criminal Sentencing, Washington Laws 1990:70–91). The two other strategies required the registration of sex offenders in the communities in which they lived (CPA, Part IV,

Registration of Sex Offenders, Washington Laws 1990:49–54) and the notification of the community that a sex offender had moved into the area (CPA, Part I, Community Notification, Washington Laws 1990:13–36).

The legislation defines a sexually violent predator as "any person who has been convicted of or charged with a crime of sexual violence and who suffers from a mental abnormality or personality disorder which makes the person likely to engage in predatory acts of sexual violence" [CPA Part X, Section 1002(1), Washington Laws 1990:97–98]. Predation refers to acts "directed toward strangers or individuals with whom a relationship has been established or promoted for the primary purpose of victimization" [Section 1002(2), Washington Laws 1990:98]. The intent of the Governor's Task Force that drafted the legislation was to make it extremely difficult to define an offender as a sexually violent predator. This intent is evident in the law itself: "The legislature finds that a small but extremely dangerous group of sexually violent predators exists" (CPA, Section 1001, Washington Laws 1990:97).

Under the act, it may be possible to prove that an acquaintance rapist is a sexually violent predator. However, intrafamilial sexual violence and abuse are not covered. In the majority of cases, the sexually violent predator will be a rapist (almost always unknown to the victim) or an extrafamilial child molester [CPA, Section 1002(4), Washington Laws 1990:98]. In all twenty or so cases to date, the predator has been male. Therefore it is not the act of rape, molestation, mutilation, or murder that is of central concern. Rather, it is the political context within which the act occurs. Under Washington's CPA, predators are primarily strangers. Husbands cannot be predators. If the victim is known to the perpetrator in any way other than in a relationship that has been established or promoted for the primary purpose of victimization, then that perpetrator cannot be convicted as a predator. The legislature did not intend that the law be applied to sexually violent husbands.

It was not the intent of the Washington State legislature to sweep marital rape and intrafamilial child abuse under the carpet by not making husbands subject to indefinite civil commitment. Rather, legislators felt that to make husbands subject to indefinite civil commitment for intrafamilial abuse would have had the effect of discouraging victims within families from reporting his abuse. The legislature reasoned that wives would not report husbands because, for example, they feared the loss of a husband's economic support if he were to be subject to indefinite civil commitment.

The main objections to the predator law were summarized in a brief of amicus curiae written for the American Civil Liberties Union by John Lafond, University of Puget Sound professor of law (see Lafond 1991). This brief was in support of appellants Andre Brigham Young and Vance Cunningham, who had been detained as sexual predators. In Lafond's opinion, the predator law is unconstitutional because it (1) authorizes lifetime preventive detention, (2) does not meet constitutional requirements for involuntary civil commitment, (3) does not require constitutionally adequate proof of danger-ousness, and (4) is too vague and does not specify constitutionally adequate commitment criteria (see Brief of Amicus Curiae in Support of Appellants Andre Brigham Young and Vance Cunningham. Supreme Court of Washington, No. 57837-1:11).

It is important to bear in mind that the legal debate about predation has remained firmly fixed on the issues of constitutionality. The protagonists did not raise the issue of systemic intrafamilial male sexual abuse of women and children, nor the perils of a predator law that focused solely on "stranger danger."

THE GENDERED NATURE OF THE
PREDATOR LAW

The legislative and media embellishment of the threat posed by predators produces a skewed analysis of sexual violence against women who, in reality, face far greater danger from the men they know (Russell 1990; Finkelhor and Yllo 1985; Radford and Russell 1992; Dobash and Dobash 1979; Hanmer and Saunders 1984; Stanko 1990). This obfuscation effect also counteracts feminist progress in the area of passing legislation that does have some beneficial effect in the lives of women (e.g., marital rape, sexual harassment, and mandatory arrest laws). The chapter returns to these coun-teracting effects in the final section.

Diana Russell's rigorous survey conducted by women interviewers with a random sample of 930 women in San Francisco revealed that among 2,588 reports of rape and attempted rape, 38 percent were committed by the husband or ex-husband, and 13 percent by a lover or ex-lover. Only 6 percent were committed by strangers. This suggests that roughly half of all rapes or attempted rapes are committed by men who are or have been in an intimate relationship with the victim (1990:67). In general, she found that sexual assaults by husbands were twice as common as those committed by strangers. Finkelhor and Yllo (1985) surveyed 323 Boston area women. They found that 10 percent of the women had been raped by their husbands or ex-husbands, compared with 3 percent who had been the victims of stranger rape (ibid.:6–7).

The prevalence of wife rape is compounded by the fact that wives may be raped more than once. Russell found that 70–80 percent of the victims of wife rape were raped more than once. In a related vein, Finkelhor and Yllo (1985:23) found that half the victims of wife rape had experienced sexual assault on twenty or more occasions.

Finkelhor (1984) reports a 600 percent rise in child sexual abuse between 1976 and 1982. Undoubtedly, this increase reflects a dramatic increase in reporting rather than a significant escalation of abuse. The recent recognition of child sexual abuse as a major social problem should not obscure the historically enduring presence of this form of child exploitation. As Linda Gordon observes, the recent "discovery" of child sexual abuse merely highlights a problem well-known to the Progressive Era and nineteenth-century social workers (1988:7). Following Gordon and other feminist arguments on child sexual abuse and incest, I argue these phenomena are best understood as part of the power relations of gender. Gordon puts it succinctly:

> One of the most striking things about incest, that most extraordinary and heinous of transgressions, is its capacity to be ordinary. . . . In the family violence case records it is a behavior of very ordinary people. . . . [I]ncest participants made sense of their behavior precisely in terms of their family positions. Men referred to their paternal rights, girls to their filial duty. Men spoke of men's sexual "needs" and their prerogative to "have" women. (ibid.:204)

In discussing the history of child sexual abuse in Great Britain, Carol Smart points to discursive tendencies that distance such abuse from known offenders such as fathers and other relatives:

> [O]ddly nourishing the complacency over abuse by fathers . . . the more concern is expressed about the threat of strangers, the less close relatives could be brought into the frame. The more child sexual abuse was depicted as a horrible pathology, the less could "ordinary" fathers be seen as enacting such deeds. (1989:52)

This displacement effect highlighted by Smart can also be seen in the definitional imperatives of Washington State's predator law. The focus on aberrance serves to distance child sexual abuse from its authentic locus, namely, the patriarchal family. As feminists have noted, the problem of child sexual abuse is the problem of male sexuality (see Herman with Hirschman 1981). Child sexual abuse is a widespread phenomenon that occurs most frequently within families. Men are overwhelmingly the perpetrators of this abuse. Russell's above-mentioned survey found that 16 percent of her sample of women reported incest occurring before the age of eighteen. Nearly all of the perpetrators in Russell's study were reported by incest victims to be men.

The link between intrafamilial sexual violence toward women and children is that both are an expression of male power within a patriarchal system of families. To argue, as the Washington State legislature did, that wives would not report intrafamilial sexual violence under a predator law, because they feared the loss of a husbands' economic support, is profoundly ironic. Here we see wives' and children's economic dependence on husbands and fathers being used as a rationale for disqualifying large numbers of sexually violent men from being predators. This rationale, embedded in the predator law, constitutes patriarchal ideology par excellence.

It is not the argument of this chapter that the victims of predators, victims' families, politicians, and criminal justice system personnel who contributed to the media construction and sensationalization of predation deliberately set out to divert attention from everyday sexual violence against women and children. Neither did the media, as claims-makers, conspire to marginalize everyday sexual violence against women and children. Rather, the media presentation of predation is best seen as an integral part of a patriarchal ideology, the power of which is most insidious when its operation is silent and largely unobserved. Nevertheless, because of the definitional imperatives of the predator law and the media sensationalization of rare one-on-one stranger violence, everyday sexual violence against women and children remains marginalized.

Before discussing the ways in which a moral panic developed around sexually violent predators, it is important to situate my argument within the broader context of feminist theories of the law and the state. While these theories await further development, some important headway has been made. According to Catherine MacKinnon: "[T]he state is male in the feminist sense. The law sees and treats women the way men see and treat women" (1987:140). Likewise, "[T]he state, in part through law, institutionalizes male power" (ibid.:141). While MacKinnon's work has been criticized as both essentialist and deterministic (see Smart 1989:66–89), she nevertheless deconstructs the objectivist posturing of liberal theories of the law, which fail to recognize the historical significance of the public/private divide. Liberal legal discourse denies the life experiences of women and subsumes them under an empiricist and allegedly gender-neutral code. The failure of the state to encroach upon the domain of domestic relations is justified under liberal law by an appeal to rights of privacy and the sanctity of the family from state interference. The hierarchical relationship between the modern liberal state and its citizenry is rooted in and based upon the nature of the patriarchal family and the historic rights of a husband over his wife and children (see Dobash and Dobash 1979; MacKinnon 1987; Aries 1962).

Carol Smart criticizes MacKinnon for seeing male power as omnipotent. According to Smart, MacKinnon's approach leaves insufficient room to theorize the resistance of women. Smart sees the law as more of a contested arena and less of a monolithic tool than MacKinnon. Although Smart acknowledges that law is androcentric, she argues that it is nevertheless possible at times for women to use the state and the law for their own benefit. Smart argues: "Yet law remains a site of struggle. While it is the case that law does not hold the key to unlock patriarchy, it provides the forum for articulating alternative visions and accounts" (1989:88). Smart's approach is consistent with the work of other feminists who have acknowledged the way the state has changed its response to the plight of women. Patriarchy is not an unchanging transhistorical phenomenon. As the machinery of the modern patriarchal state developed, divorce became easier to obtain, certain forms of legal (not de facto) discrimination were confronted, and laws were passed against wife battering and in some cases marital rape. In short, there is an ebb and flow in the area of gender legislation, which usually but not always favors the patriarchal interests of men.

In this chapter I argue that the predator law constitutes androcentric legislation that, under the guise of protecting women and children, effectively upholds the historic separation of public and private spheres. The predator law works against the feminist claim that the private is political and that the private constitutes the central locus of women's oppression. Nevertheless, following Smart rather than MacKinnon, I also suggest that this law is part of the historical ebb and flow of gender legislation. After examining the media sensationalization of sexually violent predation, this chapter concludes with a discussion of the ways in which the predator law can be seen as part of the ebb and flow of patriarchal legal discourse.

MY APPROACH TO EXAMINING THE PREDATOR LAW, ITS ENFORCEMENT, AND THE EMERGING MEDIA DISCOURSE

The central question of my analysis asks, What ideological positions benefited from the particular orientation of the predator law? Another related question inquires, How did the various discursive themes in the media support the orientation of the law and further feed into the ideology that "stranger-danger" posed an awesome threat to women and children?

I reviewed various sources to access the political themes of the predator discourse. Information for my analysis of sexually violent predation was obtained primarily through (1) analysis of legislation, newspaper articles, hard and soft news shows, and the true crime literature; (2) interviews with legal scholars and criminal justice personnel responsible for implementing the predator law; and (3) taping and transcription of the legal debates.

The analysis of newspaper articles began with the high-circulation dailies, the *Seattle Times* (*ST*) and the *Tacoma News Tribune* (*TNT*). My impressions of the ideological slant of the predator discourse were formed as a member of the public and as a working scholar living in Tacoma in the late 1980s/early 1990s. The term "predator" was first coined in 1989 by the Governor's Task Force on community protection. The *ST* picked up on the term from the task force. An initial computer search of a data base covering 150 newspapers revealed that about 90 percent of all articles on sexual predators came from the *ST*. The remaining articles took their lead from the early pieces in the *ST*. In this chapter I use those quotes that most succinctly and powerfully summarize discursive themes. Significantly, no articles or other media presentations even remotely contextualized the act of predation against the wider structure of patriarchy.

Transcripts from television shows provide the substrate for the analysis of hard and soft news stories. My content analysis of these news shows seeks to deconstruct some of the messages and explore some of the nuances and meanings of the spoken and unspoken word.

I conducted unstructured interviews with key informants. Interviewees were point-people in their respective fields (policing, law, corrections) who worked with predators and the operationalization of the predator law. Eight key informant telephone interviews were conducted with police officers (one chief, one lieutenant, three sergeants, and three detectives) from the following departments in Washington State: Seattle, Tacoma, Olympia, and Puyallup. These interviews provided insights into the perspectives of police officers and the ways they contextualized predation within their wider worldview. Discussions about the predator law were held with two prosecutors from the King County (Seattle) Prosecutor's Office, two attorneys from the Attorney General's Office, and a public defender in Tacoma. One of the key legal players in the predator discourse is John Lafond. Lafond appeared on news shows such as "ABC Nightline" and drafted the American Civil Liberties Union brief against the predator law. I discussed the predator law at length with Lafond. Finally, three telephone interviews were conducted with Washington State Department of Corrections staff.

PANICKING ABOUT SEXUALLY VIOLENT PREDATORS

Stanley Cohen (1980) used the term "moral panic" to refer to a stylized societal overreaction to vandalism and the general "disorderly" behavior of youth during the 1960s in England. Cohen identifies the importance of the media and other claims-makers in the construction of "folk devils." Moral panics serve as a form of social control since they produce an overreaction on the part of authorities and ultimately some kind of crackdown. There are a number of parallels between the panic over vandalism studied by Cohen and the "discovery" of sexually violent predation in Washington State. In many ways the construction of the sexually violent predator as a fiendishly dangerous individual could be seen in terms of a moral panic. The predator resembles Cohen's folk devil. However, the sociology of deviance and the anomie tradition that Cohen draws upon have not readily accommodated issues of gender. Consequently, this chapter employs an analytical scheme that is informed by Cohen's work, but linked much more closely to the politics of gender. Excerpts from the legal and media discourses on sexually violent predators are presented in order to expand upon the main theoretical argument that the predator law constitutes patriarchal ideology. I begin by examining the initial construction of predation and go on to analyze the rise of what I call the "decontextualized predator." These two discussions preface an exploration of the way predators made it onto prime time soft news shows.

The Initial Construction of Sexually Violent Predators

Three interrelated themes permeated the early construction of the predator discourse. First, the danger posed by predators was frequently magnified for all to see. Second, predictions were made about the potential future dangerousness of predators. Third, a symbolic linguistic code emerged to describe predators.

The Magnification of Danger.   The initial reporting of the Shriner incident in which Helen Harlow's son was attacked took the form of what Bromley, Shupe, and Ventimiglia (1979) have called an "atrocity tale." We hear of the physical mutilation alongside statements concerning the innocence of children and the ineffectiveness of the criminal justice system. The *TNT* reported that the seven-year-old son of Helen Harlow had been found in a wooded area at around 9:00 P.M. on May 20, 1989. He had been raped and his penis had been cut off. The *TNT* reported the boy "was too traumatized to speak or cry" (*TNT* 1989a). Two days later, an editorial in the *TNT* stated that this was: "a crime of unfathomable depravity. . . . How could anyone inflict such an atrocity upon a child? Why couldn't the system stop such a monster?" (*TNT* 1989b). Using the language of predation, the *TNT* then went on to note that Shriner had been "preying upon children for the last 24 years" (ibid.).

This was an inflammatory statement given that Shriner (only a suspect at the time of the newspaper article) had been incarcerated for the majority of those twenty-four years. The impression was conveyed that there were large numbers of innocent children under threat from the omnipresence of predators. One of the newspaper reports introduced the group called SAVUS (Stop All Violent Unnecessary Suffering). This group asked that the public "barrage Governor Gardner with 10,000 sneakers, each representing a child who needs protection" (*TNT* 1989e).

The aim of this barrage was to seek legislative changes that would guard against sex offenders like Shriner being released if they presented a "danger" to the community. The reference to ten thousand children in need of protection was a gross exaggeration in the context of the discussion about offenders such as Shriner. Using the acronym SAVUS was profoundly ironic, because the SAVUS group, which made initial headway in its claims-making activities by publicizing the rape and murder of Diane Ballasiotes and the mutilation of Helen Harlow's son, failed entirely to contextualize these rare acts of stranger violence against the wider backdrop of intrafamilial violence. Stop All Violent Unnecessary Suffering might have been more aptly named Stop All Violent Unnecessary Extrafamilial Suffering.

The most important point about the early media analysis of predation was that it constructed the threat posed by sexual predators such as Shriner to be more pervasive than it was. One columnist warned: "[O]ver the past 10 days, we have learned that there is no place to hide" (TNT 1989c).

Yet while no one is safe from the marauding predator and no one can hide, an unspoken exception exists. Adult men are safer because predators go for the relatively defenseless, especially women and children. Raymond Kane had murdered a woman and Earl Shriner had mutilated a small boy. All of the twenty or so "predators" confined in the Monroe Sex Offender Program victimized women and children.

Predicting Future Acts of Predation.   According to Stanley Cohen (1980), moral panics assume that deviant acts and/or atrocities will recur. Perhaps the most explicit statement of prediction in the predator discourse came from Pierce County Prosecutor John Ladenburg. He was critical of a criminal justice system that let recidivist sex offenders out after serving their time. Ladenburg was quoted as saying: "We've got to wait for the guy to commit a major offense when everybody knows he's going to re-offend" (TNT 1989b). The word "everybody" implies readers agree Shriner will reoffend and simultaneously constructs the predator as "outsider." The exclusivity of the predator derives from his depraved sexuality vis-à-vis the "normal" sexuality of the family man. An alternative opinion appeared when Dr. James Reardon, a spokesperson for the Washington State Psychiatric Association, said: "There is absolutely no credible evidence that we can predict dangerousness" (ST 1990c).

Assumptions of the eventual recidivism of newly released sex offenders underpinned the early calls for changes in the sex offender legislation. If these men were a menace, then a law was needed that informed communities of their whereabouts. Washington State's attorney general called for a law "that strips offenders of confidentiality so that they are known to their neighborhoods" (TNT 1989d).

Symbolic Language and Sexually Violent Predation. Perhaps the most powerful imagery was that of the sex predator or fiend who stalked innocent children. The predator was projected into the dark unknown beyond the bounds of existing criminality. One columnist noted: "This case is different because it gives us the opportunity to face the darkness" (*TNT* 1989c). In the "predator," the media had discovered someone with whom the criminal justice system could not cope. The *TNT* reported Tacoma School Board Vice President Cathy Pearsall "speaking at a rally attended by 175 people: 'Our young children walk this way but once,' Pearsall told the audience, which had its share of young children gazing at the balloons, the clowns and candy they had been given" (*TNT* 1989e). The reporting of the danger posed to children is imbued with a sense of legitimacy because it comes from the mouth of a school board vice president. When this danger is set alongside the carefree activities of childhood, predation assumes an even more sinister presence.

The hanging of sneakers on trees around the state capital provided a dramatic way of capturing press attention. The sneaker, as a symbol of the freedom of the child to roam, emotively evoked memories of how that same freedom can bring the child into the clutches of the predator. Helen Harlow's son had been attacked in a wooded area in South Tacoma. One resident, Linda Land, heard screams about fifteen minutes before the seven-year-old boy was found. She said that she "never allows her children to play in the wooded area where she said she found mattresses and pornographic magazines" (*TNT* 1989a). However, other residents were less eager to restrict the movements of their children. Local resident Mike Inske said that "many neighborhood children including my eight-year-old son often ride bicycles by themselves in the woods" (ibid.).

The polarization is dramatically laid out here. The carefree play of childhood, which apparently exposes the child to the dangers of the wooded areas where Helen Harlow's son was "stalked," is contrasted with a restricted childhood, which undermines the spirit of play. One observation missing here is that freedom and adventure in childhood have always been more readily available to boys than girls. Another hidden implication is the presumption of safety in the patriarchal home, which, as I argued earlier, is in fact the site of the majority of child sexual abuse.

What we begin to see through this imagery is the condensation of what Goffman (1963) called stigma. By stigma, Goffman is referring to an attribute that is "deeply discrediting." The stigmatized person is seen to be less than human. Long before Shriner was found guilty, his past record had been resurrected and he had been labeled as a sexual deviant. Bearing these observations in mind, it is easier to understand the initial reception of Shriner by local police: "The only sound during the 30 seconds Earl Shriner spent in the police station hallway after his arrest . . . came from an officer near a sergeant's desk who said, 'Get him out of here'" (*TNT* 1989a).

The Rise of the Decontextualized Predator

The construction of sexually violent predators proceeded in a manner that disconnected predators from the patriarchal culture of predation. This process of subsequent construction took its lead from the patriarchal ideology embedded in the predator law. The silence of the media on issues germane to the interests of women helped further facilitate the decontextualization of the predator.

I now examine the way initial ideological positions were consolidated and discuss the way atrocities were autopsied.

Refining and Consolidating Initial Ideological Positions.   The intensity of Shriner's stigma was continually reinforced by the dark presence of his act of castration. Perhaps the act of castration touched one of the deepest nerves in the phallocentric social body; in any case, we cannot easily discount the fact that Shriner's act of castration may have been a major contributing factor in the passage of the predator law. The atrocity tale was restated by Judge Sauriol, who handed down Shriner's sentence. Reflecting on his original signing of the search warrant in the case in May 1989, Sauriol said: "I read about the third paragraph and stopped and said this is incredible. I don't think in 37 years in the field of law I've heard of, been part of, seen a criminal offense that borders on extreme cruelty more than this one" (*ST* 1990b). Sauriol rearticulated the theme of the vulnerability of children when he observed that Shriner constituted: "A danger to the defenseless" (ibid.). The defenselessness theme was repeated on numerous occasions in the press and on local TV. In one article, a journalist summarized the central questions: "How could the abuser do this to a helpless child? How can society allow predators to be free?" (*ST* 1989b). This is a thinly disguised reference to the fact that sex offenders, like all other offenders, are released after they have served their sentence. According to the journalist, society (mistakenly) allows "predators" to be released upon completion of their term in prison. What this quote fails to acknowledge is that the "freedom" of men to prey on women underpins patriarchal relations. In a rape trial under current criminal law, juries judging the intent of the rapist still have to overcome a common belief that it is men who initiate sex. It is not a question of freeing predators, but rather a question of asking (critically) why men are free to prey on women and why this predatory behavior has not been systematically challenged by the criminal justice system.

The castration of Helen Harlow's son was revisited in the media on a number of occasions. In fact the mutilation of this seven-year-old boy received by far the widest coverage of any of the acts of the predators. Roughly half a million dollars was raised for the boy. In stark contrast in March 1990, little less than a year after the Shriner atrocity, a three-year-old girl was mutilated by an alleged predator (see *State of Washington v. Randy Russell Smith, Case Number 145324*). The girl suffered internal and external tearing of the vagina. Her injuries, like those of Helen Harlow's son, required reconstructive surgery. The press coverage of her case was relatively low key compared to the Shriner case and only ten thousand dollars was raised on her behalf. The differential press coverage and the much greater sum raised for the boy may have reflected the fact that the boy's case was the first act of predation to make the headlines. It may have reflected the fact that the Seattle-Tacoma area is far more heavily populated and has a wider readership than the Olympia area. However, the differential treatment of the boy and girl may also reflect the publicly perceived values of the penis and vagina in a patriarchal society. More recently in the case of Lorena Bobbit, we have seen how the act of castration generates enormous media attention and electrifies the already inflamed discourse on crime. We had already been informed that Shriner was a "defective delinquent" who was "mildly retarded" (*TNT* 1989e). The *TNT* informed its readers that as a child, Shriner attended a school for developmentally disabled children. His mother had said that doctors had told her that Shriner had some damage to the lower brain (*TNT* 1989d). We were told that Shriner was "emotionless" when the verdict was read at his trial. This observation appeared beneath a two-inch by one-inch drawing of Shriner, which depicted him in the likeness of a Neanderthal Man (*ST* 1990a). The point is that the reporter had no way of knowing Shriner's emotions. A more accurate statement might have been that there were no visible signs as to what Shriner was feeling. The use of the word "emotionless" underneath the drawing strongly implied that Shriner was subhuman. This implication was compounded by other statements. We learn that the only public utterance made by Shriner during his trial was "Uh-huh" (*ST* 1990a).

Autopsying Atrocities: The Road to the Predator Law. The "atrocious actions" of predators were explained in terms of individual defects and the softness of the criminal justice system. These explanations sensitized the public, politicians, criminal justice personnel, and social service workers to the "need" for a predator law. This sensitization process enabled the predator law to be passed without a dissenting vote in the state legislature. Following a discussion of these themes in the sensitization process, I address the way the enforcement of the new predator law amplified the phenomenon of stranger-danger and helped make the topic newsworthy at a national level.

Shriner's possible brain damage, his developmental disabilities, and his alleged emotionless posture all implied that he was biologically defective. Other explanations were more psychological. Treatment professionals pushed counseling and group therapy as a potential form of rehabilitation. In one report, we learn that some therapists "use aversion techniques, such as having the offender follow his deviant fantasy with a whiff of a noxious odor such as ammonia or rotting placenta" (ST 1989a). Such treatment techniques imply that sexually violent predatory behavior can be modified or eliminated through conditioning. The sexual deviant would then return to the ranks of the "sexually normal." Even if it is possible to deter this form of sexually violent predation, the conditioning approach assumes that an absence of predation results in the adoption of "normal" rather than patriarchally constructed sexuality.

Diane Ballasiotes was raped and murdered by a work release prisoner, Gene Kane, who had been previously imprisoned for two separate sexual assaults. Had he not been on work release, the Ballasiotes murder might never have happened. Her mother, Ida Ballasiotes, who obtained extensive press coverage after the Shriner incident, argued that violent sexual offenders should be banned from work release programs.

Others attacked Washington State's inadequate sentencing laws, which did not "protect" the public. For example, attempts had been made by the Department of Social and Health Services and the Department of Corrections to commit Shriner to Western State Hospital rather than permit his release. However, a Pierce County court commissioner, for reasons not stated, declined to do this (TNT 1989d). Shriner had served his full term and the state had no legal provision to further detain him. The SAVUS group, among others, sought to change this.

Another cause of the predation problem, it was argued, was that the public was not well informed of the whereabouts of released sex offenders. There was no requirement under existing law for ex–sex offenders to register in the communities in which they lived. Privacy laws meant that law enforcement agencies could not inform the public about the location of ex-offenders.

News surfaced that Shriner had served only sixty-seven days in the county jail in December 1988 for an unlawful imprisonment charge (TNT 1989a). This stemmed from an attack on a ten-year-old boy Shriner had tied to a post and beaten. The boy later escaped. In this case, Shriner was originally charged with attempted statutory rape and unlawful imprisonment. However, these two charges were plea bargained down to unlawful imprisonment. Here the plea bargain appeared to be yet another symptom of a criminal justice system gone soft.

Sensitization, Social Control and the Passage
of the Predator Law

The atrocity tales associated with predators such as Kane, Shriner, Dodd, Bundy, and the Green River Killer sensitized the public, the police, the courts, social services and the state legislature to the dangerousness of these sexually violent marauders. Police in Washington State received many more calls from the public concerning "suspicious" or potentially "predatory" individuals.

Persistent calls for the passage of tougher legislation to protect Washington State's citizens from sex offenders emerged during the immediate aftermath of the Shriner incident. These calls came from a number of sources and were directed at the legislature. At a local rally publicizing the threat posed to children by predators, Attorney General Ken Eikenberry urged Governor Booth Gardner to call a special session of the legislature to effect a number of changes in the laws related to sex offenders. Suggesting that these changes might be slow to materialize, Eikenberry told the crowd: "You people stay mad, stay committed and keep talking" (*TNT* 1989d).

Earlier that day, the newly formed group SAVUS issued its demands. The mothers of the victims of Kane and Shriner spoke in support of the SAVUS agenda. The confluence of interests between state prosecutors and SAVUS attracted considerable press attention. Helen Harlow, the mother of Shriner's much publicized victim revealed: "This isn't something that just started with my son's victimization. . . . People have been working for changes for many years. That's one of the most disheartening discoveries I've made" (*TNT* 1989d).

In the ensuing months, a Task Force on Community Protection was established. This task force produced a number of recommendations, including the indefinite civil commitment of sexually violent predators. As noted, the ensuing legislation provided a variety of strategies for dealing with sex offenders.

Enforcing the Predator Law

Police officers in Seattle, Tacoma, and Olympia were adamant that public awareness of predators had been dramatically increased from the late 1980s. One officer, who trains law enforcement personnel on sex offender issues, stated that calls were coming in over incidents that previously were not seen to be suspicious. For example, unknown cars parked near schools became the subjects of reports to police (telephone interview with Mark Mann, Tacoma Police Department, 17 March 1992).

Within police departments, we see a gearing up to deal with the new threat from predators. One police chief noted that sexual predators were the "new thing" in law enforcement (conversation with Police Chief Lockie Reeder, Puyallup Police Department, Washington, 9 April 1991). In-service training increased dramatically. In Tacoma, the police began to use counselors from the Mary Bridge Hospital's sex abuse program to interview victims. At the Olympia Police Department, Detective Nancy Gatchett reported that an additional detective had been hired to deal with sex offenses. Gatchett noted that detectives in Olympia were now much better prepared to interview victims (telephone interview, 16 March 1992).

The police were also required to register offenders and notify communities of their presence. Just over four thousand sex offenders are registered in Washington State. The state police oversee the registry of addresses. City and county police authorities have developed a classification system based on the alleged future dangerousness of newly released sex offenders. A level-one sex offender has the lowest likelihood to reoffend. He is a minimal offender. At this level, police agencies would notify each other by circulating a photograph and history of the offender. At level two, police also notify the community by informing neighborhood watches and schools that a particular offender is at large. It is at level three that the word sexual predator comes into use. Once a level-three classification has been made, news media are informed. Photographs of offenders can be released to the press and the offenders' whereabouts made known.

In spite of the objections to the constitutionality of the law, the Washington courts proceeded to process would-be sexually violent predators. As of September 1993, there were twenty-one "residents" (all men) in the Monroe facility either detained for treatment or awaiting a civil commitment trial. Profiles of fourteen Monroe reformatory residents show that nearly all of them were detained because of offenses against women and children they did not know. The offenses ranged from statutory rape, rape, and attempted rape, to indecent liberties, indecent exposure, child molestation, sexual assault, and communicating with a minor for indecent purposes. Only one of the residents had victimized acquaintances, although those acquaintance victimizations were not the reason that he was detained as a sexual predator.

The autopsying of the atrocities in terms of the defectiveness of offenders and the softness of the criminal justice system, coupled with the passage and subsequent enforcement of the predator law, all made the topic of sexually violent predation highly newsworthy. It is in this direction that my analysis now turns.

Predators and Prime Time: The Dispersion of Danger

Thousands of press articles have appeared both locally and nationally about sexual predators and hard news stories on this phenomenon are commonplace in Washington State. I will use Joel Best's (1990) distinction between primary and secondary claims-makers in order to classify the media involvement. Primary claims-makers use a certain style and rhetoric in order to attract the attention of the public. This was the case, for example, with the SAVUS group's symbolic hanging of sneakers on trees. Secondary claims-makers translate and transform the messages of the primary claims-makers (ibid.:19). As Best argues, the public's perception of a social problem comes largely from the secondary claims-makers. These secondhand claims-makers include the makers of hard news (reporting of daily developments in ongoing cases), soft news (feature stories), and popular true crime literature (in the case of predators, see, for example, Olsen 1989, 1991; Rule 1989; Smith and Guillen 1991).

In a complex manner and through a variety of media sources, the predator discourse has spread far beyond the families of the initial victims. This chapter briefly focuses on "ABC Nightline: Washington State's Sexual Predator Law" (April 26, 1991), CBS's "48 Hours: Predators" (November 20, 1991), and a "Frontline Special: Monsters Among Us" (November 10, 1992). These shows reached a wide audience and were characterized by the same sensationalism. The focus was upon the stigma of the predator, his twisted biography, and the ways in which predation might be managed.

"ABC Nightline" started by introducing Andre Brigham Young, who had been convicted of six rapes. An ABC news person was then shown talking with a prisoner:

> News person: "You have molested how many children?"
> Prisoner: "Oh, not a whole lot. About thirty or so."

Having set the scene emotionally, the show proceeded to discuss the constitutionality of indefinite civil commitment, the dangerousness of the "predator" and how we might measure it and predict it, and finally the possibility of treating predators, or at least warehousing them. "ABC Nightline" failed to note the systemic nature of sexual violence within families.

Like "ABC Nightline," the "48 Hours" special entitled "Predators" also failed to contextualize the stranger-danger phenomenon against the incidence of known-offender sexual violence. CBS correspondent Bernard Goldberg pointed out: "There is a frustration in much of America. Too often criminals seem to be winning the war on crime" ("Predators" 1991:14). Goldberg made this point as he introduced the tennis shoe brigade (SAVUS). Helen Harlow appeared and questioned the indefinite civil commitment clause. She stated a preference for life imprisonment: "Let's just lock them up, and if we could kill a few of them that would be cool" (ibid.:16).

One of the longest media presentations was a "Frontline" special entitled "Monsters Among Us," which aired on November 10, 1992. A central character in the show was Wesley Alan Dodd. Dodd made headlines nationally by requesting that he be put to death for the murder of three children. He had chastised the criminal justice system for not locking him up for a sufficient period of time. This reflexive attack on the softness of the system fed into the rhetoric of law and order advocates, who complained about lax sentencing, plea bargaining, and the seemingly endless appeals involved in executing an offender. Although Dodd was never defined by the courts as a sexually violent predator, he fit the bill perfectly. Had he not been eligible for the death penalty, Dodd could eventually have qualified as a predator and been confined at Monroe. As noted earlier, Dodd was presented as another reason Washington State needed a predator law. Had such a law been in place, Dodd may never have had the opportunity to kill three children.

"Monsters Among Us" also captured imaginations by presenting a retinue of predators who informed viewers in graphic detail of the atrocities they had committed. Dodd was introduced against the backdrop of the town of Richland, Washington, where he grew up. Correspondent Al Austin told viewers that Richland was seen as a "good place to grow up in" and an "ordinary town." He noted: "But people here, like people in other peaceful places, have learned to fear their parks and playgrounds and parking lots and homes because something happened in Richland that happens in many good places to grow up in. A monster grew up here" ("Monsters Among Us" 1992:1).

Out of this dichotomy of the "good and peaceful place" and the spawning of the "monster," Austin posed troubling questions: "How was this monster created? How could we have stopped him? How can we stop any of them?" ("Monsters Among Us" 1992:1).

"Frontline," in concert with the other prime time shows, never stopped to frame the presence of these "monsters" against the systemic sexual violence against women and children by offenders known to them. The show proceeded to expand upon the distinctiveness of the pathology of the predators. Viewers learned in great detail of Dodd's fifteen-year career as a child molester and child killer. Austin confronted what he called the startling thing about Dodd: "[H]ow ordinary he seems—small and harmless looking. The handcuffs seem unnecessary. He speaks in a matter-of-fact voice about unspeakable things" (ibid.:1). Other predators appeared on the show. Mike, for example, shared that he has been involved in three gang rapes. Correspondent Austin informed viewers that Mike "looks like anything but a rapist." He was "an ordinary looking young man like Wesley Dodd" (ibid.:3).

Viewers may have assumed that rapists possess horns. Had "Frontline" presented the research showing that rapists are much more likely to be known to the victim than to be predatory strangers though, the powerful political schism between "sexually violent predation" and "everyday sexual violence" would have disappeared. It is these continuities between predators and patriarchy that draw this chapter to a close.

PREDATORS AND PATRIARCHY: SOME CONCLUDING REMARKS

I have argued that the ideological thrust of the predator law reproduces the power relations of gender by obfuscating systemic social problems such as woman battering, marital rape, and the gendered nature of child sexual abuse. This ideological thrust inherent in the predator law has been reinforced by the sensationalist media treatment of predation. Such sensationalist treatment may have been easier because predators were "strangers," "unknown quantities," and "random threats." Notwithstanding these possible reasons for the sensationalist media embellishment of the predator law, it is the case that the social construction of sexually violent predators does not confront much more common forms of patriarchal violence that occur within families.

There has not been a conspiracy to divert attention away from patriarchal violence. It is not my argument that predators like Shriner should be ignored or their violence be seen as insignificant. Rather, it is a question of primary claims-makers, resorting to individualistic explanations that secondary claims-makers such as the news media fail to contextualize against the systemic sexual violence that characterizes patriarchal relations. This failure on the part of the media, whether conscious or not, reflects and contributes to a patriarchal discourse that reproduces the domination of men over women. My argument about predation resembles other approaches to patriarchal ideology and the media (see Tuchman, Daniels, and Benet 1978; Spender 1980, 1983; Soothill and Walby 1991) and capitalism, racism, and the media (see Hall, Critcher, Jefferson, Clarke, and Roberts 1978). All these works point to the powerful ways the media are able to frame events and social phenomena in astructural ways that often fail to comprehensively explore systemic power relations. Likewise my analysis resonates with recent work by Philip Jenkins on the social construction of serial homicide. Jenkins (1994) argues that the threat posed by serial killers has been blown out of proportion and serves the vested interests of certain claims-makers.

One theme to emerge from the predator discourse is the notion that predators prey upon multiple victims. The construction of the serial rapist and/or sexually violent predator as the most threatening rapist to women is consistent with the criminal justice system's emphasis on "forcible rape." By focusing upon "forcible rape," the criminal justice system concentrates upon sexual intercourse that occurs through the use, or threatened use, of violence. This feeds the ideological construct that sexual intercourse otherwise occurs between "consenting" partners in a manner that is ostensibly free from coercion. As noted, Russell (1990) has shown that women are much more likely to experience rape or attempted rape at the hands of husbands or ex-husbands, than they are from strangers. If the word "serial" did not refer to a perpetrator who attacked more than one victim in distinctive episodes, we might make the case that husbands, lovers, etc., would be the most likely candidates for serial rapists. Modern social science and the media have yet to invent a catchword for the husband/nonstranger who rapes the same woman on many occasions. Without wishing to impute any blame to the victims of marital/date/acquaintance rape, the paradoxical term "companionate rapist" might suffice.

The media hype about monstrous sexual violence ignores these many situations where women in intimate relationships with men are sexually abused, and unable, for a variety of reasons, to escape. This observation recalls the rather sweeping words of Catherine MacKinnon:

> Calling rape violence, not sex, thus evades . . . the issue of who controls women's sexuality and the dominance/submission dynamic that has defined it. When sex is violent, women may have lost control over what is done to us, but absence of force does not ensure the presence of that control. (1987:144)

This type of logic begins to trace links between certain forms of sexual intercourse within institutions such as marriage, rape, and sex between a sex worker and a john. In all of these encounters we see varying degrees of "nonconsent" that reflect the operation of patriarchal social structures. The offenses of the sexually violent predator can be situated at a point along this continuum, rather than being seen as aberrant and marginal vis-à-vis "everyday" interactions between men and women.

With these empirical and theoretical observations in mind, feminists have called for a number of reforms including the more stringent policing and prosecution of rape and domestic violence. Others have been keen to point out the limitations of legal change (Smart 1989; Ferraro 1993). They have also sought to explode the myth that offenders such as sexually violent predators warrant a heightening of awareness on the part of potential victims. As Betsy Stanko points out, precaution is a normal part of women's existence in a patriarchal society (1990:173–83). Crime prevention strategies advise women about "safe" living at the expense of systematically spelling out that the violence is mostly meted out by "known" and unsafe others, not strangers.

Soothill and Walby's (1991) analysis of five thousand newspapers from a forty-year period in Great Britain indicates that the reporting of sex crimes has become increasingly sensationalist. These authors also note recent feminist demands vis-à-vis the criminal justice system. However, Soothill and Walby stress that the feminist demands have been resisted and an alternative perspective has arisen. From this alternative perspective, "[S]ex crimes are dreadful, but rare, and are best dealt with by an increased law and order effort, rather than wider social reform" (ibid.:145).

The findings of Soothill and Walby raise a crucial question. Has the recent increase in the sensational reporting of sex crimes been a part of the backlash directed at feminist arguments about the systemic nature of patriarchal violence? This question is directly relevant to the predator law in Washington State. It is possible that this draconian law first appeared in Washington because of the presence of a relatively high number of nationally celebrated serial killers and predators. Doubtless, the primary claims-making of victims' rights groups such as SAVUS and the Governor's Task Force contributed greatly to the uniqueness of the Washington situation. However, I would argue that the predator law developed in part as a conservative response to the growing publicity over phenomena such as spousal abuse during the 1980s. Like police across the United States, police in Washington State were directed to be more sensitive to domestic calls. In Washington, marital rape became a crime in 1988 and new measures were introduced to address intrafamilial child abuse. As Dobash and Dobash have recently noted, Washington State has a strong commitment to altering the criminal justice response to violence against women (1992:200). For example, they observe that: "with the introduction of mandatory arrest . . . there was a fourfold increase in the number of arrests (of batterers) and a 300 percent increase in successful prosecutions" (ibid.).

These reforms were encouraged by feminist pressure. However, feminists have also pointed out that unless the structure of patriarchy is changed, reforming the criminal justice system will be little more than window dressing. In conclusion, I suggest the predator law and the gendered coverage of sexually violent predators has had the effect of counteracting the feminist push for deeper-seated reform over gender issues, by suggesting the real dangers to women and children come from freakish strangers rather than intimates or companions. It must be restated that this backlash against feminism is not something that the Washington State legislature or the media conspired to contribute to. The contribution to the backlash is more of an unforeseen twist in the ebb and flow of the predator discourse, which ends up reproducing patriarchal relations. The Washington State legislature did not go after intrafamilial "predation" because legislators feared that such an approach would reduce the reporting of intrafamilial abuse. I have noted how this rationale was underscored by patriarchal assumptions about the relationship between husbands, wives, and children.

Finally, if the predator law is not seen as part of the ebb and flow of gender legislation, then its possible adoption in other states will be challenged only on the grounds that it offends constitutional guarantees. Such a challenge takes for granted the way in which liberal law upholds the sanctity of the public/private divide, a divide that continues to work against the interests of women.

ACKNOWLEDGMENTS

The author would like to thank Ray Michalowski, Dave Rudy, Stanley Cohen, Ed Reeves, Rick Northrup, John Lafond, and Jeff Ferrell for helpful comments on various drafts of this manuscript.

REFERENCES

"ABC Nightline." 1991. "Washington State's Sexual Predator Law," show no. 2590 (26 April): Journal Graphics Transcripts.

Aries, Phillipe. 1962. *Centuries of Childhood: A Social History of Family Life.* New York: Random House.

Best, Joel. 1990. *Threatened Children.* Chicago: University of Chicago Press.

Brakel, S. J., J. Perry, and B. Weiner. 1985. *The Mentally Disabled and the Law,* 3rd edition. Chicago: American Bar Association.

Bromley, David G., Anson D. Shupe, and J. D. Ventimiglia. 1979. "Atrocity Tales: The Unification Church and the Social Construction of Evil." *Journal of Communication* 29:45–53.

Cohen, Stanley. 1980. *Folk Devils and Moral Panics,* 2nd edition. New York: St. Martin's.

Dobash, R. Emerson and Russell Dobash. 1979. *Violence against Wives.* New York: Free Press.

Dobash, R. Emerson and Russell Dobash. 1992. *Women, Violence and Social Change.* London and New York: Routledge.

Ferraro, Kathleen J. 1993. "Cops, Courts and Women Battering." Pp. 165–76 in *Violence against Women: The Bloody Footprints,* edited by Pauline Bart and Eileen Geil Moran. London: Sage.

Finkelhor, David. 1984. *Child Sexual Abuse: New Theory and Research.* New York: Free Press.

Finkelhor, David and Kersti Yllo. 1985. *License to Rape: Sexual Abuse of Wives.* New York: Holt, Rinehart and Winston.

"48 Hours." 1991. "Predators," show no. 173 (20 November). Denver, CO: Journal Graphics Transcripts.

"Frontline." 1992. "Monsters among Us," show no. 1105 (10 November). Denver, CO: Journal Graphics Transcripts.

Goffman, Erving. 1963. *Stigma: Notes on the Management of Spoiled Identity.* Englewood Cliffs, NJ: Prentice Hall.

Gordon, Linda. 1988. *Heroes of Their Own Lives: The Politics and History of Family Violence.* New York: Penguin.

Hall, Stuart, Chas Critcher, Tony Jefferson, John Clarke, and Brian Roberts. 1978. *Policing the Crisis: Mugging, The State and Law and Order.* London: MacMillan.

Hanmer, Jalna and Sheila Saunders. 1984. *Well Founded Fear.* London: Hutchinson.

Herman, Judith, with Lisa Hirschman. 1981. *Father-Daughter Incest.* Cambridge, MA: Harvard University Press.

Jenkins, Philip. 1994. *Using Murder: The Social Construction of Serial Homicide.* Hawthorne, NY: Aldine de Gruyter.

LaFond, John. 1991. Brief of Amicus Curiae in support of appellants Young and Cunningham in the Supreme Court of the State of Washington. No. 57837-I.

MacKinnon, Catherine. 1987. "Feminism, Marxism, Method and the State: Toward a Feminist Jurisprudence." Pp. 135–56 in *Feminism and Methodology,* edited by S. Harding. Indianapolis: Indiana University Press.

Olsen, Jack. 1989. *Doc: The Rape of the Town of Lovell.* New York: Atheneum.

Olsen, Jack. 1991. *Predator: Rape, Madness and Injustice in Seattle.* New York: Delacorte.

Radford, Jill and Diana Russell, eds. 1992. *Femicide.* New York: Twayne.

Rule, Ann. 1989. *The Stranger beside Me: Ted Bundy His Shocking True Story.* New York: Penguin.

Russell, Diana E. H. 1990. *Rape in Marriage.* Bloomington and Indianapolis: University of Indiana Press.

Seattle Times. 1989a. "Treating Sexual Deviants." June 18, p. A1.

Seattle Times. 1989b. "Healing the Hurt." June 19, p. E1.

Seattle Times. 1990a. "Shriner Guilty." February 7, p. A1.

Seattle Times. 1990b. "Shriner Gets 131 Years." March 26, p. A2.

Seattle Times. 1990c. "Mental Health Experts Criticize Sex-Predator Law." October 25, p. Al.

Smart, Carol. 1989. *Feminism and the Power of Law.* London: Routledge.

Smith, C. and T. Guillen. 1991. *The Search for the Green River Killer.* New York: Penguin.

Soothill, Keith and Sylvia Walby. 1991. *Sex Crimes in the News.* London and New York: Routledge.

Spender, Dale. 1980. *Man Made Language.* London: Routledge.

Spender, Dale. 1983. *Women of Ideas (and What Men Have Done to Them).* London: Ark.

Stanko, Elizabeth. 1990. "When Precaution Is Normal: A Feminist Critique of Crime Prevention." Pp. 78–83 in *Feminist Perspectives in Criminology,* edited by Lorraine Geisthrope and Alison Morris. Open University Press, UK: Milton Keynes:

State of Washington v. Andre Brigham Young. 1993. Washington State Supreme Court.

State of Washington v. Randy Russell Smith. Case Number 14532-4.

Sutherland, Edwin. 1950. "The Diffusion of Sexual Psychopath Laws." *American Journal of Sociology* 55:142-148.

Tacoma News Tribune. 1989a. "Past Sex Offender Suspect in Attack: Boy Too Traumatized to Cry by Mutilation." May 22, p. A1.

Tacoma News Tribune. 1989b. "An Offense That Calls for Outrage." Editorial. May 24.

Tacoma News Tribune. 1989c. "Fury over Mutilation Must Be Convened into Solutions." May 30, p. B1.

Tacoma News Tribune. 1989d. "Shriner Attorney Details Plans." June 21, p. B1.

Tacoma News Tribune. 1989e. "Stay Angry, Crowd Told: Violent Crime Can Be Halted, Speakers Say." June 21, p. B12.

Tuchman, Gaye, Arlene Kaplan Daniels, and James Benet, eds. 1978. *Hearth and Home: Images of Women in the Mass Media.* New York: Oxford University Press.

6

Media Misogyny
Demonizing "Violent" Girls and Women

MEDA CHESNEY-LIND

There is no denying the fact that female violence fascinates the general public at the same time that it perplexes feminist scholars (White and Kowalski 1994). Certainly, the possibility that women might begin to emulate male violence is a potent, albeit potential challenge to women's universal domination by men. The fact is, however, that girls' and women's violence is a relative rarity. As an example, women killers have accounted for about 10–15 percent of all homicides for centuries (Holmlund 1994:131), and there is even some evidence that the number of adult women killing men actually decreased rather sharply in the last few years (Dawson and Langan 1994; Bureau of Justice Statistics 1998). One estimate of this decline is 25 percent (Holmlund 1994:131).

The average citizen would likely be extremely surprised to hear this, since during the last two decades, both print and television journalists as well as other architects of popular culture have subjected us to a steady drumbeat of powerful representations of violent girls and women (Faludi 1991; Faith 1993; Birch 1994). This chapter will examine media constructions of girls' and women's violence, compare these with the realities of women's aggression, and, finally, speculate on the origins of this new fascination with unruly women.

MEDIA CONSTRUCTIONS OF GIRL'S AND WOMEN'S VIOLENCE

"They Get Right in Your Face": Discovering "Mean" Girls[1]

Shortly after a study by the American Association of University Women (1992) documented the dramatic and widespread drop in the self-esteem of girls during early adolescence, a curious thing happened in the media. There was a dramatic surge of journalistic interest in girls, often girls of color, engaged in nontraditional, masculine behavior—notably joining gangs, carrying guns, and fighting with other girls.

While arrest statistics still reflect the dominance of status and other trivial offenses in official female delinquency (for a full discussion of girls' delinquency, see Chesney-Lind 1997), these facts held little interest for media set on finding the new, "meaner" girl. Moreover, a review of girls' arrests for violent crime for the last decade (1986–1995) initially seemed to provide support for the notion that girls are engaged in more violent crime, further fueling the media firestorm. Arrests of girls for murder were up 62.4 percent, robbery arrests were up 119.6 percent, and aggravated assault was up 128.1 percent. Indeed, arrests of girls for all violent offenses (including other assaults) were up 145 percent (Federal Bureau of Investigation 1996:213).

What is going on? Are we seeing a major shift in the behavior of girls and an entry of girls into violent behaviors that were once the nearly exclusive domain of young boys? As we shall see, if all one did was read the papers, watch television, and go to the movies, the answer would be a resounding yes, but a closer look at the actual trends in girls and women's aggressive and violent behavior presents a more complex view.

"Some Girls Now Carry Guns. Others Hide Razor Blades in their Mouths"[2]: Media Hype and Girls of Color

The fascination with a "new," violent female offender is not really new. In the 1970s, a notion emerged that the women's movement had "caused" a surge in women's serious crimes, but this discussion focused largely on an imagined increase in crimes of adult women. The idea, though, was an appealing and simple concept: "[T]he movement for [women's] full equality has a darker side which has been slighted even by the scientific community. . . . In the same way that women are demanding equal opportunity in the fields of legitimate endeavor, a similar number of determined women are forcing their way into the world of major crimes" (Adler 1975a:42).

The female crime wave so vividly described by Adler (1975a, 1975b) and, to a lesser extent, by Simon (1975) was definitively refuted by subsequent research (see Steffensmeier and Steffensmeier 1980; Gora 1982), but the popularity of this perspective, at least in the public mind, is apparently undiminished.

Indeed, one of the observations to make about the "liberation" or "emancipation" hypothesis about women's offending is its resiliency as a theory of women's crime. Like other unproven, but compelling "bandwagon" notions about gender (like women's "fear of success"), this perspective is extremely popular and receives extensive press coverage. Careful refutations by other researchers never seem to attract the same media coverage or, more importantly, to dim its appeal (Mednick 1989). The emancipation hypothesis of women's crime is one of these notions, and it has the additional value of appearing to highlight unforeseen and negative consequences associated with the women's movement (Faludi 1991).

The current version of the "equal opportunity" theory of women's crime has settled largely but not exclusively on girls' commission of violent crimes, often in youth gangs. Indeed, as this section will demonstrate, there has been a flood of news stories with essentially the same theme: today girls are more violent, they are in gangs, and their behavior does not fit the traditional stereotype of girl's delinquency.

On August 2, 1993, for example, in a feature spread on teen violence, *Newsweek* had a box entitled "Girls Will Be Girls," which noted that "some girls now carry guns. Others hide razor blades in their mouths" (Leslie, Biddle, Rosenberg, and Wayne 1993:44). Explaining this trend, the article notes that "[t]he plague of teen violence is an equal-opportunity scourge. Crime by girls is on the rise, or so various jurisdictions report" (ibid.). Exactly a year earlier, a short subject appeared on a CBS program entitled "Street Stories." "Girls in the Hood," which was a rebroadcast of a story that first appeared in January 1992, opened with this voice-over:

> Some of the politicians like to call this the Year of the Woman. The women you are about to meet probably aren't what they had in mind. These women are active, they're independent, and they're exercising power in a field dominated by men. In January Harold Dowe first took us to the streets of Los Angeles to meet two uncommon women who are members of street gangs. (CBS 1992)

More recently (November 5, 1997), "ABC Primetime Live" aired two segments on Chicanas involved in gangs also entitled "Girls in the Hood" (ABC 1997) that followed two young women into their barrio for four months. The series opened with Sam Donaldson noting, "There are over six hundred thousand gang members in the United States. What might surprise you is that many of them are young women." Warning viewers that "some of the scenes you may see are quite graphic and violent," the segment featured dramatic shots of young women with large tattoos on their stomachs, youths carrying weapons and making gang signs, young women selling dope and talking about being violent, and distant shots of the covered bodies of drive-by shooting victims.

These stories were but three examples of many media accounts on violent girls to have appeared in recent years.[3] Where did this come from? Perhaps the start was an article entitled, "You've Come a Long Way, Moll," which appeared in the *Wall Street Journal* on January 25, 1990. This article noted that "between 1978–1988 the number of women arrested for violent crimes went up 41.5% vs. 23.1% for men. The trend is even starker for teenagers" (Crittenden 1990). The trend was augmented through media reports linking increasing violence to women's liberation. "For Gold Earrings and Protection, More Girls Take the Road to Violence," announced the front page of the *New York Times,* in an article that opens as follows:

> For Aleysha J., the road to crime has been paved with huge gold earrings and name brand clothes. At Aleysha's high school in the Bronx, popularity comes from looking the part. Aleysha's mother has no money to buy her nice things so the diminutive 15 year old steals them, an act that she feels makes her equal parts bad girl and liberated woman. (Lee 1991)

This is followed by the assertion that "[t]here are more and more girls like Aleysha in troubled neighborhoods in the New York metropolitan areas, people who work with children say. There are more girls in gangs, more girls in the drug trade, more girls carrying guns and knives, more girls in trouble" (ibid.). Whatever the original source, at this point a phenomenon known as "pack journalism" took over. The *Philadelphia Inquirer,* for example, ran a story subtitled, "Troubled Girls, Troubling Violence," on February 23, 1992, which asserted:

> Girls are committing more violent crimes than ever before. Girls used to get in trouble like this mostly as accomplices of boys, but that's no longer true. They don't need the boys. And their attitudes toward their crimes are often as hard as the weapons they wield—as shown in this account based on documents and interviews with participants, parents, police and school officials. While boys still account for the vast majority of juvenile crime, girls are starting to catch up. (Santiago 1992)

This particular story featured a single incident in which an African-American girl attacked another girl (described as "middle class" and appearing white in the picture that accompanies the story) in a subway. The *Washington Post* ran a similar story entitled "Delinquent Girls Achieving a Violent Equality in D.C." on December 23, 1992 (Lewis 1992). And the pattern continues to the present. As an example, the *Boston Globe Magazine* ran a feature piece entitled "The Razor's Edge," which proclaimed on its cover that "girls are moving into the world of violence that once belonged to boys" (Ford 1998), and from the *San Jose Mercury* (Guido 1998) comes a story entitled "In a New Twist on Equality, Girls' Crime Resembles Boys'" and features an opening paragraph that argues:

> Juvenile crime experts have spotted a disturbing nationwide pattern of teenage girls becoming more sophisticated and independent criminals. In the past,

girls would almost always commit crimes with boys or men. But now, more than ever, they're calling the shots. (ibid.)

In virtually all the print stories on this topic, the issue is framed in a similar fashion. Generally, a specific and egregious example of female violence is described, usually with considerable, graphic detail about the injury suffered by the victim. In the *San Jose Mercury* article, for example, the reader hears how a seventeen-year-old girl, Linna Adams, "lured" the victim into a car, where her boyfriend "pointed a .357 magnum revolver at him, and the gun went off. Rodrigues was shot in the cheek, and according to coroner's reports, the bullet exited the back of his head" (ibid.). These details are then followed by a quick review of the Federal Bureau of Investigation's arrest statistics showing what appear to be large increases in the number of girls arrested for violent offenses. Finally, there are quotes from "experts," usually police officers, teachers, or other social service workers, but occasionally criminologists, interpreting the events.

Following the earlier print media stories, the number of articles and television shows focused specifically on girls in gangs jumped. Popular talk shows such as "Oprah" (November 1992), "Geraldo" (January 1993), and "Larry King Live" (March 1993) did programs on the subject, and NBC broadcast a story on its nightly news that opened with the same link between women's "equality" and girls' participation in gangs:

> Gone are the days when girls were strictly sidekicks for male gang members, around merely to provide sex and money and run guns and drugs. Now girls also do shooting. . . . [T]he new members, often as young as twelve, are the most violent. . . . Ironic as it is, just as women are becoming more powerful in business and government, the same thing is happening in gangs. (NBC 1993)

The "ABC Primetime: Girls in the Hood" segment discussed earlier featured many of the sensationalistic aspects of the NBC story. It, though, was especially notable for its use of a white woman reporter, Cynthia McFadden, who reacted to the two young Chicanas' accounts of their complex and violent lives with outrage and moralistic hectoring. As an example, the reporter asked one of the young women "Are you a bad person?" The young woman began to answer, "I don't think so. Some people may not agree with what I say but . . ." at which point the reporter interrupted and said, "I don't think it's what you say so much as what you do. You sell drugs, you participate in gang violence, you participate in shootings, in robbings, in stabbings." Later in the same interview, in response to her expression of pride over having stolen and kept a coffeemaker during the Los Angeles riots, the reporter blurted out: "You realize that most of the people watching you want to slap you when you say that" (ABC 1997).

While much of the media focus regarding female violence has been on girls, violence committed by adult women has also attracted attention, but in a slightly different venue—the movies. As Birch notes, "[T]he rampaging female has become a new cliché of Hollywood cinema, stabbing and shooting her way to notoriety" (1994:1).

Adult Women and Violence: Popular Culture's War on Women

While the constructions of womanhood that appear in popular culture, and particularly movies, have always been problematic (Haskell 1973; Douglas 1994), the last two decades have seen a particular and determined focus on violent women. Films like *Basic Instinct, The Hand that Rocks the Cradle, Mortal Thoughts, Thelma and Louise,* and *To Die For* all feature women who kill. Indeed, if Hollywood's representation of crime were accurate, unruly women who were not busy trying to kill men would be busy stalking (*Fatal Attraction*) and sexually harassing them (*Disclosure*).

Some of these movies, particularly *Fatal Attraction* and *Thelma and Louise,* unleashed a flood of critical commentary, but most of this discussion, particularly in the case of *Fatal Attraction,* focused on the attack on modern career women rather than on Alex's (the female lead played by Glen Close) violence (see Bromley and Hewitt 1992; Babner 1992; Berland and Wechter 1992). In the case of *Basic Instinct* and *Thelma and Louise,* much of the public commentary focused on the implicit and explicit lesbian themes (and homophobia) that the films expressed (Siegal 1995; Sharratt 1992). Some of the discussion of *Thelma and Louise,* though, did touch on women's aggression. Here, the essential question was whether the film's depiction of women's violence expressed a new kind of feminism (see Schickel 1991) or was instead merely an outgrowth of the fact that the film was "a male buddy movie with two women plunked down in the starring roles" (Carlson 1991; see also Boozer 1995).

Certainly, with the mention of male violence against women (*Thelma and Louise*) and even more the links between domestic violence and women's decisions to kill (*Mortal Thoughts*), some of these movies begin to approximate a consideration of women's violence in a patriarchal context. Of course, it goes without saying that few women in the criminal justice system resemble the white, privileged, rail-thin, drop-dead beauty of Sharon Stone, Nicole Kidman, Demi Moore, and Geena Davis—all movie killers.

"You've Come a Long Way Moll"

The movies have not been the only site of media attention to adult women's violence. As with girls, the print media has also discovered violent adult women. As mentioned earlier, one of the first of these print media treatments was the 1990 *Wall Street Journal* article entitled "You've Come a Long Way Moll." This piece focused largely on increases in the number of adult women arrested for violent crimes. Opening with a discussion of women in the military, it noted that "the armed forces already are substantially integrated" and moved from this point to observe that "we needn't look to the dramatic example of battle for proof that violence is no longer a male domain. Women are now being arrested for violent crimes—such as robbery and aggravated assault—at a higher rate than ever before recorded in the US" (Crittenden 1990).

A year later came the "Hand That Rocks the Cradle Is Taking Up Violent Crime" (Kahler 1992), which focused on increases in women's imprisonment and linked this pattern to "the growing number of women committing violent crimes" (ibid.). For many feminist criminologists, these headlines were more than a little familiar. For example, a 1971 *New York Times* article entitled "Crime Rate of Women Up Sharply over Men's" noted, "Women are gaining rapidly in at least one traditional area of male supremacy—crime" (Roberts 1971).

If one compares the media hype about adult women's violence to that which targeted girls of color, many (though not all) of the same themes emerge. Clearly, though, the links to women's quest for equality (particularly in the workplace) are more at the center of the construction of adult women's violence; race seems more central to the discourse about girls' violence. And, as was the case with the first wave of media attention on the new liberated "female crook," the 1990s also found academic criminologists supplying journalists with apparent support for media constructions of women's violence as a serious and growing problem.

Academics and the Media Construction
of Crime Problems

In the seventies, it was not uncommon for articles detailing the "women and crime" problem to include an interview with Freda Adler. In an article entitled "Women Terrorists: Sisters in Crime," she is quoted as saying, "When you have increased participation of females in society . . . there is no reason why they wouldn't become involved in such things as big business, or government, or even violent crimes that men are involved in" (Klemsrud 1978).

More recently, one group of academics whose work generally supports the notion that women are engaging in more violent crime credits media coverage for their interest in the topic. The authors' "interest in women's involvement in violent street crime was initially piqued when we noted the following story in our neighborhood newspaper" (Baskin, Sommers, and Fagan 1993:403). They follow this comment by reprinting a portion of the news story, which originally appeared in The *Park Slope Paper*. This story reports, "A 34 year old . . . woman is in stable condition after being shot in the face during a robbery Monday night . . . a couple of doors from her home. . . . Two women, a 24 year old and a 26 year old . . . were arrested and charged with attempted murder, robbery, assault and criminal posses- sion of a weapon in connection with the shooting and robbery, said police" (ibid., ellipses in original).

In a series of academic articles, these authors make the general point that "women in New York City are becoming more and more likely to involve themselves in violent street crime" (ibid.:401). The first author, Deborah Baskin, was also quoted by the *New York Times* as saying about her re- search that "people are afraid of doing these studies because of the political implications" (Lee 1991). She continues, "[T]hey are afraid it will result in the over-incarceration of women. I'm more willing to go out on a limb and say from anecdotal reports and our research this is something we should be worried about" (ibid.)

What is the research evidence that supports their position? In one study (Sommers and Baskin 1992), two of the authors use arrest data from New York City (as well as arrest histories of 266 women) to argue that "black and Hispanic females exhibited high rates of offending relative to white fe- males." They further argue that "violent offending rates of black females parallel those of white males" (ibid.:191). Included in their definition of "violent" crimes is murder, robbery, aggravated assault, and burglary (which is apparently classified as a violent crime in New York City, but which is classified as a property crime by the FBI).

This pattern is explained by the authors as a product of "the effects of the social and institutional transformation of the inner city" (ibid.:198). Specifi- cally, the authors contend that "violence and drug involvement" become adaptive strategies in underclass communities that are racked by poverty and unemployment. Both men and women, they argue, move to crime as a way of coping with "extreme social and economic deprivation" (ibid.).

A second study (Sommers and Baskin 1993) further explores women's violent offending by analyzing interview data from twenty-three women who were arrested for a violent felony offense (robbery and/or assault) and sixty-five women incarcerated for such an offense. Finding a high correla- tion between substance abuse and the rate of violent crime (particularly for those who committed robbery and robbery with assault), they also note that "the women in our study who were involved in robbery were not crime specialists but also had a history of engagement in nonviolent theft, fraud, forgery, prostitution, and drug dealing" (ibid.:142). In fact, they comment that "these women are not roaming willy-nilly through the streets engaging in 'unprovoked' violence" (ibid.:154).

Just how involved these women were in more traditional forms of female crime was not totally apparent in the text of the article. In an appendix, however, the role played by a history of prostitution in the lives of these women offenders is particularly clear. As an example, the women who reported committing both robbery and assault also had the highest rate of involvement with prostitution (77 percent) (ibid.:159).

In a third paper, Baskin et al. (1993) explore "the political economy of street crime." This piece, which appears to be based on the New York arrest data as well as a discussion of the explosion of crack selling in the city, explores the question, "Why do black females exhibit such relatively high rates of violence?" (ibid.:405). Convinced that the concentration of poverty is associated positively with the level of criminal activity regardless of race, the authors then conclude that "the growing drug markets and a marked disappearance of males" combine with other factors in underclass communities "to create social and economic opportunity structures open to women's increasing participation in violent crime" (ibid.:406).

The authors go further by suggesting that traditional theories of women's offending, particularly those that emphasize gender and victimization, do not adequately explain women's violent crime. Their work, they contend, "confirms our initial sense that women in inner city neighborhoods are being pulled toward violent street crime by the same forces that have been found to affect their male counterparts (e.g. peers, opportunity structures, neighborhood effects)" (ibid.:412). They conclude that the socioeconomic situation in the inner city, specifically as it is affected by the drug trade, creates "new dynamics of crime where gender is a far less salient factor" (ibid.:417).

These authors seem to be saying that in economically devastated inner cities like New York, women's violence—particularly the violence of women of color—does not need to be contextualized within patriarchy (since gender is "far less salient" in their lives). Instead, they contend that these women (like their male counterparts) are being drawn to violence and other forms of traditionally male crimes for the same reason as men.

Here, then, is the "liberation" hypothesis turned on its head. Now, it is not presumed economic gain that promotes "equality" in crime, but rather economic marginalization that causes women to move out of their "traditional" roles. Is that really what is going on? Has there been an increase in women's participation in traditionally male types of crime, such as violent crime, particularly in the urban areas devastated by poverty and drugs? Can these changes, in turn, degender some girls and women and make them more likely to commit masculine offenses? To answer these questions, it is important to briefly review the actual evidence on girls and women's violence.

EMPIRICAL TRENDS

Trends in Girls' Violence and Aggression

As noted earlier, a review of girls' arrests for violent crime for the last decade (1986–1995) initially seems to provide support for the notion that girls are engaged in dramatically more violent crime than a decade earlier. As an example, arrests of girls for all Part One Offenses[4] were up 124.2 percent during the period 1986–1995 (Federal Bureau of Investigation 1996:213).

Serious crimes of violence are, though, only a very small proportion of all girls' delinquency, and that figure has remained essentially unchanged. Only 2.1 percent of girls' arrests in 1986 were for serious crimes of violence. By 1995, this figure had climbed to 3.2 percent (15,503 arrests out of a total of 482,039 arrests). Moreover, girls' share of serious crimes of violence (i.e., the sex ratio for these offenses) has changed only slightly during the two time periods. In 1986, for example, arrests of girls accounted for 11 percent of all arrests of youth for serious crimes of violence; in 1995, the comparable figure was 14.5 percent (Federal Bureau of Investigation 1996:213).

When exploring the dramatic increases in the arrests of girls for "other assaults" (which increased by 126.2 percent in the last decade), it is also likely that police have increasingly arrested disproportionate numbers of girls. Minor or "other" assaults can range from school yard tussles to relatively serious, but not life-threatening assaults (Steffensmeier and Steffensmeier 1980). Steffensmeier and Steffensmeier first noted an increasing tendency to arrest girls for these offenses in the seventies and commented that "evidence suggests that female arrests for 'other assaults' are relatively non-serious in nature and tend to consist of being bystanders or companions to males involved in skirmishes, fights, and so on" (ibid.:70).

The relabeling of behaviors that were once ignored or swept up under broader offense categories (like "runaway") into violent offenses, particularly assaults, cannot be ruled out in explanations of arrest rates. A review of the over two thousand cases of girls referred to Maryland's juvenile justice system for "person-to-person" offenses revealed that virtually all of these offenses (97.9 percent) involved "assault." A further examination of these records revealed that about half were "family centered" and involved such activities as "a girl hitting her mother and her mother subsequently pressing charges" (Mayer 1994).

Other mechanisms for relabeling status offenses as criminal offenses include police officers advising parents to block the doorways when their children threaten to run away and then charging the youth with "assault" when they shove their way past their parents. Such relabeling, which is also called bootstrapping, has been particularly pronounced in the official delinquency of African-American girls (Robinson 1990; Bartollas 1993), and this practice also facilitates the incarceration of girls in detention facilities and training schools—something that would not be possible if the girl were arrested for noncriminal status offenses.

Detailed comparisons drawn from supplemental homicide reports from unpublished FBI data also hint at the central rather than peripheral way in which gender colored and differentiated girls' and boys' violence. Loper and Cornell's study of these FBI data on the characteristics of girls' and boys' homicides between 1984 and 1993 found that girls accounted for "proportionately fewer homicides in 1993 (6 percent) than in 1984 (14 percent)" (1996:324). Their work shows that girls' choice of weapons differed from boys' so that in comparison to boys' homicides, girls who killed were more likely to use a knife than a gun and to murder someone as a result of conflict (rather than in the commission of a crime). Girls were also more likely than boys to murder family members (32 percent) and very young victims (24 percent of their victims were under the age of three compared to 1 percent of the boy's victims) (ibid.:328). When involved in a peer homicide, girls were more likely than boys to have killed "as a result of an interpersonal conflict"; in addition, girls were more likely to kill alone, while boys were more likely to kill with an accomplice (ibid.). The authors concluded that "the stereotype of girls becoming gun-toting robbers was not supported. The dramatic increase in gun-related homicides . . . applies to boys but not girls" (ibid.:332).

Finally, trends in self-report data of youthful involvement in violent offenses also fail to show the dramatic changes found in official statistics. Specifically, a matched sample of "high risk" youth (aged thirteen–seventeen) surveyed in the 1977 National Youth Study and the more recent 1989 Denver Youth Survey revealed significant *decreases* in girls' involvement in felony assaults, minor assaults, and hard drugs, and no change in a wide range of other delinquent behaviors—including felony theft, minor theft, and index (nonstatus) delinquency (Huizinga 1997).

But what about girls in gangs? Has there been an increase here? While official police estimates reflect extremely low numbers of girls involved in gang activity (one national estimate is that only about 3.65 percent of the names in police databases are female) (Curry, Ball, and Fox 1994:8), other estimates are significantly higher. As an example, Moore, in her important ethnographic work on gang activity in the Los Angeles barrios, estimates that fully a third of the youth involved the gangs she studied were female (Moore 1991:8).

Given the range of estimates, one might wonder whether the involvement of girls with gang life resembles the involvement of girls in other youth subcultures, where they have been described as "present but invisible" (McRobbie and Garber 1975). Certainly, Moore's higher estimate indicates that she saw girls others missed. Indeed, Moore's work is noteworthy in its departure from the androcentric norm in gang research. The long-standing "gendered habits" of researchers have meant that the girls' involvement with gangs has been discussed in relation to boys gangs (as "auxiliary") and that they themselves have often been portrayed as either sexual chattel or maladjusted tomboys (Campbell 1990); most often, in earlier decades, the girls were simply ignored.

An exception to this generalization is Quicker's study of female Chicano gang members in East Los Angeles conducted in the sixties and seventies. He found evidence that the girls he interviewed, although still somewhat dependent upon their male counterparts, were becoming more independent decades earlier than the media "discovery" of girls in gangs. The girls Quicker studied identified themselves as "homegirls" and their male counterparts as "homeboys," a common reference to relationships in the barrio. Quicker also found girls engaging in fighting with other girls, but also noted many prosocial impulses in girl's involvement in gangs (Quicker 1983).

Moore's (1991) ethnographic work on two Chicano gangs in East Los Angeles was initiated during the same period as Quicker's, but she returned to these same neighborhoods in the eighties. Her interviews clearly establish both the multifaceted nature of girls' experiences with gangs in the barrio, as well as the variations in male gang members' perceptions of the girls in gangs. First, her work establishes that there is no one type of gang girl, with some of the girls in gangs, even in the 1940s, "not tightly bound to boy's cliques" and also "much less bound to particular barrios than boys" (ibid.:27). Moore definitely records girls talking about fighting other girls in both time periods (ibid.:64–65), but she also notes that the girls in gangs tended to come from "more troubled background than those of the boys" (ibid.:30).

Moore found that significant problems with sexual victimization haunt girls' accounts of their lives but not boys'. She also documents that the sexual double standard characterized male gang members' as well as the neighborhood's more general view of the girls in gangs. Moore notes that the girl gang members were labeled as "tramps" and symbolized as "no good" despite the girls' vigorous rejection of these labels. Further, some male gang members, even those who had relationships with girl gang members, felt that "square girls were their future" (ibid.:75).

This brief review of the literature on girls and violence suggests that much of the "evidence" of an increase in girl's violence rests on shifts in arrest patterns (particularly in the area of assault) or accounts of girls in gangs. Certainly, girls in gangs report violence, but this again is a long-standing pattern, as is girls' participation in gangs. More generally, it appears that girls' occasionally violent behavior has been largely ignored or sexualized in years past when concern about girls sexuality was uppermost in people's minds (see Chesney-Lind and Shelden 1998); now that youthful violence is more topical, it is relatively easy to suddenly "discover" the girls' violence that was there all along.

Trends in Adult Women's Arrests

What of adult women's violence? Is it on the increase? Arrest data can provide a partial response. While arrests of adult women for robbery did increase by 17.1 percent between 1986 and 1995, and arrests for aggravated assault were up by 100.2 percent, arrests of women for murder actually declined by 19.6 percent (Federal Bureau of Investigation 1996:213); and all of these offenses accounted for only about 4 percent of women's arrests.

More significant were increases in arrests of women for "other assaults" (up 127.6 percent), not unlike the pattern seen in girls' arrests (ibid.). In addition, arrests of adult women for drug abuse violations increased by 91.1 percent compared to 53.8 percent for men (ibid.). As a result of these trends, arrests of women for other assaults and drug offenses have replaced fraud and disorderly conduct as the most common offenses for which adult women are arrested. These patterns certainly suggest that the "war on drugs" has had consequences for women as well as men, but what of the increase in women's arrest for assault?

First, the significant increase in women's arrests for "other assaults" is likely not the product of the decreasing salience of gender in the lives of women in poor neighborhoods or women's "emancipation." Instead, the sad fact is that much of the increase, like the pattern seen earlier with girls, is a product of mandatory arrest laws in the area of domestic violence.

Researchers certainly agree there have been increased arrests in the area of other assaults (Stark 1996; Buzawa and Buzawa 1990). Ironically, buried in this pattern is a substantial increase in the number of women arrested for assault. Briefly, as women's groups pressured police departments to implement mandatory arrest policies for domestic violence, an unanticipated consequence was that the number of women arrested for violent behavior increased rather substantially. Only a few estimates of this exist, but Buzawa and Buzawa note that in the state of Washington, "fully one-third of all [domestic violence] arrests are dual arrests" (ibid.:104). Other states report lower, but still significant rates of 11 percent (Oregon) and 17 percent (Connecticut) (ibid.:104). Buzawa and Buzawa interpret these figures as "mechanistic" interpretations of mandatory arrest policies by police, who have "historically been unsympathetic to the needs and goals of abused women" (ibid.).

Ethnographic field work conducted in the neighborhoods of Chicago (Ouellet, Wiebel, Jimenez, and Johnson 1993), Harlem (Bourgois and Dunlap 1993), and New York (Maher and Curtis 1992; Williams 1992), as well as interviews with young women in Miami (Inciardi, Lockwood, and Pottieger 1993), Harlem (Fullilove, Lown, and Fullilove 1992), and San Francisco (Schwartz et al. 1992) add an important dimension to the discussion of women, culture, and drugs in politically and economically marginalized communities. More importantly, these studies also demonstrate how women's involvement in the drug economy also increases their likelihood for arrest for such "nontraditional" offenses as robbery.

First, women's drug use is closely connected to trauma and victimization. The extensiveness of the violence in girls' and women's lives is dramatically underscored in interviews with women crack users in Harlem, most of whom were African-American. This research focused on the lives of fourteen women crack users and documented that "trauma was a common occurrence in their lives," which in turn propelled the women into drug use (Fullilove et al. 1992:277). These women's lives are full of the chaos and abuse common in neighborhoods of extreme poverty. They are also distressed and depressed at their inability to "maintain culturally defined gender roles" (specifically functioning as mothers) because of their drug use. Finally, these women are further victimized by the "male-oriented drug culture," which has developed a bizarre and exploitative form of prostitution around women's addiction to crack cocaine.

These ethnographies have clearly linked the discussion of women's patterns of drug use to women's involvement in prostitution. Since prostitution has always played such a central role in women's crime (Miller 1986; Chesney-Lind and Rodriguez 1983), it is important to now turn to the ways in which contemporary patterns of prostitution have been affected by the contemporary drug scene in certain cities, and how these two trends are, in turn, linked to women's involvement in violent behavior.

Prostitution, Drug Selling, and Violence

There is no doubt that the crack scene has clearly affected street prostitution, long a mainstay in women's survival in marginalized communities. In a study of the impact of crack in three Chicago neighborhoods, it was noted that while "street-level prostitution has probably always had rate cutters" (Ouellet et al. 1993:88), the arrival of crack and the construction of the "crack ho" has created a desperate form of prostitution involving instances of extreme degradation that had previously only been seen in extremely impoverished countries like the Philippines and Thailand (Studervant and Stoltzfus 1992; Enloe 1989).

Most women involved in prostitution, even those involved in crack-related prostitution, view their activities as "work," and feel that this work is more ethical and safer than either stealing or drug dealing (Bourgois and Dunlap 1993:104). According to this perspective, because the crack epidemic has virtually destroyed the economic viability of street prostitution in some neighborhoods, some women might even prefer to go to crack houses to get their drugs directly, rather than to risk the dangers of the streets and violence from johns who are even less well known to them than the men in the crack houses.

Not all women addicted to crack choose this path, particularly when times get hard. For this reason, crack has also changed the nature of street prostitution in neighborhoods where it is present. Maher and Curtis's (1992) work on women involved in street-level sex markets in New York notes that the introduction of crack cocaine "increased the number of women working the strolls and had a significant impact on the kind of work they did, the remuneration they received and the interactions that occurred in and around street-level sex markets" (ibid.:21). Maher and Curtis found that women involved in prostitution were also involved in other forms of property crime, like shoplifting, stealing from their families, and occasionally robbing johns as a way of surviving on the streets.

In essence, increased competition among women involved in prostitution, plus the deflation in the value of their work, has created a more hostile environment among New York streetwalkers, as well as an increased willingness to rip off johns (see also Ouellet et al. 1993). To understand this, it is important to convey the enormity of the violence that women in sex work are routinely exposed to at the hands of johns. Maher and Curtis provide many such examples. One woman they talked to told them:

> I got shot twice since I bin here. . . . [W]as a car pulled up, two guys in it, they was like "C'mon gon' on a date." I wouldn't go with that so they came back around and shot me . . . in the leg and up here. (Maher and Curtis 1992:23)

Here's another:

> I got punched in the mouth not too long ago they [two dates] ripped me off—they wanted their money back after we finished—threw me off the van naked—then hit me with a blackjack 'caus I jumped back on to the van because I wanted to get my clothes. It was freezing outside so I jumped back onto the van to try and get my clothes and he smacked me with a blackjack on my eye. (ibid.:244)

In fact, some "robbery" becomes much more understandable, when seen up close as it is in this work. Take Candy's story:

> I robbed a guy up here not too long ago—5 o'clock Sunday morning . . . a real cheek gonna tell me $5 for a blow job and that pisses me off—arguing wit them. I don't argue no more—jus get in the car sucker, he open his pants and do like this and I do like this, put my hand, money first. He give me the money I say, "See ya, hate to be ya, next time motherfucker it cost you $5 to get me to come to the window." (ibid.:246)

Although women are clearly using crack, Bourgois and Dunlap (1993:-123) found little evidence of women involved in selling the drug. Inciardi and his associates found slightly more evidence of this, noting that women (including many prostitutes) are drawn to selling crack due to its availability and low cost (unlike heroin). All agree that prostitution is still a mainstay for street women, as is petty property crime. By contrast, female violent crime and major property crime is far less frequent—even among these women—and clearly related to "heavy" crack use (Inciardi, Lockwood, and Pottieger 1993:120).

The work on women's pathways into criminal behavior, taken in total, illuminates the ways in which the injuries of girlhood produce problems that young women often solve on the streets of poor neighborhoods. That the straight and illicit economies the women find on those streets is gendered is also very clear from all these studies. In addition, it is evident that violence is a part of life in these communities, that women have always been exposed to large amounts of violence, and that women are capable of responding in ways that can be categorized as "violent." Generally, it has served the interests of the powerful to ignore or minimize women's ability to engage in violence (White and Kowalski 1994). After all, given the amount of violence women suffer at male hands, the remarkable story is that we are not more violent.

Campbell notes that the androcentric perspective on women's violence is that "violent women must be either trying to be men or just crazy" (Campbell 1993:144). What this research illustrates is the importance of placing a woman's violence within the totality of her life. Then, it is clear that "the problem of female aggression is located within interpersonal and institutionalized patterns of a patriarchal society" (White and Kowalski 1994:502).

Finally, prostitution, however renamed and reshaped, remains the major gateway to women's entry into other forms of illicit activities, since girls' and women's "capital" is still chiefly their sexuality. It is not clear that drugs play a more central role in the prostitution of the nineties than they did in earlier decades (Bourgois and Dunlap 1993), when women's drug addiction and crime went largely ignored and only the prostitution caused concern. What has changed, though, is the public response to the drug addiction and the violence that have likely always surrounded street life.

CONSTRUCTING VIOLENT WOMEN: MEDIA, MISOGYNY, AND ATTITUDES TOWARD WOMEN

Media coverage of crime and violence has increased dramatically in recent years. One content analysis of evening newscasts on the three major networks found that "crime has been by far the biggest topic of the decade," far overshadowing economic news, which placed "a distant second" (*Media Monitor* 1997:1). While links between these trends and public attitudes about crime, including women's crime, are complex, it is also the case that the number of Americans naming crime as the nation's "most important problem" increased sixfold between June 1993 and January 1994—at a time when victimization surveys and crime rates showed little change or actual decreases (ibid.).

It is certainly well documented that media function as "gatekeepers," with power to decide which current events are to become "news" (White 1950). Violence figures prominently in the reporting of deviance-related news stories and enjoys great popularity with audiences (Ammons, Dimmick, and Pilotta 1982; Fedler and Jordan 1982; Smith 1981; Combs and Slovic 1979; Antunes and Hurley 1977). Additionally, extant research demonstrates that not only do media reports disproportionately focus on and distort violent events, but that they also manufacture crime-related articles that bear little resemblance to established crime trends (Garofolo 1981; Sheley 1981; Davis 1952). Finally, Sacco (1995) notes that media reports with the strongest ideological content are the mostly likely to affect public attitudes.

The work of feminist media observers adds an important dimension to the understanding and interpretation of the patterns found in the coverage of women's crime. First, media constructions of women's activities must be understood as part of the institutional accomplishment of gender, in which some images of gender are privileged over others. Most specifically, media images of masculinity routinely reinforce "hegemonic masculinity," which emphasizes the subordination of women, authority, aggression, heterosexuality, and technical accomplishment (Connell 1987:186).

Images of "emphasized femininity" feature and privilege dependence, sociability, fragility in mating, and "acceptance of marriage and childcare as a response to labor-market discrimination against women" (ibid.:187). "Emphasized femininity" is, according to Connell, especially visible in the mass media "with an insistence and on a scale far beyond that found for any form of masculinity" (ibid.:188). Perhaps for this reason, media constructions of crime and victimization routinely feature women as crime victims, and men, particularly men of color, as criminals (Madriz 1997). Madriz goes on to note that the construction of the ideal, "innocent victim" (one the press particularly loves) is either white and upper class or a member of a minority group acting in distinctly nonstereotypical ways (a Latina honor student and class valedictorian who is killed by a mugger) (ibid.:87).

How then to construct a femininity that dares to access aggression and other elements of "hegemonic masculinity"? As this analysis has revealed, the overarching media construction of a violent woman is a woman masculinized by some form of "emancipation." This treatment may serve an important purpose—the casting out of these women from the ranks of "true womanhood," which in turn excludes them from the benefits, however dubious, of that status (Kraditor 1971). Since so many of the women portrayed in these accounts are women of color, this pattern can be seen as accessing the historic pattern of masculinizing African-American women so as to make harsh treatment, like slavery, field work, and whippings, more palatable (Horton 1998).

This tradition of excluding women of color from the ranks of "women" has a specific tradition within crime and punishment. During the Progressive Era, for example, white women were deemed worthy of "saving" and "reform," but no such intervention was considered for African-American women, who were often housed with male prisoners, placed on chain gangs, and whipped along with the men (Rafter 1990:150). In her history of women's imprisonment, Rafter quotes Frances Kellor, who toured women's prisons at the turn of the century, as saying that the African-American female offender is "first a negro and than a woman—in the whites' estimation," meaning that black women did not "benefit from the 'chivalry' extended to white females" (ibid.:134).

How exactly do media accounts accomplish this degendering of violent women, particularly women of color? One critical element is the opening piece in most print media accounts of women's violence—the description of a violent incident with a female perpetrator presented in graphic detail. This media approach to crime reporting has been categorized as "forensic journalism" by Websdale and Alvarez (1998). In their research on media accounts of "murder/suicides" (where women are lethally assaulted by male intimates), they noted that readers were almost always given extensive detail about the immediate situational dynamics within the crime, often with "dramaturgical details" about the weapon involved, the location of the wounds, and the extent of the injury (ibid.:127). In essence, the readers are told "more and more about less and less" (ibid.:126), while the larger context within which this horrific event occurred (often battering relationships of long standing) is obscured or not mentioned.

These patterns can clearly be found in the media's fascination with girls' and women's violence. When the true nature of girls' and women's violence is explored, its place in patriarchal society (and particularly its link to women's victimization and economic marginality) is a major explanatory theme. But one can look long and hard in media accounts of women's violence for any careful discussion of these issues. Instead, after the graphic, "forensic journalism," there is often an avoidance of any detail that might contextualize the girls' and women's violence that has been so vividly described. Instead, there is a rush to "experts" who explain these patterns as part of girls and women becoming more like men.

In Websdale and Alvarez's work, the larger social patterns being ignored were the links between lethal violence against women and earlier battering; in this instance, what is generally missing is the context within which women's violence is lodged (often victimization). Media treatment of women's violence, instead, tends to focus on one or two sensationalistic crimes, with considerable and sometimes graphic details on injury or injuries caused by the female perpetrator, followed by selective use of trends in arrest data, and quotes from experts who deploy either individualistic, pathological explanations or some version of the emancipation hypothesis.

Certainly, few of the news stories on women's crime and punishment and none of the movies that have represented women's violence do adequate justice to the lack of options and desperation that characterizes the lives of the women who actually commit violent acts. Beyond this, the efforts to construct women's violence as more or less equivalent to male violence (as in *Basic Instinct, Thelma and Louise,* and *The Hand that Rocks the Cradle*) or demented (*Fatal Attraction*) shift the public discourse back to crude essentialist arguments about whether "real" women are or are not capable of "male" violence. The shortcomings of this approach are clear when compared to the important work of scholars who are contextualizing women's aggression and violence in a society that is racist, capitalistic, and patriarchal.

If understanding is not the goal of the media fascination, then what is? Possibly the best way to describe this work is Faludi's term, "backlash journalism," whose chief project in the last two decades appears to have been to demonize feminists (Kamen 1991), to document the negative effects of feminism (Faludi 1991), and to construct women on the economic margins of society as the authors of their own problems. Simplistic and sensational discussions of women's violence fit perfectly into this agenda, and the work is relatively easy to do. Women's everyday violence and aggression, and its social context, have been ignored or trivialized. Instead we witness the sporadic "discovery" of rather heinous female offenders. In addition, focusing on women's violence obscures the fact that it is women's victimization, not male victimization, that has increased dramatically over the past two decades. In 1973, the women's victimization rate (for murder, rape, robbery, and assault) was less than half that of men; in 1994, the female victimization rate was two-thirds that for men. And unlike male victims of violence (where only half knew their assailants), the vast majority of women victims (78 percent) knew their assailants—generally intimately (Craven 1996:1).

Media treatments of female violence, particularly those pieces that contain strong ideological content, must be placed within the context of "patriarchal ideology" as a "system of beliefs and ideas that justify or legitimate the power of men over women" (Websdale and Alvarez 1998:137). Typically, patriarchal interests are served when women's violence is denied, minimized, pathologized, or ignored. Like the slave owners who argued the "passivity" of African-American males (Horton and Horton 1993), it is best to avoid or deny the normalcy of violent resistance among the oppressed. To further constrain women's violence, though, it may also be important that an occasional violent woman be vigorously, and publicly, demonized so that her experience will serve as a cautionary tale to all women about the profound risks associated with women accessing strategies of male violence.

Media, Crime, and Crime Policy: Going Beyond Media Misogyny

Clearly, media constructions of women's violence must be challenged by those who are most knowledgeable. Unfortunately, criminologists are rarely featured by those journalists crafting the stories (Tunnell 1998); some of this could be the product of conspiracy, but other explanations, such as the routines of production (like the pressure of the deadline) within journalism must also be considered. What is clear, though, is that feminist criminologists can no longer simply wait for the phone to ring on issues of such importance. We should, instead, engage directly in what Barak (1988) has called "newsmaking criminology" and actively seek ways to build alliances, and build credibility, with progressive journalists, to construct better coverage of crime issues.

It is my belief that such a dialogue is possible, because, simply put, crime is too big a story these days, and relegating crime coverage to the traditional "cop shop" reporter is no longer good journalism. One example of an issue surrounding women offenders is the coverage of the "boom" in women's imprisonment. Since 1980 the overall number of women in prison in the United States has quintupled (Chesney-Lind 1997). As one who does policy-related research in this area, I encouraged Adrian LeBlanc to explore this issue by examining life in what is arguably the world's largest women's prison (Central California Women's Facility). Her powerful coverage of the consequences of this trend, "A Woman Behind Bars Is Not a Dangerous Man" appeared in the *New York Times Magazine* (1996).

Related to the issue of women's imprisonment is the sexual abuse of women inmates at the hands of an increasingly male guard staff. These incidents have garnered international attention and investigation from Human Rights Watch and now Amnesty International (Human Rights Watch 1996). Recently, journalist Gary Craig (1995, 1996) did an impressive series for the *Rochester Democrat and Chronicle* on sexual abuse of women inmates in the correctional facility in Albion (for discussions of these and other media accounts, see Chesney-Lind 1997).

Concerned criminologists must actively seek ways to let journalists know what we are doing and to speak about our work in language that they, and the general public, can understand. These examples are provided to demonstrate that while the obstacles we face to successfully undertaking newsmaking criminology are profound, they are not insurmountable. As more young women enter the field of journalism and rise to the rank of editor (Kosicki and Becker 1996), one hopes that articles that normalize male aggression while demonizing female agency might become less appealing.

ACKNOWLEDGMENTS

The author would like to thank Katie Fujiwara Clark for her generous assistance in the preparation of this chapter, and Neil Websdale and Jeff Ferrell for their very helpful suggestions on various drafts of the manuscript. Portions of this chapter have appeared in the author's book, *The Female Offender.*

NOTES

1. Jones (1994).
2. Leslie, Biddle, Rosenberg, and Wayne (1993).
3. While my convenience sample of media stories is admittedly incomplete, I have been tracking the issue of girls' and women's crime since the early seventies, and I have been clipping articles during the last three decades. Moreover, because some regard me as a national expert on the subject of girl and women offenders, I am often in touch with journalists, who interview me and then send me copies of their published articles. Knowing of my interest, colleagues from around the country also send me articles from their papers.
4. Defined by the FBI as murder, forcible rape, robbery, burglary, aggravated assault, larceny theft, auto theft, and arson.

REFERENCES

ABC. 1997. "Girls in the Hood," on "ABC Primetime Live," 5 November.

Adler, Freda. 1975a. "The Rise of the Female Crook." *Psychology Today* 9:42–46, 112–114.

Adler, Freda. 1975b. *Sisters in Crime.* New York: McGraw-Hill.

American Association for University Women. 1992. *How Schools Shortchange Girls.* Washington, DC: AAUW Educational Foundation.

Ammons, L., J. Dimmick, and J. Pilotta. 1982. "Crime News Reporting in a Black Weekly." *Journalism Quarterly* 59:310–13.

Antunes, G. and P. Hurley. 1977. "The Representation of Criminal Events in Houston's Two Daily Newspapers." *Journalism Quarterly* 54:756–60.

Babner, Liahna. 1992. "Patriarchal Politics in *Fatal Attraction.*" *Journal of Popular Culture* 26(3, Winter):25–35.

Barak, Gregg. 1988. "Newsmaking Criminology: Reflections on the Media, Intellectuals, and Crime." *Justice Quarterly* 5:565–87.

Bartollas, Clemens. 1993. "Little Girls Grown Up: The Perils of Institutionalization." Pp. 469–82 in *Female Criminality: The State of the Art,* edited by C. Culliver. New York: Garland.

Baskin, Deborah, Ira Sommers, and Jeffrey Fagan. 1993. "The Political Economy of Female Violent Street Crime." *Fordham Urban Law Journal* 20:401–17.

Berland, Elaine and Marilyn Wechter. 1992. "Fatal/Fetal Attraction: Psychological Dimensions of Imagining Female Identity in Contemporary Film." *Journal of Popular Culture,* Winter, 26(3):35–46.

Birch, Helen, ed. 1994. *Moving Targets: Women, Murder, and Representation.* Berkeley: University of California Press.

Boozer, Jack. 1995. "Seduction and Betrayal in the Heartland: *Thelma and Louise.*" *Film Quarterly* 23(3, July):188–97.

Bourgois, Philippe and Eloise Dunlap. 1993. "Exorcising Sex-for-Crack Prostitution: An Ethnographic Perspective from Harlem." Pp. 97–132 in *The Crack Pipe as Pimp,* edited by Mitchell Ratner. New York: Lexington.

Bromley, Susan and Pamela Hewitt. 1992. "Fatal Attraction: the Sinister Side of Women's Conflict about Career and Family." *Journal of Popular Culture* 26(3, Winter):17–25.

Bureau of Justice Statistics. 1998. "Violence by Intimates: Analysis of Data on Crimes by Current or Former Spouses, Boyfriends, and Girlfriends." NCJ-167237, March. Washington, DC: USGPO.

Buzawa, Eve S. and Carl G. Buzawa. 1990. *Domestic Violence: The Criminal Justice Response.* Newbury Park: Sage.

Campbell, Ann. 1990. "Female Participation in Gangs." Pp. 163–82 in *Gangs in America,* edited by Ronald Huff. Newbury Park, CA: Sage.

Campbell, Ann. 1993. *Men, Women, and Aggression.* New York: Basic Books.

Carlson, M. 1991. "Is This What Feminism Is All About?" *Time,* 24 June, p. 57.

CBS. 1992. "Girls in the Hood," on "Street Stories," August 6.

Chesney-Lind, Meda. 1997. *The Female Offender: Girls, Women and Crime.* Thousand Oaks, CA: Sage.

Chesney-Lind, Meda and Noelie Rodriguez. 1983. "Women Under Lock and Key." *Prison Journal* 63:47–65.

Chesney-Lind, Meda and Randall G. Shelden. 1998. *Girls, Delinquency, and Juvenile Justice,* 2nd edition. Belmont, CA: Wadsworth.

Combs, B. and P. Slovic. 1979. "Newspaper coverage of causes of death." *Journalism Quarterly* 56:837–43, 849.

Connell, R. W. 1987. *Gender and Power.* Stanford, CA: Stanford University Press.

Craig, Gary. 1995. "Videotaped Frisks Anger Women Inmates." *Rochester Democrat and Chronicle,* 8 April, p. 1A.

Craig, Gary. 1996. "Advocates Say Nude Filming Shows Need for New Laws." *Rochester Democrat and Chronicle,* 23 March, p. A1.

Craven, Diane. 1996. "Female Victims of Violent Crime: Selected Findings." Washington, DC: Bureau of Justice Statistics.

Crittenden, Danielle. 1990. "You've Come a Long Way, Moll." *Wall Street Journal,* 25 January, p. A14.

Curry, G. David, Richard A. Ball, and Robert J. Fox. 1994. *Gang Crime and Law Enforcement Record Keeping.* Washington, DC: National Institute of Justice.

Davis, F. J. 1952. "Crime in Colorado Newspapers." *American Journal of Sociology* 57:325–30.

Dawson, J. M. and P. A. Langan. (1994). *Murder in Families.* U.S. Department of Justice, Bureau of Justice Statistics Special Report. Washington DC: U.S. Government Printing Office.

Douglas, Susan J. 1994. *Where the Girls Are: Growing Up Female with the Mass Media.* New York: Random House.

Enloe, Cynthia. 1989. *Bananas, Beaches and Bases: Making Feminist Sense of International Politics.* Berkeley: University of California Press.

Faith, Karlene. 1993. *Unruly Women: The Politics of Confinement and Resistance.* Vancouver: Press Gang.

Faludi, Susan. 1991. *Backlash: The Undeclared War against Women.* New York: Crown.

Federal Bureau of Investigation. 1996. *Crime in the United States 1995.* Washington, DC: U.S. Department of Justice.

Fedler, F. and D. Jordan. 1982. "How Emphasis on People Affects Coverage of Crime." *Journalism Quarterly* 59:474–78.

Ford, Royal. 1998. "The Razor's Edge." *Boston Globe Magazine,* 24 May, p. 13.

Fullilove, Mindy, Anne Lown, and Robert Fullilove. 1992. "Crack Hos and Skeezers: Traumatic Experiences of Women Crack Users." *Journal of Sex Research* 29(2):275–87.

Garofolo, J. 1981. "Crime and the Mass Media: A Selective Review of Research." *Journal of Research in Crime and Delinquency* 18:319–50.

Gora, JoAnn. 1982. *The New Female Criminal: Empirical Reality or Social Myth.* New York: Praeger.

Guido, Michelle. 1998. "In a New Twist on Equality, Girls Crimes Resemble Boys." *San Jose Mercury,* 4 June, p. 1B.

Haskell, Molly. 1973. *From Reverence to Rape: The Treatment of Women in the Movies.* New York: Holt, Rinehart and Winston.

Holmlund, Christine. 1994. "A Decade of Deadly Dolls: Hollywood and the Woman Killer." Pp. 127–51 in *Moving Targets: Women, Murder, and Representation,* edited by Helen Birch. Berkeley: University of California Press.

Horton, J. O. and L. E. Horton. 1993. "Violence, Protest and Identity: Black Manhood in Antebellum America." Pp. 80–97 in *Free People of Color,* edited by J. O. Horton. Washington, DC: Smithsonian.

Horton, L. E. 1998. "Ambiguous Roles: The Racial Factor in American Womanhood." In *Identity and Intolerance,* edited by Dietmar Schimer and Norbert Finsch. New York: Cambridge University Press.

Huizinga, David. 1997. "Over-Time Changes in Delinquency and Drug Use in the

1970's and the 1990's." Research Brief of the Denver Youth Study, University of Colorado, Boulder.

Human Rights Watch. 1996. *All Too Familiar: Sexual Abuse of Women in U.S. State Prisons.* New York: Human Rights Watch.

Inciardi, James, Dorothy Lockwood, and Anne E. Pottieger. 1993. *Women and Crack-Cocaine.* New York: Macmillan.

Jones, Andrea. 1994. "They Get Right in Your Face: Are Girls Turning Meaner?" *Utne Reader* (July/August):54–55.

Kahler, Kathryn. 1992. "Hand That Rocks the Cradle Is Taking Up Violent Crime" *Sunday Star-Ledger,* 17 May, p. A3.

Kamen, Paula. 1991. *Feminist Fatale.* New York: Donald I. Fine.

Klemsrud, Judy. 1978. "Women Terrorists, Sisters in Crime." *Honolulu Star Bulletin,* 16 January, p. C1.

Kosicki, Gerald M. and Lee B. Becker. 1996. "Annual Survey of Enrollment and Degrees Awarded." *Journalism and Mass Communication* 51:4–14.

Kraditor, Aileen S. 1971. *The Ideas of the Woman Suffrage Movement 1890–1920.* Garden City, NY: Anchor.

LeBlanc, Adrian. 1996. "A Woman Behind Bars Is Not a Dangerous Man." *New York Times Magazine,* 2 June, p. 34.

Lee, Felicia R. 1991. "For Gold Earrings and Protection, More Girls Take the Road to Violence." *New York Times,* 25 November, p. B7.

Leslie, Connie, Nina Biddle, Debra Rosenberg, and Joe Wayne. 1993 "Girls Will Be Girls." *Newsweek,* 2 August p. 44.

Lewis, Nancy. 1992. "Delinquent Girls Achieving a Violent Equality in D.C." *Washington Post,* 23 December, p. A1.

Loper, A. B. and D. G. Cornell. 1996. "Homicide by Girls." *Journal of Child and Family Studies* 5:321–33.

Madriz, Esther. 1997. *Nothing Bad Happens to Good Girls.* Berkeley: University of California Press.

Maher, Lisa and R. Curtis. 1992. "Women on the Edge: Crack Cocaine and the Changing Contexts of Street-Level Sex Work in New York City." *Crime, Law and Social Change* 18:221–58.

Mayer, J. 1994. "Girls in the Maryland Juvenile Justice System: Findings of the Female Population Task Force." Presentation to the Gender Specifics Services Training, Minneapolis, Minnesota.

McRobbie, A. and J. Garber. 1975. "Girls and Subcultures." In *Resistance Through Rituals: Youth Subculture in Post-War Britain,* edited by S. Hall and T. Jefferson. New York: Holmes and Meier.

Media Monitor. 1997. "Network News in the Nineties." 11(3):1–6.

Mednick, Martha. 1989. "On the Politics of Psychological Constructs: Stop the Bandwagon, I Want to Get Off." *American Psychologist* 44:1118–23.

Miller, Eleanor. 1986. *Street Woman.* Philadelphia: Temple University Press.

Moore, Joan. 1991. *Going Down to the Barrio: Homeboys and Homegirls in Change.* Philadelphia: Temple University Press.

NBC. 1993. Diana Koricke in East Los Angeles. "World News Tonight," 29 March.

Ouellet, Lawrence J. W., Wayne Wiebel, Antonio D. Jimenez, and Wendell A. Johnson. 1993. "Crack Cocaine and the Transformation of Prostitution in Three Chicago Neighborhoods." Pp. 69–95 in *The Crack Pipe as Pimp,* edited by Mitchell Ratner. New York: Lexington.

Quicker, J. C. 1983. *Homegirls: Characterizing Chicano Gangs.* San Pedro, CA: International University Press.

Rafter, Nicole Hahn. 1990. *Partial Justice: Women, Prisons and Social Control.* New Brunswick, NJ: Transaction.

Roberts, S. 1971. "Crime Rate of Women up Sharply Over Men's." *New York Times,* 13 June, p. 1.

Robinson, Robin. 1990. "Violations of Girlhood: A Qualitative Study of Female Delinquents and Children in Need of Services in Massachusetts." Unpublished Ph.D. dissertation, Brandeis University, Waltham, Massachusetts.

Sacco, V. F. 1995. "Media Constructions of Crime." *Annals of the American Academy of Political and Social Sciences* 539:141–51.

Santiago, Denis-Marie. 1992. "Random Victims of Vengeance Show Teen Crime; Troubled Girls, Troubling Violence." *Philadelphia Inquirer,* February 23, p. A1.

Schickel, R. 1991. "Gender-Bender." *Time,* 23 June, p. 52.

Schwartz, Sandra K., et al. 1992. "Crack Cocaine and the Exchange of Sex for Money or Drugs." *Sexually Transmitted Diseases* 19:7–13.

Sharratt, Christopher. 1992. "Hollywood Homophobia." *USA Today Magazine,* July, p. 93.

Sheley, J. F. 1981. "Crime, Crime News, and Crime Views." *Public Opinion Quarterly* 15(1):492–506.

Siegal, Carol. 1995. "Compulsory Heterophobia: The Aesthetics of Seriousness and the Production of Homophobia." *Genders* 21(Spring):319–39.

Simon, Rita. 1975. *Women and Crime.* Lexington, MA: Lexington.

Smith, S. J. 1981. "Crime in the News." *British Journal of Criminology* 21(3):289–95.

Sommers, Ira and Deborah Baskin. 1992. "Sex, Race, Age, and Violent Offending." *Violence and Victims* 7(3, Fall):191–201.

Sommers, Ira and Deborah Baskin. 1993. "The Situational Context of Violent Female Offending." *Crime and Delinquency* 30:136–62.

Stark, E. 1996. "Mandatory Arrest of Batterers: A Reply to Its Critics." Pp. 115–49 in *Do Arrest and Restraining Orders Work?* edited by E. Buzawa and C. Buzawa. Thousand Oaks, CA: Sage.

Steffensmeier, D. and R. H. Steffensmeier. 1980. "Trends in Female Delinquency: An Examination of Arrest, Juvenile Court, Self-Report, and Field Data." *Criminology* 18:62–85.

Studervant, Saundra Pollock and Brenda Stoltzfus. 1992. *Let the Good Times Roll: Prostitution and the U.S. Military in Asia.* New York: New Press.

Tunnell, Kenneth. 1998. "Reflections on Crime, Criminals, and Control in Newsmagazine Television Programs." Pp. 111–22 in *Popular Culture, Crime and Justice,* edited by Frankie Bailey and Donna Hale. Belmont, CA: West/ Wadsworth.

Websdale, Neil and Alexander Alvarez. 1998. "Forensic Journalism as Patriarchal

Ideology: The Newspaper Construction of Homicide-Suicide." Pp. 123–41 in *Popular Culture, Crime and Justice,* edited by Frankie Bailey and Donna Hale. Belmont, CA: West/Wadsworth.

White, D. M. 1950. "The 'Gatekeeper': A Case Study in the Selection of News." *Journalism Quarterly* 27:383–90.

White, J. W. and R. M. Kowalski. 1994. "Deconstructing the Myth of the Nonaggressive Woman: A Feminist Analysis." *Psychology of Women Quarterly* 18:487–508.

Williams, Terry. 1992. *Crackhouse: Notes from the End of the Line.* New York: Penguin.

7

"The War Against Women"
Media Representations of Men's Violence Against Women in Australia

ADRIAN HOWE

This chapter explores the way in which one Australian newspaper represented men's violence against women and children in a series called "The War Against Women" in 1993. Notwithstanding widespread media coverage of men's violence, "The War" series responded with a shock-of-the-new reaction to statistics and reports indicating widespread domestic violence and sexual assaults in Victoria, Australia. The chapter comments critically on the newspaper's discursive construction of the problem of men's violence and its attempt to represent that violence as a war.

In 1993, when I was overseas, I missed a war in my home state of Victoria, Australia. This war was not reported overseas. In fact, it was reported in only one local newspaper. In June 1993, *The Age,* published in Melbourne and widely regarded as Australia's leading daily, gave three weeks of coverage to "The War Against Women." Reading the back copies, I discovered that it was a strange kind of coverage, not what one usually expects of war stories. But, of course, this was not a real war and the coverage was actually a series—one that would "disturb you" by presenting "the shocking reality of domestic violence" ("He's Finally Stopped Beating His Wife" 1993).

"The War Against Women" series offers a unique opportunity to examine representations of violence against women in a mainstream Western press. After all, the newspaper's full-page advertisement pronounced that it intended to cover "every aspect of violence including domestic violence, rape, the court system and male attitudes" (ibid.). Typically, this was overstating its case. But my interest in "The War" series is not in assessing the success—whatever that might mean—of *The Age's* self-proclaimed project

From: Adrian Howe, *Violence Against Women* 3(1), pp. 59–75, © 1997 by Sage Publications Incorporated. Reprinted by permission of Sage Publications.

of depicting the reality of domestic violence. My project is rather the Foucauldian one of exploring how one of the most pervasive and widely researched social issues of late twentieth-century Western societies—men's violence against women and children—is being "put into discourse" (Foucault 1979:11) in the mainstream media. That is, my interest is in the question of representation, which, from a Foucauldian perspective, is always a question of power/knowledge.[1] More specifically, I am concerned here with how the feminist discovery, or rather rediscovery, of domestic violence is translated into a human interest story or, more simply, into news. How, precisely, is three decades of Western feminist work to make men's domestic violence a public issue being appropriated in the 1990s by Australian mainstream media discourses? Before answering these questions, I present several representative examples from the series.

"THE WAR AGAINST WOMEN": READ ALL ABOUT IT

Day 1 (June 3, 1993)

"War Against Women: A Special Investigation" began on the front page of *The Age* on June 3, 1993. Our attention is grabbed by the headline: "Epidemic of Violence on [*sic*] Women." The article informs us that

> male violence against women in Victoria is at epidemic levels and rising. It is so widespread that some experts believe it cannot be seen as exceptional behavior by men. (Dixon and Magazanik 1993)

The first page of "The War" provides a smorgasbord of violent scenarios. At the top of the page, little boxes encapsulate the main points: There have been in Victoria more than fourteen thousand family violence calls, an increase of 26 percent from the previous year; 40 percent of applications for emergency intervention fail; only 8 percent of men who breach intervention orders are jailed; and 39 percent of homicides stem from domestic conflicts. Just below is a photo of a woman with pictures of her two dead children. The article, "Reign of Terror Ended in Murder," explains that they were killed by their father during an access visit but that his violence during the marriage was not disclosed during his murder trial nor reported in the press. "The War" series sets out to fix this, declaring, "Many women trapped in families by male violence are constantly in fear of how far the violence will go. Often it goes as far as death" (Dixon 1993a).

This report of the killing of two children in a domestic context on the first page of "The War" series serves at least two functions. First, it helps to establish the seriousness of the problem of domestic violence. Second, it buttresses the idea of calling domestic violence a war. What is a war, after all, without death? Moreover, what sort of war coverage does not have a map? "Pattern of Violence," a map representing "calls to police about domestic incidents" (ibid.) in the Melbourne metropolitan area and country districts appears in the middle of the front page of Day 1. Its purpose seems to be that of suggesting that violence is worse in less affluent areas of Victoria—a suggestion that gives rise to speculation about the causes of domestic violence. "Perhaps economic hardship, poverty and unemployment are contributing factors, adding to family pressures and explosions of violence" ("The Pattern of Violence" 1993).

Speculation as to the causes of wars is a staple of mainstream journalism. Indeed, the causation question is the centerpiece of Day 2 of "The War." As for "explosions of violence" (ibid.)—what is a war without explosions?

Day 2 (June 4, 1993)

So much for the first day of "The War." Day 2 reports on the findings of a poll conducted in May 1995:

> An estimated 321,000 Victorians are direct victims of domestic violence and more than half a million say they know someone in their immediate family who is a victim. (Muller 1993a)

The results of the poll (taken using a sample of 603 voters) indicate that 75 percent of the adult population say domestic violence is widespread and nearly 90 percent say it is serious. Is men's violence against women ever justified? Fifteen percent said yes, if a partner (read: woman) is having an affair; 8 percent said yes if a partner (read: woman) refuses to have sex, and 6 percent said yes if a partner/woman "fails to fulfill household duties" (ibid.).

Day 3: The Men's Story (June 5, 1993)

Saturday, June 5: Day 3 of "The War" but not a moment too soon, apparently, to tell the men's story on the front page of *The Age*. A photo of a man who, for years, violently assaulted his wife appears on the front page with the caption, "Ricky: 'I knew I was doing wrong.'" Ricky is attending a men's counseling group where he is learning to be "assertive, not aggressive" (Magazanik 1993a). The next article bears the headline, "The Question Is: Can the Men Change?" According to one consulting psychologist in the field, counseling for men "could only be the first step, and was not the answer to family violence on its own." Besides, to be effective, the men had to "want to change." On the other hand, we are advised that the women's refuge services have been opposed to resources being placed in counseling services for men, their priority being women's safety (Dixon 1993b).

It is only Day 3, but already the editors feel the need to editorialize on "The War." They declare that the results of the survey on domestic violence are "shocking" and "not just because they show that domestic violence is so widespread that calling it an epidemic is not an exaggeration." Also, the widely shared view that such violence is justified in some circumstances "shows that this epidemic will not be brought under control until a basic truth about it is acknowledged by the whole community: that men who beat the women they live with are committing crimes" ("Domestic Violence Is Criminal Assault" 1993).

Day 7 (June 10, 1993)

Day 7 of "The War" presents articles that are more diverse. One reports on the sexism that ethnic women face in court. The study, by three domestic violence workers' groups, involved a six-week survey of applications to magistrates' courts by women from non-English-speaking backgrounds. It found that these women were subjected to sexual and racial discrimination by Victorian magistrates, who focused on the behavior of the victim and her culture, rather than on the violence of the male partner.

> Some magistrates unwittingly perpetuate racist assumptions about the prevalence of domestic violence in ethnic communities as opposed to the perceived harmony of Australian society. (Dixon 1993c)

Day 10 (June 16, 1993)

Here begins Part 2 of "The War," a part devoted to sexual violence. A newspaper poll reveals that sexual violence was pervasive in the state: "More than a quarter of a million Victorians are victims of sexual assault and 41 percent of them are victims of domestic violence" (Muller 1993b). Further,

> most of these victims are women. On these figures, one woman in every eight in Victoria has been sexually assaulted. This represents more than 200,000 Victorian women. A similar number are victims of domestic violence and an estimated 100,000 of them are victims of both. (ibid.)

Sexual assault is thus widespread and serious and is recognized as such by eight out of ten men and nine out of ten women. Indeed, only 4 percent of people say it is not a serious problem. However,

> In contrast to the social patterns of domestic violence, where the incidence is markedly higher among people of lesser education, sexual assault occurs

across the socio-economic spectrum at virtually the same level-about 8%. (ibid.)

Importantly, the poll revealed that no less than 95 percent of respondents were aware of recent sexist comments made by Australian judges in rape trials, and 88 percent of these thought that judges were out of touch with community attitudes (ibid.).

There is also a report that the governor-general of Australia does not believe that Australia has become more violent. Speaking at a national conference on violence, the governor-general (who until this time was not known as an expert on violence) also expressed concern about the possible danger to the public "caused by an epidemic of journalistic hysteria." Interestingly, he singled out *The Age's* "The War Against Women" series as an example (Willox 1993).

Day 12 (June 18, 1993)

"Most Rapists Go Free: Survey" reports a national survey on rape, which indicated the "hidden nature and silence" (Milburn 1993) of rape victims. Another article reports on research on the sexual violence of ten- and eleven-year-old boys in schools. It is reported that teachers were increasingly concerned about sexual harassment in schools, a problem said to be "rife throughout the school system" (ibid.). Indeed, a national report on school policy identified sexual harassment as "a daily fact of life for Australian schoolgirls" (ibid.).

Day 16 (June 23, 1993)

On Day 16, the final day of the war, we read a story about a woman who had many hours of counseling at a Center Against Sexual Assault—a place where "they believe the woman no one else will believe." Although she deeply regrets going to the police, she is making a sexual harassment claim against her employer and the accused man. She will also seek crime victims' compensation (Dixon 1993d). Finally, there is a report on feminist demands for rape law reform (Magazanik 1993b).

There ends "The War Against Women."

A CRITICAL READING OF "THE WAR"

Familiar as I am both with reports about the prevalence of domestic violence and also with the public discourses about men's violence, I found

reading "The War" series to be a dispiriting experience. Lulled by its lugubri-
ous prose into a debilitating lethargy, I found myself asking: Why should a
poststructuralist feminist, one who refuses essentialized notions of women
and men, bother with a newspaper series that takes for granted fixed gender
categories? Why should a theorist who is politicized about racialized representations of gender relations in hegemonic Anglo-Celtic texts dignify with
critique a text that is based on an unacknowledged racial whiteness and
which refers, in a predictable tokenism, to "ethnic women"?

Besides, I reasoned, do we really need another feminist media watch? A
wide range of feminist analyses of media presentations of gendered issues,
including violence, are available (for example, Cockburn and Loach 1986;
Farrell 1995; Howe 1989; Johnson 1995; Kozol 1995; McDermott 1995;
Rhode 1995; Smart and Smart 1978; Young 1990). In the end, however, I felt
constrained by my methodological and political commitment to analyzing
the ways in which violence against women is discursively produced to order
my reaction to "The War" series into some sort of coherent response. Here
then are some observations on *The Age's* coverage of "The War Against
Women."

"The War" series draws attention to a local manifestation of one of the
most pressing and intractable social problems in late twentieth-century
Western societies: men's violence against women and children in public
places and, even more pervasively, in the so-called private sphere. Notwithstanding *The Age's* shock-of-the-new reaction, the issue of men's violence
has been a matter of public debate in Australia since the 1980s. Indeed,
domestic violence had received extensive coverage in *The Age.* The wom-
en's refuge movement had worked for over a decade to get men's violence
against women recognized as a public issue in Australia. In Victoria, their
efforts were rewarded in 1987 with a Crime (Family Violence) Act, which
was designed to increase protection for victims of violence and sexual assault in the home. In addition, a spate of mass killings in Victoria had led to
public pressure for an inquiry into "the causes of increased violence in
Australia" (Conroy 1988).

By the time *The Age* reported on the establishment of Australia's first
national inquiry on violence in October 1988, men's violence against wom-
en and children in the home had become a regular feature. For example,
The Age reported on the research of the first National Committee of Violence under the headlines, "Violence Is Part of the Nation's Culture" and
"Greatest Risk of Violence 'Occurs at Home'" (Rau 1989). This research
showed that family killings accounted for 40 percent of homicides, that 25
percent of all homicides were marital killings, and that "violence is widely
tolerated in the Australian community" (Rau 1989:6). What, then, can account for the newspaper's selective amnesia—the profound forgetting of its
own reportage of domestic violence when it attempted to shock its readers

with "The War Against Women"? Was it the sheer magnitude of a problem that will not disappear? Or was it simply the popular media's lust for sensationalism?

Amnesia in relation to men's violence against women and children is not a phenomenon unique to the Australian press. Wendy Kozol has recently commented that North American national media are "continually redis-covering (and forgetting)" the pervasive problem of domestic violence in the United States, "despite their own coverage of this topic since the 1970s" (1995:646). My concern here is not to speculate about the reasons for this collective amnesia but to point out that "The War" series fits perfectly into this pattern of discovery/forgetting/rediscovery of men's pervasive violence against women.

Given that critical perspectives on the social construction of crime and the production of crime news are still minority views within criminology schools in Australian universities, it is hardly surprising that a mainstream newspaper would present a series on domestic violence within the limited framework of masculinist criminological positivism. Despite efforts by criti-cal criminologists to challenge both the cultural dominance of common-sense, hegemonic understanding of crime as deviance, and the obsession with causative factors, positivistic approaches to the crime problem pervade popular and media discourses. When it comes to analyzing gendered issues in relation to criminality, profound ignorance of feminist theoretical inter-rogations of sex/gender issues over the past twenty-five years compounds the difficulty for a mainstream reporter trying to get a grip on critical per-spectives regarding men's violence. Conventional approaches to sex/gender issues are devoid of an analytical framework or even a language that can express and face the issue—the issue of men's violence.

Most problematically, commonsense approaches to crime rely on taken-for-granted analytical categories. Men, women, and gender roles are pre-sumed to be fixed categories, and tired, old misogynist stereotypes are in-voked to explain men's violence. The most standard one—men lose control because women provoke them—is relied on in *The Age's* sexual assault survey, reproduced in the poll results and then recycled in the press. Thus,

> In the face of what is clearly a general abhorrence of sexual assault, 14 percent of people said men could not always by blamed because women sometimes provoked them. (Muller 1993b)

But what else could be expected when the question put in the poll was this:

> Which of these statements comes closest to your view: men cannot always be blamed for sexual assault because women sometimes provoke them into

such behavior, or there can be no justification for sexual assault, no matter what the situation is? (ibid.)

Further, the *sex* of *sex crime* is never problematized in mainstream discourses. For example, on the front page on Day 10 we find an article about an eighteen-year-old woman murdered in what police believe was a sex attack. This police hypothesis was apparently based on the fact that robbery had been ruled out as a motive and that her body had been found "only partly clothed," although she had not been raped (Tobin 1993). In Australia as in other Western jurisdictions, a partly clothed female body signifies a sex attack, notwithstanding a lack of evidence of a sexual assault. But is domestic violence, which frequently involves sexual assault, a sex crime? It is not clear whether *The Age* sees any connections between routine domestic violence and sex attacks. The feminist concept of a continuum of men's violence (Kelly 1987) is nowhere in evidence here.

Consider, too, the first poll taken for "The War" series. The respondents were asked for their views of the causes of domestic violence. The answer: money troubles, 41 percent; alcohol, 33 percent; unemployment, 15 percent; and family history, 13 percent (Muller 1993a). However, these replies, which are made to stand for "public perceptions," are found to "differ dramatically" from the views of the chosen experts (Painter 1993). These experts include a feminist academic, a feminist lawyer, and a feminist activist, all of whom point to men and men's attitudes toward women as the problem. Further, in what turns out to be one of the most insightful comments in "The War" series, one journalist (ibid.) notes that

causes seldom identified by respondents in the poll but frequently referred to by experts include the media portrayal of women and men, men's inability to control their own anger and the lack of gender equality in society

This writer adds that

The divergence between public and expert opinion underscores widespread ignorance and confusion about the cause of male violence in Australian society.

The reporter here touches on one of the key issues attached to the representation of violence, namely, the chasm that separates feminist knowledge of men's violence from public understandings of that violence. Indeed, this chasm is so vast that it begs the question of why *The Age* bothered conducting a poll at all. We already know how widespread domestic violence is. What exactly is gained by asking people their view of the causes?

The reporters, however, fail to mediate this chasm, caught up as they seem to be in "taking the public voice"—that is, presuming to speak for the majority of the public (Hall, Critcher, Jefferson, Clarke, and Roberts 1978:63)—and uncomfortable as they seem to be with feminist opinions. For example, a spokeswoman for the Domestic Violence and Incest Resource Center is represented as saying that men are "solely responsible for their violence" (Painter 1993). This statement is read by the reporter as flatly contradicting the view of another expert, a male psychologist, who declares that the mateship ethos is misogynist and a "repository of sexist attitudes" (ibid.). From a feminist perspective, it is difficult to see the contradiction here.

Again, according to the Day 2 report, the findings of the poll reinforce key patterns that have emerged from other studies of domestic violence. These findings include some that are recognizable to feminist analysts but others that are not. Thus it is claimed that "women are twice as likely as men to be victims"—an underestimation, surely, given their own so-called finding that only 7 percent of male respondents said they were victims (Muller 1993a). Further, domestic violence "tends to be kept a dark secret" (ibid.). By whom? Certainly not by the many women survivors of domestic violence nor by the Australian women's refuge movement, which has been actively campaigning about men's violence in the home for two decades. The reporter also wants to insist that whereas domestic violence "appears in all sections of the community, there is evidence that the incidence is greater among those people with less education" (ibid.). This finding is based on the fact that a higher proportion of those respondents who had received only primary education, compared with a university education, reported incidents of domestic violence (ibid.).

The section on class is among the most confused in the series. Consider the "Pattern" map based on the number of domestic incident calls that police receive in a given year. The accompanying text reads:

> No one knows how common domestic violence is or why it seems to be increasing. On the face of it, the map . . . seems to suggest that violence is worse in less affluent areas in Victoria. Perhaps economic hardship, poverty, and unemployment are contributing factors, adding to family pressures and explosions of violence. ("Pattern" 1993)

Domestic violence is being constructed here as a problem afflicting less affluent classes as a result of pressures that might manifest in explosions. But this view is immediately contradicted:

> But while most experts agree that domestic violence occurs right across the community, researchers are unclear about how concentrated it might be in different levels of society. (ibid.)

Clearly, the journalists, and apparently the researchers, are of two minds about the location of domestic violence. They want to say it is concentrated in working-class suburbs, but neither their research nor their map supports that finding.[2]

If the journalists are confused about the geographic and class location of domestic violence, "what keeps many men and women together in relationships is an unfathomable mystery" ("Men and Violence" 1993) for the editors of *The Age*. They are puzzled, too, that their poll indicates that more women than men believe that violence is justified when the housework is not done:

> Despite the feminist revolution of the past two decades, many people in our society still believe that relationships between men and women do not need to be between equals, that power can still be a male prerogative, that women essentially have to be submissive. ("Domestic Violence" 1993:10)

Evidently the editors have not read Gramsci (1991), let alone kept abreast of more recent Foucauldian elaborations of his theory of hegemony and its application to sex/gender relations (for example, Holub 1992). To feminists, what keeps many men and women together in relationships is no mystery—structural inequality and hegemonic heterosexism (Collier 1991:432) account for a great many otherwise "mysterious" heterosexual relationships, just as hegemonic masculinity helps explain the taken-for-granted status of men's social position and men's viewpoints (Connell 1987; Thornton 1989). Under conditions of gendered inequality and hegemonic masculinity, women frequently share men's viewpoints, adopting their masculinist perspectives as their own. In this way, such loaded viewpoints become normative, and feminist and other radical perspectives are dismissed as extreme.

A key dilemma for "The War" series journalists was that much of its expert opinions on men's violence came from feminist researchers, feminist lawyers, activists, and refuge workers. For example, one feminist expert declared that "it is the normality of it, as opposed to the abnormality of it that makes it such a challenging and complex problem" (Dixon and Magazanik 1993). Another said that Australia rated among the top four of five Western industrialized nations in terms of violent crime against women (ibid.).

Such comments were sure to provoke a knee-jerk reaction. Indeed, the question of whether violence is normative for men was to become a major subtheme of "The War" as journalists at a mainstream newspaper attempted to grapple with the ways in which feminist experts were putting men's violence into discourse. Their reaction was swift. By Day 3, *The Age* editors were devaluing the opinions of their own experts by declaring that domestic violence "is not normal behavior":

> Many women, especially feminists, believe that attacks on women—by strangers or partners—are the responsibility of all men: that all men are capable of such behavior and, indeed, are complicit in it, even if they do not

themselves behave that way. This is a view which achieves nothing apart from providing some women with an outlet for their understandable anger. ("Domestic Violence" 1993)

Furthermore, domestic violence is "aberrant behavior in which women sometimes acquiesce." So men are not responsible for men's violence, and men are not complicit in other men's violence, but women sometimes are complicit in such violence and feminist views are extreme, although they do provide an outlet for understandable anger. Here, old standbys of masculinist commonsense understandings of gender relations are reproduced as editorial opinion in a valiant effort to counter the views of the feminist experts consulted for "The War" series.

One measure of the effect of the series on readers is the letters page on Day 7, which was almost entirely consumed by "The War." The lead letter was written by members of Men Against Sexual Assault, who agree with feminists that men have "a responsibility to work toward ending men's oppressive behavior to women" ("How All Men Can End a War Against Women" 1993). They also agree that

> violence against women by men will only end when we as men place such a taboo on this behavior and it is regarded by all men as a shameful and unmanly way to behave. (ibid.)

Other letters divide fairly evenly along congratulatory and condemnatory lines. Some letters praise "The War" series for "lifting the lid on domestic violence" and challenging many myths about men's violence against women. Women correspondents find a space in which to say that

> the "epidemic" of male violence in Victoria cannot be explained by calling it "aberrant behavior." Only by linking male violence to broader issues of gender and masculine identity can we understand why it is so widespread. (Emerman 1993)

Male correspondents, however, complained that men have "become an easy target" of a "faddish male-bashing exercise." What about "the emotional cruelty" that women inflict on men ? In how many of the "incidents of male-against-female domestic violence" was there "a dose of female-against-male taunting and emotional cruelty" (Oldis 1993)? Other letters echo these and similar themes. For example, the "Salem-style witch-hunt of the Spencer Street feminists continues unabated" (Rugg 1993). Yet another male takes issue with the term, *war against women:*

> The frequency of male-to-female violence is appalling; however, most men are innocent and cannot be held responsible. *War* implies organized conflict. A great problem exists, but there is no war. (Ford 1993)

In response to these antifeminist opinions, *The Age* published two more editorial opinions, both masterpieces of trepidation. On Day 15, the editors insisted that "this newspaper has never suggested that all men commit acts of violence against women" ("Men and Violence" 1993). Moreover, they insisted that the suggestion that all men are responsible for violence against women was "counter-productive and silly" (ibid.). On the other hand, they were not about to apologize for calling domestic violence an epidemic. After all, their survey showed that one in eight women were victims of domestic violence and:

> nowhere near that proportion of the population is infected with the AIDS virus and yet virtually everyone agrees that the incidence of AIDS in our Community warrants calling it an epidemic. What is the difference?—violence is a human problem, but the fact is that, overwhelmingly, men are the perpetrators. Not all men, but men nevertheless. All of us have to come to terms with that fact. (ibid.)

The final editorial in the series is another angst-ridden attempt to negotiate a way through the impasse of the overwhelming evidence that men's violence is a pervasive social problem and hostile reactions to the reporting of such evidence. It begins with a justification for running a three-week series examining rape and domestic violence:

> In both areas it is predominantly men who are the perpetrators and women who are the victims. We have upset some men and made them question fundamental assumptions about the way they relate to women. For this, we do not apologize. If some men are uncomfortable with what they have read, we understand their feelings. We too, have been shocked by just how widespread violence against women is. ("Listen to Women" 1993)

The editors hoped that the series had "prompted men to confront a problem," namely that "the frightening reality to come out of the series is that most violence against women is carried out not by strangers, but by men they know: husbands, lovers, acquaintances" (ibid.). They were aware that some men, including the governor-general of Australia, "have felt aggrieved" by the fact that the series was called "The War Against Women." It seemed to imply that *The Age* was taking "a pro-feminist position on violence." The editors, however, agreed that this is not a war waged by all men against all women. Still, although they did not want to "widen the gap between men and women," they believed that "the onus is on men to help make the streets and homes safe for women" (ibid.). In the final analysis, then, the editors managed to insist, albeit reluctantly, that men's violence was a reality. Still, for all the effort to put this reality into discourse, it turned out to be something of a phony war; the sort of war one has when there is no real war.

How did this mainstream Australian newspaper put men's violence against women into discourse? The short answer is: hegemonically. It deployed representational strategies or "strategies of recuperation" (Alcoff and Gray 1993:262), such as editorial disclaimers, to minimize men's responsibility for their own actions and distance its purportedly neutral view from that of feminist extremists. The effect was to reinscribe its critique of men's pervasive violence against women within hegemonic narratives of gender relations in which women acquiesce in domestic violence, feminists vilify men, and men as a group are much-maligned and not to be held accountable for the behavior of a small, aberrant minority. The message is ultimately one of helplessness: Domestic violence is a war that cannot be won. What other meaning should we take from the many stories of helplessness, victimization, and death at the hands of men? Further, how telling is the story told on the final day of "The War" about a woman who was not believed and who wanted to tell young women not to report sexual assault to the police? Finally, what is gained by calling men's pervasive violence against women a war? *The Age* hoped that it would underscore the pervasiveness of the violence and the seriousness of the problem. But most people, as their polls showed, already know this, and those who do not, far from being convinced by the war analogy, argue vehemently that it serves to exaggerate what is, in their uninformed view, a small problem of male violence, which, in any event, is provoked by women and even justified in some circumstances.

Was the "War Against Women" series one that disturbed me, as it claimed it would? The answer is yes, but not in the way that *The Age* intended. I knew that men's violence against women and children is pervasive. What disturbs me is the way in which the media appropriate feminist knowledge of and activism against men's violence and then translate it into digestible material for a mainstream readership. What disturbs me is realizing how far mainstream media coverage of men's violence has to go before it can begin to fathom the depth of the problem of men's violence, let alone work out what to do about it.

NOTES

1.   See especially Foucault (1979) and his interviews in Gordon (1980). I elaborate on my Foucauldian methodological approach in Howe (1994).

2.   I wish to thank Mariastella Pulvirenti, a social geographer, for her insightful comments about the "Pattern" map.

REFERENCES

Alcoff, L. and L. Gray. 1993. "Survivor Discourse: Transgression of Recuperation?" *Signs* 18:260–90.

Cockburn, C. and L. Loach. 1986. "In Whose Image." Pp. 15–26 in *Bending Reality: The State of the Media,* edited by J. Curran, J. Eccleston, G. Oakley, and A. Richardson. London: Pluto.

Collier, R. 1991. "Masculinism, Law and Teaching." *International Journal of the Sociology of Law* 19:427–51.

Connell, R. W. 1987. *Gender and Power.* Sydney: Allen & Unwin.

Conroy, P. 1988. "Inquiry on Violence Established." *The Age,* October 17, p. 1.

Dixon, R. 1993a. "Reign of Terror Ended in Murder." *The Age,* June 3, p. 1.

Dixon, R. 1993b. "The Question Is: Can Men Change?" *The Age,* June 5, p. 1.

Dixon, R. 1993c. "In Law Ethnic Women Face Sexism: Report." *The Age,* June 10, p. 4.

Dixon, R. 1993d. "A Woman Police Wouldn't Believe." *The Age,* June 23, p. 4.

Dixon, R., and Magazanik, M. 1993. "Epidemic of Violence Against Women." *The Age,* June 3, p.1.

"Domestic Violence Is Criminal Assault." Editorial. 1993. *The Age,* June 5, p. 10.

Emerman, M. 1993. "Linking Broader Issues." Letter to the editor. *The Age,* June 10, p. 14.

Farrell, A. E. 1995. "Feminism and the Media: An Introduction." *Signs* 20:642–45.

Ford, D. 1993. "Appalling, But It's Not a War." Letter to the editor. *The Age,* June 10, p. 14.

Foucault, M. 1979. *The History of Sexuality,* vol. 1. London: Allen Lane.

Gordon, C. 1980. *Michel Foucault: Power/Knowledge, Selected Interviews and Other Writing, 1972–1977.* Brighton, UK: Harvester.

Gramsci, A. 1991. *Prison Notebooks.* New York: Columbia University Press.

Hall, S., C. Critcher, T. Jefferson, J. Clarke, and B. Roberts. 1978. *Policing the Crisis: Mugging, the State, and Law and Order.* London: Macmillan.

"He's Finally Stopped Beating His Wife." 1993. *The Age,* June 2, p. 20.

Holub, R. 1992. *Antonio Gramsci: Beyond Marxism and Postmodernism.* London: Routledge.

"How All Men Can End a War Against Women." Letter to the editor. 1993. *The Age,* June 10, p. 14.

Howe, A. 1989. "Chamberlain Revisited—the Case against the Media." *Refractory Girl* 31/32:2–8.

Howe, A. 1994. *Punish and Critique: Towards a Feminist Analysis of Penalty.* London: Routledge.

Johnson, L. A. 1995. "Forum on Feminism and the Media: Afterword." *Signs* 20:711–19.

Kelly, L. 1987. "The Continuum of Sexual Violence." Pp. 46–60 in *Women, Violence, and Social Control,* edited by J. Hanmer and M. Maynard. Basingstoke, UK: Macmillan.

Kozol, W. 1995. "Fracturing Domesticity: Media, Nationalism, and the Question of Feminist Influence." *Signs* 20:646–67.

"Listen to Women." Editorial. 1993. *The Age,* June 22, p. 15.

Magazanik, M. 1993a. "Exchanging One Kind of Control for Another." *The Age,* June 5, p. 1.

Magazanik, M. 1993b. "Call for Reform on Rape Evidence." *The Age,* June 23, p. 4.

McDermott, P. 1995. "On Cultural Authority: Women's Studies, Feminist Politics, and the Popular Press." *Signs* 20:668–84.

"Men and Violence." Editorial. 1993. *The Age,* June 16, p. 10.

Milburn, C. 1993. "Sex Battle Lines Drawn Up in Primary Schools." *The Age,* June 18, p. 3.

Muller, D. 1993a. "321,000 Are Victims, Survey Finds." *The Age,* June 4, p. 1.

Muller, D. 1993b. "Sexual Violence: 262,000 Victims, 41% at Home." *The Age,* June 16, pp. 1, 6.

Oldis, M. 1993. "Men Have Become Easy Targets." Letter to the editor. *The Age,* June 10, p. 8.

Painter, J. 1993. "Widespread Differences over Causes." *The Age,* June 4, p. 8.

Rau, C. 1989. "Violence Is Part of the Nation's Culture." *The Age,* February 13, p. 6.

Rhode, D. L. 1995. "Media Images, Feminist Issues." *Signs* 20:685–710.

Rugg, K. 1993. "Solutions Beat Shame." Letter to the editor. *The Age,* June 10, p. 14.

Smart, C. and B. Smart. 1978. "Accounting for Rape: Reality and Myth in Press Reporting." Pp. 87–103 in *Women, Sexuality, and Social Control,* edited by C. Smart and B. Smart. London: Routledge and Kegan Paul.

"The Pattern of Violence." 1993. *The Age,* June 3, p.1.

Thornton, M. 1989. "Hegemonic Masculinity and the Academy." *International Journal of the Sociology of Law* 17:115–30.

Tobin, B. 1993. "Sex Attack May Have Preceded Girl's Murder." *The Age,* June 16, p. 1.

Willox, I. 1993. "Hayden Slates Media Stance." *The Age,* June 16, p. 1.

Young, A. 1990. *Femininity in Dissent.* London: Routledge.

8

Detecting Masculinity

GRAY CAVENDER

INTRODUCTION

Criminology's scope of intellectual inquiry occasionally changes. What was taken for granted becomes problematic by focusing on the definitional and the political/economic aspects of lawmaking and lawbreaking. The labeling perspective and critical criminology problematized issues of crime and criminality that had largely been ignored; even criminology as a discipline was problematized (Cavender 1995). Feminists criticized criminology's neglect of women, and brought to the discipline new insights about the relationship of women, crime, and law (Jurik 1998). This focus initially meant the study of women criminals and victims, and women's disproportionately low rates of crime. Feminist criminologists further recognized that issues of gender apply to men and men's crimes.

These shifts in criminological thought facilitated two more recent transformations: an interest in the relationship between masculinity and crime, and an interest in cultural criminology. These "new areas" are the backdrop of this chapter.

By making gender relevant, feminist criminologists problematized the relationship between crime and masculinity (Newburn and Stanko 1994). It was conventional wisdom that men committed a disproportionate amount of crime. This fact was so commonplace that crime's gendered aspects remained largely invisible. However, Jack Katz, in *Seductions of Crime: Moral and Sensual Attractions in Doing Evil* (1988), noted the relationship between masculinity and crimes like armed robbery. Criminologist James Messerschmidt made this relationship more explicit in *Masculinities and Crime: Critique and Reconceptualization of Theory* (1993). As Messerschmidt argues, aspects of social life from work to crime provide opportunities for boys and men to reproduce and construct masculinity. Other criminologists currently explore the relationship between masculinity and crime (Hobbs 1997).

The second shift, the emergence of a cultural criminology, draws upon critical criminology's interest in ideology, and upon the tenets of cultural studies. Critical criminology's focus on ideology challenged the neutrality of law and "criminal" as inherent categories; it also problematized the very consciousness with which we think about the crime problem. The notion of ideology is also central for cultural studies.

According to cultural theorist John Fiske, "Cultural studies is concerned with the generation and circulation of meanings in industrial society" (1992:284). Fiske assumes that culture is constituted by society's meanings, and that these are best understood in terms of social structure and its history. In turn, meanings help to hold that structure in place. Fiske agrees with Stuart Hall, Raymond Williams, and other cultural historians that our social relations, indeed, our very social identities, depend upon the meanings and the frameworks of knowledge that allow us to make sense of our experiences (ibid.:285).

Cultural studies draws upon a range of scholarship from feminist theory to film theory. Much of the focus is on popular culture, which circulates images and ideologies that continually reproduce and transform our culture. Because some of these images deal with crime, cultural studies is relevant to criminology.

The importance of cultural studies and of masculinity is evident in recent criminological work. Jeff Ferrell and Clinton Sanders, in *Cultural Criminology*, argue that "the everyday collective practice of criminality and the criminalization of everyday life . . . are cultural enterprises" (1995:7). They stress the links among style, popular culture, and criminalization campaigns. Others emphasize the interconnections of crime, masculinity, and popular culture. Richard Sparks (1996) notes that crime films circulate images of masculinity. However, criminology has failed to address such films or the gendered implications of their standard characters, e.g., hero, villain, cop, or private eye (ibid.). Sparks suggests that these films are relevant for criminology: their images of crime and masculinity are a compelling part of our culture.

In this chapter, I employ these new currents in criminological thought in an analysis of crime and masculinity as depicted in popular culture. Specifically, I consider how two classic crime films of the 1940s, *Murder, My Sweet* and *Blue Dahlia,* depict crime and masculinity. I compare the depictions in these 1940s films with representations of crime and masculinity in two contemporary films, *Die Hard* and *Blink.* Through this comparative cultural analysis, we can see how Hollywood circulates ideologies about crime and images of masculinity, and how these representations have changed over time.

Before turning to the analysis, I review the literature that deals with crime and masculinity, in fact and in fiction. I in turn offer a brief methodological comment, and provide a synopsis of the four films.

CRIME AND MASCULINITY IN FACT AND IN FICTION

James Messerschmidt (1993) maintains that crime is a resource for "doing masculinity." Messerschmidt makes this provocative statement as he explores the fact that boys and men commit more crimes and more serious crimes than do girls and women. However, he notes that criminologists rarely discuss the gendered implications of this fact; attention to gender usually means an analysis of women and crime (ibid.:2). Messerschmidt's intellectual project is to put men under the criminological lens by "articulating the gendered content of men's behavior and of crime" (ibid.:62). His ideas about crime and masculinity are grounded in gender studies.

Gender studies scholars see gender as a social construction. Candace West and Don Zimmerman (1987) argue that gender is an emergent property of social interaction. They use the gerund "doing gender" to emphasize how attitudes and situations are managed in a manner that is considered to be gender-appropriate; gender becomes an ongoing accomplishment. The social construction of gender underlies Messerschmidt's claim that crime is a resource for "doing masculinity."

Robert Connell (1993b:xi) agrees that crime is a "strategy of masculinity." He notes that there is not merely one masculinity; there are many "ways of enacting masculine gender" (ibid.). Although there are many masculinities and femininities, some predominate over others. He suggests that in any historical period there are two idealized gender types: hegemonic masculinity and emphasized femininity. Their defining features change over time.

Connell notes that these changing features produce crises in masculinity. Prior to World War II, masculinity was defined more by physical strength and dominance. In terms of work, notions of craft and skill were important. Since World War II, however, masculinity increasingly has come to be defined in terms of expertise and technical knowledge (1993a:610); the "organization man" is an important image in work. These defining features are those most associated with white, upper-class ideals of masculinity. Struggles over masculinity entail not only gender issues but also dimensions of social class, race, and sexual orientation (Connell 1995:55, 76). Masculinities associated with white working-class men, gay men, and men of color tend to be subordinated.

Today, hegemonic masculinity is characterized by heterosexuality, the subordination of women, authority, aggression, and technical knowledge. Emphasized femininity is subordinate to hegemonic masculinity. It is characterized by dependence, sexual receptivity and fragility, motherhood, and sociability (Connell 1993a). Though these images appear to be natural, they are socially produced (West and Fenstermaker 1995).

Although Connell uses the term "hegemony," which implies consent, albeit manufactured consent, he notes that physical violence supports hegemonic masculinity (1987:184). This lends credence to Messerschmidt's claim about crime and masculinity. Connell also suggests that the media reinforce dominant images of gender. For men, "hegemony often involves the creation of models of masculinity which are . . . fantasy figures" (ibid.).

Connell's views on gender, hegemony, and the media are consistent with media scholarship. Todd Gitlin (1982) suggests that the media, especially entertainment media, deal with potentially disruptive issues in ways that are compatible with dominant social meanings. In Gitlin's view, the media are a part of the manufacture of consent—hegemony. He notes, however, that hegemony is never fully accomplished. The very existence of dominant systems of meaning presumes potentially oppositional meanings. Thus, hegemony is a process: meanings are continually reproduced and negotiated, and there are efforts to contain oppositional meanings.

John Thompson (1990) makes a similar point on a related matter: ideology. The media circulate and reinforce society's dominant ideological messages. Again, the existence of such messages presumes the possibility of resistance: audiences or certain groups within audiences may engage messages in unexpected ways. Thompson does suggest that it is easier for audiences to accept socially preferred meanings, and that even contrary meanings reference dominant ideological positions. Additionally, over the long run preferred messages tend to become ingrained in our identities, for example, in what it means to be masculine or feminine. But, identities are also dynamic. Even so, despite the ever-present potential for resistance, Thompson suggests that media messages tend to stabilize and reinforce existing power relations (1995:214).

Cultural studies scholars often study ideology through genres. Genres are taxonomies or classifications of cultural productions such as novels and films. Their formulaic elements—standard plots, situations, and characters—are ideal for social analyses that address ideology generally, or ideological shifts over time. This is true for U.S. films, which are largely driven by genre (Maltby 1995).

The crime genre is a fertile site for analyses of ideology, and several scholars have produced thoughtful work in the area (Knight 1980; Mandel 1984; Thompson 1993). The genre, almost by definition, addresses ideological issues: crime, typically a deviation from social norms, motivates the plot. Character development works in tandem with plot. Standard characters include loathsome villains who are a social threat and heroic detectives who fight them. By identifying with heroes, audiences indirectly identify with the social order. The genre's long-standing popularity means that its ideologies reach a wide audience (Surette 1998).

The crime genre is also an ideal site for analyses of gender. Women have been successful in writing crime fiction, and there are interesting analyses of this work (Klein 1992; Munt 1994). However, men dominate the crime genre. Indeed, in the typical plot, a woman exists as either a "good girl" love interest or a femme fatale, a dangerous woman who threatens the hero.

The figure of the male detective, from Sherlock Holmes through Thomas Magnum, is a defining image of the genre. He often is portrayed as an iconoclastic loner; yet his strong internal morality reflects, albeit in a highly individualized fashion, society's dominant sense of justice (Cavender 1998). This figure is an idealized representation of hegemonic masculinity, although different class positions are apparent. He is an aggressive, authoritative figure who exhibits intelligence, skill, daring, and often physical prowess. Usually, women are subordinate to and in love with him. The detective is the repository of dominant notions of both justice and masculinity.

On both dimensions, however, a note of caution is in order. While there is a sense of justice defined in terms of dominant ideologies, the detective often treats the law and the police in a derisive fashion, and sometimes dominant social institutions are critiqued. There are complexities in terms of gender. In some films, masculinity is virtually a caricature. In others, even the hero reveals negative aspects of masculinity. These are clearly complex matters that are negotiated as a part of the narrative of a film.

While crime narratives may be complex, the genre's basic elements are relatively simple. A crime drives the story. The detective must put things right by apprehending and/or killing the villain. His pursuit of this resolution provides the audience's pleasure. Dorie Klein (1992) summarizes the genre's simplicity: there is a crime, a detective, and a quest.

Two of Klein's elements provide the framework for this chapter. In the analysis that follows, I consider the depiction of the crime and the detective figure in two 1940s films and two contemporary films. The analysis is designed to yield insights into images of masculinity and ideologies about crime, then and today. As Sparks (1996:358) notes, although fictional, these images and ideologies nonetheless capture our attention; they also reinforce existing views about masculinity and crime.

METHODS

My analysis is based upon an in-depth qualitative, cultural analysis of four films: *Murder, My Sweet* (1945), *Blue Dahlia* (1946), *Die Hard* (1988), and *Blink* (1994). I chose the films because crime is a central aspect of their narrative, and a Hollywood leading man stars in each.

Critics include *Murder, My Sweet* and *Blue Dahlia* as key productions in the film noir cycle (Hirsch 1981). *Murder, My Sweet* stars Dick Powell as private eye Philip Marlowe. The film features the detective's trademark voice-over narrative (ibid.). *Blue Dahlia* stars Alan Ladd. Ladd is not a detective, but his character is implicated in, and he tries to solve, a murder. The film is a classic post–World War II production: Ladd and others are returning veterans, a feature that figures in the narrative (Schrader 1996).

Die Hard stars Bruce Willis as New York City Cop John McClane. *Die Hard* is a good representation of the action movie; it features an action hero and an array of violent special effects. The action movie, like the spy thriller, is a subgenre of the crime genre (Bennett and Woollacott 1987). *Blink* stars Aidan Quinn as police detective John Hallstrom. *Blink* represents the serial killer subgenre.

I note three methodological caveats. First, my analysis of these films is best described as interpretative. Although my analysis is informed by other scholarship and research, it is not in the criminological tradition of theory-testing based on quantitative data analysis. Rather, it is in that tradition of cultural studies that focuses on the text of cultural productions (Kellner 1995). Second, in part, my analysis is a retrospective interpretation: I analyze two films from the 1940s using contemporary tenets of film theory and cultural criminology. Third, in my interpretative analysis I forgo that variety of cultural studies that analyzes how audiences actually engage films. Such research generates many insights, not the least of which is the recognition that audiences are not passive; they actively engage the films they see (Fiske 1994). Notwithstanding such insights, it is also useful to analyze the discourses within films and the connections between such discourses and the cultural meanings they represent (Joyrich 1996).

I had viewed each film several times before this research, so I was familiar with their plots. However, as I viewed each film for this research, I took notes about the plot and about details that related to key research themes. I also used the tape counter, which allowed me to return to each film for direct quotes, visuals, or other relevant matters.

My primary research theme focuses on how these films depict crime and masculinity. Drawing upon Klein's (1992) statement about the elements of the crime genre, I use as my organizational framework the detective and the crime. I begin the analysis with synopses of the four films.

SYNOPSES

Murder, My Sweet.   Private eye Philip Marlowe is hired on two seemingly unrelated cases: To locate Velma Valento, Moose Malloy's ex-girlfriend, and to accompany Lindsay Marriott as he buys back a jade necklace that was stolen from Mrs. Helen Grayle. Marriott is murdered; the police suspect Marlowe. Marlowe is hassled by the police, beaten, drugged, and offered money to drop the jade case. He develops a romantic interest in Helen, who is married to the wealthy Mr. Grayle, and in Ann, Mr. Grayle's daughter. Marlowe realizes that the two cases are interrelated: Velma is Helen; she faked the jewelry theft to foil a blackmailer who knew her identity. Mr. Grayle kills Helen, and he and Moose kill each other. In the final scene, Marlowe rides away with Ann.

Blue Dahlia. George, Buzz, and Johnny are Navy veterans returning from World War II. Johnny finds his wife, Helen, at a party with her lover, Eddie Harwood, a shady character. Unremorseful, she tells Johnny that she killed their son in a drunken car wreck. When she is murdered with Johnny's gun, the police suspect him. Johnny tries to discover who killed her. Johnny meets Joyce; there is a romantic attraction. He learns that she is Harwood's estranged wife. Harwood's thugs capture Johnny, who has learned that Harwood is wanted for murder. Johnny escapes; Harwood is killed. Suspicion falls on Buzz for Helen's murder. Buzz suffers from blackouts due to a war injury and could have killed Helen; he does not remember. Johnny proves that Buzz is innocent. The police kill the apartment security man, who killed Helen. In the final scene, Buzz and George leave so that Johnny and Joyce can be alone.

Die Hard. New York City cop John McClane is in Los Angeles to visit his wife, Holly, who has left him for her career; she uses her maiden name, Gennero. Heavily armed terrorists, led by Hans Gruber, take over the Nakatomi Corporation building, and hold thirty hostages, including Holly. The terrorists really are thieves, out for 640 million dollars in negotiable bonds. McClane eludes and kills many of them. The police and the FBI are bureaucratic fools, except for LAPD sergeant Al Powell, who is in communication with McClane. They bond. McClane saves the hostages. Sergeant Powell, who in the past lost his resolve when he mistakenly killed a thirteen-year-old boy, saves John by killing the last villain. Holly retakes the name Holly McClane. In the final scene, she and John kiss.

Blink. Detective John Hallstrom, who is drinking with other cops in a club, is smitten by violinist Emma Brody. As she and her band play, he does a strip tease but fails to get her attention because she was blinded as a child by her angry mom. Emma undergoes transplant surgery. The surgery is successful, but she experiences lagged flashbacks, i.e., an event that she sees might not register as "seeing" until later. She sees (and also smells) a man who murdered her upstairs neighbor. The crime resembles another murder. Serial killer Neil Booker is avenging his dead sweetheart, whose donated organs are being transplanted to other women. Hallstrom must protect Emma and solve the case. They have sex; this compromises his investigation and her safety. Booker traps Emma, but she kills him. In final the scene, John is at a nightclub with his and Emma's friends, watching her play.

THE DETECTIVE

The detective is the crime genre's central character. The audience delights in the detective's nuances of personality and investigative skill. The detective is a heroic, almost mythic individual. Because the detective is so often a man, his portrayal reflects that constellation of traits that comprise an ideal of hegemonic masculinity that is specific to the film's historical period.

The 1940s was a rich decade for crime genre films. French critics called them "film noir" because of the sense of darkness that permeated them (Vernet 1993). Scholars locate film noir's look, plots, and characters in the post–World War II era. Male veterans returned home to find that women had done the jobs that had been a defining feature of their masculinity (Krutnik 1991). With some women reluctant to give up these positions, there was competition for work. In addition, men who did not go to war had prospered. Not only were veterans "behind," the economic system was becoming more corporate, which further eroded the sense of mastery that had defined "a man's place;" conformity, not craftsmanship, was emerging as the measure of success (Reid and Walker 1993). The heroes in those 1940s films had to overcome obstacles as they tried to be men in the postwar United States, while at the same time conforming to the expectations of the crime genre.

Philip Marlowe (*Murder, My Sweet*) and Johnny Morrison (*Blue Dahlia*) epitomize the male protagonists in these films. They are tough, daring men who can handle any situation. Marlowe is equally comfortable with Moose Malloy, a huge, dimwitted man who could crush him, or Jules Amthor, an intelligent psychic consultant and blackmailer. Similarly, Johnny handles himself well as a war hero who is the center of a crowd's attention, or in a fight with the dangerous Eddie Harwood, whom he defeats.

Women are subordinate to these men both physically and romantically. Sometimes, Marlowe and Johnny manhandle women. Marlowe grips Ann's hands as he searches her purse. Johnny threatens Helen with a gun when he learns how their son died. Women also look upon them with desire. Helen Grayle tells Marlowe, "Hmm, you've got a nice build . . . I hope you don't mind, I'm sizing you up." Joyce picks Johnny up and wants him to stay with her, perhaps for the night.

Other men look upon Marlowe and Johnny with respect. Marlowe and Johnny evidence the courage and the inner morality that characterize the genre's hero (Cawelti 1976). They survive threats and beatings, and refuse to "drop the case." Marlowe explains, "He [Marriott] gave me a hundred bucks to take care of him, and I didn't. I'm just a small businessman in a messy business, but I like to follow through on a sale." Johnny makes a similar comment, "Even if we weren't happy, Helen was my wife. The man who killed her isn't going to get away with it." These are men of honor.

A part of the crisis in the troubled negotiation of masculinity that these films address is the emergence of a mass society. Marlowe and Johnny are idealized depictions of this crisis. In their character development, both men seem to be "antiestablishment" at some deep level. They are loners with no institutional affiliations: Marlowe was fired from the DA's office "for talking back." Johnny, a navy lieutenant commander, is now a civilian. Marlowe's status affects his relations with the police. A detective tells him, "It ain't personal, we don't like you." Marlowe in turn dislikes and distrusts the police; he wisecracks and works against them. Johnny does not trust the police, either. He fears that if they capture him, they will stop looking for Helen's killer. His status as a former naval officer implicates him: a police bulletin refers to the navy top coat that he wears. To avoid capture, he throws away the coat, and, by so doing, symbolically puts the navy behind him.

Film noir not only depicts the police in a negative light, but questions other social structures and institutions, including capitalism and social class (Vernet 1993). The wealthy, men like Grayle, are weak and their excesses cause problems. Grayle's marriage to Helen, a younger woman, causes trouble. Marlowe works for him, but has disdain for his wealth: at Grayle's mansion, Marlowe plays hopscotch on the checkered marble floor; he lights a cigarette with a match struck on a sculptured cherub's butt. Psychology and the emerging therapeutic state also are critiqued. Jules Amthor uses the information that he learns in therapeutic sessions to blackmail women "who come to him with broken-down libidos." A psychiatrist holds Marlowe prisoner and gives him drugs to find out what he knows.

Although Marlowe and Johnny are capable, experienced men, they, like other characters in 1940s films, are not in control of the situations they encounter (Krutnik 1991). *Murder, My Sweet* depicts this in a visual manner: many scenes, including the opening scene, create a sense of visual disorientation. Marlowe loses control when he is knocked unconscious or drugged. When Ann accuses him of not knowing which side he is on, Marlowe answers, "I don't know which side anybody is on; I don't even know who's playing." Johnny makes a similar comment to Joyce, "I don't know anything. I don't even know your name." Indeed, we know her name only from the screenplay; her name is never mentioned in the film.

The sense that these men are not in control sometimes goes a step further: they are out of control (Reid and Walker 1993). Especially in *Blue Dahlia,* the war is implicated. Early in the film, Buzz argues with a soldier in a bar and grabs him in a judolike choke hold. Later, when Johnny grabs Helen and hurts her, she says, "Maybe you've learned to like hurting people." The notion that these veterans violently overreact to situations is a key part of the film's narrative. Indeed, it seems that Buzz may have killed Helen because of a war-related head injury.

A profound alienation thus abounds in both films, among all the characters, but especially the heroes. When Ann accuses Marlowe of enjoying seeing people torn apart, he says, "They're headed for it anyway; you're headed for it." Johnny exists in an equally alienated universe. His naval career over, he has a farewell drink with George and Buzz, and wistfully toasts, "Well, here's to what was." The events that follow confirm that his war experiences held a clarity that civilian life lacks. When Joyce gives him a ride, she claims to be headed to Malibu, but they drive aimlessly in the rain. Johnny tells her, "You were trying to run out on yourself, like me."

George and Buzz are drifting, too. George is a lawyer, but there is no mention of work for him or Buzz. Even their living situation reveals the postwar uncertainty of veterans. They room together in a small apartment, which was George's before the war. Buzz says that they were lucky to get it. In contrast to George and Buzz who are back to where they were before the war, Eddie Harwood, who did not go to war, has a successful nightclub, the Blue Dahlia; Buzz and George are envious.

Marlowe and Johnny are heroes, but only to a degree. Marlowe realizes that Velma and Helen are one and the same, but he is not fully in control and she gets the drop on him; Grayle kills her. Marlowe is unconscious when Moose and Grayle kill each other. Johnny is a partial hero. He proves Buzz's innocence, but does not know that "Dad" Newell, the house detective, killed Helen. The police deduce that, and kill Dad. Marlowe and Johnny "get the girl," but there is much that is unresolved. Marlowe is blind at movie's end, and there are no immediate prospects for Johnny.

There are commonalties and differences between *Murder, My Sweet* and *Blue Dahlia,* the 1940s noir films, and *Die Hard* and *Blink,* the contemporary films that I analyzed. While the formulaic conventions of the crime genre produce some commonalties, the genre does change with time, as do the characteristics and images of masculinity.

As in the 1940s films, there are issues today that challenge men's identities (Horrocks 1994). The success of the women's movement, ideologically and occupationally, threatens some men. Some have responded with what Susan Faludi (1991) calls a backlash. Moreover, beginning in the 1980s and continuing into the 1990s, corporate America has downsized, forcing men and women out of jobs. This has produced economic insecurity and has also undermined one of the defining features of masculinity: work (*New York Times* 1996; Martin and Jurik 1996). *Die Hard* and *Blink* thus offer the genre hero, but in a manner that acknowledges today's ongoing crisis of masculinity.

The conventions of the genre require a tough, heroic man (Cawelti 1976). John McClane is such a man in *Die Hard*. Like Marlowe, McClane is comfortable with a range of characters. When he learns that Argyle, the African-American limousine driver, is nervous because it is his first day on the job, McClane puts him at ease, noting that it is his first limo ride. McClane sits up front with Argyle and they discuss McClane's situation with his wife. McClane is equally at ease with Holly's boss, the head of the Nakatomi Corporation. John Hallstrom is less the mythic hero, but equally comfortable with characters ranging from a neighborhood kid to his lieutenant.

Where Marlowe and Johnny reflected a 1940s masculinity by being "worldly wise," McClane and Hallstrom evidence the technical knowledge and expertise that are elements of hegemonic masculinity today. McClane and Hallstrom are not small businessmen like Marlowe, they are police experts. Sergeant Powell recognizes McClane's specialized police knowledge of phony IDs and weaponry. McClane avoids capture because of his creative technical abilities; he even makes a bomb. Hallstrom is an expert, too. He discovers the connection among the killer's victims, and explains it in detail to other detectives and his lieutenant. Emma Brody says that he is "good at his job."

McClane and Hallstrom display hegemonic masculinity in their relations with women. Women are subordinate to them. Hallstrom manhandles Emma, pinning her to the floor and the wall. He tells Emma that he is protecting her; he doubts that she can protect herself. While McClane does not manhandle women, he protects Holly and the hostages. McClane and Hallstrom also are the objects of women's desire. As McClane deplanes, a flight attendant gives him the eye. Holly, who is estranged from and exasperated by McClane, nonetheless wants him to stay with her, "The kids would love to have you at the house. I would, too." Hallstrom also is an object of women's attention. In the scene that opens the film, a woman watches him dance; they end up in bed. When Emma explains why she is not attracted to her eye surgeon, she says, "I just can't see Dr. Pierce that way . . . my eyes are filled with someone else."

Interestingly, McClane and Hallstrom are more sensitive to women than are Marlowe or Johnny. McClane tells Powell that he should have been more supportive of Holly's career. Hallstrom is a more complex man than the 1940s heroes. He lets Emma into his world; near the film's end, he waits for her with her dog. These characterizations exemplify Sparks's (1996) observation that contemporary film heroes emote and suffer and care.

Other men respect McClane and Hallstrom. When the terrorists learn of McClane's presence, one of them speculates that he is a security man, but Gruber knows that McClane is more than that. When an LAPD deputy chief hassles McClane, Sergeant Powell tells him, "I love you; so do a lot of the other guys [street cops]." In *Blink,* the other detectives assume that Hallstrom will have his way with Emma. They exhort him to "sink the salami"; his lieutenant tells him to "just go ahead and fuck her, and get on with the case."

McClane and Hallstrom are driven by the inner morality that characterizes the genre hero. McClane draws upon the tradition of the American cowboy, a forerunner of the detective (Cawelti 1976). When Gruber belittles him as "another orphan of a bankrupt culture who thinks he's John Wayne," McClane says, "I was always . . . partial to Roy Rogers." He tells Sergeant Powell to call him "Roy." Hallstrom, too, is driven by a sense of "what is right." He likes Emma and does not want to "just fuck her." When another victim is murdered, he feels badly and redoubles his efforts.

Despite the similarities, the heroes in the four films differ on an important dimension: where Marlowe and Johnny walked through an urban landscape alone and alienated (Jameson 1970), McClane and Hallstrom are connected to others. McClane is married with children. Hallstrom has friends; the film begins as he drinks with them in a club.

More important, McClane and Hallstrom are cops. McClane and Hallstrom not only wear badges, their morality reflects a cop's working personality. When asked why he did not move to LA with his wife, McClane says, "I'm a New York City cop. I've got a six month backlog of New York scumbags I'm trying to put behind bars." Later, he and Powell bond and call each other "partner." Hallstrom says that being a cop is what he does best.

Perhaps the emerging mass society against which those 1940s heroes were juxtaposed has now fully arrived. What remains of their "outsider" status is the genre's now standard portrayal of the rogue cop who gets the job done by breaking bureaucratic rules (Sanders and Lyon 1995:32). *Blink* offers a scene common to cop movies: Hallstrom and a lieutenant yell at one another. McClane has similar interchanges in *Die Hard.* The frustration with a rule-bound society appears in a scene in which McClane grasps a terrorist, who says, "You won't hurt me . . . there are rules for policemen." McClane answers, "That's what my captain keeps telling me," and breaks the terrorist's neck.

Die Hard and *Blink* critique the police bureaucracy and other institutions. When McClane tries to warn the LAPD about the terrorists, they note that his call is on an unauthorized frequency, and threaten him with another bureaucracy, the FCC. The FBI's predictable procedures are the crux of Gruber's plan to steal the bonds. Indeed, the LAPD and the FBI are depicted as a collection of reckless, bureaucratic fools. The media and media experts also are critiqued. In one scene, a TV expert explains the Helsinki syndrome (hostages identifying with captors). Accompanying his dialogue is a shot where a terrorist drags off the body of a victim. In that scene, the TV news anchor also does not know where Helsinki is. Later, a TV reporter forces his way into Holly's home and interviews her kids; the interview reveals to Hans that she is McClane's wife, endangering her. *Blink*'s plot wherein a serial killer murders an organ donor's recipients raises concerns about medical science.

McClane and Hallstrom are insecure heroes. McClane fears flying. Holly has left him for a career that is more highly paid than his occupation. He expresses doubts that he will escape. Hallstrom also exhibits weakness. He is drunk in the opening scene; this later embarrasses him with Emma. He fails to believe her when she reports a murder. When he cannot solve the case, the lieutenant says, "This guy's out there laughing at you; he's beating you." Emma, not Hallstrom, kills the killer. In *Die Hard,* Sergeant Powell saves McClane by killing a terrorist.

The four films address issues of masculinity, and are true to the genre. Women are subordinate to Marlowe, Johnny, McClane, and Hallstrom. The detectives, even McClane and Hallstrom who are cops, are nonconformists; they are men with whom the audience, at least other men, can identify. They are heroic, if imperfect. Definitions of masculinity were in flux in the 1940s, and so they are today. These films reflect those uncertainties, even as the heroes aspire to extant notions of hegemonic masculinity.

CRIME

Crime drives the plot in this genre. It creates a narrative tension whose resolution restores social order. The audience takes pleasure in this, but it is a pleasure of a distinctly ideological sort: an identification with order. Jon Thompson suggests that "fictions of crime offer myths of the experience of modernity" (1993:2). These are mythic stories of threat and resolution. In this section, I will consider the crimes in these four films on two levels: crime as a social disruption and woman as a disruption to masculinity.

Things are rarely as they seem in the two 1940s films; false identities abound. Although this is a standard convention of the crime genre and of film noir, it adds to the sense of disorientation in the films. By today's standards, these films are not very violent. In *Murder, My Sweet,* five people are killed, only one of these on camera; Marlowe kills no one. Motivations include blackmail, anger, and the prevention of other crimes. In *Blue Dahlia,* four (possibly five) people are killed, and three of these are on camera; Johnny kills one person in self-defense. Motivations include blackmail, self-defense, and police duty.

The situation is different in the contemporary films. Although greed motivates the villains in *Die Hard,* both it and *Blink* ground their plots in something akin to urban legends. Like urban legends, their plots reflect the fears and insecurities of modern society. In *Die Hard,* heavily armed terrorists (even if only thieves that act like terrorists) take hostages in a corporate office building. The police and the FBI are unprepared for their violent, well-planned crime. In *Blink,* a serial killer kills to undo the donation of organs. Perhaps the film reflects discomfort with the ethics of harvesting organs. Serial killer films, a common subgenre of the crime film, reflect a world populated by irrational forces (Epstein 1995).

The contemporary films are more violent than the 1940s films. In *Die Hard,* nineteen people die, all on camera; McClane kills eight of them. Motivations include greed, self-defense, and police duty. In *Blink,* six people die. Only the murderer dies on camera; we do see the body of a victim, nude in a bathtub, in a fairly lengthy scene. Hallstrom kills no one.

Crime represents both a direct physical and a larger social threat in these films. Women are a threat also. This is a standard portrayal in the male-centered crime genre. It is to this threat that I now turn.

Only *Murder, My Sweet* presents the classic femme fatale: Velma/Helen. She is trouble from the outset: we see only her leg extending provocatively into our field of vision. She is a poseur and a temptress. Her presence is key to the film's tension. She uses sexual wiles to tempt Marlowe to help her kill Amthor. Even as she kisses Marlowe, she is a threat: she steals his gun during their embrace. She is, to use Ann's words, "evil, all evil."

In *Blue Dahlia,* Helen epitomizes the postwar threat to masculinity. She is uninterested in Johnny's war experiences; she does not know who George and Buzz are; she had an affair while he fought; she derisively calls him "hero." Helen rejects her life as a proper wife and mother, "We lived in a five-room house and I did the laundry. And I never went anywhere cause I had a kid . . . I don't have a kid anymore." When Johnny asks her to stop drinking so that they can discuss their future, she laughs, "I take all the drinks I like, anytime, anyplace. I go wherever I want to with anybody I want. I just happen to be that kind of a girl." She explains that he is not paying for the drinks, a reference to the business she started in his absence. Helen is a bad woman, liberated, and beyond Johnny's control.

In *Murder, My Sweet* and *Blue Dahlia,* even the women who are proper love interests are problematic. Ann lies about her identity when she meets Marlowe. Later, she offers him money to drop the case, and says, "I'm not corrupting you, surely you've been bought off before." Marlowe likes her, but cannot be sure if she genuinely cares for him or is manipulating him to drop the case. In *Blue Dahlia,* Joyce is not trustworthy either. She is Harwood's estranged wife and might still be loyal to him.

In their resolution, both films preserve masculinity. The bad women die in a manner appropriate to their transgressions. Grayle, the cuckolded husband, kills Helen in *Murder, My Sweet.* Dad Newell, who has been blackmailing Helen in *Blue Dahlia* because of her affair, kills her. Ann, in *Murder, My Sweet,* has already shown the proper signs of subordination. When Marlowe escapes from a sanitarium, she cooks for him after he opens a jar for her. As the film ends, she helps him to get home. Joyce's position is also at her man's side in *Blue Dahlia.* Unlike Helen, she knows that Buzz and George are important to Johnny.

In *Die Hard* and *Blink* there are no femme fatales, though women are a threat to masculinity. Holly's career takes priority over her role as McClane's wife. She has moved her children to LA; indeed, McClane's visit to LA sets in motion *Die Hard's* narrative. Holly uses Gennero, her maiden name, which troubles McClane. She works late, leaving her kids in the care of a nanny. Her lifestyle is juxtaposed with McClane's nostalgic references.

Emma Brody is a threat to Hallstrom's masculinity in *Blink.* In one scene, she and a woman friend discuss what sex was like when Emma was blind. Emma says that she was in control and pulled the man into her fantasy. When she is attracted to Hallstrom but he resists, she says, "Someday that dam you build is going to break, detective." Later, in a club, he watches her play the violin and is drawn to her. His interest in her makes him "cross the line," and affects his work. The lieutenant tells him, "You've stuffed your instincts in the trunk, and your dick is driving the car." When Emma tells Hallstrom that she loves him, he pulls away from her and blames another murder on their liaison. She embarrasses him at work. In a final woman-as-threat scene, Emma shoots the killer, but in a superimposed shot, also sees (kills) the image of the mother who blinded her.

Masculinity also is restored to its proper place in the resolution of *Die Hard* and *Blink,* though, as I mentioned earlier, in some respects it is a more sensitive masculinity. In *Blink,* Hallstrom has helped to set things right. He tells Emma that she needs a man she can control, and that he is not that kind of man. But he writes a poem for her. As the film ends, he and their friends (a kind of family) watch her in a club as she plays and sings.

Although *Die Hard* also exhibits this heightened sensitivity, it is somewhat more heavy-handed in its resolution of the crisis of masculinity. In what is perhaps the ultimate reaffirmation of hegemonic masculinity, Sergeant Powell, in slow motion, draws his pistol and kills a villain who is about to kill McClane. In that act, Powell's lost masculinity is redeemed in blood (see Gibson 1994). McClane also saves Holly as Gruber tries to drag her with him out of a high window. In one of the final shots, Holly punches the TV reporter who interviewed the kids, perhaps violating gender expectations, but restoring her place as mother. When McClane introduces her to

Sergeant Powell as Holly Gennero, she corrects him, "Holly McClane." She is back where she belongs.

CONCLUSION

Movies are entertainment. However, like other aspects of popular culture, movies, especially crime films, do more than entertain. They circulate ideologies—about good and evil, order and disorder—and images of masculinity and femininity.

Genres are predictable and formulaic, but they also reflect and reproduce emerging social contexts. They reflect the hopes and joys, the fears and insecurities of their time. For this reason, for what they tell us about right and wrong, men and women, genres and genre films are worthy of study.

The 1940s crime films combine character, plot, and technique to engage in positive social criticism. These films, now called film noir, present plots in which the corrupt social institutions of an emerging mass society are aligned against the individual. The individual is depicted heroically in the figure of the detective who fights these larger forces. Also aligned against this hero is Woman, whether the classic femme fatale (Velma/Helen in *Murder, My Sweet*), or the "new woman" post–World War II (Helen, the bad wife/bad mother in *Blue Dahlia*). The detective plays out these critiques and insecurities in a manner that conforms to the conventions of the crime genre.

Contemporary crime genre films still reflect and reproduce the social context, embedding ideology in plot and character in ways that often go unnoticed (Cavender 1998). Yet, times have changed. *Die Hard* and *Blink* reflect the forces that produced a backlash against the women's movement. These forces include the successes of the women's movement and the economic decline that began in the 1980s. Masculinity, like the corporate labor force, has been downsized. In *Die Hard,* McClane's wife has left him for her career at a Japanese corporation in LA. In *Blink,* Hallstrom cannot "commit" to Emma. Her love scares him and hurts his work.

These films are only images on the screen, but they project insights that are relevant for criminology. These films traffic in ideology, which includes beliefs about and fear of crime and other social concerns. They also depict images of masculinity and femininity, in their hegemonic forms, and in alternative forms as well. They depict masculinity in crisis at two different periods in our history. And yet, because Hollywood prefers happy endings, all's well that ends well, at least at the movies.

But of course, all is not well. Perhaps crime is merely a metaphor for other social problems. Official statistics show a decline for some serious crimes, but crime persists as a problem of public concern. The same may be true for masculinity. Men's economic security is filtered, metaphorically, through the illusion that women, not global capital, have taken the jobs.

In any case, crime genre films will no doubt continue to circulate ideologies about crime and images of hegemonic masculinity as the films continue to evolve. While some conventions of the genre will remain unchanged, social context will change and so will the genre. This is already underway. Notable films of the not-too-distant past address gender issues in ways that differ from the four films that I have analyzed. *Fatal Attraction,* for example, is a man's worst nightmare: a femme fatale, crazed by the ticking of her career woman's biological clock, attacks a nice (if philandering) guy and his family. In *Thelma and Louise,* women fight (and shoot) back at the men who would victimize them. In *Fargo,* a pregnant woman sheriff solves the crime; Frances McDormand, the actress who played this character, won an Academy Award.

Similarly, shifting racial/ethnic demographics are increasingly an issue in the crime film. The hero in *Devil in a Blue Dress* is an African-American man who must confront racism in the LAPD and in city politics; his motivation is a desire to own his own home. In *Lone Star,* the sheriff solves a crime, but along the way deals with interracial romance and the fact that he does not really want to be a sheriff.

These crime genre films, like those analyzed in this chapter, exemplify "doing gender." They also "do race." However, because the social context has shifted, they address and engage these social constructions in new ways. At the same time, even these recent films reproduce many of the standard conventions of the crime genre. Fundamentally, they remain true to the notion that the detective has a quest to solve a crime. But, as in *Murder, My Sweet, Blue Dahlia, Die Hard,* and *Blink,* a part of that quest is also the search for what it is to be a man. In that sense, one theme that will predictably continue in the crime genre is the enterprise of detecting masculinity.

ACKNOWLEDGMENTS

I appreciate helpful comments from Jeff Ferrell, Neil Websdale, and Nancy Jurik.

REFERENCES

Bennett, Tony and J. Woollacott. 1987. *Bond and Beyond: The Political Career of a Popular Hero.* New York: Methuen.

Cavender, Gray. 1995. "Alternative Criminological Theory: The Labeling Perspective and Critical Criminology." Pp. 349–67 in *Handbook of Criminology,* 2nd edition, edited by J. Sheley. Belmont, CA: Wadsworth.

Cavender, Gray. 1998. "In the Shadow of Shadows: Television Reality Crime Pro-
gramming." Pp. 79–94 in *Entertaining Crime: Reality Television Programs,* edit-
ed by M. Fishman and G. Cavender. Hawthorne, NY: Aldine de Gruyter.
Cawelti, John. 1976. *Adventure, Mystery, and Romance.* Chicago: University of
Chicago Press.
Connell, Robert. 1987. *Gender and Power.* Stanford, CA: Stanford University Press.
Connell, Robert. 1993a. "The Big Picture: Masculinities in Recent World History."
Theory and Society 22:597–623.
Connell, Robert. 1993b. "Foreword." In *Masculinities and Crime: Critique and
Reconceptualization of Theory,* James Messerschmidt. Lanham: Rowman &
Littlefield.
Connell, Robert. 1995. *Masculinities.* Berkeley: University of California Press.
Epstein, Su. 1995. "The New Mythic Monster." Pp. 66–79 in *Cultural Criminology,*
edited by J. Ferrell and C. Sanders. Boston: Northeastern University Press.
Faludi, Susan. 1991. *Backlash: The Undeclared War against Women.* New York:
Crown.
Ferrell, Jeff and Clinton R. Sanders. 1995. "Crime, Culture, and Criminology." Pp. 3–
21 in *Cultural Criminology,* edited by J. Ferrell and C. Sanders. Boston: North-
eastern University Press.
Fiske, John. 1992. "British Cultural Studies and Television." Pp. 284–326 in *Chan-
nels of Discourse: Television and Contemporary Criticism,* 2nd edition, edited
by R. Allen. Chapel Hill: University of North Carolina Press.
Fiske, John. 1994. *Media Matters: Everyday Culture and Political Change.* Min-
neapolis: University of Minnesota Press.
Gibson, William. 1994. *Warrior Dreams: Paramilitary Culture after Vietnam.* New
York: Hill and Wang.
Gitlin, Todd. 1982. "Prime-Time Ideology: The Hegemonic Process in Television
Entertainment." Pp. 426–54 in *Television: The Critical View,* 3rd edition, edited
by H. Newcomb. New York: Oxford University Press.
Hirsch, Foster. 1981. *Film Noir: The Dark Side of the Screen.* New York: Da Capo.
Hobbs, Dick. 1997. *Bad Business: Professional Crime in Modern Britain.* Oxford:
Oxford University Press.
Horrocks, Roger. 1994. *Masculinity in Crisis: Myths, Fantasies and Realities.* London:
St. Martin's.
Jameson, Fredric. 1970. "On Raymond Chandler." *Southern Review* 6:624–50.
Joyrich, Lynne. 1996. *Re-Viewing Reception: Television, Gender, and Postmodern
Culture.* Bloomington: Indiana University Press.
Jurik, Nancy C. 1998. "Socialist Feminism, Criminology, and Social Justice." Pp. 30–
50 in *Social Justice/Criminal Justice: The Maturation of Critical Theory in Law,
Crime, and Deviance,* edited by B. Arrigo. Belmont, CA: West/Wadsworth.
Katz, Jack. 1988. *Seductions of Crime: Moral and Sensual Attractions in Doing Evil.*
New York: Basic Books.
Kellner, Douglas. 1995. *Media Culture: Culture Studies, Identity, and Politics be-
tween the Modern and the Postmodern.* London: Routledge.
Klein, Dorie. 1992. "Reading the New Feminist Mystery: The Female Detective,
Crime and Violence." *Women and Criminal Justice* 4:37–62.

Knight, Stephen. 1980. *Form and Ideology in Crime Fiction.* Bloomington: Indiana University Press.

Krutnik, Frank. 1991. *In a Lonely Street: Film Noir, Genre, Masculinity.* London: Routledge.

Maltby, Richard. 1995. *Hollywood Cinema.* Oxford: Blackwell.

Mandel, Ernest. 1984. *Delightful Murder: A Social History of the Crime Story.* Minneapolis: University of Minnesota Press.

Martin, Susan and Nancy C. Jurik. 1996. *Doing Gender, Doing Justice: Women in Law and Criminal Justice Occupations.* Thousand Oaks, CA: Sage.

Messerschmidt, James. 1993. *Masculinities and Crime: Critique and Reconceptualization of Theory.* Lanham: Rowman & Littlefield.

Munt, Sally. 1994. *Murder by the Book: Feminism and the Crime Novel.* London: Routledge.

New York Times. 1996. *The Downsizing of America.* New York: Times Books.

Newburn, Tim and Elizabeth Stanko, eds. 1994. *Just Boys Doing Business? Men, Masculinities and Crime.* London: Routledge.

Reid, David and Jayne Walker. 1993. "Strange Pursuit: Cornell Woolrich and the Abandoned City of the Forties." Pp. 57–96 in *Shades of Noir,* edited by J. Copjec. London: Verso.

Sanders, Clinton R. and Eleanor Lyon. 1995. "Repetitive Retribution: Media Images and the Cultural Construction of Criminal Justice." Pp. 25–44 in *Cultural Criminology,* edited by J. Ferrell and C. Sanders. Boston: Northeastern University Press.

Schrader, Paul. 1996. "Notes on Film Noir." Pp. 53–63 in *Film Noir Reader,* edited by A. Silver and J. Ursini. New York: Limelight.

Sparks, Richard. 1996. "Masculinity and Heroism in the Hollywood Blockbuster." *British Journal of Criminology* 6:348–60.

Surette, Ray. 1998. *Media, Crime and Criminal Justice: Images and Realities,* 2nd edition. Belmont, CA: West/Wadsworth.

Thompson, John. 1990. *Ideology and Modern Culture.* Stanford, CA: Stanford University Press.

Thompson, John. 1995. *The Media and Modernity: A Social Theory of the Media.* Stanford, CA: Stanford University Press.

Thompson, Jon. 1993. *Fiction, Crime, and Empire.* Urbana: University of Illinois Press.

Vernet, Marc. 1993. "Film Noir on the Edge of Doom." Pp. 1–31 in *Shades of Noir,* edited by J. Copjec. London: Verso.

West, Candace, and Don Zimmerman. 1987. "Doing Gender." *Gender and Society* 1:125–51.

West, Candace, and Sarah Fenstermaker. 1995. "Doing Difference." *Gender and Society* 9:8–37.

IV

Constructions of Subculture and Crime

9

Wild Life
Constructions and Representations of Yardies

KARIM MURJI

This chapter is concerned with representations and constructions of "black criminality" and specifically "yardies" in Britain. It draws on ideas about racialization that begin with a view of "race" as a socially and culturally constructed category. From this perspective, racist discourses are seen as generating, and seeking to fix or essentialize, "race differences" as the principal marker of boundaries between groups of people. In recent years "cultural difference" has become one of these boundaries. A "new racism" based on cultural rather than biological differences emerged in the 1970s (Barker 1981). Conventional notions of genetic superiority and inferiority were supplanted by beliefs about the incompatibility of different cultures. Cultural difference became a code for race and depictions of the "culture" of ethnic or racial minorities became a means for simultaneously denying, while implicitly reasserting, racial hierarchies through which racism is veiled or "smuggled" back in. A "differential" or "culturalized" racism emerged in the writings of conservative commentators and politicians, where accounts of "black crime," often linked to "cultural pathology," were employed to demarcate cultural difference as a hard and fast boundary that separates "us" from "them."

It has been argued that liberal, and sometimes radical, perspectives have also offered problematic, often essentialized, representations of black culture. Because of this, the dividing line between reactionary and would-be progressive approaches has sometimes been a thin one. As an illustration, consider this passage:

> Among cultural minorities within the United States, historically there have been higher rates of unemployment and poverty level existence. . . . [C]haracteristics and stresses of poverty, such as feelings of hopelessness, alienation, and powerlessness [are] high correlates of chemical abuse within African-American communities. Youth raised in these communities are often subjected to a culture of origin that appears to tolerate and support the trafficking and use

179

of chemicals for non-medical purposes. . . . This does not imply that all members of low income communities succumb to or tolerate the abuse of chemicals. In fact, the majority of people in these communities do not. Yet, in terms
of prevention or intervention program development, the visibility and acces-
sibility of trafficking and use does impact the culture and lifestyle evolution in
many of these communities. It is evident historically that the trafficking of
illegal chemicals within minority communities has served to fulfill some of the
economic needs of a population that was systematically and legally ostracized
from the job market. Over time, the culture has adapted to a situation thrust
upon them but not accepted by the majority. (Griswold-Ezekoye 1986:209–10)

As an example of the use of a "cultural deficiency" model to explain
initiation into drug use this is not uncommon (Dorn and Murji 1992). Less
acceptably, it equates race with culture by conflating African-American
communities with cultural minorities. Regarding drug use as an effect or
consequence of social and economic pressures probably marks this out as a
liberal perspective. But as culture is seen as a determined outcome of structural forces, a sense of agency, as well as the possibility that drug use has
wider meanings, including pleasure (Katz 1988), tends to be lost. Most
problematic is the view that there has been a seemingly embedded cultural
adaptation that tolerates the "trafficking and use of chemicals." This employs
a malignant and dangerous form of culturalism and a pathological view of a
"black drugs culture." To the extent that this implies the "Otherness" of this
culture, it is close to, rather than critical of, New Right and other forms of
new racism.[1]

Indeed I will argue that all kinds of texts on the yardies, whether of liberal
or illiberal intent, that seek to "understand" yardie violence, or "explain" its
social and economic origins, can also be seen to lead to much the same
outcome. In doing so, they serve to differentiate "the Other," whose activities or presence demarcate "them" from "us." This reinforces boundaries
rather than questioning their construction and character. Edward Said has
argued that the languages, cultures, writings, and people of "the East" have
been built up into a distinctive way of "seeing" the Orient as "different"
from, or opposed to, the West. Thus the "exoticism" and "decadence" of the
East were contrasted with the morality of the West. These differences, or
subject-constituting positions, shape mutually constitutive relations between
civility and the uncivilized, the clean and the dirty.[2] What is most questionable is the way this model introduces boundaries or lines that serve to
demarcate groups of people, in the same way that "race thinking" seeks to
institute essentialized boundaries between "racial" groups. Such processes
recur in different contexts and forms. To take the example of drugs again, the
Advisory Council on the Misuse of Drugs (ACMD)[3] has alluded, implicitly
using control theory, to some sort of cultural blanket acting to prevent or
contain drug problems among Asian communities. But while "Asian" cul-

ture is seen as strong and offering protection, the culture of African-Caribbean groups is seen as somehow lacking or deficient. The denigration of the latter finds its corollary in the idealization of the former (Pitts 1993). Or put another way, "Asians have culture, West Indians have problems" (Benson 1996).[4]

A key starting point for examining racialized constructions of black crime is the work of Hall, Critcher, Jefferson, Clarke, and Roberts (1978). In the 1970s the media and moral entrepreneurs were the key players in naming and framing the "new" crime of "mugging." In focusing upon the operation of the control system in identifying and constructing this crime, rather than the behavior of those labeled, Hall et al. drew upon the social constructionist approach to social problems. For present purposes the crucial point is that, as mugging or street crime came to be constructed as a particular racialized crime, mostly committed by young black men and against white victims, it became a means for accentuating the Otherness of both the crime and of blacks; and during a period when "popular racism" was on the rise and politicians sought to mobilize a consensus for more law and order in the process of constructing the authoritarian state. Gilroy (1987a) has further analyzed discourses on race, crime, and nation. Perceptions of the "weakness" of black culture and family life—often attributed to the absence of a father or authority figure, or sometimes, to a lack of respect for the law and English traditions of civility—have served to define blacks as "lesser breeds without the law," as the Other who stand outside what(ever) it means to be English or British. This discussion indicates that there are several overlapping layers of Otherness in play, as race, crime, culture, and geography are mutually coded (Giroux 1996). Race or blackness acts as an Other that gives rise to fears about particular people and places. Race has also been a medium through which fears and anxieties about crime are focused and given a recognizable shape (Hall et al. 1978; Gilroy 1987a; Keith 1993). Furthermore, Kohn (1987) has suggested that racism and xenophobia shape complex fears about drugs. The discovery of the yardies in the 1980s meant that the "black drug trafficker" became the latest in the gallery of racialized characters linking race to vice, mugging, disorderliness, violence, and now drugs.

Using a number of sources I examine representations of yardies as a dangerous and violent group originating in Jamaica and now "over here." Taking representation to refer to "the significance of the construction . . . of ethnic identities through the production of images and narratives in visual and written texts of 'popular' and 'high' culture" (Rattansi 1994:58), I have drawn freely from a wide variety of texts: police and law enforcement documents from Britain, Canada, and the United States, newspaper reports and books by journalists, and television and radio reports. I argue that there is a striking degree of agreement between them so that, taken together, they amount to a form of "closed text" in which space for alternative representations has been squeezed out. They constitute hyperreal circles of repetition that generate self-referencing "truths" from which it is not possible to identify a causal chain or generative text. A principal source of information is sometimes clear, where assistance from the police or a particular police officer is acknowledged. Yet there are writers who appear to stand outside that circle of information but still reproduce much the same story. There obviously are some differences of detail and style between these texts, but there are enough similarities to make the lines between fact and fiction, or even reportage and invention sufficiently blurred to evade any neat divisions. These texts compete to most "faithfully" represent the excesses of yardies. For example, *Blood Posse* (Baker 1994) is marketed with the promise that it is "the real thing, written by somebody who's really been there." The prototype for such books was Victor Headley's (1992) novel *Yardie,* a tale of drugs, sex, guns, violence, and gang wars.[5] It was treated as, and adopts, a realistic format, particularly in the quasi-sociological accounts of social conditions in Jamaica. The success of the book was such that the covers of other novels use bylines such as "Here's the real Yardie!" as a selling point.

The concordance between these sources may be regarded by some as a marker of their verisimilitude rather than as the problem that I understand it to be. In examining social problems some writers seek to contrast "objectivist" versus "constructed" accounts. This has at times led constructionists into comparing the latter with, or against, the former (for example, Reinarman and Levine 1989). But contrasting "representation" and "reality" creates the difficulty that such methods are "always obliged in the final instance to refer and contrast 'representation' to the arbitration of 'the real' and . . . hence [are] unable to develop a full theory concerning the operations of ideology within all representational systems" (Watney 1987:41).[6] Reality is subject to discourses of representation and, consequently, the media cannot be seen simply in terms of distortion and misrepresentation. Rather, as Stuart Hall says, the media plays "a part in the formulation, in the constitution, of the things they reflect. It is not that there is a world outside, 'out there', which exists free of the discourse of representation. What is 'out there' is, in part, constituted by how it is represented" (quoted in Giroux 1996:51). Hence, I do not think that it would be helpful to see representations of yardies as either police discourses or media/journalistic accounts. Rather, they are mutually imbricated. As Ferrell and Sanders (1995:308) suggest, "media presentations, real-life events, personal perception [and] public policies . . . spiral about each other in a complex, mutually affecting, and ever-changing structure of inter-relationships." In focusing on construction and representation I am not looking directly at the impact of these on social audiences, though the preceding would suggest that audiences do not "stand apart" from producers. Moreover, to the extent that they are intertextual, the sources to which I refer can be regarded as each other's "audience."

For contextual purposes, it may be useful to state that, in Britain, crack has remained largely a cottage industry and that levels of crack and cocaine use have remained relatively low, behind heroin, which is below ecstasy, let alone the most widely used illegal substances such as amphetamines and cannabis (Shapiro 1994). Guns and violence, whether related to drugs or not, have never figured to anything approaching the levels found in parts of the United States. In 1994 there were 729 homicides, peaking at 753 in 1995 and declining by about 10 percent to 681 in 1996. The most common method of killing was the use of a sharp instrument. Shooting accounted for only 8 percent of homicides. In the early 1990s firearms were reported to have been used in 0.2 percent of all crimes and in 3 percent of violent crimes. The homicide rate is 1.3 per 100,000 population, among the lowest in Western Europe, while, at 7.4 percent, the rate in the United States was more than five times greater.[7]

DRUGS, RACE, AND NATION

Historical associations between race and drugs have been extensively explored in the United States (Musto 1973; Helmer 1975) and to some extent in Britain (Kohn 1987, 1992). In recent years, crack cocaine has been the drug most commonly associated with African-Caribbean communities, and especially yardies. The picture of crack as a distinctively "ethnic" drug was apparent in an infamous speech by DEA agent Robert Stutman. In spite of calling it an "equal opportunity drug," he told the British Association of Chief Police Officers (ACPO), "Right now crack is controlled by a fairly large number of organisations, basically of two ethnic backgrounds, Dominicans and Jamaicans. . . . [T]he Jamaicans have taken over control of much . . . of the United States. . . . I don't have to tell any of you that you have a large number of Jamaicans in this country" (Stutman 1989:7). Countless links between crack and Jamaicans in particular followed, culminating in a police description of yardies as threats to the "very security and stability of the nation" (quoted in *The Guardian*, 3 February 1997:1).[8]

In policing terms, connections between race and drugs are integral and not merely incidental. In the 1970s a Metropolitan Police specialist unit was set up on the basis that drugs and immigration were necessarily connected:

> [T]wenty five years ago . . . it [drugs] was directly relatable to illegal immigration, it was the illegal immigrants who were predominantly bringing the drugs through, hence the reason that the NDIU [National Drugs Intelligence

Unit] if you look at its history was formerly known as the Central Drugs and Illegal Immigration Unit. (quoted in Dorn, Murji, and South 1992)[9]

The association between drug trafficking and illegal immigration has since become a routine part of official discourse. Since the 1980s both have frequently been linked in the same sentence with terrorism (Clutterbuck 1990) especially in the context of increasingly strict immigration control, racially defined, and the building of a "Fortress Europe" policy that has pooled efforts to control the movement of "undesirables" to keep everyone, from refugees to terrorists, out of the "safe European home." The policy has been described as a form of racism "which cannot tell one black from another, a citizen from an immigrant, an immigrant from a refugee—and classes all Third World peoples as immigrants and refugees, and all immigrants and refugees as terrorists and drug dealers" (Sivanandan, quoted in Read and Simpson 1991:2).

CONSTRUCTING THE IDENTIKIT

Interest in the yardies emerged in the 1980s when the police and the media began to monitor and highlight the development and activities of what was already being described as a "black mafia." The yardies were said to be leaving Jamaica after the political fallout there in the early 1980s and entering Britain and North America, usually unlawfully: the "majority of posse members are illegal aliens" according to an intelligence report from the Royal Canadian Mounted Police (RCMP 1988:27). Indeed, illegal immigration became one of the key motifs of the yardie profile or identikit: "The Yardie idea of status focuses on four factors: You have to have a gun; money; drugs to sell—and you must have the ability to travel freely, and that usually means false passports" (*Evening Standard,* 22 October 1993, p. 5). Through "ethnic networks" or sheer violence, yardies were seen as establishing themselves as criminal kingpins in British cities (and, in the shape of posses, in American ones as well). An internal British police report characterized yardies as:

> Jamaican born males who, by the use of extreme violence, including murder, are dominating the drugs trafficking, prostitution, gaming clubs, both legal and illegal and possibly the black popular music industries. They inflict their violence with firearms and sharp instruments, in particular machetes and flick knives. (NDIU, undated)

The NDIU report rather confusingly moves between presenting a caricature and seeking to deny it. It states: "There is no criterion which can be used to identify a criminal of West Indian origin as being a Yardie." But it adds, "from those [yardies] already identified, certain similarities have emerged":

> He would have been born in Jamaica, probably about 1950; he would have entered the UK usually from the late 1970's direct from Jamaica or via the USA; he will be involved in black reggae-type music; he will have a violent past, not necessarily found in previous convictions; it is known for him to be polite to police officers when being arrested and during any subsequent interview; he may, when being interviewed, simulate low intellect. (NDIU, undated)

A memorandum from the Metropolitan Police reflects the above:

> Many of those involved [in drugs distribution] are Jamaican illegal immigrants who have no fixed addresses but who are bound by their Jamaican origin and reggae culture and who travel from one location to another with regularity. Such is their nomadic lifestyle that serious offences, for example murders, have been, and will continue to be committed wherever the cultural bandwagon happens to stop. (Metropolitan Police 1989:47)[10]

The allegedly near-seamless link between yardies and "reggae culture" illustrates a distinctively cultural construction of criminality (Ferrell and Sanders 1995). All of this apparently constitutes a rolling "cultural bandwagon" in which, presumably, crime and drugs are indissolubly linked with culture, music, and clubs.

The unpublished report does qualify the broad-brush cardboard-cutout: "The above points are purely indications. It would be most inadvisable to use them as a 'check-list' when attempting to identify a Yardie." Nonetheless, the identikit portrait of a new breed of organized black criminal in Britain has been widely reproduced, resulting in textual closure between police reports [the RCMP, NDIU, and the U.S. Bureau of Alcohol, Firearms and Tobacco (ATF) use virtually identical images and phrases], journalism (see Silverman 1994; Small 1995; Thompson 1995a; Davison 1997), and, as mentioned above, various fictional works traded as infotainment (for example, Headley 1992, 1993). A refection of all these blurred boundaries is apparent when a book that exists to provide factual data about race in Britain can state, without qualification: "A Yardie is a member of an organized crime institution with its roots in Jamaican politics that has become increasingly involved in drug dealing in the 1980s–90s" (Skellington 1996:74).

In addition to connections between race, crack, violence, and guns, a number of interrelated themes emerged in press accounts: aggression, sexual promiscuity, and conspicuous consumption, in the form of fast cars and showy jewelry. As some of these terms suggest, it is significant that yardies are not just racialized but also sexualized, in ways that reaffirm stereotypes of "dangerous black masculinity" as potent, threatening, and elemental. In this picture of masculinity in excess, they are "oversexed" as well as "over here." At the same time, yardies are also infantilized. The head of a Metropolitan Police specialist unit on crack said: "They [yardies] have a big thing about shiny, large calibre handguns in bright colours" (quoted in the *Daily Telegraph,* 22 June 1993, p. 19). Such childish images are strikingly similar to the conception of the "normal primitive":

> His goals are sensual and immediate—satisfying his physical and sexual needs without inhibition. There is little regard for the future. . . . His loyalties are with a group that has little purpose in life, except surviving with a minimum of sweat and a maximum of pleasure. He has the ten-year old boy's preoccupation with prowess and "being a man" [but] unfortunately, he lacks the boy's external restraint and supervision. (Swigert and Farrell 1977:19)

Above all, the rise to power of the yardies was linked to their domination of one commodity: crack cocaine. The apparent characteristics of the drug—an intense rush and feelings of excitability—are mirrored in the erratic and unpredictable behavior attributed to yardies, establishing a homology between the drug and its main sellers/users. Hence, crack tales combined a dizzying depiction of black men with a fondness for guns and extreme violence, loose living, and a fragile valuing of their own and other people's lives. Yardies are said to have an attitude that "life is short but sweet" (Thompson 1995b:5) or, more bluntly, "sociopathic recklessness" (*Newsweek* 1988:22).[11] This has been presented as wreaking havoc on black communities and inner-city areas, furthering a spiral of decline. These themes are discursively too intertwined to disentangle, but I will highlight some of the main features in representations of yardies as Other.

YARDIES IN OUR BACKYARD: THE INVASION

Contemporary accounts combine the Otherness of both drugs and race in an image of yardies and crack cocaine as twinned menaces from without that have spread within. The use of the invasion metaphor to describe drugs parallels discourses where black and Asian immigration has been described as an "alien invasion" that threatens to "swamp" Britain (Barker 1981). Similarly, drugs are commonly described as "flooding" into Britain, which is at risk of being "awash" with them (Kohn 1987). Underlying these terms are notions about contagion and pollution that recur in racist discourses (Goldberg 1993). They run right through chronicles of yardies and crack, implying a racial "stain" on a hitherto uncontaminated and unspoiled landscape. For instance, a *Newsweek* feature (1988:24) contained a section, "A Jamaican Invasion in West Virginia." As with other examples of this type of reportage, there is an image of an unsullied, perhaps even idyllic, community that has been tainted by drugs and blacks:

> With its tidy clapboard houses and neat apple and peach orchards . . . West Virginia seems far from the mean streets normally patrolled by drug gangs. But over the last three years, an invasion of Jamaican drug dealers has turned the home of the Mountain State Apple Harvest Festival into a mecca for cocaine.

The image of the external invasion operates at levels other than the despoiling of the pure. It can also be applied to "ghetto" areas, as when the *Sun* (25 May 1989) reported that "ruthless yardie gangbosses" were sending their best recruits "to peddle crack on Britain's inner-city estates"; or when a more highbrow newspaper refers to yardies "making their presence felt . . . [by] pumping crack into black housing estates" (Davies 1997:2). The threat from such areas, which do not have so far to "fall," is that contamination may seep out and infect "us." Moss Side in Manchester—described as "England's Bronx" by Silverman (1994)—has been extensively featured as an area where "gun gangs rule the rat runs" (*Times,* 29 June 1993, p. 7). A fearful image of Moss Side as a infectious place that risks polluting the rest of the city is summed up in the view that it was

> inescapably exerting its irresistible criminal influence on what local common sense wants to see as a relatively non-criminal city. The presence of Moss Side . . . symbolis[ed] the presence not just of a racial Other . . . but also of a specific kind of violent criminality, signified in particular by discussion of the "Yardie," implicitly linked into the "international drugs and firearms trade." (Taylor, Evans, and Fraser 1996:206)

The status of Moss Side typifies Lash and Urry's (1994) conception of the "wild zone" as "a field of disorder and ungovernability [that] signifies an area of the without-law(s)" (Stanley 1996:105). Race and place become intertwined as features that demarcate the boundaries of civility, distinguishing the respectable from the disreputable. "Yardie gun culture" (Davison 1997) causes Moss Side to deteriorate from bad to worse, while an "invasion of Jamaican drug dealers" (*Newsweek* 1988) leads to the alien defilement of the hitherto untainted Mountain State, as "this violent group of international criminals are [now] present and organised in our very own backyards" (Brennan 1994:16). In both cases, all "indigenous" crime is neatly obscured.

POLICING YARDIES: ETHNIC CLOSURE

Police accounts suggest that a major problem in policing yardies is that they are difficult to distinguish within black culture. We have already seen references to their role within the "black popular music industries" and "black reggae-type music." These invoke an image of "ethnic closure," so that police officers simply cannot tell who is and is not a yardie, because they are so easily concealed within black communities. The ethnically challenged police are simply unable to distinguish the law-abiding from the lawless, thus coming close to the view that "all blacks look alike." Having left Jamaica to "go foreign" (Brennan 1994) yardies are apparently able to hide themselves with ease:

> Once in a foreign country the individual can easily be absorbed into the local community making their detection difficult. Once abroad the Jamaican criminal merely acts in an identical way as if he were on the streets of Kingston, Jamaica. (ibid.:15)[12]

Similarly, the Interpol Secretary-General has written that criminals are able to hide within "immigrant" peoples by using "ethnic customs, backgrounds, fears and language" (Kendall 1990). In this way the police, seemingly impervious to accusations of criminalizing whole communities, provide themselves with the legitimation for targeting entire neighborhoods and communities, as well as black clubs because they may be used as cover, just in case there might be some yardies hiding among them. Black culture is treated as being indistinguishable from a culture of crime. Assertions such as the view that everyday behavior in black communities is indistinguishable from that in Kingston, Jamaica, reveals rather more about the mind-set and outlook of some police officers than about yardies. Hence it is unsurprising that:

> Today virtually every black criminal in Britain is seen as a Yardie, or at the very least suspected of having Yardie links. When black drug dealer Sammy Lewis shot and wounded a detective . . . the incident was immediately reported as a Yardie crime (in fact Lewis was born in Reading, his parents were from Barbados and he had never been to Jamaica in his life). (Thompson 1995b:5)[13]

Indeed it is not only all blacks who are now being inclusively characterized as the Other; the dangers go even beyond identifiable racial minorities. The NDIU report said: "It is of interest to note that . . . tenuous links have been established between the Yardies and/or close associates with members of the Israeli criminal fraternity, the Angry Brigade and the IRA" (NDIU, undated). So the Others are not discrete but rather coalescing into a single all-powerful enemy, "the rest," who seemingly stand against "the West" (Hall 1992).

A vision of ethnic closure is evident in other facets of drugs policing. During the 1980s drug enforcement began to "chase the money" rather than just drugs (Dorn et al. 1992). Some police officers working on money laundering wrote of their discovery of "hawala" and "chiti" banking, techniques said to be commonly employed by Indians and Asians in lieu of identifiable paper records. The "inscrutability" of these "ethnic customs" thus presents a challenge to what is, by implication, constructed as a monoethnic, monocultural police force. At the same time, there is also an insinuation that these devious methods are characteristic of the "wily oriental," and as Gilroy (1993) has pointed out, this can be invidiously contrasted with a view of blacks as "dumb savages."

A further aspect of the "impenetrability" of yardies/ethnic drug trafficking networks is apparent in the use of informants. In 1988 the Metropolitan Police set up Operation Lucy to look into organized black crime in Britain. This was merged into the Crack Intelligence Coordinating Unit, which as Operation Dalehouse, gathered all information about crack and targeted drug-related violence. Criticism that the crack market was too small to justify such a specialist response, and evidence that crack sales and use had not approached American levels, led to the unit's winding up in 1992.[14] However, this did not mean that yardies were no longer of interest to the police. Rather the strategy had changed, as police and Customs sought to recruit informants from within the yardies. The rationale for this can be surmised from this statement: "Because of their [yardies/posses] tightly organized operations and high mobility, it is virtually impossible to utilize undercover agents" (RCMP 1988:29).[15] This trait was taken to mean that enforcement agencies could not use their own officers or established informants in undercover work. Thus there is an image of a "tight knit" or "clannish, cunning and extraordinarily violent" group as *Newsweek* (1988:21) puts it. The difficulty in penetrating the yardies is due to their operating on a seemingly "tribal" basis. Such conceptions are reaffirmed by tracing posses back to particular neighborhoods in Jamaica from which they are said to take their name, as also expressed in "turf wars," where gangs are defined according to geography/neighborhood. These ways of understanding yardies are evident to some extent in all of the sources that I am drawing upon. In at least two instances, however, the informant strategy has imploded, once disastrously so. In the case of informant Eaton Green, it emerged that:

> for more than two years he had been a paid Scotland Yard informant and his handlers [police officers] had allowed him to bring known Yardies into the country. . . . Other detectives came across evidence of the crimes Green says he committed while on Scotland Yard's payroll, but [the detectives] were

blocked from investigating them by his handlers who wanted to keep their informer on the streets. It is understood that Green has admitted that he routinely used a firearm, committed armed robberies, bought and sold large quantities of crack cocaine, and ran protection rackets. . . . He was never prosecuted for any of these offences, and was finally brought to book only when he committed the armed robbery in Nottingham where his handlers were unable to protect him. (Davies 1996)

Such use of informants is prohibited under Home Office guidelines (see Dorn, Murji, and South 1992; Davies 1996, 1997). So too is the unofficial policy of "squeal deals," where people under threat of deportation from Britain have been allowed to remain in return for acting as informants for the police and/or Customs. Nonetheless, in another case it became evident that the police had permitted a man to stay so that he could act as an informant on the yardies, despite a Home Office order that he should be deported. During this period, this individual committed various crimes, including rape and murder, which eventually led to his conviction (Davies 1997).

EXPLAINING YARDIES: A CULTURE OF VIOLENCE

The alienness of yardies or posses is supplemented by a list of seemingly unique features. Paramount among these is the recurring theme of "extreme violence" (*Newsweek* 1988:22); the ATF reports that posses have a "propensity for violence" (RCMP 1988), while the ATF director says: "These gangs are the most vicious and violent groups local law enforcement has ever encountered. They don't hesitate to kill for any reason and they don't care who gets caught in the crossfire" (Drug Enforcement Report, March 8, 1988:5). Similarly, a British police officer echoes the view that "the[y] are a unique group of criminals, their illegal activities . . . are reinforced by ruthless violence" (Brennan 1994:15). Having been well-established by enforcement officials the same refrain is repeated as journalistic reportage or as fictional glamour. A journalist adds that yardies are "using guns and knives with terrifying spontaneity" (Davies 1997:2). Guns are not simply a means to an end but a status symbol and a source of pleasure. Under the headline, "Drug Gangs Relish Dice with Death," a police officer was reported to have said: "The gangs actually enjoy the buzz that comes from the fear of being shot at or the sense of power when carrying a gun. They revel in the 'respect' that goes with having money, access to drugs and a gun. They love to pose or posture; their sense of well-being comes from 'status'" (quoted in *The Guardian,* 13 May 1993, p. 4). And the violence is allegedly random (see Brownstein 1995), and as likely to be directed at "their own kind," as *News-*

week reports that reggae clubs have "a well deserved reputation for frequent homicides" (1988, p. 26).

A number of television and radio productions on yardies have chosen to go to Jamaica. These documentaries commonly seek to explain that yardies originated from a period of political conflict and patronage between various factions. This is often combined with a report of the social and economic climate in Jamaica, such as the lack of legitimate job opportunities. Both factors are used to explain a "drugs and guns" culture in Jamaica in a way that many liberals might find appealing. However, attempts to make a culture of violence understandable can end up reinforcing the idea that violence is somehow a cultural proclivity, or "in their roots," something for which we might expect someone to discover a gene sooner rather than later. This is not entirely flippant, as I suggest that culture is here being regarded almost as deterministically as biology sometimes is. For Thompson: "Yardies are simply a class apart, born as they were from an environment in which violence is the norm" (1995b:5). Since yardies are from a violent society, visiting Jamaica to look for "root causes" of yardie violence can simply reaffirm that a "foreign import" has been brought in by these "outsiders." Once again, there are similarities here with the "normal primitive," an official imagery that Swigert and Farrell deduce from diagnostic typing of homicides in the United States, which "suggests a group of people whose style of life and innate attributes predispose them to violence" (1977:19; see Hawkins 1987).

Another explicit contrast serves to attest to the Otherness of yardie/posse violence. The domination of white gangsters such as the Krays and the Richardsons in 1960s London has been eulogized as a basically stable, ordered, and hierarchical criminal culture in which everyone knew their place and kept to it. But disorganized crime, accompanied by guns and violence (its randomness exemplified in the "drive-by shooting" and the danger to innocent bystanders; see Brownstein 1995) exemplifies a culture of instability.[16] The excitable effects of crack are allegedly mimicked in the erratic behavior of yardies. As Stanley points out:

> The "controlled" gang violence of the 1960s and the 1970s has declined in favour of new and more arbitrary forces of violence. Where gang rule provided a veneer of respectability in the distribution of the criminal activities of protection, gambling and vice . . . the dominant commodities are now drugs and guns implicating embryonic Jamaican Yardie . . . influence. (1996:103)

Another exercise in differentiation is observable when *Newsweek* also stresses exceptionality: "Jamaican posses are far more violent than the Mafia" (1988:22).[17] Yardies are therefore sufficiently strange to make earlier criminal networks seem tame by comparison. For Clutterbuck the comparison between yardies and the Italian mafia is misleading because the former have no mysticism and honour, "just the power and security derived from membership of a violent criminal community able to hold its own with guns and knives" (1995:72). While there may, in the 1990s, be quantitative as well as qualitative changes in the extent and form of drug-related violence, reasons for this are in fact more likely centered around market competition than ethnicity (Dorn et al. 1992; Brownstein 1995).

It could be added that a reputation for violence may be as significant as any actual deeds. A "rep" can serve many purposes (Bourgois 1995; Katz 1988). One of these is the reasonably obvious one of status enhancement, which may also be seen as an element of cultural performance: "Many young blacks of various ethnic origins play up their own, usually non-existent, links with the Yardies in order to reinforce their own reputations. There have even been some cases of Nigerian and Ghanian drug dealers attempting to affect Jamaican accents in order to enhance their status" (Thompson 1995b). Another is that being famed for violence may be useful for intimidating other criminals, something that Woodiwiss (1988) argues occurred in the period of prohibition. The idea of an all-powerful criminal mafia may also have been useful in "buying off" law enforcement officials and politicians. In any case, Woodiwiss adds, suggestively, that such a reputation was useful for two other groups: the media because it made for better stories, and the police because it emphasized the size of the task they faced.

PICTURING THE YARDIE: LIFESTYLES OF THE RICH AND INFAMOUS

Turning to another level of representation, it is notable that accounts of yardies use very similar photographs. The most common depiction features black men, their eyes "blacked out," displaying gold jewelry and posing with one or more handguns. One of the first of these was in the *Observer* magazine when its front cover featured a black man posing with two firearms. The text next to it read:

> He makes his money from drugs. He wears the profits in a neckchain. He loves fast cars but his women are just "baby mothers". Cross him and he'll blast your head away. He is one of a frightening new network in Britain.

The article titled "Heirs to the Krays" (Sweeney 1989) featured a full-page picture of a black man toting a submachine gun in each hand. The text contains a slightly more measured approach but most striking are the headline, photographs, and the "yardie profile" set off from the main text with its tale of large amounts of cash, a fondness for "classy German cars," and "many girlfriends . . . who are treated very badly." The iconography is sufficiently well established so that the yardie connection does not particularly need to be spelled out. Thus, a feature on "The Dealers in Death" in the Metropolitan Police newspaper, the *Job* (8 July 1994, pp. 8–9) uses pictures of gun-toting blacks, with barely a mention of crack and none of yardies, to connote threat/menace. These images could well be read as the criminalization of subcultural style (Ferrell and Sanders 1995). Alternatively, I prefer to see this as the operation of a signifying system in which race is coded to denote criminality and dangerousness (see Goldberg 1993; Giroux 1996).

As we have seen, the composite portrait of yardies includes a predilection for a high-profile lifestyle. In the late 1980s it was rumored that the German car company BMW had moved to control secondhand car sales because of a concern that their cars had acquired an image as the "drug dealer's car," a key motif of conspicuous consumption among successful dealers (see Chambliss 1994; Miller 1996). Given the relatively high risk for black men of being stopped by the police, especially when "out of place" in high-status cars, it would appear that a representation of yardies as blithely seeking publicity and public visibility suggests that while they may be violent and dangerous, they are basically dense, or at least criminally unprofessional; again, the dumb savage. In another version of the same theme, featuring a repeat of the invasion motif, it has been reported that yardies targeted Britain because it is "easy" (for example, "Yardie Gangsters See London as Soft Touch," *Evening Standard,* 22 October 1993, p. 5; "Crack Trade Turning to 'Safe' Britain," *Guardian,* 2 July 1994, p. 8)—with yardies thus presumably ignorant of the fact that Britain has some of the toughest penalties for drug trafficking in Europe (see Dorn et al. 1992).

By way of contrast, an account by "James," a black man convicted for drug trafficking, is noteworthy. James does not quite fit the yardie profile we saw earlier: he was born in the late 1950s and brought up in Britain. Because he has been involved with what the police call "reggae-type music" he could, like Sammy Lewis (mentioned above), be mistakenly thought to be a yardie, or at least to have some connections with them. Interviewed in prison, he told me about some basic measures that he took to minimize the risk of being stopped by the police:

> You don't go out there totally willy nilly, I did take precautions, for instance you get yourself a decent car not something ostentatious like a BMW, but a Ford or something. You dress decently and go to places where there's no trouble. It's trying to do everything that the drug stereotype wouldn't do.

James may not be exceptional in his approach to dealing drugs, but his way of working does differ significantly from images of the yardie. In place of the gang or posse he describes himself as a "one man operation" and a "smuggler, period." He rules out involvement with selling drugs at a retail level because that would have increased the risks. Despite his personal concerns about cocaine as the drug that had become stereotypically linked to black men, his decision to deal in it was informed by a basic businesslike attitude, which could be (and sometimes is) applied to yardies too:

> In my case it was a rational decision to smuggle cocaine. One, I knew people in America I could get it from. Two, the returns on your investment are very high. Third, the quantities you can carry in relation to how much you can get for it.

IRONIES AND CONTRADICTIONS

The demonization of the yardies has produced some ironic consequences.[18] The "folk devil" image acquired a certain cachet and, in some cases, yardie status became something to aspire to rather than to live down. In the late 1980s T-shirts were available in London street markets with the single word, "Yardie," below a picture of a muscular black man, akin to a character from the TV program "The A-Team."[19] This led some officers to express concern that the yardie label had become fashionable and that the yardie image was creating an alternative role model: "It has been found that many West Indian males will identify themselves as a Yardie in order to enhance their reputations among the West Indian criminal fraternity" (NDIU, undated).[20]

I have adopted a skeptical and critical outlook in examining representations of yardies. In doing so, I do not wish to be seen as claiming that there are no black people involved in drug trafficking and crime. Rather, I concur with the view that "images and representations of black criminality . . . achieve a mythic status" (Gilroy 1987b:118). A seemingly casual racialization serves to establish the boundaries of propriety. When the dangerous minority are referred to in terms of nationality, race, or ethnicity, they easily coalesce into an all-encompassing Other "them" who threaten "us." For example, an article about the decline of the Mafia concluded with this warning about new threats emerging to fill the void: "As well as the growing influence of the ruthless Russian gangs, Chinese Triads and Japanese yakusa compete for spoils. On the west coast of the United States, Korean gangs are active alongside Mexican organised crime collectives which recruit from the smaller street gangs of young disaffected Latinos" (Guardian, 4 January 1997, p. 2). Similarly, Newsweek (1988:21) identifies "black gangs, Hispanic gangs, Asian gangs and gangs drawn from specific nationality groups."

That this is something more than a matter of crime discourses becomes clear in a broader context. For example, Huntington's (in *Guardian,* 23 November 1996, p. 23) clash of civilizations thesis maintains that:

> Western people have far more in common with each other than they have with Asian, Middle Eastern or African people. . . . Promoting the coherence of the West means both preserving Western culture *within* the West and defining the limits *of* the West. [It] requires . . . controlling immigration from non-Western societies . . . and ensuring the assimilation into Western culture of the immigrants who are admitted.

Naturally, the view that the West has spread its civilizing values to the rest of the world has been contested. More notable for now is the view that all "non-Western" Others pose a threat to Western values and civilization, and the insinuation that the West was once (and, for Huntington, seemingly still is) undivided, before the "outsiders" came in. When the Other is characterized so comprehensively, the argument that the terms used refer only to a "tiny minority" seems rather ineffectual. For example, Thompson (1995a:5) prefaces his tale of *Gangland Britain* with the statement that "in every case, organised criminals make up only a fraction of a percentage of the population—[I] do not seek to tar every Jamaican, Colombian, Sicilian or Asian with the same brush, it [this book] merely focuses on the tiny underworld element within each group." But since the rest of his book concentrates on "ethnic" criminal enterprises and uses descriptions such as "Jamaicans" and "Asians," it is difficult to see precisely who is not being tarred by his brush.

I have argued that a number of crude clichés of yardies are propagated from a variety of sources. These representations have a peculiar cultural character that is questionable at best and probably better described as dangerous, particularly in the climate of culturalized racism that I mentioned at the outset. Representations of yardies are akin to cartoon images, and I will end by looking at some slippages or "dislocations" (Rattansi 1994) in the cartoonlike construction process. Postcolonial discourse analysis by writers such as Homi Bhabha has drawn attention to the chronic instabilities of racialized dichotomies. We have already seen that yardies are apparently impenetrable and unfathomable, while at the same time some police officers are treated as experts on yardie culture. The problem of this strangeness/familiarity dichotomy is mirrored in a number of other respects: yardies can be characterized as both dumb and wily, as simple and sophisticated, as uniquely foreign and as inheritors of an indigenous tradition. Yardies, on the one hand, appear to be driven by "elemental needs" to be violent, powerful, and sexually promiscuous. This "base" conception of them suggests a somewhat primal and uncivilized set of instincts. They are like the "primitive man

. . . [who] has little, if any, education and is of dull intelligence" (Swigert and Farrell 1977:19). Yardies like to make themselves conspicuous by wearing gaudy jewelry, posing for photographs with automatic guns "in bright colors," and being seen in BMWs. To the extent that all this makes them more visible, yardies are therefore obtuse—and simpletons. They act as if they are (still) in Kingston, Jamaica, unaware that such behavior could make them look more out of place than "at home." Yet it seems that their stupidity cannot be taken for granted, as "it is not unknown for them to feign low intelligence" (NDIU, undated) to trick police officers.

Similar contradictions surface. Yardies apparently operate in ways that are plain, even crude: "The workings of the group are very simple. They are after fast money which the drug market provides. Their violence, utilisation of firearms, ease of travel to escape detection all assist in perpetuating their operation" (Brennan 1994:14). Similarly, according to the NDIU: "The MO [Modus Operandi] used by the Yardies will not require a great deal of explanation, as the one crime they could never be accused of is 'subtlety.' With the aid of sound systems (discos), the Yardies infiltrate clubs [and] displace existing staff. The venue then becomes one more outlet for the sale of drugs." But all their naivete, lack of sophistication, and visibility does not seem to make them any easier to police. On the contrary, stories appear regularly about the police fighting considerable odds: "Police Fight to End the Yardie Reign of Terror" (*Sunday Times,* 1 August 1993, p. 5). "[Scotland] Yard revamp to beat gangland" (*Times,* 28 June 1993, p. 1). The "Jamaican posses are . . . a national problem. It is only through an unrelenting, unified and flexible approach by all levels of law enforcement that we can combat the threat of Jamaican posses" (RCMP 1988:29). For *Newsweek:* "Outmanned, outgunned and outspent, the cops are fighting back as best they can" (1988:26). Hence a view that yardies are disorganized and unlike professional criminals is forced to co-exist with an image of ultraprofessionalism in their use of "ruthless violence" and their ever-increasing sphere of influence and activities. In other paradoxical oppositions, yardies are "unique" but they are also "heirs" to an "indigenous" criminal tradition (see Sweeney 1989). And in trafficking cocaine they are economically rational, but in their lifestyles cultural dupes.

Processes of boundary construction are significant in revealing the contradictory ways in which race and crime are coded through culture. Although the divisions are not fixed, they are important when read in a wider political context of racialization and criminalization (for example, Keith 1993). The partitions serve as performative artifacts within particular narratives and practices, in which "it is the divisions themselves that are in a process of being consumed and reproduced" (Munro 1997:4).

POSTSCRIPT

An inquiry carried out for chief police officers in Britain (reported in the *Independent,* 12 January 1996, p. 4) found: "Contrary to previous reports, organisations such as Triads, the Mafia, Yardies and Russian criminals, pose little national threat. . . . The report also says that the powers of foreign-influenced outfits are greatly exaggerated, particularly with Jamaican 'Yardie' gangsters."

ACKNOWLEDGMENTS

My thanks to Jeff Ferrell, Neil Websdale, and Steven Groarke for helpful suggestions on an earlier draft. None of them should be held responsible for any errors in this chapter.

NOTES

1. In contrast, Ruggiero (1995) has argued that, to the extent that the illicit economy mirrors the structure of the licit economy, we would expect blacks in the main to be at the lower end of criminal hierarchies, just as they mostly are in the legitimate world. This makes the visibility of black drug sellers in some streets and areas understandable without resorting to a culturalist explanation.

2. In contrasting "the West" with the Orient, Said can be accused of homogenizing the former and obscuring its own fractures and fissures (Rattansi 1994).

3. The ACMD is a body made up of a variety of experts on drugs. It was established under the 1971 Misuse of Drugs Act to advise the government on aspects of drug policy.

4. There is a broadly similar distinction made in the United States, where Asians (albeit from Southeast Asia rather than the Indian subcontinent, as in Britain) are seen as a "model minority," placing them above "underclass" blacks and Latinos in a racial hierarchy.

5. There are two other books in the series: *Excess* (1993) and *Yush!* (1994). In them Headley acknowledges criticism of him for glamorizing drugs and guns.

6. The difficulties are not resolved by the idea from constitutive criminology of seeking to insert a "truer" picture or "replacement discourses" (Barak 1995).

7. These figures apply to England and Wales only. They are for deaths initially recorded as homicides, some of which are later reclassified. For instance, of the 681 offenses first recorded in 1996, 54 were not regarded as homicides by 1997. Homicide includes murder, manslaughter, and infanticide, the latter being significant as children aged less than one are most at risk. (Source: *Home Office 1997.*)

8.   Previously Mike Bennett, chairman of the Metropolitan Police Federation, said on a TV program that some members of the black community posed the greatest threat to law and order. When he was criticized for this, he said that he meant yardies ("Sane Policing Is Going out of the Window," *Daily Mail,* 6 May 1994).

9.   This quote is from an interview with a senior officer from the National Drugs Intelligence Unit. The NDIU was established as a central intelligence point for information about drugs. In 1992 it was absorbed into the National Criminal Intelligence Service, which has a wider function (Dorn et al. 1992).

10.   It is important to avoid the simple replacement of one broad brush approach with another. While most of the police and journalistic works I make use of are indistinguishably similar, there is reason to believe that the police response should not be seen as homogeneous or undifferentiated. Some officers both in localities and centrally played down the idea of yardies as a black mafia (Keith 1993; Small 1995).

11.   As an example of the tautological nature of yardie discourse, consider this remark by the head of Operation Dalehouse: "They [yardies] have a philosophy that it is a short life but a sweet one" (quoted in Campbell 1994:260).

12.   Small (1995:391) describes Brennan as "one of the world's leading authorities" on the subject of Jamaican criminals.

13.   Small (1995) mentions that the Jamaican embassy in London expressed concerns about the blanket catchall representation of yardies.

14.   There are indications of an internal struggle within the police. The shooting of a beat/patrol officer in south London in October 1993 was widely reported as linked to yardies/a crack or drugs deal that he had interrupted. This led some officers to complain that the Metropolitan Police had closed its crack intelligence unit too soon; alternatively, other officers said that antidrug operations had increased even if the specialist response to crack had been scaled down. They also argued that levels of drug-related violence were low, especially compared to the United States (see *Guardian,* 23 October 1993, p. 3).

15.   Similarly an ATF agent says "Jamaican crime activity . . . [has] moved right into the mainstream and they are very difficult to infiltrate" (quoted in *Narcotics Control Digest,* 3 July 1991, p. 5).

16.   For instance: "Yard warning to drug gangs: Met chief acts over crack wars on streets" (*Evening Standard,* 22 October 1993, p. 1).

17.   See also "Crimes and Misdemeanors" (*Guardian,* 29 April 1993), in which a New York district attorney says that, as the mafia declines, gang power "is shifting to the Colombian cartels, to the unbelievably violent Jamaican posses, to the street-level Dominicans."

18.   Included among these ironic consequences are mobilizations for law and order among black communities (see Murji 1998:Chapter 7). Other examples are mentioned in *Newsweek* (1988) and Dorn and Murji (1992).

19.   Another T-shirt twisted the storyline by depicting a white male police officer in riot gear with the words "New Scotland Yardie."

20.   Similarly, an officer in London's Chinatown expressed reluctance to see all or any criminal activity there as a sign of Triad activity, because "I was conscious of the enhancing effect the term 'Yardie' had on the street credibility of low-level drug

dealers and street thugs in north and south London council estates." (quoted in *Police Review,* 21 June 1991, p. 1261).

REFERENCES

Baker, Philip. 1994. *Blood Posse.* London: Picador.

Barak, Gregg. 1995. "Media, Crime, and Justice: A Case for Constitutive Criminology." Pp. 142–66 in *Cultural Criminology,* edited by J. Ferrell and C. R. Sanders. Boston: Northeastern University Press.

Barker, Martin. 1981. *The New Racism.* London: Junction.

Benson, Susan. 1996. "Asians Have Culture, West Indians Have Problems." Pp. 47–56 in *Culture, Identity and Politics,* edited by T. Ranger et al. Aldershot: Avebury.

Bourgois, Phillippe L. 1995. *In Search of Respect.* Cambridge: Cambridge University Press.

Brennan, John. 1994. "'The Yardies'—Organised Crime in Our Own Backyards." Pp. 14–16 in *Drugs and Criminality.* Report of ACPO National Drugs Conference. London: ACPO.

Brownstein, Henry H. 1995. "The Media and the Construction of Random Drug Violence." Pp. 45–65 in *Cultural Criminology,* edited by J. Ferrell and C. R. Sanders. Boston: Northeastern University Press.

Campbell, Duncan. 1994. *The Underworld.* London: BBC Books.

Chambliss, William J. 1994. "Policing the Ghetto Underclass." *Social Problems* 41:177–94.

Clutterbuck, Richard L. 1990. *Terrorism, Drugs and Crime in Europe after 1992.* London: Routledge.

Clutterbuck, Richard L. 1995. *Drugs, Crime and Corruption.* Basingstoke: Macmillan.

Davies, Nick. 1996. "Yard's Yardie Is Too Hot to Handle." *Guardian,* May 1, p. 7.

Davies, Nick. 1997. "Police Yardie Scandal" and "How the Yardies Duped the Yard." *Guardian,* February 3, pp. 1, 2–4.

Davison, John. 1997. *Gangsta: The Sinister Spread of Yardie Gun Culture.* London: Vision.

Dorn, Nicholas and Karim Murji. 1992. *Drug Prevention.* London: ISDD.

Dorn, Nicholas, Karim Murji, and Nigel South. 1992. *Traffickers: Drug Markets and Law Enforcement.* London: Routledge.

Ferrell, Jeff and Clinton R. Sanders. 1995. "Toward a Cultural Criminology." Pp. 297–326 in *Cultural Criminology,* edited by J. Ferrell and C. Sanders. Boston: Northeastern University Press.

Gilroy, Paul. 1987a. *There Ain't No Black in the Union Jack.* London: Hutchinson.

Gilroy, Paul. 1987b. "The Myth of Black Criminality." Pp. 107–20 in *Law, Order and the Authoritarian State,* edited by P. Scraton. Milton Keynes, UK: Open University Press.

Gilroy, Paul. 1993. *Small Acts.* London: Serpents Tail.

Giroux, Henry A. 1996. *Fugitive Cultures.* New York: Routledge.

Goldberg, David. 1993. "Polluting the Body Politic." Pp. 45–60 in *Racism, the City and the State,* edited by M. Cross and M. Keith. London: Routledge

Griswold-Ezekoye, Stephanie. 1986. "The Multicultural Model in Chemical Abuse Prevention and Intervention." Pp. 203–29 in *Childhood and Chemical Abuse,* edited by S. Griswold-Ezekoye et al. New York: Haworth.

Hall, Stuart. 1992. "The West and the Rest." Pp. 275–320 in *Formations of Modernity,* edited by S. Hall and B. Gieben. Cambridge: Polity.

Hall, Stuart, Chas Critcher, Tony Jefferson, John Clarke, and Brian Roberts. 1978. *Policing the Crisis.* London: Macmillan.

Hawkins, Darnell. 1987. "Devalued Lives and Racial Stereotypes." Pp. 189–205 in *Violence in the Black Family,* edited by R. L. Hampton. Lexington: D.C. Heath.

Headley, Victor. 1992. *Yardie.* London: X Press.

Headley, Victor. 1993. *Excess.* London: X Press.

Headley, Victor. 1994. *Yush!.* London: X Press.

Helmer, John. 1975. *Drugs and Minority Oppression.* New York: Seabury.

Home Office. 1997. *Criminal Statistics, England and Wales, 1996.* London: Stationery Office.

Katz, Jack. 1988. *Seductions of Crime: Moral and Sensual Attractions in Doing Evil.* New York: Basic Books.

Keith, Michael. 1993. *Race, Riots and Policing.* London: UCL.

Kendall, Raymond. 1990. "The International Problem of Criminal Gangs." *International Criminal Police Review,* March–April, pp. 2–5.

Kohn, Marek. 1987. *Narcomania.* London: Faber & Faber.

Kohn, Marek. 1992. *Dope Girls.* London: Lawrence & Wishart.

Lash, Scott and John Urry. 1994. *Economies of Signs and Space.* London: Sage.

Metropolitan Police. 1989. "Memorandum of Evidence." Pp. 47–50 in *Drug Trafficking and Related Serious Crime.* Report of the Home Affairs Committee, Vol. II. London: HMSO.

Miller, Jerome. 1996. *Search and Destroy.* Cambridge: Cambridge University Press.

Munro, Rolland. 1997. "Ideas of Difference." Pp. 3–24 in *Ideas of Difference,* edited by K. Hetherington and R. Munro. Oxford: Blackwell.

Murji, Karim. 1998. *Policing Drugs.* Aldershot: Ashgate.

Musto, David F. 1973. *The American Disease: Origins of Narcotic Control.* Oxford: Oxford University Press.

NDIU. Undated. "Black Organised Crime—The Yardies." Unpublished internal report, National Drugs Intelligence Unit, United Kingdom.

Newsweek. 1988. "The Drug Gangs." *Newsweek,* March 28, pp. 20–27.

Pitts, John. 1993. "Thereotyping." Pp. 96–117 in *Racism and Criminology,* edited by D. Cook and B. Hudson. London: Sage.

Rattansi, Ali. 1994. "Western Racisms, Ethnicities and Identities." Pp. 15–86 in *Racism, Modernity and Identity,* edited by A. Rattansi and S. Westwood. Cambridge: Polity.

RCMP. 1988. *Monthly Digest of Drug Intelligence Trends.* October. Ottawa: Author.

Read, Mel and Alan Simpson. 1991. *Against a Rising Tide.* Nottingham: Spokesman.

Reinarman, Craig and Harry G. Levine. 1989. "The Crack Attack." Pp. 115–37 in *Images of Issues,* edited by J. Best. Hawthorne, NY: Aldine de Gruyter.

Ruggiero, Vincenzo. 1995. "Drug Economics." *Capital and Class* 55:131–50.

Shapiro, Harry. 1994. "The Crack Report." *Druglink,* September/October.

Silverman, Jon. 1994. *Crack of Doom.* London: Headline.

Skellington, Richard. 1996. *"Race" in Britain Today,* 2nd edition. London: Sage.

Small, Geoff. 1995. *Ruthless: The Global Rise of the Yardies.* London: Warner.

Stanley, Christopher. 1996. *Urban Excess and the Law.* London: Cavendish.

Stutman, Robert. 1989. "Crack Stories from the States." *Druglink,* September/October, pp. 7–9.

Sweeney, John. 1989. "Heirs to the Krays." *Observer,* June 25, pp. 25–30.

Swigert, Victoria Lynn and Ronald A. Farrell. 1977. "Normal Homicides and the Law." *American Sociological Review* 42:16–32.

Taylor, Ian, Karen Evans, and Penny Fraser. 1996. *A Tale of Two Cities.* London: Routledge.

Thompson, Tony. 1995a. *Gangland Britain.* London: Hodder & Stoughton.

Thompson, Tony. 1995b. "Yardies: Myth and Reality." *Guardian,* September 19, p. 5.

Watney, Simon. 1987. *Policing Desire.* London: Methuen

Woodiwiss, Michael. 1988. *Crime, Crusades and Corruption.* London: Pinter.

10

Punky in the Middle
Cultural Constructions of the 1996 Montréal Summer Uprisings (A Comedy in Four Acts)

LAURAINE LEBLANC

In the summer of 1996, the Montréal street population, including its punk community, twice rose up in defiance of the police: the first time, punks allegedly pillaged shops; the second, they occupied a public park after hours, resulting in over seventy arrests. These uprisings,[1] characterized as "riots" in some media coverage, punctuated mounting tension between street kids and police throughout the summer. As the rest of the world geared up for an Atlanta Olympic summer, the game of "monkey-in-the-middle"[2]— in which punks, police, and politicians (always under the watchful eye of the media), hurled and dodged accusations and blame—occupied the street kids and the police at the site of the 1976 Olympics. This game, however, had less to do with the Olympics' "power of the dream" and more with the power of social authorities in constructing attributions of deviance.

In the immediate aftermath of these events, various claims-makers pointed fingers through the medium of print journalism. Punks denounced extreme leftist anarchist groups for capitalizing on tensions between punks and police. Investigative journalists argued that the police instigated the events at the root of these uprisings. Columnists blamed bar owners, the police, and politicians. City councillors argued that the mayor's laxness was the source of ongoing tensions. In the end, however, media constructions of punks as the key players in the uprisings meant that punks bore the brunt of the blame. Montréal newspapers featured front-page pictures of broken shop windows and bizarrely coifed protesters, while the metropolitan sections of the newspapers investigated the punk lifestyle, and editorial columnists weighed in with their analyses of the uprisings. Through a process of accusation by media attention, the print media constructed these events as a "punk problem."

In this chapter, I explore the ways in which the major francophone print source of the city of Montréal, *La Presse,* chronicled these events. (Refer to Table 10.1 for a timeline of events and reports.) To do so, I construct this

Table 10.1.   Timeline of Events and Reports

Date	Event	Report
May 17	Police arrest punks, and others "riot" along boulevard St-Laurent	
May 19		"Punks Wreak Havoc" characterizes events as a "riot," on front page
May 21		"The Riot on the Main" presents punks' point-of-view
May 22		Columnist Pietrowski's "The Squeegees Counter-Attack" blames everyone but punks
May 26		"Zero Tolerance for Punks" features police in riot gear
May 31		"Curfew at Place Emilie-Gamelin" reports on rezoning of Berri Square and on petition against this (does not mention punks)
July 10		"Increased Police Presence at Berri Square" reports community policing and punks' fears of police repression
July 26	Punks hold a car wash, raising $1,180 to repay uninsured store owners	
July 27		"Punk Car Wash" photo runs on front page "Car Wash for Forgiveness" foreshadows second uprising at later protest
July 29	Food Not Bombs protest against rezoning of Berri Square results in over 75 arrests	
July 30		"The Conflict Grows" characterizes the second uprising as a "demonstration" Columnist Lavigne's "Which Is Your Gang?" favorably compares punk lifestyle to yuppie lifestyle
July 31		"Agitators at the Root of Sunday Night Mayhem at Former Berri Square" reports punks' contention that "Démanarchie" was at the root of conflicts with police "Beating Police at Their Own Game" reports punks tape-recording police Gravel's editorial "The Real Victims" points the finger at Bourque's administration

(continued)

Table 10.1. (*Continued*)

Date	Event	Report
August 3		"Black Hair, Green Thoughts" explores punk authenticity "There is Punk . . . and Punk" introduces the permutations of punk "Smack and Death" documents ravages of heroin and antidrug lobbies in punk "Forbidden Grass" summarizes the events of the past summer
August 14		"Former Berri Square: A Clean-Up That Left Stains" reports the police origin of the "merchants'" petition

study of media construction of crime and deviance as a play in four acts involving four players: the city administration, the police, the media, and the punks. In presenting journalistic coverage of the happenings of that summer, I analyze these texts and examine how such reports established successive culpabilities by alternately casting each group of actors as the guilty party. I argue that such coverage suggests an alternative to the attribution of media as prime instigators of "moral panics" (Cohen [1972] 1980). Using this single media source, I construct a case study of the ways that complex interactions between media, police, and community members construct marginal youths as "folk devils" (ibid.). Further, expanding on Angela McRobbie and Sarah Thornton's (1995) work on moral panics in a multi-mediated world, I examine the ways in which multiple voices within media sources can simultaneously undermine constructions of authority and collude with them in constructing subcultural deviance as a social problem. The game is afoot . . .

MISE-EN-SCÈNE

The action unfolded in Montréal, a city of roughly two million inhabitants located on an island in the St. Laurent Seaway in Québec, Canada. Built on an extinct volcano, Mont Royal, the city had seen its share of flare-ups: the 1970s terrorist/revolutionary acts of the antifederalist séperatiste movements (Fédération de Libération du Québec) and the Stanley Cup riots of the late 1980s. This bilingual and multicultural city had also been the site of ongoing tensions, conflicts, and conflagrations between francophones and anglophones centering around the Québec national holiday of St-Jean-Baptiste (June 24) and Canada Day (one week later, July 1), as well as two referenda on provincial secession from Canada. To this inventory, Montréalers now added the "punk riots" of the summer of 1996.

THE CAST

The Administration of the Garden-City

Pierre Bourque, former director of the Montréal Botanical Garden, was elected mayor of the Montréal Urban Community (MUC) in 1994, coming to power partly on a promise of urban renewal and beautification—a promise to turn the city of winter into a summer garden. With the ongoing decline of the Canadian dollar and the postreferenda exodus of anglophone residents and businesses, Montréalers feared a loss of prosperity, recognized a rise in crime and homelessness, and wanted someone to clean up downtown. Certain areas of the city—the downtown corridors along Ste. Catherine street and boulevard St. Laurent, "the Main"—had long been colonized by the homeless, by artists and hippies, and by subcultural youths of all stripes. Small green spaces such as Carré St. Louis and Berri Square, areas of city parks (Parc Jeanne-Mance, Parc Lafontaine), and vacant lots and boarded-up buildings had for some time been the stomping grounds of punks, street musicians, and drug dealers, as well as shelter for runaways.

In cities all over the globe, youths and the homeless colonize such "marginal spaces," appropriating them for their underground economies, and employing them to construct everyday forms of resistance to subordination (Smith 1995). These geographical "cultural spaces" then become sources of contention for police and city administrators on one side, and for marginalized actors on the other (Ferrell 1997). The city seeks to obscure/obliterate the urban embarrassment of poverty and dissent, while squatters and other folk try to retain their sole source of resistance and place of shelter (their accommodations). Until recently, this appropriation of cultural space by Montréal's homeless and subcultural residents had been tolerated as another aspect of the vibrancy of this multicultural city. With the election of the gardener-mayor, this struggle to weed out these unwanted urban outgrowths had come to Montréal.

Montréal Urban Community Policing

Taking its cue from the success stories on the crackdown on "quality-of-life" crimes emerging from New York City, the Bourque administration, in its drive to clean up Montreal, strongly advocated proactive or "community" policing. Originating in the late 1980s, community policing functions by

> (1) diagnosing and managing problems in the community that produce serious crimes; (2) fostering closer relations with the community to facilitate crime solving; and (3) building self-defense capabilities within the community itself. (Moore, Trojanowicz, and Kelling 1988:2)

Note that this definition does not state, nor does it imply, that community policing occurs in response to the needs of "the community." Rather, this process simply begins with the police "diagnosing" problems in the community, thus providing police with broad discretionary powers. Communication with this community merely comes into play during the "management" of such problems—crime solving and self-defense. Because such community policing is based on addressing potentially criminogenic situations, it broadens the mandate of police to address any number of social ills—most often interpreted in the embodiment of social undesirables—before they (inevitably?) lead to crime. In response to Bourque's call for a cleaner downtown, the Montréal Urban Community police adopted such a strategy of community policing.

The Media and the Medium

The role of the media in detecting and constructing deviance is well-documented.[3] As a central actor in interpreting public perceptions and opinions, the media play an important role in defining deviance and enforcing social controls. Through the routinized practices of news reporting—finding a story, interviewing regular sources, writing in a journalistic style—news media ideologically buttress relations of ruling, supporting the hegemonic power structure of the society in which they are embedded. When pursuing news stories, reporters not only rely upon their own "objective" observations, but upon "sources." The legitimacy of these sources' social standing determines their reliability; thus as media rely upon elite sources, they both draw legitimization from and legitimate these as authorities—a circular process of authority production (Sigal 1986). In cases involving deviance, the media thus privilege the voices of those in "legitimate" institutions (i.e., police, psychiatrists, politicians) over those of "deviant" actors.

The role of news media in both shaping and representing public perception and action is most clearly shown in reportage of deviance, and especially of subcultural youth deviance (Sanders 1990). Critical perspectives on crime and deviance have therefore focused especially on the study of news media constructions of, and community responses to, such deviance. Stan Cohen's ([1972] 1980) ground-breaking analysis of the "moral panic" incited by news reports of British beachfront clashes between Mods and Rockers in 1964 still stands as the standard for such research. In documenting the ways in which discourses of authority (media, judiciary, community) represented these events, Cohen showed that these authorities colluded in exaggerating the events' seriousness, all the while ensuring the continuation and dissemination of such deviance. Cohen's study thus presented a model that highlights the ways in which social authorities and media cooperate in the construction of deviance. This perspective has recently been further augmented in such works as Jeff Ferrell's (1996) *Crimes of Style,* Clint Sanders's (1990) *Marginal Conventions,* Ferrell and Sanders's (1995) *Cultural Criminology,* and the present volume.

Spectacular forms of subcultural deviance served as fodder for the Montréal media in the summer of 1996. These events, occurring on the east— primarily French-speaking—side of the city and involving both francophone punks and authorities, garnered much more attention from the francophone than from the anglophone press. Montréal is currently served by three francophone newspapers: *Le Journal de Montréal,* a colorful tabloid-style paper catering mainly to working-class readers; *Le Devoir,* a "higher-end" paper catering to the upper and upper-middle class; and *La Presse,* the main paper serving the island of Montréal and its suburbs. Like many of its anglophone and American counterparts, *La Presse* offers a full-size layout, multiple sections (i.e., local news, world news, living, travel, sports), and a full-color front page, as well as a full-color weekend comics section. All of these papers offered coverage of the 1996 summer uprisings, with *La Presse* proffering the most copious coverage.[4]

The Punk Monkeys

The final and most visible player in these events of summer 1996 was the punk subculture of Montréal. Originating as a music-based subculture in the mid-1970s, punk has always presented itself as an oppositional youth subculture, one remarkable for its use of stylistic innovation in the creation of tools of "sartorial terrorism" (Carter 1992) with which to wage its "semiotic guerilla warfare" (Hebdige 1979) against mainstream culture. Wearing their unnaturally colored hair in gravity-defying mohawks, sporting deliberately torn T-shirts, bondage gear, and black leather, cursing, spitting, and vomiting in public, punks constructed a mass affront to dominant cultural mores, and created a "reflexive" subculture challenging nearly everyone's sartorial, vocational, political, and moral norms (Levine and Stumpf 1983). After "enjoying" a brief term of media attention and fashion co-optation in the late 1970s, the punk subculture returned underground in the 1980s, reinventing itself as "hardcore." By the 1990s, punk had made its way around the globe and developed a number of variants. The most remarkable of these was a schism between the generic "punk rockers" espousing the original brightly colored fashions and ideologies, and "gutter punks," itinerant youths more intent on hopping trains, dumpster diving, and squatting in abandoned buildings than on maintaining the proper punk "look."

The Montréal punk scene differs little from scenes anywhere in North America. Overwhelmingly anglophone in its early stages in the 1970s, the Montréal punk scene today is almost entirely French-speaking. As in other scenes, the 1990s saw the emergence of gutter punks in Montréal, with runaway and throwaway kids adopting the muted khakis, grays, and blacks of the gutter punk style, as well as gutter punk activities and lifestyle. Thus, like other North Americans, Montréalers are treated to the spectacle of gutter punks panhandling, hanging out, squatting, sleeping in parks, and washing car windshields for spare change. Unbeautiful and unwanted, these punks were not public flora of the garden city (not "the flowers in your dustbin" of the Sex Pistols' anthem "God Save the Queen"), but rather public fauna: noisome, bothersome beasts, pigeons without wings, squirrels without charm. Something had to be done

ACT 1: LET THE GAMES BEGIN

Scene 1: The "Riot"

It was Friday night, May 17 1996, and the Bar SO Cafe, a popular punk hangout, was hosting a show. More punks than could fit into the venue had come, and they milled about outside. Mingling with the crowd, four plain-clothes police officers attempted to arrest two punks who had outstanding fines for the offense of "squeegeeing"—washing car windshields for spare change (actually, the charge was obstruction of traffic). Seeing their friends stuffed into police cruisers, a number of punks left the show and protested. The next day, the major media outlets in Montréal reported that 250 punks poured down boulevard St. Laurent, vandalizing forty businesses and damaging fourteen civilian-owned vehicles and three police cars. One hundred and fifty police officers were called out to quell the "riot." One police officer and the doorman of Bar SO Cafe were slightly injured. Nine punks were arrested.

This news made the front page of the Sunday, May 19, edition of *La Presse,* with the headline "Punks Wreak Havoc—[Mayor] Bourque Promises That Bars Will Be Closely Monitored" (Gervais 1996) accompanied by a photograph of a shattered storefront window. The article immediately characterized the events of the weekend as a "riot" (using the word "*émeute*"), invoking images of random violence, terrorism, and mob mentality. Accordingly, the article focused first on the damage incurred, featuring interviews with shop owners. Mohammed Fenni, proprietor of a crafts shop, compared the uprising to the sack of Rome: "It's discouraging, we work hard for a living and we are sacked and robbed by vandals. Besides the damages to my window, they stole works worth many thousands of dollars" (ibid.). The front-page coverage in *La Presse* then turned to the response of city government; assigning blame, the area's council member, Michael Prescott, pointed to the mayoral administration: "There are almost 75 bars in my district, that's too many. Yesterday, it was punks, but often it's 'clean-cut' people who are a little too drunk who holler and vandalize" (ibid.).[5] In the same article, the mayor responded by reassuring store owners that the bars would be more closely monitored.

Thus, in this initial report of the first punk uprising, *La Presse* had already characterized the acts of the punks as a "riot." However, the blame on punks for this incident had been somewhat attenuated by the brinkmanship of the city councillor and the mayor, and further calls for action centered on city zoning (fewer bars) and better policing (closely monitoring bars). The construction of the events, therefore, led to a number of potential leads into follow-up stories: the bar scene was out of control; some city councillors were at odds with the mayor; shopkeepers were recovering their losses; police would monitor bars more closely. However, *La Presse* followed up on none of these leads—as it turned out, it was not the bars that were more closely monitored . . .

Scene 2: Making Meaning

Two days after the initial report of the uprising, *La Presse* followed up not by investigating the city's admitted difficulties in regulating bars, but by investigating the local punks—surely a more interesting, marketable target. A third-page article appeared on May 21, "The Riot on the Main—A 'Squeegee Revolt'?" (Pineau 1996), running under a photograph of a menacing mohawked male punk grimacing and gripping a squeegee. The body of the article, however, was less sensationalistic, reporting that entrepreneurial punks desirous of making money in order to eat, drink, and be merry had taken to the streets of Montréal armed with squeegees, making up to ten dollars an hour washing windshields and encountering police repression.

Interviewing punks for the first time, *Le Presse* reporter Yann Pineau ultimately took a more sympathetic tack than did the original articles on the "riot." Pineau's article began by referring to these events: "Since Friday night's riot on St. Laurent, a certain animosity reigns between the MUC police and the Montréal punks. But the increasing number of squeegee virtuosi (the rubber broom used to wash car windows) adds fuel to the fire" (ibid.). He continued in an expository vein: "In fact, for several months, the police have been much more strict with the punks who, for a few dollars, wash windshields at certain street corners in the city. The fines for obstructing traffic are commonplace, and rare are the punks who can pay the hundreds of dollars it costs each time they are caught by the police" (ibid.). Pineau then interviewed punks on their perceptions of the events said to have precipitated the uprising: "I got three [fines] in one month," said one. Another added: "When you have a warrant (for arrest following an unpaid fine) and they catch you, you spend two or three days inside [jail]. . . . I'd rather that than pay, plus they feed you, but it costs the government a lot of money for nothing!" (ibid.).

Remarkably, Pineau's piece for *La Presse* not only drew on punks as sources, but on a spokesperson for a subcultural organization as well. Alain Dufour, head of the local grassroots political group of punks (Ligue Antifasciste Mondiale, or World Anti-Fascist League) argued that the punks' disaffection was understandable, predictable, and would be repeated unless authorities began to respect their cultural space:

> We can expect further incidents of this type. . . . Saturday night, I saw police officers giving tickets to all the punks they encountered, with the excuse that they weren't moving along. If the police decide to start an all-out war against them, it won't be over soon. We're miles from community policing! Punks defy authority and we're seeing an upsurge in the movement. 'No Future' [a nihilistic punk catch phrase from a Sex Pistols' lyric] is stronger than ever. (ibid.)

Dufour called for police to find solutions "other than repression," a sentiment echoed in the conclusion of the article by council member Michael Prescott, who called for the establishment of a "police-punk committee" and demanded a report from the Public Safety Commission concerning Friday's uprising.

This foray into punk culture began by explicitly linking the uprising of May 17 to the punk subculture, thus casting the issue as a "punk problem." This representation, coupled with the lack of follow-up articles on bar monitoring or city politics, clearly cast punks as central players in this uprising, explicitly linking fines for obstructing traffic to the uprising of May 17. However, the tone of the article was not condemnatory, but rather sympathetic. Pineau gave voice to the punks, allowing them to air their interpretation of "police repression" without calling on any police representative, for example, to explicate the "punk menace" or to describe the police's intent in leveling fines against and imprisoning squeegeeing punks. In addition, the punks' own calls for freedom from police repression played nicely into more mainstream advocacy for free market economy and lessened taxpayer burdens. Thus, paradoxically, while this article explicitly constructed punks as the deviant causes of the "riot," it also humanized members of the subculture and allowed them media access with which to denounce their perceived oppression, and in turn to legitimate their actions on May 17. Thus, *La Presse* simultaneously vilified the punk "rioters" and presented the other side of the story from the subcultural sources themselves. This early attribution of blame was cemented in the article by the inclusion of city councillor Prescott's call for the establishment of a "police-punk committee" (the aim of which was probably not to facilitate *punks'* monitoring of police!), firmly casting urban uprisings as a direct result of subcultural deviance.

The next day, the media's more sympathetic vein continued in an editorial by regular columnist Natalie Petrowski, who liberally assigned blame to all parties involved—save the punks!

> First of all, the Friday night riot, as all riots, including the [1986] Stanley Cup riot, is the work of a minority of hotheads and morons, a breed we find as often among the punks as we do among beer drinkers, bridge players, golfers, and Denver boot installers.
>
> Friday night's riot is also the work of a booker of punk shows, who rented an overly small venue.
>
> Friday night's riot, finally, is the fault of the cops who endlessly hunt squeegeers and stick them with fines. . . .
>
> If [punks] frighten Mr. and Mrs. Average, who have never seen anything in all their lives, we should offer Mr. and Mrs. Average an introductory course in urban living at the end of the millennium. And, finally, if, as some claim, the squeegeers bang up car hoods when their tips are too small, let's point them out to the cops and leave the rest alone.
>
> Punks and other squeegeer types maybe choose to be different, but that's no reason to blame them for all sorts of things. (Petrowski 1996)

This second wave of reporting and editorializing, this processing and interpreting of events, ultimately contradicted the original *La Presse* coverage of the uprising. Whereas the original account focused on officials' reactions and store owners' lamentations, the inclusion of punk voices in the second round added an element of "human interest," resulting in calls for tolerance and understanding. Further, as a columnist rather than a reporter, Petrowski was able to criticize police and politicians, upon whom she was not dependent for sources.

Thus, the reports immediately following the initial report of May 19 presented yet another aspect of mediated contradiction: the way that different voices in a single media outlet can both legitimate and criticize authorities. Nonetheless, in focusing on the punks' experiences of police repression the media began to cement the perception of these uprisings as a "punk problem." Rather than focusing on the lead from the first story—the city's liberal granting of bar permits, or the police's mismanagement of the Friday night crowd—*La Presse,* while ultimately sympathetic to the punks, published follow-up pieces that explicitly linked the "riots" closely to the punks. Why did *La Presse* choose to follow this lead, rather than its leads on police and municipal blunders? Could it be that the punks really were at the root of the problem, or was it rather that misbehaving teenagers with shaved heads bearing slightly menacing squeegees make better copy? No matter how sympathetically these punks were depicted, *La Presse*'s decision to cast them, rather than police or politicians, at the center of the controversy would doubtless lead to further repercussions.

Scene 3:   The Crackdown

La Presse's focus on the punk players in these scenes extended into its reporting on police efforts to prevent further uprisings. Thus, on page A3 of the May 26 edition of *La Presse,* a photograph of eight police officers in riot gear—helmets on heads, nightsticks in hands—ran with the caption:

> The Montréal Urban Community police is not laughing, and did not appreciate that some 250 punks swept over Boulevard St. Laurent last week, attacking around forty businesses along their way. In order to prevent any repetition of these events, the police kept an eye out for trouble on Friday to Saturday night on Rachel Street and boulevard St. Laurent, not far from the bar frequented by punks. No one was arrested, but many punks were persuaded to quickly vacate the area. (*La Presse* 1996)

This photograph ran under the headline, "Zero Tolerance for the Punks," casting punks as some sort of dangerous substance in its echo of "zero tolerance" drug enforcement practices. The deployment of these riot-geared officers, and its media coverage, reflected a nonevent: there were no further riots, and the most that could be said is that some citizens were "persuaded" to abandon their Friday night leisure.

As it cited no police spokesperson and ran without an accompanying article, it remains unclear from this caption whether the rhetorical link between punks and riots was still the work of the paper, or whether this imagined relationship was now the focus of the police's efforts as well. What *La Presse* interpreted as zero tolerance for punks might indeed have been the police's response to Mayor Bourque's call for closer monitoring of bars. The only indication that punks were the targets of this riot-geared police contingent was the newspaper's report that punks were "persuaded" to leave the area, without mention of any other persons likewise "persuaded." The police were not quoted as stating that their intent was to police punks exclusively, but what this caption, this headline, and the accompanying photograph clearly illustrated was that police efforts at protecting the public were perceived to be directed toward punks, rather than toward bar patrons in general. Running counter to the leads of its original report, *La Presse* now firmly interpreted and constructed the uprisings of May 17 not as a problem of policing nor as one of city mismanagement, but rather as one of deviant, possibly dangerous, youth.

Scene 4:   From Dangerous to Ludicrous

The punks' next move was (perhaps) unintentionally ironic: in a heartfelt effort to raise money to reimburse local shopkeepers for the damage incurred in the uprising, the very youths who had been harassed for washing windshields, who had been vilified for smashing cars, now made up for it by . . . holding a car wash. On July 27, over two months after the initial events, the punks made the front page of *La Presse* again, this time with the headline "Punk Car Wash" (Guay 1996) accompanying a photograph of the ubiquitously squeegee-wielding male punk. The accompanying page 3 article, "Car Wash for Forgiveness" (Clément 1996), related that the event had been engineered by a youth group overseen by an organization that feeds the homeless. The article stated that the punks "wanted to show that not all these kids are 'bums': they may do stupid things, but they can also be generous" (ibid.). The punks raised $1,180 to help uninsured local merchants recoup their losses. This met with some gratitude, but more trepidation; shop owner Mohammed Fenni, who had been interviewed in the May 17 article, was again quoted, admitting that this was "a good action," all the while adding a cautionary note: "They are honest. . . . But we can't turn back the clock. It's regrettable. I hope they won't do it again, because it's discouraging. The day before yesterday, a neighboring business had its window broken" (ibid.).

This report on the punks' attempts to make amends for the damages incurred during the riots underscored the attribution of responsibility. Thus, while initial reports had blamed the city's laxness, the police's ineptitude, and bar owner's irresponsibility, only the punks were reported making reparations. In addition, the article, while celebrating the punks' act of contrition, still cast punks as deviants, reporting that "not *all* these kids are 'bums'" and printing Fenni's implication that punks were now to be suspects in any act of vandalism in the area. This cautionary tone was especially reinforced at the article's conclusion, which stated that the group Food Not Bombs had organized a rally to be held the following night in order to protest a curfew instituted at Berri Square. Once again, tensions between merchants and punks had been growing, with *La Presse* stating that the city's curfew had been imposed "ever since the bordering business owners complained about

the presence of 'the punks' near their stores" (ibid.). Thus, an article reporting on an effort at reconciliation between the community and the vilified
punks ended by predicting further trouble: a curfew, a rally, and, possibly, a
protest? Would this lead to another "riot"? Once again, the punks' appropriation of cultural space, this time not the street corners of the underground
squeegee economy but a public park, was being contested. Can you say
"foreshadowing"?

ACT 2:   THE PEACE BETWEEN THE WARS

Scene 1:   Get Them Where They Live

In the interstice between the first uprising and the car wash of contrition
(see timeline in Table 10.1), city administrators had been at work, but not,
once again, monitoring bars, as they had promised. Instead, Bourque's
beautification plan had again targeted the cultural space of the punks, rezoning Berri Square, a popular punk hangout. Berri Square used to be a
smallish green space in the heart of the East side of the city's business
district, surrounded by bank headquarters, a university, government offices,
mall entrances—the concrete buttresses of modern capitalism. It offered a
balm for the bank teller's fluorescent-irradiated eye, a salve for the bureau-
crat's cubicle-enclosed soul, a space for the store clerk to grab a quick
smoke, and a haven for the homeless punk to hang out and sleep. The space
itself was still there, physically unchanged, but with one stroke of the
mayor's pen it had been reconceptualized into a park, Place Emilie-
Gamelin.

This seemingly minor change to the city's urban plan was initially reported in a short article on page A3 of *La Presse* on May 31, 1996. Unaccompanied by photographs, and nowhere using the word "punk," the short
article "Curfew at Place Emilie-Gamelin" (Laberge 1996) simply stated that
the "regulars" would henceforth be denied access from midnight to six A.M.
Prior to this, as Berri Square was not a park, it had no closing time. Because
it had no closing time, "the ordinances governing public parks, notably that
which prohibits entry between midnight and six A.M., did not apply, and
police were unable to drive out the fauna[!] which occupies it at night"
(ibid.). Sammy Forcillo, city council member representing the neighborhood
surrounding the square, argued that the area was infested with prostitutes
and drug dealers at night. In the article, he was quoted as stating that "these
people" need professional attention, something that community organizations can provide with the assistance of police. He hastened to add: "We are
not asking the police to use strong-arm tactics. . . . Rather, we are asking

them to use preventative strategies" (ibid.). Thus, the first call for community policing of the area emerged in the voice of a city official.

However, in this same article Laberge quickly dispelled any appearance that this decision to rezone the area occurred in response to community needs; the article went on to add that the transformation of Berri Square into Place Emilie-Gamelin had been undertaken by the city council without consulting community members. Laberge reported that a petition denouncing the Bourque administration was being circulated. In part echoing Bourque's election-day botanical rhetoric, this read:

> What is the use of having a large beautiful garden if one cannot take advantage of it? . . . The status change will mean that police can issue fines to those who set foot in it to eat, skate, or walk their dogs. . . . In short . . . this decision was taken without consulting the park's users. Until they are consulted . . . the Bourque administration should back off. . . . We know that Mayor Bourque wants to turn Montréal into a garden . . . but that is no reason to take the ground out from under us! (ibid.)

The originators of this petition remained unnamed, but those in the know would recognize that it was the punks who made most frequent and active use of the park, and that it was they, not bourgeois dog walkers nor yuppie inline skaters, who would experience the greatest police harassment. Why did *La Presse* not choose to bring this to the attention of its readers? Why was the city's reappropriation of punks' cultural space not spelled out here, as it was in the later article on the punk car wash? The unnamed petition writers quoted in the article also implicitly challenged the notion of "community," the backbone of community policing: Who was the community? Was it the constituents ostensibly represented by Sammy Forcillo? Was it the local merchants whose businesses bordered the park? Was it the "fauna" who occupied the park? Once again, ironies abound: the namesake of the park, Emilie Gamelin, was an advocate for the homeless.

Scene 2:   Your Community Calling

Although punks were not explicitly named either by *La Presse*'s reporter or by the city administration in their decision to impose the park curfew, the city's intent seemed clear to the originators of the petition cited in the May 31 report: get rid of the verminous punks. The above-noted report on the punk car wash of July 27 stated that the curfew had been in the works "ever since the bordering business owners complained about the presence of 'the punks' near their stores" (Clément 1996). Over five weeks after the May 31 report on the rezoning, on July 10, *La Presse* reported "Increased Police Presence at Berri Square"[6], adding, "Youth Fear the Start of a 'Punk Hunt'"

(Grandmont 1996a). The article ran on page A4, accompanied by a photograph of police officers facing punks in the park, a sign of community policing: "Downtown Montréal police have adopted a more 'community-based' approach in dealing with the youth fauna[!] found particularly in Berri Square by assigning four police officers as of tomorrow" (ibid.). After weeks of discussing police motivations with regard to punks, *La Presse* finally turned to a source in the MUC police, quoting André Lemaire, adjunct commander of the local precinct: "One of the ways of dealing with the [punk?] problem is to always have the same officers on the same beat. . . . They will know the punks and the store owners and they will be able to create a sort of bridge between them and the other officers in the precinct" (ibid.). To this, Michel Beaudoin, precinct commander, was quoted as adding, "It will reassure the store owners, who will see one or two officers, and it will reassure the people who would like to go have a smoke in the park. . . . Maybe the people who will dare venture in there now will realize that these kids are not as dangerous as they thought" (ibid.). Apparently, one of the aims of community policing, according to the MUC sources cited in the article, was to provide buffers between ostensibly frightened citizens and others who pose no threat to them.

Grandmont concluded that police had no intention of initiating the "punk hunt" feared by youth. ("Although it may disappoint some shop owners," he added.) The article implied that police intended to initiate a conciliatory discourse, of sorts, quoting Lemaire once more: "Not all punks are trash. We have problems with a few people, but the vast majority of them are reasonable" (ibid.). The article also reflected punks' discomfort with this approach at community policing, citing one as fearing that "it is only a facade the better which to prepare a wave of repression" (ibid.). Grandmont turned, penultimately, to punks themselves: "How do you expect us to be friends with [the police] if they keep giving us fines at the drop of a hat?" (ibid.) Another added, "They'll come in here and in two weeks, there won't be anyone [punks] left because everyone will have gotten hassled" (ibid.). Commander Beaudoin, however, had the honor of the last word, asserting, "We try to avoid confrontation because it never pays. We are feeling our way through, there's no cookbook that tells you that when you have a hundred punks somewhere, you have to do this, this, and that" (ibid.).

The rhetoric of community policing reported in *La Presse* added another element to the construction of punk deviance: the point of view of the police. The language used by police was especially evocative. Police spokespersons stated that the officers "will know the punks and the store owners" and that the police presence would bring others to "realize that these kids are not as dangerous as they thought" and perhaps even bring community members to agree with the police point of view that "not all punks are trash"—damning punks by the faint praise that punks are not, in fact, actual devils. Commander Beaudoin's lament that "there's no cook-book that tells you that when you have a hundred punks somewhere, you have to do this, this, and that" underscores the police's intent to police *punks,* not the park itself. Thus, hidden behind the rhetoric of maintaining the peace—by fostering communication, by assuring the public that punks are not monsters, and by bridging the gap between punks and nonpunks (merchants and other park users)—is the assumption that punks are a threat, one that requires police intervention. The rhetoric of community policing evidenced in these quotes revealed an iron fist in an all-too-transparent velvet glove. The punks, who reported fears of further police repression, understood this, fearing that the rhetoric of community policing was little more than a further excuse for differential law enforcement, rather than an effort to encourage everyone to just get along.

ACT 3:   BLACK NIGHT, WHITE RIOT

Scene 1:   The Demonstration

It was midnight, Monday July 29, at Berri Square—no, Place Emilie-Gamelin—and punks had gathered at the behest of Food Not Bombs, and with police permission, for a civil action, a protest against the rezoning. For twenty days, the MUC police had "community policed" the park with its four "Officer Friendlys." Then, the second uprising—hinted at in *La Presse*'s coverage of the punk car wash two days before—broke out. The front page headline of *La Presse* (this time, unaccountably devoid of photographs) of July 30 read: "The Conflict Grows—Punks and Police Confront Each Other in the Middle of the Night at Former Berri Square" (Legault and Perreault 1996). The paper reported that some three hundred youths (only about half of them punks, despite the headline) had occupied Place Emilie-Gamelin that Monday night. Initially a protest organized by Food Not Bombs and authorized by the police, the event had been supervised by "a few dozen police officers from station 33, and others called in for reinforcements" (ibid.). The demonstration ostensibly turned ugly when police responded to the decision of some protesters to set a piece of wood on fire in the middle of a paved path around 5:00 A.M. With the police moving in, the protesters dispersed into the surrounding streets, where more police reportedly awaited them. Reporters Jean-Benoit Legault and Mathieu Perreault de-scribed the events of the following hour as punks playing "a game of hide-and-seek with the police force in the neighboring streets" (ibid.). They con-cluded: "Toward 5:30 A.M. [i.e., half an hour before the end of the curfew], the trap closed on the youths in the middle of the park" (ibid.). Seventy-seven protesters were arrested between 5:30 and 9:00 A.M., brought to the precinct, and issued fines of $115 "for having been in the park after closing" (ibid.).

Many immediately questioned the police's handling of the protest and of ensuing events. The same article that reported the demonstration and its aftermaths carried the protests of those arrested: "Those who wanted to go home had to play cat-and-mouse in order to get out of the quad. Of course, they had to return to the park, thus committing an offense" (ibid.). An attorney representing some protesters likewise added, "Indubitably, the Québec Code of Penal Procedures was not respected. In cases such as this, fines must be issued on site. Arrests are only called for in cases where there are problems in determining identification" (ibid.). The police retorted that arrests were required due to the difficulty of issuing so many citations at one time: "When the security of the people and of the park is imperiled, we must intervene" (ibid.). *La Presse* also cited other officers, who "maintain that in the presence of anarchists who have no respect for public property, a certain reaction is inevitable" (ibid.).

Perhaps more interesting than what *La Presse* reported was what it omitted. Unlike its accounts of the previous uprising, the newspaper refrained from describing this event as a "riot" ("*émeute*"), using, instead, the word "démonstration." In fact, the reporters twice referred to games—hide-and-seek, cat-and-mouse—when referring to the conflicts between police and protesters, casting the event as play, rather than as a potential danger to citizens. In addition, although seventy-seven protesters were arrested, this article failed to mention what (if any) actual percentage of those arrested were punks. Perhaps the most telling omission, however, was the failure of the newspaper, in this report, to refer to the "riot" of six weeks before. The July 27 report on the punk car wash had foreshadowed punks' involvement in this protest, linking the May 17 uprising to this later event. Yet, the reporting of the actual event made no reference to the May uprising. However, despite these omissions, *La Presse*'s coverage further instilled the sense of this second uprising as a "punk problem." In the headline and throughout the article, *La Presse* reporters described the adversaries of the police as punks, even though only about half of the protesters were punks, a fact that was stated only in the body of the text.

Scene 2: Pointing Fingers

Once again, as it had in the reports of May 21 ("Riot on the Main") and July 10 ("Increased Police Presence at Berri Square"), the tenor of *La Presse*'s coverage conflicted with authorities' depictions of the events. Rather than endorsing the MUC police's "law and order" attempts at "community policing," the newspaper produced coverage sympathetic to the punks, quoting them and their "representatives" in articles, as well as printing another columnist's (Lavigne 1996) favorable depiction of the punks' car wash of July 26. Further, *La Presse* sent reporter Charles Grandmont to cover the human interest side of the story—the punks—from their own point of view. Following this second uprising, police, punks, and politicians played yet another round of monkey-in-the-middle, once again hurling accusations and blame.

On July 31, on the third page of the first section, *La Presse* published a photograph of three punks relaxing on a fire escape (read: urban fauna in natural habitat), and introduced a new, shadowy player in the uprisings. According to these participants in the protest of July 29, shady "agitators" were at the root of the Berri Square unrest. Indeed, Grandmont reported that the putative existence and presence of these "extreme leftists" united punks, police, and the local youth outreach program in collective finger-pointing: "The turmoil that erupted early Monday in the former Berri Square was inspired by a core of extreme-leftist militants and of extremist punks, and not by the marginal youths who habitually frequent the area in relative tranquillity" (Grandmont 1996b). André Lemaire, adjunct commander of the local precinct, stated,

> The people who were running it were not our regular punks[!]. . . . We arrested two people about 35–40 years old who were really activists, one of whom recently participated in a demonstration organized by the elderly.[7] Out of the 78 people arrested, many were youths passing through Montréal. They were not the kids that we usually work with. (ibid.)

Marina Boulos, director of a local youth organization, described the role of these "radical forces":

> At the start, everyone was having fun, they were playing guitars, they were singing, there was no problem. . . . Everything was very calm, but there were others, people from the extreme left and associated with 'Démanarchie' [described as an anarchist group] who started looking for trouble at about 3 A.M. We didn't know any one of all the people arrested. (ibid.)

A punk concurred: "They were trying to get the kids into their game so that it would be the kids who take the shit. They know about their frustration and they're trying to exploit them" (ibid.). The city administration further concurred with the police, punks, and youth organization leaders, with city council representative Sammy Forcillo stating, "I am in favor of defending these young punks. . . . They are not the ones making trouble, it's the others who exploit their vulnerability" (ibid.). For once, then, the players were united in designating a new "middleman" in their game: the shadowy "extreme leftist anarchist" forces of Démanarchie.[8]

Even were protest warranted, the *La Presse* article elaborated, its focus should be other than police repression. Grandmont's report then argued, "While the relationship between police and marginal youths was getting on the right track, the events of Sunday night have escalated tensions one notch" (ibid.). He then once again quoted the adjunct commander of the local precinct arguing that the punks (and, implicitly, the media) should take their protests not to the police, but to city hall: "[The police] cannot decide ourselves that the municipal ordinance no longer applies" (ibid.). Local city council representative Sammy Forcillo, when approached, denied any consideration of reversing the rezoning of the former Berri Square: "For the moment, it is status quo on the issue" (ibid.). He followed this with an open-ended suggestion that the city should provide these discontented youth with alternative cultural space, by finding them a vacant building that they could transform into a "punk house."

In introducing the extreme leftists of "Démanarchie" as the new folk devils (once again, a lead that went nowhere and was quickly dropped), this report heralded the beginning of a new relationship between punks and authority figures. The police argued that the protesters arrested "were not the kids that we usually work with," rhetorically casting the punks as coworkers, in a sense acknowledging that the "nuisance" posed by the punks was a necessary component of police work (no cops without crooks). The city councillor declared himself in favor of defending "these young punks," and even proposed the establishment of a "punk house"—a type of city-sanctioned squat? With the introduction of Démanarchie as the folk devil, the punks became a sort of pet project for the police, the city councillor, and the media. The goal appeared to have been greater understanding, and reform.

Scene 3: Reporting as Ethnography

As had happened following the first uprising in May, while initial articles identified a culprit (not, in this case, a city administration lax with bar permits, but a more exciting extreme leftist anarchist group), the media failed to follow on initial leads and instead focused once again on punks and their lifestyle. This time, *La Presse* reporter Charles Grandmont became both an ethnographer of and apologist for the local punk scene. In the following four days, from July 31 to August 3, he produced short descriptive articles about the punk subculture and lifestyle, including a piece about some punks' decisions to use tape recorders to document police harassment ("Beating the Police at Their Own Game," Grandmont 1996c). Grandmont also documented the pressing issue of punk authenticity, arguing in a front page article titled "Green Hair, and Black Thoughts—In the World of Punks

There Are 'Tourists' . . . and the Real Ones" (accompanied by a photograph of happy, smiling punks; Grandmont 1996d) that "[t]he biggest problem of Montréal punks is not the police[!]. It's fashion. Hard to be a non-conformist when everyone copies you" (ibid.). He introduced readers to the variety and richness of the punk subculture in "There Is Punk . . . and Punk" (Grandmont 1996e) stating: "All punks have one commonality: they refuse to conform. Beyond that, things get complicated. A new tendency has emerged in punk. It perfectly fits these 90s kids. Non-violent, anti-racist, pacifist, eco, granola, vegetarian: here are the crusty punks" (ibid.). Grandmont added to this fashion litany the sad tale of one punk girl's descent into heroin addiction and prostitution ("Smack and Death," Grandmont 1996f), and concluded with a hopeful note, citing the existence of an antidrug punk faction, "Punx Not Junx," and its effort to clean up the punk scene. Both the crusty punk and heroin girl stories ran accompanied by photographs of punks hanging out in their natural habitat: Place Emilie-Gamelin.

Grandmont's stories humanizing the punk lifestyle were not alone in *La Presse*'s exculpatory coverage. On July 31, the newspaper ran an editorial by Pierre Gravel (1996) on "The Real Victims" of the "riots": "Everyone came out a loser last weekend . . . except, of course, those who, in the shadows, exploited the real vulnerability" (ibid.) of the punks—once again, this shady group of extreme leftist anarchists. While exonerating the punks ("not all punks are necessarily savages[!]") and the police ("who honestly try to do a difficult job"), Gravel once again pointed fingers at the city administration. Accompanying this editorial was a caricature of Mayor Bourque in the guise of a squeegee-toting mohawked punk, and referencing his frequent absences from the city. Reprinted from the coverage of the previous uprisings,[9] this caricature both made explicit reference to the first uprisings, and once again underscored attempts to lay blame on the city administration for failing to properly address these ongoing conflicts between police and punks.

Scene 4: Summer-y Conclusion

The final die was cast in characterizing the events of the summer as a "punk problem" on August 3. In the same full-page spread describing the joys and miseries of punk, Grandmont concluded *La Presse*'s coverage of the civil unrest and the punk subculture with a short article summing up the events of the past summer. In his final piece on the subject, "Forbidden Grass" (Grandmont 1996g), he summarized the current state of affairs: "The punks love downtown, but downtown, or at least its shopowners, does not love them" (ibid.). Grandmont reported that police had ceased leveling fines at punks, and that punks were beginning to move along to other parks, just as they had in previous years, when police had driven them out of other cultural spaces they had made their own. There were no more mentions of possible "punk houses," no more talk of extreme leftist anarchist groups, and no more calls for the city administration to rescind its decision on the rezoning of Place Emilie-Gamelin. Grandmont's report signaled the conclusion of the summer uprisings: defeated, the punks conceded the disputed territory to the police and city authorities.

ACT 4:   THE PLAY'S THE THING

Scene 1:   *The Conscience of the King*

Grandmont's dénouement of the "punk riots" was not to be his final word on the summer's events. However, his last report, one finally laying blame on a single player in the uprisings, ran unaccompanied by photographs of punks (happy or snarling), caricatures of the mayor, or even the word "punk" in the headline, and appeared in the back of the first section of the August 14 edition. Titled "Former Berri Square—A Clean-Up That Left Stains" (Grandmont 1996h), Grandmont's article began with this statement: "The storekeepers' petition that precipitated last spring's 'clean-up' of former Berri Square was initiated by the police of station 33, who were seeking support before forcefully intervening against the punks" (ibid.). Grandmont reported that under the guise of community policing, the Montréal Urban Community police force was somewhat more proactive than it ought to have been. Citing a report from the community newspaper *Vox*, Grandmont wrote:

> Since last March, the police have taken the initiative in meeting with the store owners of Place Dupuis [Mall] and those bordering [Berri] square. Not all agreed in assigning blame to the marginal youths, but the Merchant's Association of Place Dupuis nevertheless agreed to start a petition in support of police intervention. (ibid.)

This document reportedly read, "This petition supports the efforts of station 33, which will attempt to clear Berri park [*sic*] of all its undesirable elements and finally return the park to its residents [*sic*]" (ibid.). Grandmont reported that the store owners claimed to have returned the petition to the local precinct after having signed the document at the instigation of the police.

Under questioning by Grandmont, adjunct commander André Lemaire—who was quoted in a July 31 report stating that "[the police] cannot decide ourselves that the municipal ordinance no longer applies"—was unable to produce the original petition. Nor could the officer identified by the merchants as the originator of the petition be reached for comment, as he was "recovering from an injury sustained during an arrest" (ibid.). Grandmont then reported that the initial request made to city council to revise the zoning of Berri Square from a square to a park also originated with the police of station 33. The report then concluded that the police's actions in instigating a petition and requesting a rezoning ordinance "raises questions concerning the limitations of the community approach that the MUC police force is implementing" (ibid.). Unfortunately, these questions were not to be addressed in this or in any subsequent report, and after weeks of media attention, the whole issue of responsibility for the summer uprisings was no longer front page news—too late to fully exculpate the punks.

DÉNOUEMENT

What had begun as a "riot" seemingly instigated by angry punks in mid-May had, by mid-August, ended with a buried call for further investigation into the pitfalls of community policing. In the course of reporting these events, La Presse had accused, or carried accusations against, the city administration, bar owners, punks, the police, and extreme leftist anarchists. At the same time, however, the newspaper had provided in-depth coverage of the only group they repeatedly sought to exculpate, thereby solidly linking the uprisings with this spectacularly deviant group of punks. Despite early leads on city hall's laxness with liquor permits and later references to "extreme leftist anarchists," La Presse chose to simultaneously exonerate yet bring attention to the punk scene. The newspaper repeatedly printed editorial apologia, routinely blamed the city administration and police for tensions and explosions between punks and police, and regularly pointed fingers at shady anarchists. All the while, La Presse provided in-depth profiles of punks and the punk lifestyle, highlighting both the deviance and conformity of the punk subculture and bringing the punk scene, once again, to the forefront of public consciousness. How would that summer's events thus be remembered? Would this be remembered as a summer of city administrators' bungling? Or perhaps as a season marked by police repression of citizens? Or would it instead leave its mark as the summer the punks rioted?

I have characterized the events of the summer of 1996 as a play, as this image best captures the roles and the comedy, irony, and drama undertaken by the various groups involved. I have also described these events as a game in order to highlight the sometimes comic, ultimately ludicrous nature of these uprisings and their subsequent interpretations. From the punk car wash, to games of hide-and-seek and cat-and-mouse played by police and punks in the predawn hours in the Berri Square environs, to the subsequent finger-pointing and attributions of responsibility, these events seemed most like performances designed to entertain the house-bound public between televised bouts of the Olympics. After all, no one was seriously hurt, the punks moved along, and the city's green space was preserved for the use of "legitimate" residents; no harm done, and a little sensationalism thrown in. Yet ultimately, these events raise serious questions about the role of police in the community, and the role of the media in the cultural construction of crime and deviance.

Under the rubric of "community policing," the Montréal Urban Community police allegedly *engineered* a crackdown on what it perceived to be a community problem: punks in Berri Square. Given free reign by the city administration, in the guise of a rezoning ordinance, the police targeted these youth, and masterminded a "community call to action" to establish a community need for their predetermined tactics. The sequencing of these events raises a number of questions concerning the viability of "community policing": Who is part of the community "protected and served" by the police? Definitions of "community" aside, is it the role of the police to call attention to issues deemed criminogenic, even though the community may not perceive them as such? Should the police participate in the legislative process, requesting rezoning in order to facilitate policing? Ultimately, does the differential enforcement that is the backbone of community policing (i.e., ticketing the jaywalking punk, but not the jaywalking businesswoman) serve the interests of the community?

The events of the summer of 1996 provided even clearer illuminations of the complex role of the media in shaping public perceptions of deviance and social control. Unlike the relatively uniform media and authority discourses surrounding the Mod-Rocker conflicts of Stan Cohen's ([1972] 1980) research, the media in this instance were as likely to challenge the authorities as they were to collude with them. Recently, Angela McRobbie and Sarah Thornton (1995) have argued that such inconsistent coverage is symptomatic of a multimediated world. Today's "moral panics," they argue, are characterized not by agreement on the part of media, police, and politicians as moral entrepreneurs, but rather by competition among players in order to establish theirs as the dominant version of events. Thus, we see city council members challenging the mayoral administration, police being challenged by city administrators, and the media alternately blaming the disenfranchised, the city, and the police. Rather than presenting a united front, these traditional arbiters of deviance create conflicting discourses in their race to establish culpability in response to civil unrest and in the construction of social problems (just as there are no cops without crooks, there are no newspapers without news).

In addition, McRobbie and Thornton argue that the growing number and types of media outlets (mass, niche, and micromedias) add to the multitude of voices offering competing interpretations of events. This dissonance is augmented by the one factor that McRobbie and Thornton omit: the multiple voices of a single media outlet. *La Presse*'s coverage of the 1996 Montréal summer uprisings offered many such competing accounts. The news coverage of the *La Presse* reporters was united in casting punks as the central players in these events, even as the editorial content of the paper largely exonerated the punks while blaming police and politicians. Nonetheless, *La Presse*'s repeated forays into punk culture offset their more muted calls for mayoral action, for police accountability, and for investigations into anarchist groups. In one sense, then, this media source presented a single voice in casting these events as a "punk problem"—a type of accusation by media attention.

However, *La Presse* also created a type of cognitive dissonance by presenting not conflicting accounts of the events, but conflicting interpretations. Early accounts of the first uprising drew solely on the interpretations of police, city council members, and local store owners, describing the first uprising as a "riot," and thus invoking images of uncontrolled violence. Later accounts privileged the voices of the punks, often adopted their perspective of "police repression," and thereby described the second uprising as a "demonstration" or as a "revolt." By shifting their presentation to incorporate punks' perspectives in contrast to the accounts offered by the police, *La Presse* reporters subtly called into question the authority of the police to interpret, much less control, these events.

In its reporting on the 1996 Montréal summer uprisings, *La Presse* issued both condemning and celebratory depictions of punks, creating a dissonance within its own editorial coverage. In its exposé of the police's responsibility in constructing the conditions precipitating these uprisings (including unfairly ticketing the punks, approaching the city to rezone Berri Square, and approaching the merchants with a petition), *La Presse* positioned itself at odds with certain agents of social control. Further, in reporting city council members' critiques of the police and the mayor, *La Presse* aided in fragmenting whatever united front that may have existed among agents of social control. In offering contradictory interpretations, mass media such as *La Presse* become instrumental in challenging the monolithic ideal of hegemonic social control, pitting moral entrepreneurs against each other rather than allowing them to present a single authoritative voice. However, the newspaper's coverage also played into the construction of disenfranchised youth as social problem by focusing its substantive reporting on the punks themselves, rather than on, for example, conflicts between city councillors and the mayor, or collusions between the mayor's agenda and that of the police.

The 1996 Montréal summer uprisings thus did more than illuminate conflicts between punks and authorities. The "punk riots" brought to light an increasingly complex web of contradictions in media constructions and representations of subcultural deviance, as well as raising important questions around cultural issues of defining community, creating social problems, and constructing community policing. Further, while this chapter presents a convoluted set of interactions between the powerful and disempowered, its analysis of *one* media source's role in constructing and challenging imputations of deviance seems relatively simple and straightforward when compared to the complex effects of intersecting print, television, radio, and computer media matrices. In the end, the cultural construction of deviance is not as simple as a schoolyard game of monkey-in-the middle, with well-defined roles and rules. Rather, it is a dangerous, interminable game played in and around constantly shifting and contested cultural spaces. In this game, there are never any clear winners, only losers.

ACKNOWLEDGMENTS

The author would like to thank Jeff Ferrell, Neil Websdale, Terrie Leblanc, Ludovic Leblanc, and Neil Brouillet for their help with this chapter. Writing was funded in part by a 1996-1997 American Dissertation Fellowship from the American Association of University Women.

NOTES

1.   Though the media characterized these as events and riots, and punks appear to have represented them as revolts against police repression, I use the term "uprising" throughout this chapter as a political alternative to the more politically charged "riot" and "revolt."

2.   Also known as "keepaway," this schoolyard game requires three players and a ball. One player, the "monkey" in the middle, stands between the other two confederates, who throw the ball back and forth to each other. The objective of the confederates' game is to keep the monkey from catching the ball; the objective of the monkey's game is to catch it. As a metaphor in this chapter, the monkeys are the punks (hence my title), the confederates are the police, the news media, and the city government, and the ball is blame, deviance, power—and perhaps the truth?

3.   See, for examples of this, Cohen ([1972] 1980), Cohen and Young (1974), Ericson, Baranek, and Chan (1987), and the present volume.

4.   All articles analyzed in this chapter were taken from *La Presse,* and all quotes are my own translations.

5.   Prescott's comment about "clean-cut" rioters may be a veiled reference as well to the 1986 and subsequent Stanley Cup riots, when sports fans (nearly the perfect antithesis of punks) vandalized downtown Montréal, overturning police cars

and city busses, following the Montréal Canadiens' Stanley Cup wins and losses. Prescott's comment was also echoed by columnist Natalie Petrowski (1996), who remarked that behaviors characterized as criminal and subcultural (vandalism and violence) are not the prerogative of punks. Both imply that it is the behavior of "rioters," rather than their subcultural affiliation, that should be addressed.

6.   Note the use of the old nomenclature for the area—a political decision, or simply a device to facilitate readers' recognition?

7.   Note Lemaire's tacit acknowledgment that police not only monitor such demonstrations, but retain data on the identities of those who participate in rallies supporting causes of social justice.

8.   The very name of this group invokes, in French, the words *"démon"* (demon), *"demain"* (tomorrow), *"démarcher"* (to protest or act) and *"anarchie"* (anarchy).

9.   I remain unable to locate the first run of this caricature, and hence have not included it in my Act 1 analysis.

REFERENCES

Carter, Angela. 1992. "Ups and Downs for the Babes in Bondage." *New Statesman and Society* 5:xiv–xv.

Clément, Eric. 1996. "Lave-o-thon pour se faire pardonner." *La Presse,* July 27, p. A3.

Cohen, Stanley. [1972] 1980. *Folk Devils and Moral Panics.* London: MacGibbon and Kee.

Cohen, Stanley and Jock Young, eds. 1973. *The Manufacture of News: Deviance, Social Problems, and the Mass Media.* London: Constable.

Ericson, Richard V., Patricia M. Baranek, and Janet B. L. Chan. 1987. *Visualizing Deviance: A Study of News Organization.* Toronto: University of Toronto Press.

Ferrell, Jeff. 1996. *Crimes of Style: Urban Graffiti and the Politics of Criminality.* Boston: Northeastern University Press.

Ferrell, Jeff. 1997. "Youth, Crime, and Cultural Space." *Social Justice* 24:21–38.

Ferrell, Jeff and Clinton R. Sanders, eds. 1995. *Cultural Criminology.* Boston: Northeastern University Press.

Gervais, Raymond. 1996. "Des punks font du grabuge—Les bars seront surveillés de près, promet Bourque." *La Presse,* May 19, p. A1.

Grandmont, Charles. 1996a. "La police plus présente au square Berri—Les jeunes craignent voir s'ouvrir une 'chasse aux punks.'" *La Presse,* July 10, p. A4.

Grandmont, Charles. 1996b. "Des agitateurs à l'origine du grabuge de dimanche soir à l'ex-square Berri—L'extréme gauche tente de rallier les punks à sa cause." *La Presse,* July 31, p. A3.

Grandmont, Charles. 1996c. "Battre les policiers à leur propre jeu." *La Presse,* July 31, p. A3.

Grandmont, Charles. 1996d. "Cheveux verts, idées noires—Dans le monde des punks il y a les 'touristes' . . . et les vrais." *La Presse,* August 3, p. A1.

Grandmont, Charles. 1996e. "Il y a punk . . . et punk." *La Presse,* August 3, p. B5.

Grandmont, Charles. 1996f. "Smack et mort." *La Presse,* August 3, p. B5.

Grandmont, Charles. 1996g. "L'herbe interdite." *La Presse,* August 3, p. B5.

Grandmont, Charles. 1996h. "Ex-square Berri: un nettoyage qui laisse des taches." *La Presse,* August 14, p. A8.

Gravel, Pierre. 1996. "Les vraies victimes." *La Presse,* July 31, p. B2.

Guay, Christian. 1996. "Lave-auto punk." *La Presse,* July 27, p. A1.

Hebdige, Dick. 1979. *Subculture: The Meaning of Style.* London: Methuen.

La Presse. 1996. "Tolérance zero pour les punks." May 26, p. A3.

Laberge, Yvon. 1996. "Couvre-feu à la place Emilie-Gamelin." *La Presse,* May 31, p. A3.

Lavigne, Lucie. 1996. "C'est quoi ta gang?" *La Presse,* July 30, p. A5.

Legault, Jean-Benoit and Mathieu Perreault. 1996. "Le conflit prend de l'ampleur—Punks et policiers s'affrontent en pleine nuit a l'ex-square Berri." *La Presse,* July 30, p. A1.

Levine, Harold G. and Steven H. Stumpf. 1983. "Statements of Fear Through Cultural Symbols: Punk Rock as a Reflexive Subculture." *Youth and Society* 14:417–35.

McRobbie, Angela and Sarah L. Thornton. 1995. "Rethinking 'Moral Panic' for Multi-Mediated Social Worlds." *British Journal of Sociology* 46:559–74.

Moore, Mark H., Robert C. Trojanowicz, and George L. Kelling. 1988. "Crime and Policing." *Perspectives on Policing* 2:1–13.

Petrowski, Nathalie. 1996. "Les squeegees contre-attaquent." *La Presse,* May 22, p. A5.

Pineau, Yann. 1996. "L'émeute de la Main: une 'revolte du squeegee'?" *La Presse,* May 21, p. A3.

Sanders, Clinton R., ed. 1990. *Marginal Conventions: Popular Culture, Mass Media, and Social Deviance.* Bowling Green, OH: Bowling Green State University/Popular Press.

Sigal, Leon V. 1986. "Sources Make the News." Pp. 9–37 in *Reading the News,* edited by R. K. Manhoff and M. Schudson. New York: Pantheon.

Smith, Michael P., ed. 1995. *Marginal Spaces: Comparative Urban and Community Research,* Vol. 5. New Brunswick, NJ: Transaction.

11

Freight Train Graffiti
*Subculture, Media, Dislocation**

Contemporary "hip hop" graffiti—today the dominant form of public graffiti and illegal public art in the United States, Europe, and elsewhere—took shape some twenty-five years ago as a distinctly local and urban phenomenon. Emerging in the Bronx and other New York City boroughs as part of a home-grown hip hop culture, this form of nongang graffiti was developed by inner-city kids as a stylized system of subcultural status and street-level communication (Castleman 1982; Ferrell 1995a, 1996; Lachmann 1988). "Tagging" subcultural nicknames on walls and subway cars, painting larger two-dimensional "throw ups" and still larger, multicolored "pieces," hip hop graffiti "writers" and the "crews" they organized illicitly remade New York City's public spaces and public meanings.

Soon enough, though, the aesthetic codes and wildly stylized images of hip hop graffiti began to spread from New York City to other large cities and small towns in the United States, to the urban centers and isolated villages of Europe, and to Australia, New Zealand, and Japan (Chalfant and Prigoff 1987). A number of social and cultural forces facilitated the dissemination of hip hop graffiti from the heart of New York City to the heartlands of the United States and other countries: films like *Style Wars!* (1985) and *Wild Style* (1983), early "style manuals" like Cooper and Chalfant's photographic book *Subway Art* (1984),[1] the covers of countless hip hop/rap cassettes and CDs, low-budget (and later high-budget) graffiti photo magazines, European and U.S. art dealers, and more recently the proliferation of graffiti sites on the Internet. In the past few years, yet another powerful and illegal form of cultural dissemination has become popular within the subculture: the widespread painting of hip hop graffiti on outbound freight trains, as a means of sending graffiti images out from their initial, circumscribed points of production and into wider circulation through countryside, cities, and towns.

* From *Justice Quarterly* vol. 15, no. 4 pp 101–122. Copyright © 1998 by the Academy of Criminal Justice Sciences. Reprinted with permisssion.

As I will explicate in this chapter, freight train hip hop graffiti can thus be understood as an important development within a broader phenomenon: the ongoing work of the hip hop graffiti underground—a deviant/criminal subculture organized by a marginalized population possessing few traditional economic and political resources—in successfully broadcasting itself, and its forms of organization and meaning, across wide geographic and cultural expanses. In fact, despite well-funded, high-profile, nationally coordinated legal and political campaigns against graffiti that have emerged in the past two decades, and that have increasingly incorporated severe legal sanctions and aggressive enforcement procedures (Ferrell 1995a, 1996), the hip hop graffiti subculture has not withered; it has instead continued to gain visibility, to develop, and to spread. As I will demonstrate, this ongoing, against-the-odds dissemination of hip hop graffiti and its subculture, through freight train graffiti and other techniques, has in turn been facilitated by dynamics that are distinctly postmodern, and even anarchistic, in nature: the do-it-yourself construction of dislocated symbolic communities, the invention of mediated intertextuality and multiple audiences, the triumph of image and style over time and place. And, as I will also show, it is precisely these postmodern and anarchistic dimensions of freight train graffiti and other hip hop graffiti practices that construct them as successful subcultural endeavors; that position them as significant challenges to traditional mechanisms of legal and social control; and that, ultimately, raise essential questions as to the nature of deviant and criminal subcultures.

DISLOCATED IMAGES, DISLOCATED METHODS

In two years of research into the emerging phenomenon of freight train graffiti, I have attempted to circulate as widely as the graffiti itself. Wandering from location to location, I have time and again plowed through high weeds and across swampy ditches to get at freight trains parked, or rolling to a stop, along rural sidings and in railyards outside small and large communities in Arizona, Texas, Missouri, Kansas, Oklahoma, Nevada, New Mexico, Utah, and California. My research on freight train graffiti has been muddied not only by the marshy ditches separating me from the trains, though, but by the geographic and cultural distance separating freight train graffiti from its producers. In setting out to study, along with the freight train graffiti itself, the dislocation of the graffiti from its original point of production, I have confronted an obvious irony: the immediate subject of my research is now, by definition, hundreds or thousands of miles from its initial context of meaning. For a researcher committed and accustomed to sharing

situations with subjects of study, to achieving a level of firsthand criminological *verstehen* with them (Ferrell 1997a; Ferrell and Hamm 1998), this
situation has created a certain crisis of meaning and understanding. How is a
researcher to interrogate the meaning of an image, to avoid simply assuming
or imposing a facile understanding of it, when the producer of that image
remains unavailable for interrogation? While this dilemma could not easily
be resolved—indeed, should not be fully resolved, given the multiple, disjointed meanings to be discussed subsequently—it could be addressed
methodologically in two ways. First, extensive prior knowledge of the graffiti
underground, and of the complex, widely used system of symbols, stylized
references, and visual codes within which it operates, established the epistemic foundation for research. By taking this knowledge along with me into
the field, I, like graffiti writers nationwide, could continue to participate in a
subculture of style, to maintain a symbolic copresence, even with no one
else nearby, and thus could establish with some certainty the meaning of
freight train graffiti in this cultural context. Second, I was subsequently able
to translate this subcultural understanding into various unobtrusive measures (Webb, Campbell, Schwartz, and Sechrest 1966; Klofas and Cutshall
1985) by which to evaluate the specific dynamics of freight train graffiti
production and circulation.

As a starting point, eight years of research in hip hop graffiti undergrounds
around the United States and Europe have taught me that, almost without
exception, graffiti writers leave behind a variety of subcultural discards as
they undertake and complete their work. Caught up in the adrenalin of the
moment, focused on executing a stylistically complex piece while negotiating the darkness and watching for street toughs and police officers, writers
are hardly likely to seek out the nearest trash can, or to pack out what they
pack in. Sites of graffiti painting are thus generally identifiable by discarded
spray cans, spray can tops, and markers; empty beer cans and forty-ounce
beer bottles; cigarette butts and spent cigarette packs; residual paint from
malfunctioning spray cans and the testing of spray nozzles; and other indicators of subcultural activity.[2] In two years of research on freight train graffiti,
though, such indicators have not been found. In situation after situation,
tags, throw ups, and pieces on freight trains exist without the usual retinue of
objects associated with their production—and thus seem, quite clearly, to
have been relocated from their initial site of production. In this regard, the
subtleties of an unusual case are instructive. Near the Arizona/New Mexico
border, in a decidedly rural area, along a stretch of siding I discovered
discarded Krylon cans and various test patches of paint sprayed on and
around the tracks—all quite typical point-of-production findings. The paint,
though, did not match any of the graffiti painted on the freight cars parked
along this same siding. Thus, a seemingly causal connection—indicators of

graffiti writers' unusual presence in a remote rural area, and graffiti on a train nearby—was not a connection at all; and in fact, both the graffiti that the writers had apparently painted and the graffiti on the parked train had moved on down the line since their original and separate execution.

In addition, the dynamics of urban graffiti undergrounds are such that tags, throw ups, and pieces seldom exist in isolation. Hip hop graffiti functions as an ongoing public conversation, a cycle of symbolic interaction, among writers. Writers carefully choose locations for their work that hold preexisting subcultural status, and that are therefore likely to be visited and utilized by other writers. Writers in turn tag near other writers' tags, as a way of achieving a sort of symbolic copresence with them; write complimentary remarks near well-executed pieces or, alternatively, cross out ("diss'") or paint over ("go over") inferior works; and execute pieces one near the other to create subcultural "walls of fame." Yet in visits to countless freight train graffiti locations, evidence of such situated, collective activity has almost never been found. With very few exceptions,[3] specific tags, throw-ups, and pieces on freight cars—identifiable by the distinct styles of each writer or crew, and by the type and color of paint used—are not reproduced in the surrounding area. Likewise, writers who have tagged or pieced in the surrounding area have not tagged or pieced on the cars, or responded in the usual way to existing graffiti on them. As with the absence of subcultural discards, this divergence from usual subcultural practices seems clearly to indicate that the on-site freight train graffiti has originated elsewhere, and that its ongoing circulation in any case leaves little time for response from local writers.

A final divergence from traditional subcultural practices provides perhaps the clearest indication that freight train graffiti is not only portable, but intended to be portable by its creators. When hip hop graffiti writers tag, they write their own subcultural nicknames (their "tags"), and often the name (or three letter abbreviation) of the crew to which they belong. Similarly, when they piece, they sign the completed piece with the tags of those who have worked on it, and with the full or abbreviated name of the crew(s) with which they are affiliated. This convention is so widespread and so widely accepted that I have found its use, without variation, in countless local graffiti undergrounds throughout the United States and Europe: writers consistently and precisely identify themselves and their work by their tags and by their crew names. With freight train graffiti, though, there exists a new element not seen before: here, writers identify themselves not only by their tags and crew names, but by their cities or areas of residence. Time and again, I have discovered city of origin tagged alongside tag and crew names on freight trains, and freight train pieces signed with individual, crew, and city identifiers. In addition, writers have begun to write three-digit telephone area codes alongside tags or pieces, as further signification of geographic origin and identity. The mere fact of a writer tagging his/her city of residence or area code suggests an understanding and intention on the writer's part that the graffiti will be relocated out of that area; the fact that the vast majority of these geographic signatures are indeed found in other, far-removed urban or rural locations confirms this pattern.[4]

Over the past two years, then, this has been my primary methodology: tracking down instances of freight train graffiti on rural sidings, in small towns, and in small-town and big-city railyards, and subsequently "reading" this graffiti for unobtrusive indicators of origin, dislocation, meaning, and intentionality. In addition, I have during this period interviewed graffiti writers, local residents, and railroad officials as to their perceptions and understandings of this graffiti. Here, however, I've confronted a methodological problem that parallels problems graffiti writers themselves face in executing freight train graffiti: the remarkable power of the railroads to control access to their trains and their personnel (see Sagarin 1973; Coles 1997). My negotiations for entry into various railyards around the country have led to limited, temporary access at times, no access at others. Worse, my repeated attempts to set up formal interviews with railroad officials and workers have consistently been denied, either through direct refusal or through endless rounds of bureaucratic deflection. Two methodological tactics have emerged in response. First, I have conducted a number of informal "non-interviews" with railroad officials while being told by them that no interviews are allowed, and with security personnel while being told by them that I must leave their railyards immediately. Second, I have conducted innumerable unapproved forays into the railyards, running across rows of tracks, sneaking between rail cars, dodging private police and surveillance systems, and thus replicating in some small way the risks faced by those whose tags and pieces I study (see Ferrell 1996, 1997a; Ferrell and Hamm 1998). Appropriately enough for a subject of study defined by its dislocation, my methodology has allowed me not only a certain stylistic copresence with writers far away, but a certain sharing in the immediacy of risks taken by them long ago.

REPRODUCING THE CULTURAL CONTEXT

While the widespread writing of hip hop graffiti on freight trains appears to be a relatively recent phenomenon, and one that creates new methodological and epistemic challenges for those who attempt to understand it, this practice emerges out of broader traditions of spatial mobility and subcultural dislocation that have characterized hip hop graffiti, and other forms of graffiti, for many years. As such, freight train graffiti both reproduces the cultural milieu in which it exists, and reinvents this milieu as it expands its geographic and symbolic boundaries.

In the United States and elsewhere, trains have historically served as a significant medium of the disenfranchised, appropriated by "outsiders" of all sorts to transport themselves and their subcultures. For decades hoboes and other transient populations have utilized freight trains as means of found transportation, and have developed out of this endeavor elaborate subcultures that incorporate complex systems of "hobo graffiti" written on and around the trains. As will be seen, this endeavor continues today, and regularly interweaves with the practice of hip hop train graffiti. Similarly, throughout the early part of the twentieth century members of the Industrial Workers of the World (the Wobblies)—many of them itinerant workers by trade—systematically "rode the rails" in the western United States, utilizing freight trains to move between and to organize hobo camps, and to transport themselves from one strike situation to the next (see Kornbluh 1988:65–93). And recently, a new group centered in the northwestern and southern United States—the Freight Train Riders of America (FTRA)—has begun to garner police and media attention for its alleged criminal activities, and for the FTRA graffiti now written on countless freight trains and railway overpasses (see Matthews 1997; Murphy 1997; Rivers 1997).

The emergence and development of hip hop graffiti has likewise been interwoven with the technology and culture of train transportation. Early in the subculture's formation, tags and pieces were written on New York City subway trains; the interconnection was such that much early hip hop graffiti terminology referred directly to subway cars ("whole car" or "window-down" pieces, for example), and such that the first, definitive book on hip hop graffiti was entitled *Subway Art* (Cooper and Chalfant 1984). As the subculture has subsequently developed in Europe and Australia, passenger trains, passenger train stations, and walls bordering train lines have become the focal point for tags, throw ups, and pieces; writers regularly utilize this form of transportation, and in turn know that other writers will see images left on and around it (see Henkel, Domentat, and Westhoff 1994; van Treeck and Todt 1995; Chalfant and Prigoff 1987). Moreover, given the social ecology of inner cities in the United States, railyards themselves have in many cases become conveniently located "playgrounds" for graffiti writers. Thus, in a recently published glossary of San Francisco Bay Area graffiti terminology, Walsh lists the term "yard," and defines it as "usually a train yard or similar place where writers frequent to do graffiti" (1996:135). And in Denver—prior to the recent redevelopment of the old railyards area into a sports/entertainment complex—local writers created "walls of fame" along railyard retaining walls; converted an abandoned locomotive turning house into the "Bomb Shelter," an informal (and illegal) "graffiti museum;" hitched rides on slow-moving freights, as a means of gaining free transportation or eluding pursuing police officers; and painted in the railyards a tribute to Jack Kerouac, denizen of another, similarly mobile subculture.[5]

In terms of both its day-to-day practice and its cultural referents, then, hip hop graffiti has from the first emerged in a context of subcultural mobility and of portable and transitory images circulating between subcultural members. Speaking of early subway graffiti in New York City, a writer recalls that "we would see some fine cars go by . . . knowing there were masters out there we'd never seen. We knew them as artists before we got to know them as men" (in Lachmann 1988:241). Freight train graffiti expands this circulation of subcultural images and identities—and it expands it so widely that, in the majority of cases, writers may see, appreciate, and learn from each other's art, but in fact never be able to traverse vast geographic distances and get to know each other "as men." As with other dimensions of the graffiti underground, freight train graffiti puts subcultural identities and images in motion, and shapes their meaning in transit.

Moreover, hip hop graffiti has consistently interwoven subcultural mobility with the reconstruction of social and cultural space (Ferrell 1997c)—that is, with the reshaping of meaning in public domains. When writers tag and piece, they work to remake the visual landscapes and symbolic codes of public life, converting abandoned abutments into "walls of fame," alley walls into ongoing sites of symbolic interaction, and—much to the chagrin of local business and political leaders—a carefully designed aesthetics of authority into an aesthetics of disorder and play (Atlanta and Alexander 1989; Ferrell 1996). Writers in turn measure their success at this endeavor not only by standards of stylistic innovation, but by degrees of spatial expansion and risk. Since the early days of the graffiti underground, writers have acquired subcultural status by "going citywide"—by tagging widely enough that their tags are visible throughout the various neighborhoods of a city. More recently, writers have invented the vertical equivalent of going citywide: "tagging the heavens" (Ferrell 1995a:79, 81) or "map[ping] the heavens" (Walsh 1996:134). In tagging the heavens, writers elevate their status by elevating their tags—by tagging at the highest possible spot on buildings, billboards, and freeway signs. In doing so, they earn subcultural respect and visibility in two ways: first, by producing tags that are in fact highly visible from surrounding locations, and second, by demonstrating a willingness to take illegal and often life-threatening risks to produce these tags. In Denver, for example, local graffiti legend Eye Six is known not only for tagging the heavens, but for his "hang and tag" technique: climbing to the top of a billboard or building and then hanging off, holding on with one hand and writing with the other, so as to tag a spot of the greatest possible inaccessibility and status. Freight train graffiti thus provides a significant extension of these existing dynamics; it allows writers to remake the cultural meanings of freight cars, railyards, and ultimately distant social spaces, and allows those who have previously expanded their subcultural reach by tagging the heavens or going citywide to now "go nationwide." Arrested for painting a piece on a railroad tankcar, a Chicago writer was questioned by a police detective as to his motives: "So I asked him, 'Why paint a railroad car?' He said it was because the whole country will see it" (in Royko 1996).

In all of this, we see the ongoing expansion and elaboration of a subculture. Some twenty-five years after its emergence in New York City, the world of hip hop graffiti has not only provided expansive deviant (and in many cases nondeviant) careers for its members (Becker 1963; Lachmann 1988); the subculture itself has followed a career path of remarkable spatial and cultural expansion. Driven early on by films, books, and music, this dynamic quickly spread hip hop graffiti from the boroughs of New York to large and small cities throughout the United States and Europe, and resulted in the precise reproduction of stylistic codes and conventions in these new locations. In the past few years, this expansion has continued, not only with the growing popularity and scope of freight train graffiti, but with underground "graffiti tours" now regularly shuttling taggers between the United States and Europe, high-quality graffiti magazines gaining readership in the United States, Europe, and Japan, and graffiti websites proliferating on the Internet. Along with magazines, books, and films, these websites can be seen as providing an elaborate latticework of communication for graffiti writers, allowing writers in far-flung locations to send images and identities out into a world beyond their immediate reach (see Chervokas and Watson 1998).[6] But the same can be said, of course, for freight train graffiti; it serves as the Internet for the other half.

AN ETHNOGRAPHY OF IMAGES

One result of this subcultural expansion, then, is a world—both rural and urban—increasingly awash in freight train graffiti. In just two years of research, I have photographed many hundreds of examples of such graffiti throughout the western and midwestern United States, and watched as fast-moving trains have carried many thousands more beyond my photographic reach. In this mobile research I have discovered a pattern that I have previously documented (Ferrell 1995a, 1995c, 1996) in research on local hip hop graffiti undergrounds across the United States and Europe: a remarkable consistency of style across locations. No matter what its geographic origins or present location, hip hop graffiti on freight trains exhibits the same distinct subcultural conventions, the same shared codes of subcultural meaning, as does other hip hop graffiti. Precise formats for tagging, throwing up, and piecing; specific conventions of lettering, shading, and coloring; shared techniques for individual and crew identification—all indicate to the informed observer the unequivocal presence of hip hop graffiti and, more broadly, the ongoing work of a subculture defined by both wide dispersion and tight stylistic organization.

This subcultural clarity is in some ways confounded, though, by the complex contexts in which freight train hip hop graffiti is found. Hip hop graffiti on trains is frequently written around, beside, and over a plethora of non–hip hop graffiti; and this non–hip hop graffiti is itself at times written over or alongside existing hip hop graffiti. Town and place names, political commentary, playful alterations of railway signs and notices, stylized drawings, informal advertisements, the graffiti of Latino/a, African-American, and neo-Nazi/skinhead gangs—all regularly appear on the same freight trains that carry hip hop graffiti. The most common non–hip hop train graffiti, though, is a type often denoted as "hobo graffiti": typically, careful white or black line drawings accompanied by notations of name, place, and date. Thus in July 1997, in the Fort Worth, Texas, railyards, hip hop tags and pieces and skinhead graffiti share freightcar space with a white-lettered warning, TROUBLE UP AHEAD TAKE CARE MY FRIENDS "R"E ARTHLEUS 8-95 LOVE 4 ALL JERRY LIVES, accompanied by a line drawing of a smiling face. On another car, three names and dates had been left in white lettering: WILD MAN 10-93, inside a drawing of a signpost shot through by an arrow; MR. BASS 2-26-93; and, in faded white, 6-86 DENVER KID, with another smiling face. Here also are three sets of images I have come to know well in my travels. A series of line drawings depicts a distinctive, square-jawed face covered by a large cowboy hat; under one is written SORROW FLOATS COGBILL BURIAL; under another, PAEAN TO A PEON (REDWOOD THRONE); under a third, DOWN BY LAW DIPLOMATS. PANCHO OF THE FRISCO is here also, just as I have found him in the Winslow, Arizona, railyards and elsewhere, his white-lettered name dated on one car 9-15-94 / 1-24-95 / 8-9-95, and on an adjacent car 6-19-96. And, not at all surprisingly, THE RAMBLER is here as well, with his distinctive line drawing of an effervescing champagne glass, and his location and date, PORT OF BEAUMONT TEXAS 7-1-90.

While particular instances of hip hop graffiti on freight trains themselves maintain a sharp stylistic consistency, then, they at the same time exist within a larger swirl of inconsistent textual and contextual frameworks, in intentional and unintentional conversation with other images and messages. As such, hip hop graffiti on trains comes to reside within layers of accreted images, and in turn takes on layers of meaning through temporary juxtapositions, accidental configurations, and transitory ironies. These intertextual dynamics take a number of forms. First, as already suggested, instances of hip hop graffiti on individual freight cars often exist in juxtaposition with other hip hop tags and pieces, with other forms of graffiti, and with altered or unaltered official signs and notices. Second, as freight trains are made up in the yards, instances of hip hop graffiti on particular cars come to be juxtaposed with hip hop or non–hip hop graffiti on adjacent cars, thereby creating in many cases temporary, unintended, and eclectic "walls of fame." Third, fast-moving trains in open urban and rural areas, and slow-moving trains in railyards, often pass other moving or parked trains, creating striking, transitory convergences and divergences of graffiti images. Fourth, similar intertextual effects are created as tagged or pieced trains pass through rural settings, small towns, urban neighborhoods, and railyards, creating momentary ironies and juxtapositions with local imagery.[7] Finally, of course, these dislocated dynamics begin again, with new layers of image and meaning added and subtracted as freight cars and freight trains are reshuffled, occasionally repainted, and moved in and out of new locations.

Only in this context of dislocation—of hip hop tags, pieces, and throw ups disconnected from original dynamics of production and reconnected to shifting frameworks of meaning—is it appropriate to present a sample of research results, a brief ethnography of images found. Like the broader subcultural practice they represent, the cases included here capture particular patterns of meaning and style, but in doing so follow no set temporal or geographic order; as with Vonnegut ([1968] 1988), they have come "unstuck in space and time:"[8]

December 24, 1996. Muleshoe, Texas. Los Angeles hip hop graffiti comes to West Texas. On a siding in front of a grain elevator, a freight car features two large throw ups by LSD—the LOCKIN SHIT DOWN crew out of L.A. One of the throw ups is now partially obliterated by a rail car number painted over its top edge. The other is signed by one of the crew's writers: SICK.

July 22, 1997. Fort Worth, Texas. As he is escorting me out of the Union Pacific railyards, a security official suggests that my time might in any case be better spent in the Burlington Northern Santa Fe yards north of town: "They probably have more graffiti, because they go through L.A."

June 30, 1997. Tehachapi Loop, above Tehachapi, California. A long freight train slowly winds its way up the loop. Car after car is written over with hip hop graffiti, hobo markings, and other images. On one car is the tag of a Los Angeles crew: INF SMERK LA 94.[9] On another car covered in three hip hop pieces, a writer apologizes for the most poorly executed of the three: SORRY TOO FUCKIN DARK + WINDY. The square-jawed face with the big cowboy hat is on this train also, in two places: under one image is written COLLAGES TOUR BRITISH ISLES; under the other, POINTLESS REPETITION NLR. And THE RAMBLER is here, his champagne glasses signed

THE RAMBLER GILA BEND ARIZONA 3-22-95 and THE RAMBLER MAURICEVILLE TEXAS 4-9-92.

April 27, 1997.   Rural area ninety miles west of Albuquerque, New Mexico.   Parked on a siding, a green tanker car features a large, multicolor piece by the METROE SMS KREW out of Portland, Oregon. Painted around the time of Halloween, 1996, the piece includes an elaborate Halloween jack-o'-lantern, stenciled interior images, and a series of tagged messages, among them IT'S MY BIRTHDAY BIG 18??? and HAPPY HALLOWEEN. Despite the technical brilliance of the piece, the writers have also included a disclaimer of sorts, much like the one found next to the piece on the Tehachapi Loop: TO COLD TO LATE TO SOAR.[10]

Hobo graffiti covers many of the other cars on this siding. BIG BUBBA 88! LETS GO! adorns one car; 4-96 BUSTER, with a peace sign attached to the T, is written on another. On down the line of cars is a face topped with a crown, and the words SALVAGE KING TRUE HEIR TO SALVAGELAND; nearby is a line drawing of a steaming cup of coffee, with MUD UP written inside it. PHOTO-BILL is also here, his name elaborated with text: @MEDIUM 6-94 OBSCURA 6-94 AT LARGE. And, of course, THE RAMBLER is present as well.

July 22, 1997.   Fort Worth, Texas.   In the Union Pacific railyards sits a freight car covered by two hip hop pieces. Both apparently the work of the same writer, one piece is done in yellow and white, the other in aqua and white. A bit of white-line hobo graffiti is written next to them: LIL BUBBA 12/29/96. Could LIL BUBBA be connected in some way to BIG BUBBA, found three months earlier and a thousand miles away, and dated eight years before this graffiti? And what of the numerous hip hop tags found on a car nearby—BADGE, CODE, TRIGER, and others, signed PASADENA'S TOP ARTISTS? Are these writers from Pasadena, Texas; Pasadena, California; or some other, unknown Pasadena?

April 19, 1996.   Reno, Nevada.   Across a small road from the Nugget Casino—in plain view of the blackjack tables and nickel slots, should the tourists ever look up—the Reno railyards themselves seem a sort of tourist destination for graffiti. On a faded orange boxcar, beneath a SEARCH throw up, Search has written FROM SPRINGFIELD, MASS TO RALEIGH, NC. On a car nearby, a white and blue NEM throw up is signed N.Y.C. NEMS ESCRES. On other cars, conversations and critiques are underway. A tanker car carries Melonone's neatly tagged condemnation: FUCK THESE CHEMICALS! MELONONE. On a freight car, the official ANY ROAD sign has been altered to read ANY TOAD; on another, WORK WORK WORK has been printed in white below the Santa Fe Railway emblem. Across the way, another boxcar carries a tagged message for the Los Angeles Police Department: CHINGA SU MADRE LA POLICE. GRAFFITI LIVES ON. But another car presents, alongside the carefully printed name of the alternative band RAGE AGAINST THE MACHINE, a second message in a different hand: TAGGERS SUCK.

July 26, 1996.   Rural area twenty miles south of Kansas City, Missouri. Individual and crew tags frame two large throw ups on a gray freight car. Also tagged is an appropriate invitation: ALL ABOARD . . .

December 24, 1996.   Clovis, New Mexico.   A long freight train is parked on the outskirts of town. On one car is a COS throw up, signed CANADA 96.[11] Another car carries a hip hop tag written over faded, Latino/a gang-style graffiti, and beside this a message, written hobo-style: KS. GOV. BILL GROVES IS A CHILD MOLESTER. Other cars are written over in various combinations of Latino/a gang-style graffiti, hip hop tags, and hobo markings; among the hobo signatures are LADY IN RED ROBIN DENVER COLO, 98° PHX KID, and, on most every car in this long train, THE RAMBLER.

July 30, 1996.   Fort Worth, Texas.   Hip hop throw ups and pieces decorate many of the cars in the Union Pacific yards. One freight car carries a black and white CL throw up, tagged CHICAGO FUSE. A few cars down, Fuse has reproduced this throw up, but in a sloppier fashion, and tagged GOTTAGO SWITCHMANS COMING . . . FUSE. 1995. Once again, THE RAMBLER is present also, writing FORT BEAUMONT or PORT OF BEAUMONT and various dates beside his champagne glasses. One champagne glass, though, is unusual: The Rambler has drawn it five or six times the usual size, and written beside it in large script THE RAMBLER PORT ALLEN LA. Next to this oversized image on one side are two crude drawings of nude women; on the other side, a hip hop writer has painted a surprised face and a series of exclamation marks, and has tagged a question: IS THIS ART?

June 12, 1997.   Winslow, Arizona.   David Riker, Administrative Specialist, Arizona Division, Burlington Northern Santa Fe Railway, is telling me the bad news. Since my last visit with him, corporate headquarters has decided that I won't be allowed to conduct interviews in and around the Winslow yards: "They don't want you talking to the crews here." He does allow himself one observation, though, in reference to the countless trains that pass through his yards: "Seems like a lot of the graffiti is all the same person, the same style."

CULTURAL AND THEORETICAL TRAJECTORIES

The widespread writing and circulation of hip hop graffiti on freight trains, the dislocation and relocation of graffiti images as they move through various contexts of meaning, the geographic and symbolic expansion of the hip hop graffiti subculture through this and other avenues—all suggest that freight train graffiti traces not only an emergent subcultural practice, but a series of broader cultural and theoretical trajectories as well. These trajectories point to the power of images that are located within a deviant or criminal subculture, and at the same time dislocated from it, in widening the scope and reach of the subculture. Relatedly, they highlight the prowess of a deviant or criminal subculture like the hip hop graffiti underground in fluidly constructing and reconstructing the cultural spaces and media through which it operates, and the audiences for whom it performs. Most broadly, these trajectories expose a set of postmodern and anarchistic dynamics that challenge both conventional notions of legal and social control, and conventional understandings of deviant and criminal subcultures.

Certainly hip hop train graffiti advances and expands the ongoing work of graffiti writers and other "outsiders" (Becker 1963) in the often illicit remaking of *cultural space.* As graffiti writers repaint freight cars with elaborately stylized designs, encode them with complex subcultural symbols, and send them out across the country, they reshape the meaning of the freight cars and freight trains themselves and, at least temporarily, reshape the public meaning of the various locations through which the trains pass. Like street cruisers, low riders, homeless "gutter punks," gang members, and pirate radio operators, freight train graffiti writers contest and reconstruct the meaning of everyday life, and develop their own everyday identities, by "appropriat[ing] marginalized areas" (Sanchez-Tranquilino 1995:76; see Baca 1995) and creating in and around them collective codes of alternative symbolism and public style. Like street cruisers, gang members, and gutter punks, freight train graffiti writers in turn share and contest this cultural space with others engaged in their own work of reconstruction and communication (Bright 1995). Intentionally and unintentionally, freight train graffiti writers maintain ongoing public conversations with distant graffiti writers, hobos, skinheads, and railroad workers and officials, and thus find their own visual vocabularies of motive and meaning (Mills 1940; Cressey 1954) recontextualized within the public discourse of others. And, like street cruisers and gutter punks, freight train graffiti writers operate in opposition to and on the run from police officers and private security personnel—personnel whose job it is, increasingly, to protect not only private and "public" property, but the public meanings, the aesthetics of authority, inscribed in it (Ferrell

1996, 1997c; Herbert 1997; Merrifield and Swyngedouw 1997; Rotenberg and McDonogh 1993).[12]

In this work of illicitly remaking cultural space, freight train graffiti writers also remind us of the various, complex forms that *media* may take, and of often unnoticed links between media and crime. From the first, hip hop writers were adept at utilizing subways and subway cars as found media of subcultural communication; today, they employ freight trains, and their far wider networks of movement, as a medium for the nationwide dissemination of images and identities. In one sense, then, graffiti writers utilize and construct freight trains as situated media—that is, as a channel of communication situated within the subculture, and thus outside the usual orbit of mass culture and mass media. In other senses, though, freight train graffiti transcends its situated context. To begin with, as seen throughout this chapter, freight train graffiti regularly and predictably becomes desituated, as it is dislocated from its original point of production and broadcast along a far-reaching and relatively unpredictable circuitry of movement. Moreover, the freight trains that serve as a medium for this graffiti are in many ways no less a part of the corporate universe, and thus no less a medium of "mass" communication, than are the Internet and the television networks. The recent merger of the Burlington Northern and Santa Fe Railways, for example, has both expanded and confined hip hop writers' dissemination of freight train graffiti in much the same way that the merger of Disney and ABC has expanded and confined the dissemination of television writers' creative efforts. Finally, like all public hip hop graffiti, freight train graffiti regularly becomes image fodder for graffiti magazines, graffiti websites, network news reports, fashion productions, print and televisual advertisements, textbook covers, and other mass media products, which in turn cycle back through the subculture as they come to the attention of writers. Whatever the ultimate outcome of this mediated spiral, though, writers remain well aware of its immediate impact. As Jose Quiroz, publisher of *Night Crawler* graffiti magazine, recently announced on MTV's "Authority Sucks" program (1996): "Most graffiti writers nowadays like freight trains. It's the biggest graffiti movement right now. Do your piece on a freight train, it's gonna go all across the country."

As with all media of communication, freight train graffiti also calls into question the nature of its *audience*. Certainly the audiences for mass media and popular culture presentations of crime and criminality have come under increasing scholarly scrutiny of late (Bailey and Hale 1998; Barak 1994; Ferrell and Sanders 1995; Kidd-Hewitt and Osborne 1995; Surette 1998). The widespread practice of hip hop graffiti, and particularly hip hop freight train graffiti, suggests that criminologists might in addition wish to investigate more carefully the audiences generated by everyday criminality, and by criminal subcultures themselves. As have writers throughout the history of hip hop graffiti, freight train hip hop writers define other writers as their intended or imagined audience; while they are of course aware that those outside the subculture will see their work, they are primarily concerned with its visibility for, and evaluation by, other writers. Especially in the case of freight train graffiti, though—with its wide dissemination and profound dislocation—intended audiences intersect in time and space with those unintended; as this chapter has begun to show, the audiences for freight train graffiti are as fluid as the graffiti itself, by turns discrete and overlapping, contradictory and confounded. As intended, distant writers are in fact likely to see and appreciate an instance of hip hop train graffiti as it moves cross-country, or finds the end of the line. But others—railway crews and officials, hobos, truck drivers, ranchers, small-town residents, law enforcement personnel—are as likely to see the graffiti, and to understand it in quite different ways. The meaning of hip hop train graffiti thus remains slippery and uncertain, sliding between time, place, and audience.

Hip hop freight train graffiti suggests broader cultural and theoretical trajectories as well. First, as demonstrated throughout this chapter, hip hop train graffiti embodies a host of social and cultural dynamics typically collected under the rubric of *postmodernism,* and thus presents for criminologists the particular contours and challenges of what we might label "postmodern criminality." With hip hop train graffiti, we see the temporary triumph of alternative or illegal images over the prescribed substance and meaning of everyday life, and over structures of legal control and private property. At the same time, we glimpse the powerful portability and plasticity of these "free floating" images and signs as they become dislocated both from localized legal control, and from their initial local contexts of production. As part of this pervasive dislocation, we see also an ongoing, impermanent collage of unintended juxtapositions and accidental ironies, as hip hop images circulate in conversation with hobo markings, gang graffiti, railway notices, and countless other hip hop and non–hip hop images along "networks . . . of connections, contact, contiguity, feedback and generalized interface" (Baudrillard 1985:127).

With hip hop freight train graffiti, we thus witness a criminal world taking shape within a spiral of mediated meaning—a spiral defined not only by ongoing intertextuality (Schwartz and Friedrichs 1994:229), but by a looping hyperreality where "images refer to other images" (Manning 1998:38). Further, we see the dispersion and multiplication of the audience for this sort of criminality, and the stylized decentering of individual and group identity within it; for graffiti writers and others "caught up in the communication membrane . . . the realization of your 'self' slips into the construction of an image, a style" (Chambers 1986:11; see Hennessy 1995). Finally, as these processes come together, we witness not static criminality, but the endless, uncertain interweaving of meaning, image, and crime within a swirl of dislocated communication—that is, within a postmodern universe defined by "flux, non-linear change, chance, spontaneity, intensity, indeterminacy, irony, and orderly disorder" (Milovanovic 1997:6; see Milovanovic 1996).

Hip hop freight train graffiti thus presents a postmodern politics and epistemology—a postmodern praxis—lodged in the dynamics of everyday life, and situated within a criminal subculture of marginalized status. It reveals a type of postmodernism defined not by the arid incest of literary criticism or the insularity of intellectual debates, but by grounded moments of illicit creativity that construct for those involved an elaborate, expanding universe of symbolic communication. In postmodern terms, freight train graffiti and other hip hop graffiti practices create for their participants a "subaltern counterpublic," a "parallel discursive arena where members . . . invent and circulate counterdiscourses" and "expand discursive space" (Fraser 1995:291). These practices function, in other words, to "transcend designated spheres of activity" (Baca 1995:138), and thus to create a "postmodernism of resistance" (Foster 1985:xii).

As such, freight train graffiti can be seen to embody also the situated, antiauthoritarian politics of *anarchism.* Engaging in a collective enterprise of self-invention, self-determination, and "direct action" (Goldman 1969; Kropotkin 1975), writers construct out of little more than spray paint, trespass, and the railroads' rolling stock a complex network of shared identity and subcultural meaning. In so doing, writers reject their roles as passive consumers of mass culture and mass media; violate conventional legal definitions and legal controls of public and private property; undermine, for themselves and others, the taken-for-granted aesthetics of cultural space; and, in the process, engage "the exhilarating and dangerous task of postmodernity, the telling of new stories, the invention of new worlds" (Tomlinson 1989:56). In classic anarchist fashion, this ongoing practice of visual sabotage, self-invention, and do-it-yourself resistance creates a distinct subcultural and communal orientation for the writers, and at the same time a distinct disorientation for others as it circulates through changing contexts of meaning (Ferrell 1994, 1995a, 1996, 1997b, 1997c). In a fashion common to both postmodernism and anarchism, this practice sets in motion a playful "debunking of predictability and permanence" (Arrigo 1995:452), and an ever-expanding "ethics of disorder" (Second of January Group 1986:5).

Ultimately, then, the wide proliferation and dislocation of hip hop freight train graffiti, and the postmodern and anarchic trajectories traced by such graffiti, raise some significant questions regarding a basic criminological concern: the nature of criminal and deviant *subcultures.* In the hip hop graffiti underground generally, and with freight train graffiti specifically, subcultural dynamics generate both widespread spatial dislocation and precise stylistic organization. For graffiti writers, the subculture exists not simply as a residue of shared physical space, but as a larger community of meaning, an exploding cultural universe of collective symbolism and style that in many ways transcends space and time (Ferrell 1991, 1995b, 1996). Freight train graffiti, of course, continually expands the boundaries of this cultural universe, and poses for criminologists a boundary question of another sort: Can those who have never met, but who have conversed, long-distance and secondhand, within a shared symbolic community, be considered inhabitants of the same subculture?

If the answer is affirmative—and the phenomenon of hip hop freight train graffiti certainly suggests that it is—some criminologists would note with concern the ease by which the practices of deviant or criminal subcultures are disseminated, and would point to fluid dislocations of image and style as the ready medium for this dispersal. Like-minded criminal justice practitioners would no doubt agree, and might add that traditional techniques of prevention and enforcement, grounded as they are in static conceptions of crime, criminals, and criminality, today seem all but overwhelmed by subcultural worlds swirling with impermanent imagery, renegotiated meaning, and ongoing self-invention. Other criminologists, more attuned to the dynamics of crime and resistance than those of crime and control, might instead marvel at the ingenuity of graffiti writers and other "outsiders" in constructing collective networks of symbolic meaning, and thus collectively engineering an escape from the claustrophobic constraints of isolation and marginality. Still others inclined to theoretical refinement might develop from Sutherland and Cressey (1978) the notion that criminal behavior can be learned not only interpersonally, but intertextually; and might explore the ways in which delinquent subcultures (Cohen 1955) mobilize widespread symbolic resources in constructing common solutions to their members' shared frustrations. But in any case, for hip hop graffiti writers the trains move on, and inscribe by their movement an emergent circuit of subculture, media, and dislocation.

ACKNOWLEDGMENTS

The author thanks Marilyn McShane, Rasta 68, Alex Seago, Neil Websdale, Ralph Weisheit, and Frank Williams III for insights and information; and David Riker of the Burlington Northern Santa Fe Railway for his assistance.

NOTES

1.   Published in an international graffiti magazine, a review of a new book on hip hop graffiti noted that this book "could and should influence Writers now and for

generations to come, with at least the same impact that *Subway Art* did for thousands of youths, in hundreds of cities across the world" (Prime 1997:4).

2. See Ferrell (1996:65–66) for more on the meaning and nature of these discards.

3. In one exceptional case, tags on fixed structures in and around the Winslow, Arizona, railyards were found to match the tags on some freight cars in the yards, thus indicating that at least a very small portion of the freight train graffiti there had been produced locally (June 1997).

4. In one unusual case, the location identifier tagged with a throw up did in fact match its present location. On a freight car photographed in the Fort Worth, Texas, rail yards (July 1997), a writer had thrown up "SET!", tagged "SET" next to it, and tagged below it "FORT WORTH, TEXAS" and "THIS TIP SUCKS" (in reference to a defective spray paint nozzle).

5. Train tunnels have likewise become graffiti playgrounds, and sites for informal graffiti galleries and museums, in New York City and elsewhere. See for example Freedom's "The History of Graffiti" metamural in an abandoned train tunnel beneath Riverside Park in New York City (in Chalfant and Prigoff 1987:13); see also Walsh (1996:64–69).

6. The website *Art Crimes: The Writing on the Wall* (http://www.graffiti.org) provides an excellent overview of graffiti-related images and information on the Internet. It also incorporates a wide-ranging gallery of train graffiti, and offers links to hundreds of other Internet graffiti websites from around the United States and the world. Among these websites—many of which also include train graffiti images and information—are *Wall Rockers Anonymous* (http://members.tripod.com/Oar1RTD/index-3.html), *Minneapolis Graffiti and Public Art Photo Gallery* (http://www.geocities.com/Athens/Parthenon/7474/graffitti.html), *The Internet's Ghetto* (http://www.geocities.com/Paris/Bistro/7187), and *sAmer'z gRaffiti hEdz* (http://members.tripod.com/sameism).

7. While in the Winslow, Arizona railyards, for example, I have many times witnessed trains covered with tags, throw ups, and pieces slowly passing walls covered in local hip hop and gang graffiti—and passing also in front of a small railway building, featuring a sign reading SANTA FE RAILWAY CRIMESTOPPERS 1-800-432-6932.

8. These case accounts are also at best limited translations of visual environments and vocabularies into the domain of the written word.

9. Los Angeles or L.A. signatures were also found affixed to hip hop graffiti in the Winslow, Arizona, railyards (July 1996).

10. In April 1998 a student researcher found and photographed this same tanker car and METROE SMS KREW piece parked on a siding in Flagstaff, Arizona. Her photographs revealed that, at some time during the intervening year since I had discovered the piece west of Albuquerque, New Mexico—and now a year and a half after it had been painted in Portland, Oregon—the piece had been partially crossed out ("diss'd") by other writers.

Regarding freight train graffiti writers' public disclaimers and apologies, see similarly the disclaimer noted in note 4. Likewise, a freight car found in the Fort Worth, Texas, Union Pacific railyards (December 1997) featured throw ups by various New

Orleans writers, and the disclaimer REAL DARK 'N' SLOPPY. For more on this phenomenon of public disclaimers and apologies among hip hop writers, see Cooper and Chalfant (1984:38) and Ferrell (1996, 1997a:5).

11. Exactly one year later—December 24, 1997—a freight car parked on the outskirts of Odessa, Texas, features another tagged, cross-border message from Canada: TAKE FIVE CANADA. WHEEL CHAIR FUNK. ONE CONTINENT ONE LOVE FROM CANADA.

12. A remarkable example of this remaking of cultural space, and confrontation with the aesthetics of authority, is found in a German graffiti crew's "bombing" of a bomber—that is, their painting of tags and pieces on a military fighter plane, and the bombs it carries; see Henkel et al. (1994:35).

REFERENCES

Arrigo, Bruce. 1995. "The Peripheral Core of Law and Criminology: On Postmodern Social Theory and Conceptual Integration." *Justice Quarterly* 12:447–72.

Atlanta, C. and G. Alexander. 1989. "Wild Style: Graffiti Painting." Pp. 156–68 in *Zoot Suits and Second-Hand Dresses,* edited by A. McRobbie. Houndmills, UK: Macmillan.

Baca, Judith F. 1995. "Whose Monument Where? Public Art in a Many-Cultured Society." Pp. 131–38 in *Mapping the Terrain: New Genre Public Art,* edited by S. Lacy. Seattle: Bay.

Bailey, Frankie Y. and Donna C. Hale, eds. 1998. *Popular Culture, Crime, and Justice.* Belmont, CA: West/Wadsworth.

Barak, Gregg, ed. 1994. *Media, Process, and the Social Construction of Crime: Studies in Newsmaking Criminology.* New York: Garland.

Baudrillard, Jean. 1985. "The Ecstasy of Communication." Pp. 126–34 in *Postmodern Culture,* edited by H. Foster. London: Pluto.

Becker, Howard S. 1963. *Outsiders: Studies in the Sociology of Deviance.* New York: Free Press.

Bright, Brenda J. 1995. "Remappings: Los Angeles Low Riders." Pp. 89–123 in *Looking High and Low: Art and Cultural Identity,* edited by B. J. Bright and L. Bakewell. Tucson: University of Arizona Press.

Castleman, Craig. 1982. *Getting Up: Subway Graffiti in New York.* Cambridge: MIT Press.

Chalfant, Henry and James Prigoff. 1987. *Spraycan Art.* London: Thames and Hudson.

Chambers, Iain. 1986. *Popular Culture: The Metropolitan Experience.* London: Methuen.

Chervokas, Jason and Tom Watson. 1998. "Graffiti Artists Tag the Web Wall." *CyberTimes: The New York Times on the Web,* January 2. (http://www.nytimes.com/library/cyber/nation/010298nation.html).

Cohen, Albert K. 1955. *Delinquent Boys: The Culture of the Gang.* New York: Free Press.

Coles, Robert. 1997. *Doing Documentary Work.* New York: Oxford University Press.

Cooper, Martha and Henry Chalfant. 1984. *Subway Art.* London: Thames and Hudson.

Cressey, Donald R. 1954. "The Differential Association Theory and Compulsive Crime." *Journal of Criminal Law and Criminology* 45:49–64.

Ferrell, Jeff. 1991. "The Brotherhood of Timber Workers and the Culture of Conflict." *Journal of Folklore Research* 28:163–77.

Ferrell, Jeff. 1994. "Confronting the Agenda of Authority: Critical Criminology, Anarchism, and Urban Graffiti." Pp. 161–78 in *Varieties of Criminology: Readings from a Dynamic Discipline,* edited by G. Barak. Westport, CT: Praeger.

Ferrell, Jeff. 1995a. "Urban Graffiti: Crime, Control, and Resistance." *Youth and Society* 27:73–92.

Ferrell, Jeff. 1995b. "Style Matters: Criminal Identity and Social Control." Pp. 169–89 in *Cultural Criminology,* edited by J. Ferrell and C. R. Sanders. Boston: Northeastern University Press.

Ferrell, Jeff. 1995c. "The World Politics of Wall Painting." Pp. 277–94 in *Cultural Criminology,* edited by J. Ferrell and C. R. Sanders. Boston: Northeastern University Press.

Ferrell, Jeff. 1996. *Crimes of Style: Urban Graffiti and the Politics of Criminality.* Boston: Northeastern University Press.

Ferrell, Jeff. 1997a. "Criminological Verstehen: Inside the Immediacy of Crime." *Justice Quarterly* 14:3–23.

Ferrell, Jeff. 1997b. "Against the Law: Anarchist Criminology." Pp. 146–54 in *Thinking Critically About Crime,* edited by B. MacLean and D. Milovanovic. Vancouver, BC: Collective.

Ferrell, Jeff. 1997c. "Youth, Crime, and Cultural Space." *Social Justice* 24:21–38.

Ferrell, Jeff and Mark S. Hamm, eds. 1998. *Ethnography at the Edge: Crime, Deviance, and Field Research.* Boston: Northeastern University Press.

Ferrell, Jeff and Clinton R. Sanders, eds. 1995. *Cultural Criminology.* Boston: Northeastern University Press.

Foster, Hal. 1985. "Postmodernism: A Preface." Pp. ix–xvi in *Postmodern Culture,* edited by H. Foster. London: Pluto.

Fraser, Nancy. 1995. "Politics, Culture, and the Public Sphere: Toward a Postmodern Conception." Pp. 287–312 in *Social Postmodernism: Beyond Identity Politics,* edited by L. Nicholson and S. Seidman. Cambridge, UK: Cambridge University Press.

Goldman, Emma. 1969. *Anarchism and Other Essays.* New York: Dover.

Henkel, Olivia, Tamara Domentat, and Rene Westhoff. 1994. *Spray City: Graffiti in Berlin.* Germany: Schwarzkopf.

Hennessy, Rosemary. 1995. "Queer Visibility in Commodity Culture." Pp. 142–83 in *Social Postmodernism: Beyond Identity Politics,* edited by L. Nicholson and S. Seidman. Cambridge, UK: Cambridge University Press.

Herbert, Steve. 1997. *Policing Space: Territoriality and the Los Angeles Police Department.* Minneapolis: University of Minnesota Press.

Kidd-Hewitt, David and Richard Osborne, eds. 1995. *Crime and the Media: The Post-Modern Spectacle.* London: Pluto.

Klofas, John and Charles Cutshall. 1985. "Unobtrusive Research Methods in Criminal

Justice: Using Graffiti in the Reconstruction of Institutional Cultures." *Journal of Research in Crime and Delinquency* 22:355–73.

Kornbluh, Joyce L. 1988. *Rebel Voices: An IWW Anthology.* Chicago: Charles H. Kerr.

Kropotkin, Peter. 1975. *The Essential Kropotkin.* New York: Liveright.

Lachmann, Richard. 1988. "Graffiti as Career and Ideology." *American Journal of Sociology* 94:229–50.

Manning, Peter. 1998. "Media Loops." Pp. 25–39 in *Popular Culture, Crime, and Justice,* edited by F. Bailey and D. Hale. Belmont, CA: West/Wadsworth.

Matthews, Mark. 1997. "Train Tramps Ride Rails of Crime." *Police: The Law Enforcement Magazine* 21:14–18.

Merrifield, Andy and Erik Swyngedouw, eds. 1997. *The Urbanization of Injustice.* New York: New York University Press.

Mills, C. Wright. 1940. "Situated Actions and Vocabularies of Motive." *American Sociological Review* 5:904–13.

Milovanovic, Dragan. 1996. "Postmodern Criminology: Mapping the Terrain." *Justice Quarterly* 13:567–610.

Milovanovic, Dragan. 1997. "Postmodernist versus the Modernist Paradigm: Conceptual Differences." Pp. 3–28 in *Chaos, Criminology, and Social Justice: The New Orderly (Dis)Order,* edited by D. Milovanovic. Westport, CT: Praeger.

Murphy, Kim. 1997. "Brotherhood May Have Deadly Control Over Rails." *The Arizona Republic (Los Angeles Times),* September 20, p. A1.

Prime. 1997. "Style Writing from the Underground." *Graphotism International* 9(Spring):4.

Quiroz, Jose. 1996. Interview with Jose Quiroz, Publisher, *Night Crawler Magazine.* MTV, "Authority Sucks" (April 30).

Rivers, Robin. 1997. "Hobo Band Blamed in 300 Transient Deaths." *The Arizona Republic (Spokane Spokesman-Review),* September 13, p. A25.

Rotenberg, Robert and Gary McDonogh, eds. 1993. *The Cultural Meaning of Urban Space.* Westport, CT: Bergin and Garvey.

Royko, Mike. 1996. "Art may Be in Eye of Beholder; Graffiti Sticks in the Craw." *Chicago Tribune,* September 24, p. 3.

Sagarin, Edward. 1973. "The Research Setting and the Right Not to Be Researched." *Social Problems* 21:52–64.

Sanchez-Tranquilino, Marcos. 1995. "Space, Power, and Youth Culture: Mexican American Graffiti and Chicano Murals in East Los Angeles, 1972–1978." Pp. 55–88 in *Looking High and Low: Art and Cultural Identity,* edited by B. J. Bright and L. Bakewell. Tucson: University of Arizona Press.

Schwartz, Martin D. and David O. Friedrichs. 1994. "Postmodern Thought and Criminological Discontent: New Metaphors for Understanding Violence." *Criminology* 32:221–46.

Second of January Group. 1986. *After Truth: A Post-Modern Manifesto.* London: Inventions.

Surette, Ray. 1998. *Media, Crime, and Criminal Justice,* 2nd edition. Belmont, CA: West/Wadsworth.

Sutherland, Edwin. H. and Donald R. Cressey. 1978. *Criminology,* 10th edition. Philadelphia: Lippincott.

Tomlinson, Hugh. 1989. "After Truth: Post-Modernism and the Rhetoric of Science." Pp. 43–57 in *Dismantling Truth: Reality in the Post-Modern World,* edited by H. Lawson and L. Appignanesi. New York: St. Martin's.

van Treeck, Bernhard and Mark Todt. 1995. *Hall of Fame: Graffiti in Deutschland.* Moers, Germany: Edition Aragon.

Vonnegut, Kurt. [1968] 1988. *Slaughterhouse-Five.* New York: Dell.

Walsh, Michael. 1996. *Graffito.* Berkeley, CA: North Atlantic.

Webb, Eugene J., Donald T. Campbell, Richard D. Schwartz, and Lee Sechrest. 1966. *Unobtrusive Measures: Nonreactive Research in the Social Sciences.* Chicago: Rand McNally.

V

Constructions of Policing and Control

12

Reflections
The Visual as a Mode of Social Control

PETER K. MANNING

INTRODUCTION

Social theory and criminological thought remain haunted by the ghosts of the nineteenth century, and imaginative exploration is required to recast theories of symbolic interaction, communication, and control. Interactionist theory featuring concepts of identity, self, and biographical continuity seems of dubious validity in a era shaped increasingly by electronic information technology and mass communications. In addition, social control theories generally take little account of the symbolic, especially the visual, in explicating processes of social control.

Clearly, reasons exist for these gaps in theorizing. Jay (1993) argues persuasively that the visual was less significant than the written for early-twentieth-century writers, and suggests that this heritage has shaped theorizing subsequently (Berman 1982). Recent developments (Foucault 1977; Poster 1990a; Cohen 1985; Lyon 1994; Bogard 1996) now require exploring the subtle connections between reflections, both interpersonal and in the media, the visual, and control. Theories of the self, and of social control and deviance, it is argued here, should be connected to the interactional contexts of self-viewing, watching, and performing, collectively and individually, as well as to modes of control, surveillance, and simulation now commonly found in work, consumption, and mass leisure.

In what follows I consider the "visual in social organization," focusing especially on television and other screens, and their roles in shaping interaction, the self, and the other; the presence and prevalence of screens as a source of reflection; and the social control implications of negotiating public and private visual experiences, particularly in the arenas of policing, medicine, and the workplace. Conclusions about the implications of the visual for self and social control and the future of the mediated self and social control follow.

THE VISUAL IN SOCIAL ORGANIZATION

The significance of the visual in social relations changes as societies differentiate and mass communications proliferate (Benjamin 1969; Berman 1982). I review now the several powerful forces that have produced this result.

Durkheim ([1915] 1961) taught us that social differentiation and integration arise through concrete interactions leading to a division of labor and that the collective conscience is strengthened by symbolic representations that both reflect and express "society." Concrete, embodied, and visible presence is the touchstone of preliterate and preindustrial societies, and activates self-control (Nadel 1953), even as representations of the collective conscience are salient.

The real, or social reality, was seen as grounded in some fundamental epistemological basis—that of personal experience. This meant that in industrialized societies, representations and the real were distinguished. Although there is a rich literature on representations and doubles, and mimesis (Auberbach 1953) analogously, originals and copies were seen as distinct, in part because surface features (size, quality, color, texture, hue) varied, and the idea of a defining consensual reference point existed. Now, even the notion of copy is elastic and dubious (Benjamin 1969; Eco 1990:174–202). The notion of an "original" becomes dubious; an "original" is submerged by the hundreds of ways available to copy it (Benjamin 1969). The surface features of a digitalized transmission, "data," can be encoded or encrypted and decoded in many ways to produce sound, graphics, images, or text, and they, in turn, can be reproduced or "materialized" variously. What is "real" is determined not by the data (sound, pictures, text, or graphics) but by the code(s), bandwidth, and the embodiment of the bits when displayed (Negroponte 1996:60–61).

The key concept, "reflection," itself suggests a realizable substance or grounding; but modern reflection seems notoriously elusive, resembling more a revolving set of mirrors than a matter of perspectival representation. Copying and screening, synthetic versions of "originals," have interactional implications because they move social life away from the material world and even nominal notions of "truth." Goffman (1974:8), for example, assumes a primary face-to-face reality as a grounding for other more abstracted experience. This links his ideas indirectly with symbolic interactionism, in which the self develops through identification with significant others and then the generalized other representing social control or society at large (Mead 1934).

It appears now that the "self" is perhaps "selves," and is more protean and malleable, even "decentered," and the "other," variously socially located (Goffman 1974:524–39). The self and other, once bounded by commonsense limitations or the "embeddedness" of action in social relations, are now more likely to be "disembedded" (Giddens 1990:53). Knowledge and reflection, rather than tradition and long-standing conventions, guide conduct; space and time are segregated. National boundaries, social and personal locations are less significant. These developments cast doubt on the viability of the Meadian notions, in part because the "other" is now more likely to be seen as a result of the media, or "mediated" in some respect.

Experience, perhaps since television, results from both face-to-face communication and in a dialectic between technologically produced and distributed images and culturally sanctioned forms (Ewen 1988; Poster 1990b). The preponderance of stranger-stranger interactions and technologically mediated interactions has implications for social control. Social integration may reflect a "working consensus" (Goffman 1959:10) represented (and simulated) across time and space and enacted through complex interactive exchanges. This results in part because interaction is increasingly orchestrated on the basis of trust and where the source of the message is unknown or of low or dubious validity. These features, acting in high-tech, commodified societies, alter the meaning of the visual because not only is trust implicit, but the "others" may not be seen, smelled, touched, or even heard, or are figures created by media realities such as celebrities.

Postmodern societies manifest new forms of interaction, social control, and integration, and the massification of experience, both its thin and elusive character and its homogenization, proceeds apace (DeBord 1990). Style and substance are disconnected (Ewen 1988) in art, architecture, and social relations because deep knowledge is unavailable and performance and appearance are the most useful and salient clues to meaning. These new forms are problematic because they are now reflected and reflected upon. Reflections are opportunities to assess what is seen, heard, smelled, or touched, whether arising from others directly or indirectly. Media transformation and dissemination of images now produce a myriad of both personal and societal level reflections.

While all societies reflect upon themselves through collective symbolism, and set moral boundaries, modern societies reflect, in part through mass communications and information technology, and then reflect upon their reflections. This reflective capacity is a distinguishing feature of postmodern or postindustrial societies.

Reflection is both concrete in the sense that we see ourselves in actual screens now proliferating, and abstract, a product of a consideration of the past and future meanings of our conduct and the responses of others. History is only the having-been-present, not a binding constraint.

Screens and Reflections

An avenue into modern reflection and reflective processes is to explore how screens, as the apparent manifestation of reflection, multiply our experiences. The development of still photography, primitive viewing machines such as the stereopticon, and later the Viewmaster allowed us to see images of ourselves; these became dynamic with the invention of the hand-held "movie" camera and then the videocam. This technology transformed self-viewing from still to moving, and from moving to virtually on-line—as when a video camera is connected to a television screen so that images are repro-duced "live" as they are captured.

We see ourselves now on many quite different types and sizes of screens. Some are in public settings, others more private. We watch alone, indirectly with others while interacting with people via screens, and in groups and in masses. Screens (or "monitors") glow in schools, bars, vans and buses, busi-nesses, stadia, airports, supermarkets, cafes, and on people. Consider some examples of how we see ourselves: on telephone LED screens showing the number dialed, time of the call, and line used; in movies and in the movies via identification; on screens suspended above an operating table revealing the interior of an opened body; on similar screens in supermarkets showing dizzying views of vast parking lots; in screens in bars, department and appliance stores, and airports; on a living room television screen; in words strung out across a computer monitor, reseen, retrieved, and edited; on small screens mounted on the back of a seat in airplanes; on multiple "windows" showing aspects of a self in "Windows 95 or 98"; on massive screens suspended high above arenas; and in recycled images, such as photographs or slides, stored and shown on a film-processing or copy ma-chine, or received via fax. These suggest a range from very public to more "private" screening experiences. Pagers, laptops, personal organizers, and multipurpose instruments (phones called "Cyberdisplay" with internet con-nections), all have microscreens. Other hand-held or strapped-on devices, video games, global positioning instruments, microtelevisions, personal heart monitors, and elaborate watches have displays—some with tiny screens and menus changed by the push of a button, such as using a com-puter, playing video and computer games (hand held, laptop or on home or office micro-computers), or watching TV, a VCR-video, or a hand-held tele-vision. The "other" seen may be the self, even as the self watches with others.

These are visible screens. Others are not. We do not know who is watch-ing and filming us through one-way glass in a supermarket or department store, but it may be consequential; on multiscreen surveillance monitoring rooms in large buildings. Many routine transactions, at toll booths, banks, and ATMs are filmed. Caller I.D. devices show caller information to the person called. Here the other sees the self as the other, but the self is unaware of being watched or filmed.

Clearly, the context of watching affects the experience, but there is little research on the meaning of the experience, its social grounding, the social networks in which screens are lodged (Wellman 1997; Turkle 1984), or the long-term consequences of such watching and being watched (and being watched watching). Given these quite different and sometimes mixed modes of reflection, the question is not the presence or absence of reflection, but how and why a particular form of reflection is created, our knowledge of it, and its consequences for social control.

External Commercial Controls

Our capacity to reflect and reflect upon reflection is amplified massively by such ubiquitous screens, and behind them, networks of information technology, and commercial entertainment media. This is a vast, expensive, agglomerated market-driven industry. These screens, like everyday social activity, are filled by arbitrary, i.e., culturally motivated, signs that float without clear referents, yet are rationally constructed to stimulate and simulate feelings, to motivate, entertain, inform, and persuade. Such created signs and associated discourse, designed by advertising companies, public relations firms, and corporations, are widely and almost immediately disseminated to potential buyers and targeted markets by information technology. This is combined with the passive and active accumulation of computerized data by credit card companies, credit-checking companies, home-shopping networks, mail order companies, and active "agents" for "personalized" shopping and services. The proliferating visual aspects of societies are driven in large part by accumulated capital and markets in commodities that are created, distributed, and sold using the mass media and information technology. The distribution of images is now a very lucrative commercial industry.

The media are an industry with political implications, as well as reproducing culture, selectively representing the world, and selling goods and services. The media act in subtle, indirect, and direct ways as conduits of social control, surveillance, monitoring, and classification. They are a fundamental mechanism in active social control, i.e., the selective enforcement of norms through sanctioning in a network of communicants.

THE PRESENCE AND PREVALENCE OF SCREENS AS A SOURCE OF REFLECTION

Screens, especially those showing the mass media and EMC (electronic mass communications), are present everywhere and everywhere present. I should like to take "television" as the quintessential example of the mass visual media, and draw inferences from its features. Virtually every American home has a television—and the average is 2.2 color television sets per home. Some 78 percent of American homes feature a VCR (letter to the editor, *New York Review of Books,* 16 June 1997). The purpose of "programming" is to embed advertising. The television-related industries finance, create, produce, distribute, and facilitate commercially produced images. Many images (with sound) are produced, marketed, and sold for home consumption. Consider here rented or purchased videos, cable television, pay-for-view television shows, laser discs and multimedia discs, and images available through the Internet or watched via a "computer."

In addition, other screens exist. There were some 120 million computers worldwide in 1996, a number that may have doubled by 1998. Some 35 percent of American families have computers (in 1994, 65 percent of new computers sold were for home use), and 50 percent of American teenagers have a home computer (Negroponte 1996:8). There are four thousand host servers (Internet service providers, ISPs) on the Internet, growing at the rate of 20 percent a year (ibid.:182), and some twelve million users of America-On-Line (AOL) alone (*New York Times,* hereafter *NYT,* 2 July 1998). Negroponte estimates one billion users by the year 2000 because websites double every fifty days, and a new one appears every four seconds (1996:233)!

Although the presence of screens and reflections is formatted, structured, and driven by "media logic," the selectively processed content has important impacts on viewers, especially as audiences become accustomed to the formats and content conventions. All visual media, especially television, represent the external world in a stylized, mannered, and aesthetically shaped fashion. Television both captures and transforms the external world. Television employs formats and genres (style and content) to capture attention and entertain (Gronbeck 1997). These genres are often conflated (news + entertainment = infotainment); intermingled (television programs show people watching movies and commenting on them; television news programs show scenes from O.J. Simpson's video explaining what "really" happened, and then have legal experts comment on his comments); simulated ("Cops" footage, although edited and reorganized, and with voice-over narration at some points, is presented as naturally occurring or "real policing"); confused and confusing (a warning shown at the beginning of a television movie: "Although this is a work of fiction, it is based on real events"); and new genres are created such as the "Stupid Videos" show, constituted by recycling home videos for mass entertainment. Mass media create and authoritatively reify social forms, modify and mix communicational genres in confusing fashion (Fiske 1987).

Modern society produces images about images, or frames other images in complex rapid fashion, especially in the form of "media looping" (Manning 1998), while the Internet is an obvious, fast, copy machine. The problem of modern industrial society is not the absence, production, transmission, or storage of information, but the definition, meaning, and value of "dig-italized" information, and the saturation-level presence of images and infor-mation. Wisdom or knowledge is buried in a heap of factoids.

The media avidly monitor and reflect on each other's reflections: they specialize in embedding images one inside the other, creating nested social realities, recycling them, looping and transforming the images and stories, and shaping and reshaping themes found in other media (ibid.). In this way, they quote each other without reference to the validity of the "original" or first source or image, quote, inference, or claim, while claiming that "protec-tion of sources," "freedom of the press," and "professional ethical standards" are operating. In this sense, the media are self-referential (they refer to themselves) rather than a "mirror," and a self-contained autopoietic system. They have mastered the notion of a "spin" or a "take" and take the conflation of spin and persuasion for granted. "The notion that this is the age of spin rests on the premise that everything, including the truth, is potentially an instrument of manipulation" (Gladwell 1998:69).

Having characterized television as the quintessential mass media form, it is important to focus on the role of the visual in social control. All of the above points suggest subtle forms of social control in the sense that they shape, reward, sanction, and reify some kinds of selves and others selec-tively. The shaping and rewarding appears to be based on the growing influence of the market in goods, services, and commodities on watching, even as playful use and sociability are sustained. The workings of television, and perhaps of other screens, are the nexus within which both instrumental and expressive conduct take place.

Television and Framing

"Television" is seen within a frame, a fabrication, or framing of the real, understood as being intended to entertain. Television is a mannered realistic presentation of fabrications. Framed apart from everyday life, it is also deep-ly grounded in it. Television is a special kind of framing: a cognitive-definitional process by which a segment of experience is isolated cogni-tively, labeled, and set aside as an instance of something (a social form generally), or as Goffman put it, a clue to the question, "What is going on here?" (1974:10–11).[1]

An analysis of how people manage to see television as showing the "real" in convincing, realistic fashion, reveals by analogy how any social activity is seen as real. While viewers upon reflection recognize that television is a social creation, and recognize the techniques and forms used to convey reality (Kappeler, Blumberg, and Potter 1993:24–26; Fiske 1987), once in the television frame, the motivated aspects of image-presentation are suppressed. The backstage "workings" implied by knowledge of how television uses technology to transform everyday activities into images are bracketed. Framing serves to systematically and intentionally isolate strips of activity.

Television is also perceived, interpreted, and interpolated within the viewers' social worlds (Fiske 1987; Taylor and Mullan 1986). These may be many, if the experience is shared: the pop celebrity world, the "mall" culture, academic life, and the elite intellectual life on both coasts. Viewers manage to grasp and maintain a dualistic vision: their own interpretation of the meaning of events and a general typification of events in the "real world." As in the theater, viewers willingly suspend disbelief in a set of recognizable yet unseen cognitive mechanisms.

Perceptions and use of the mass media create a loose boundary between "the real" (as represented) and the imagined (as a result of watching). A dialectic arises between "the real" and the "imagined," and is critical to understanding television's role in social control. The cognitive work of viewers, in their isolation or together, is a "hidden link" between television as an entertainment industry with a supple and powerful technology and television as experienced. If television is to "work," make money for networks, and maintain their shares of the viewing market, it must be seen and understood as both information and entertainment. This characterization does not obviate the infrastructures that convey screen realism. The conditions under which "information," sports, or "news" programs create, frame, or encode, social activities as realistic media events are discernible to audiences. Audiences can identify and define, redefine and respond to these genres in complex ways.[2]

Information networks and television simulate private, intimate interpersonal relations by facilitating visual connections, accessible at any time day or night across nations and cultures, and embed messages in a variety of culturally sanctioned forms—games, storytelling, conversation, and browsing or surfing (Herz 1995, 1997). However, the messages are stripped of setting, present others, and are not readily validated. Source and context are omitted. Electronic two-way communication does not require a "valid" personal identity, real address, or even a socially legitimated self, although each may exist. Such shared social identities may lead to expanded social networks (Kendall 1998).

Visual experiences such as television are powerful, even though, or perhaps because, the precise workings of such imagery are not well understood. Television's power comes from its counterintuitive presentation of time and space unfolding before the viewer's eyes (Williams 1974). This powerful capacity frees the signs displayed from social constraints and makes the experience labile, or easily nudged into hyperreality (Poster 1990a, 1990b). Violating the logic of causality, it represents itself as presenting the present, or the now, immediately. Watching television is an engaging experience that combines the "real," the might-be real, the surreal, and the fantastic. The quality of the interface between the screen and the person varies from distance and detachment to close attachment and intimate, almost embedded involvement, and is patterned by whether the viewing is interactive or passive.

The content (color, speed, texture, movements, camera angles) of television and the style with which the image is presented affect the meaning of the experience of watching. Television's effect on personal relations is most striking when it seeks the immediate and thrusts itself into (symbolic) personal space, showing intense human reactions to disasters, serial murders, or grand accomplishments. It also mimics the immediate, showing its own effects, people's reactions to the aggressive intrusion of cameras, video crews, lights, microphones, and the interviewers.

Viewing amplifies some emotions, and it provides a niche, or place for emotionally lodged selves. Television is rooted in the emotional preconditions and predispositions of modern life, and reproduces experiences meaningful to the viewer's self. Television is a powerful projective source from which emotions are read and read-off (Goffman 1959). The fabrication of intimate realities is television's forte.

Interaction on screen, or even watching television, in dialogue with viewers' readings, produces redundant, cybernetic, emotional, and expressive communication that provides a kind of "back channel" self-affirmation. Representation and reflection are central to the self-consciousness of modern society, but this self-consciousness is itself a function in part of media amplification, the reality-producing capacity of television—its socioemotional power—and the workings of other electronic forms of connectedness. Let us now examine how private and public visual experiences shape the self.

THE SOCIAL CONTROL IMPLICATIONS OF NEGOTIATING PUBLIC AND PRIVATE VISUAL EXPERIENCES

The effects of the visual vary with the social context. Private experiences differ from semiprivate watching experiences and the experience of watching together. The once "private" can be converted to quasi-public or public displays. Dogs (in England) serve as camera carriers. Carrying head-mounted video cameras, they are sent into buildings to look for suspects, bombs, or other evidence. Thus the shadows of social control appear in media use within given institutions such as the police. In what follows, I will also explore the way they surface in medicine and in the workplace.

As an entree into these shadows of social control I turn to the effects of cameras watching the self. They may show a person, peer into the self or body, or watch without knowledge of the watched. This latter is a rather different experience than seeing a self unfolding on a screen based on one's choices. These images, once captured, have many uses, but they are often used in social control. Cameras and screens on which the images are shown serve to convert the previously intimate or private semipublic to "data" processed in modern service industries. They are used to make visible otherwise quasi-private behavior, often without the awareness of the person, to control and punish, to stimulate consumption, and to protect individuals from legal action.

Policing

The police use of videos indicates the influence of visuals on "service" (Manning 1996b). Quasi-public behavior is now captured without permission by cameras in many settings:

- Shopping and traveling are filmed via cameras, and often hidden cameras film people in shops, subways, parks, train stations, squares, supermarket parking lots, and malls, and at stop signs and lights.
- Leisure activities (crowds at football matches in England, walks in the park) are filmed, often by hidden cameras.

These filmed records, edited and monitored, may be used to find villains, shown for purposes of identifying and naming suspects, and used in court as evidence.

Other filming of police work serves to monitor police as well as citizens:

- Traffic stops for "drunk driving" (captured once an officer with a video camera mounted in the car stops a driver). These serve as deterrence and controls on officer's behavior and are used to support police claims, deny liability, establish evidence, and influence juries.
- All police actions outside the car. The New Jersey State Police will soon have video cameras in all their vehicles (*NYT*, 16 June 1998). Florida's Volusia County Sheriff's Department and Maryland state troopers are being monitored for the proportion of black drivers stopped (*Lansing State Journal*, hereafter *LSJ*, 28 May 1997).
- The inside of jail cells, police offices, and lobbies are surveilled by stationary cameras.
- Routine police work—booking prisoners into jail, transmitting images and records from police station to jail, sending fingerprints and photos

electronically to the FBI, and filming police raids and critical incidents.

Some police visuals are used for public relations. For example:

- Several city police departments permit the filming of the TV show "Cops," but retain editing and censorship rights before the films are edited and shown (Hallett and Powell 1995).
- The Portland, Oregon, Police Bureau, and many others, maintain web-sites on the Internet that include maps, diagrams, statistics, and pictures.
- The FBI has placed some 16,000 pages of case files on the Internet (www.fbi.gov) and plans to post a total of 1.3 million pages. This is said to serve those members of the public requesting information un-der the Freedom of Information Act (*LSJ*, 17 June 1998).
- Many of the above police-produced videos, or news film, in turn, are given to television stations, looped or recycled, and shown on the news, feature programs, and documentaries.
- Some city police (e.g., Lansing, San Diego, Chicago) are increasingly using geomapping to produce graphics, tables, and maps of crimes, calls for service, and neighborhood characteristics, thus rendering mi-croscopically the aesthetics of a "neighborhood," police precinct, or city. These visuals are then used to inform citizens of their current problems. The Chicago police department considered installing termi-nals in stations with the mapping function for public use.

These powerful surveillance technologies can also be used by citizens to bring events to the attention of the police, or used against the police themselves.

- Two Michigan school districts have equipped more than half their buses with sound and video cameras that the drivers can monitor (*LSJ*, 1 December 1997).
- Citizens have produced videos initiating criminal investigations and arrests—the most famous being the beating of Rodney King by mem-bers of the LAPD, but also including films of the hazing of marine recruits (*LSJ*, 1 February 1997).
- An African American ex–LAPD officer cruises around Los Angeles with $15,000 worth of video equipment in his van, hoping to film an illegal stop and or search (*LSJ*, 28 May 1997).
- Dr. Jack Kervorkian, the master of assisted suicide in Michigan, has given police videos showing people killing themselves without his presence as a way of protecting himself against charges of homicide.

Medicine

Medicine uses videos to diagnose, examine, monitor and carry out treatments. As a result of these developments, one can now have active visual knowledge of some aspect of the internal structure of one's own body, even during the course of surgery.

- Patients are permitted to watch their own operations, "on line," in progress. Above the patient in the operating room is a screen on which the patient, doctors, and assistants can view an operation.
- Patients are given films of their operations so they can replay them for families and friends. These are perhaps even more powerful when the person observed can observe the inside and (perhaps flawed) workings of his/her heart, colon, anus, or vagina.
- These same films can be archived and used for diagnostic procedures. They are visual records that will guide the next operation if needed.
- If a father with a camera occupies the delivery room during a child's delivery, he might film the screen, the operating room, baby, and mother. The patient or mother sees herself being filmed as well as seeing her insides out. However, videos of childbirth in hospital, like police videos, become evidence, part of the "quality control" and civil liability of the medical profession. Some hospitals now ban fathers-with-videocameras from delivery rooms (LSJ, 19 June 1998).
- Operations can be carried out at a distance. In laser heart operations, knife and camera both penetrate the heart, but the chief surgeon may not be in the operating room with the patient but miles away viewing the operation via video camera and a computer that assists the surgeon guiding the knife. Doctors using laser procedures can in theory be in Alaska connected via computer, cameras, and fiber optics to doctors and a patient operated on in Louisiana.
- Video cameras and sound equipment are used to monitor a fetal heartbeat, and the tapes and graphics produced can be given to the patient.
- Magnetic imaging records and CAT scans can be filmed and shown in three dimensions. Pregnancy tests, and other medical signs and tests, may reveal a person's inner state, but do not visually display the body in a reproducible form.
- All such visuals can of course be transmitted digitally across the world in seconds.

Deeper modern penetration into a person is consistent with the widening of the social control net, and the potential for a widely surveilled citizenry (Foucault 1977; Cohen 1985). These detailed institutionally sanctioned and produced pictures can be used to classify, diagnose, control, and regulate masses of people. One could say that metaphorically the citizen, the patient, and the police and physicians are exposed, made transparent to various degrees, and rendered as the objects of a specialized field of knowledge relations. These machines exteriorize the inner body, including the heart, but when depicting conduct, it could be said that the soul is exposed, made overt.

The Workplace: A Quasi-Public Experience of the Visual

How does social control operate using visual means at work? Images serve to deter and control workers' behavior and regulate work processes. This occurs whether workers are aware they are being surveilled, think they are being surveilled, or are unsure. Many workers in the workplace are tracked using cameras and digitalized images. Surveillance on the job, through computer tracking of the operators' activities (*NYT*, 22 June 1997), recording of voice communication, filming of private and public spaces, bar coded and filmed entries and exits and records of such movements, is now quite easily accomplished. Legal protections, especially at work, are emergent and confusing. Employees were generally aware of these, but developing forms of control are invisible, and unknown, based on information technology (Thomas 1994). For example, employers can read off the webstream of an employee by examining the sites visited on the Internet; "cookies" as they are called, monitor the extent of game playing and either "zap" the games, or limit access via software (*LSJ*, 11 May 1998). Employees can develop countertactics if they are aware of being monitored (*LSJ*, 11 May 1997; ads for Power Book, *Newsweek*, 25 August 1997). Internet dialogues, E- and voice mails have been the basis for prosecution and firing of employees: an employee was awarded punitive damages from a company by a court because every morning when she turned on her computer, a pornographic image danced about and greeted her. An investigative journalist claimed to have access to voice mail (it is unclear as yet if he did, or if it was stolen) within a corporation as a part of his investigative reporting.

Many expressive interchanges (interpersonal relations: gossip, office politics, and friendships) shift locus to E-mail and the web; a folklore grows around mistaken communications and foul-ups. Meetings may focus less on information exchange and more on rituals of solidarity and expressive sharing (virtual office). New technologies mediate interactions, e.g., voice mail, E-mail, answering machines, and faxes. If fewer face-to-face interactions serve as ontological anchors, pinning people down to obligations and audiences, new etiquettes and rituals are devised to control mediated interactions.[3] Menus further distance callers from personal contact (even a human voice) and play Barry Manilow tunes as you wait. To reach a human voice, one has to work through a series of options and a "touch tone tango" results, recycling and redialing to reach the electronic space desired. Accessing records and data can require you to reveal your age, mother's maiden name, social security number, and other details, all of which a tinny voice informs you "may be tape recorded for purposes of quality control and for your own protection." For example, consider the controlling effects of menus on 800 lines; the algorithms and grammars of "hot lines" for computer support; the means to screen calls, or the ambiguous etiquette of answering machines. Consider that due to phone menus human communication with an "operator" is now a default option. On the other hand, technology simulates previously nonexistent intimacy that was limited because of physical distance or hardship.[4]

The sorts of filters and screens erected around people are less substantial physically (offices now have moving "work stations," flimsy mobile panels, and easily shifted furniture) but are also proliferating electronically. Think of the lag in answering E-mails, the barriers possible with cellular phones, pagers and answering machines, voice mail and a "voice mail box." In Lansing, Michigan, for example, callers seeking to speak to the chief of police (you will probably reach his staff in any case), must push their way through no less than six menus.

The skills needed to meet the impersonal demands of successful mediated communication may reduce the importance of face-to-face interpersonal relations and reduce the skills needed. Interpersonal relations, once relied on to provide problem solutions, and "emotional work," are obviated or reduced while electronic barriers arise between tasks and outcomes e.g., "The computers are down and we can't respond to your problem now." Multiple modes of communication with colleagues develop. Networks of collective action extend quickly beyond organizations via E-mail, pagers, the web, faxes, express mail, and cellular phones. New lags and ambiguities in communication result. Power-dependence (who owes what to whom when) is symbolized by lagged responses and patterned ambiguities in response.

The combination of the personalization of the computing experience, the commodification of information as property, and the corporate and university definition of "time" and "electronic space" as theirs means that efforts are made to control the use of games (and eliminate them via software); check for "illegal software"; block access to some web pages; and for the FBI (and local police) to assign agents to play roles on computers as "pedophiles" and "porn dealers" to entice "real pedophiles" and "real porn dealers" to act illegally and be subject to arrest and prosecution. A reporter searching for stories can be seen as child pornographer and a reporter (*NYT*, 7 July 1998). One can also resist being monitored and watched. Decentralization of authority and work facilitated by electronic connections is increasing. People work at home, or on the road, through links to others via screens, computers, cellular phones, fax, E-mail, and the web. Such work requires coordination through shared meanings, working consensus, and interactions even while the instrumental dimensions of communication are apparently elevated. The social networks created in this kind of labor climate are potentially meaningful (Wellman 1997). Negroponte writes, perhaps hopefully, "The value of the network is less about information and more about community" (1996:163). In short, information technology does not reduce the need for modes of social integration and expressive interactions; it may increase it (Weick 1995). Forms of workplace organization based on computer technology lead to new styles of problem solving and an oral history culture may develop around these new shared practices (ibid.).

THE IMPLICATIONS OF THE VISUAL
FOR SOCIAL AND SELF CONTROL

Mass media, in their entertainment, information provision, and service modes, are now combined in megacompanies, and their effects are not benign. Their impacts are diffuse, and electronic communications technology is not a passive actor in social control. Its links with government and market stimulation and sustenance are just being explored.

A variety of developments in social control and in the modern electronic visual media suggest that social control, or the marking of norms and values with the aim of changing behavior, is being subtly changed. My focus, for purposes of the summary, is the social location of the self.

The Self

With respect to future issues of social control and social construction of images of good and evil, deviance and crime, consider how the confusion of social realities now rules the media and private interpretations. "Real" is a function of some kind of difference, some base against which it is judged. It presumes some conventional notion about "firstness" and original, and what is a copy or reproduction of some kind. This seems a dubious distinction today (Eco 1990:174–202).

The self, which in Meadian thought (Mead 1934) is a holistic, integrative notion, is subject to fragmentation, at least by the software of computing and the experience of viewing television. However, interpersonal communication has a tenacious holism about it that resists reducing it to a single channel or mode of communication. Memories interweave what is seen, heard, felt, and smelled. It is easy to float off into hyperreality while watching a screen. This perhaps is the basis for "virtual therapy," in which a patient wears "a helmet containing video monitors and is wired to a high-speed computer that adjusts life-like images in response to the wearer's movements" ("On the Computerized House," *Parade USA Weekend,* 18–20 July 1997).

Self While Watching.   Differences arise again, because contrasts between "realities" can be confusing. Virtual realities (those created on a screen), or cyberrealities (social worlds created visually as in video games, hypertext constructions, and fantasy games), and directly experienced realities, can create ironies, or may clash—be inconsistent or even patently paradoxical. Ironies emerge because what is seen on a screen, what is known via past experience, what paperwork may reveal, and what is reported from the scene verbally often differ. This multiple-realities problem is characteristic of all formal tracking systems whether computer-assisted dispatch (CAD) in policing, navigational aids in aviation, or ship-based radar. The confusion cuts two ways: those caught and captured by these monitoring systems and those who monitor, use, and interpret them. Watching can produce a confusion of boundaries between public and private space because one can quickly be in fantasy space, historical space, dramatic space, information retrieval space, sport or games while physically watching or at "the keyboard."

The Self Interacting.   Public-private "conversations" raise questions about personal and interpersonal relations (privacy, familial obligations). What is now truly "private"? Soap opera stars and news readers generate apparent confusion in audiences, who conflate the person, the actor, the role played, his/her relations to others in the cast and in real life, and the associated emotions, character traits, biography, and skills. Self-control is made problematic by the multiplex "others" with whom one interacts via electronic media. The generalized other and the audience shift in quality and imagination. The self-other dialogue is now mediated, literally and figuratively.

The Self Observed.   The conflation of public and private means that confessionals, falls from grace, "outing" and other forms of stripping people of privacy and confidentiality run rampant in the society. While it treads a thin line between perversion, voyeurism, and "instant news," television easily penetrates the once private and personal (*NYT Magazine,* 5 July 1998).

The Self and the Other.   Media act as a direct form and forum of social control (Altheide 1996; Manning 1996b). The media argue for a right to know while at the same time they protect their sources and fabricate stories, persons, and evidence. They act to control the icons of the age, setting them up to better knock them down. The media collude with respectable authorities when it is convenient. Think here of the collusion of the media in hostage situations, in spreading disinformation and misinformation from the police concerning investigations, and in uncritically naming suspects in crimes, e.g., the Richard Jewell crucifixion by the media following his finding of the bomb at the Atlanta Olympics in 1996. More benign versions of this are television shows such as "60 Minutes" and "20/20," which lie to gain access to targets of their investigation. Media gain access to police records using the Freedom of Information Act, and then show the results, e.g., CNN's airing of the horrendous 911 call from a terrified Nicole Brown Simpson to the LAPD when her husband was threatening her.

We witness numerous links between various media substrates and the criminal justice system. For example, the *National Enquirer* purchased pictures of O.J. Simpson wearing the Bruno Magli shoes (used as evidence in the civil suit by the Brown and Goldman families against Simpson). The *New York Times* and the *Washington Post* printed the Unibomber's manifesto. In a similar vein, Court TV and CNN bring "live" and filmed court cases into the living room, edited and interspersed with "talking head" experts and "hosts." Their comments vary from expressive, concerning the mood and telegenic properties of the jury and the lawyers, to the legal and quasi-legal. Many of the authors who appeared on television analyzing the Simpson criminal trial, e.g., Jeffery Tobin, Dominic Donne, and Vincent Bugliosi, were also writing books on the media's treatment of the trial! Johnny Cochran, once a defense counsel to O.J. Simpson, now has a nightly cable show, "Cochran and Friends," in which he comments on ongoing court cases and interviews guests and experts. The man who was exposed on the Jenny Jones show as being the object of a homosexual crush later shot his admirer and was convicted of murder (*Detroit News,* 27 July 1997).

Television has indirect deterrent and punishment effects. "America's Most Wanted" leads to an escapee being captured, "Crime Stoppers" leads to a conviction, and suspects are turned in after showings of *America's Unsolved Mysteries.* Fear of crime is more correlated with hours of television watching than actual crime rates in an area (Taylor 1996). In more direct personal use, a Connecticut nursery school has a camera in its web site so parents can observe their children and their children's caretakers (*LSJ,* 12 April 1998, 8 July 1997). Japanese parents bug their children's school bags (*LSJ,* 17 June 1998).

The Moody Self in Spaces.   Displayed selves are produced through a variety of mechanisms and moods. The "self" constructed by computer-aided technology that maps the consumption preferences for music, books, cars, or theater is not the eroticized self watching naked pictures of Madonna downloaded from the Internet, or interacting on the NIJ (National Institute of Justice) listserv about burglar alarms or bicycle patrols, or the self in E-mail contact with academics around the world.

The Decentered Self. The most salient space in some public interactions becomes electronic space, rather than social space occupied by others. Cellular phones convert restaurants and movie theaters to phone boxes. Hospitals sell windows with views of the desert or sunset for patients who can afford them. People can enter "chat rooms" and create names, identities, interests, and shared values with others, work in fantasy locales, or participate on-line on MTV as videos are played. Personal video games allow players to chose characters, roles, moods, and strategies while playing (Fine 1983; Herz 1997). The screen is nominally the other. The latest electronic game, Tomagotch ("cute little egg" in Japanese), allows one to "grow a baby" over several months by caring and feeding. Better care leads to a healthier baby, even if it is a computerized doll used in a local high school (*LSJ*, 28 February 1998). Some 4,000,000 electronic matchmaker beepers are being marketed in Japan—both beep if carried when someone of the opposite sex approaches (*NYT*, 4 June 1998).

The Self Controlled by Others in E-Space. Social control on the Internet, for example, is emerging slowly as a dialogue between commercial interests seeking to commodify and control the space and access to it so as to facilitate low-cost and semiprivate business transactions. New institutional rules about privacy, protection of children, viruses, "spam" or excessive E-mail, search engines and their value, and the related issue of "content filtering" [a euphemism for censorship (Agre 1998)] are being developed. There are continuing efforts to shield sites, create blocks for children, or develop special sites, but all have the potential to be used for other purposes. For example, if a specialized children's site is created, marketers can then monitor and shape children's tastes and preferences. The federal government is shaping the debate by its concerns for national security, protection of "intellectual property," the "clipper chip" for encryption, and developing its own supersecure defense-based Internet system.

This analysis suggests something about the role of the visual in social control in postmodern societies and suggests its limits. Because of the salience of Electronic Mass Communications (EMC), and other changes in social relations, the self and the other have a particularly ambiguous status. The idea that the participant in an interaction is always expressing a single "self" or even a series of selves validated by others is clearly dubious. Many selves are created and destroyed in and through on-screen reality. Cyberspace, the combination of perception and computer actions, is a new socio-electronic space. It is difficult to establish the nature of the "social" on the basis of such evidence, since it is endlessly constituted and reconstituted by synthetic visual creations. The growth of new spaces, and the power of electronic means to control work and leisure, and shape politics and consumption, is a new frontier for studies of social control. How such inferences will be incorporated into symbolic interactionism, and cultural and media studies generally, is suggested by Bogard (1996). Its influence in criminology, police studies, and social control theory is yet to be seen.

ACKNOWLEDGMENTS

My analyses of television and politics (Manning 1996a), media and reflexivity (Manning 1996b), and media looping (Manning 1998) are published. Some of these ideas on social control in work were rehearsed at the Security 2010 Conference. I am very grateful to Neil Websdale and Jeff Ferrell for their painstaking editorial suggestions and often felicitous agreement with my ideas. Materials used here are drawn for the most part from everyday life—my experiences, stories told to me, newspaper and magazine clippings, as well as scholarly sources.

NOTES

1. Goffman saw framing as a property of social structure, not a social-psychological function such as the definition of the situation. Some ambiguity remains about the locus of framing: individualistic and interpretive, or structural and formal. Importantly in this context, Goffman was aware of the potential for a "symbolizing spiral" in which symbols reference other symbols and other symbolic worlds, creating a multiple and "laminated reality" (Goffman 1974:156ff.) without an easy end point. He explicitly rejects the idea that "all the world is a theatre," noting that a theatre had better have parking lots and coat hooks. Goffman (ibid.:8) omits from his analysis (by implication) all technologically mediated interactions. He rooted his framework in a fundamental baseline of primary reality, embodied face-to-face interaction.

2. Clearly, the sense-making of viewers is a retrospective-prospective process. The provisional coding of images is not based exclusively on surface features. Interpretation entails "the documentary method" (Mannheim 1960; Garfinkel 1967: Chapter 3), a highly reflexive method of sense-making that takes an instance and relates it to an underlying pattern while using the pattern to order further instances. How viewers see some television as framing, sometimes capturing the "real," is a complex process considered elsewhere (Manning 1996a). Research suggests that television experience is shaped by where (public or private space) and with whom

(alone, with a small group of friends, with bar patrons or other viewers of a pay-for-view boxing match held in a huge auditorium, for example) one watches, and meanings are shaped by viewers' gender, class, and ethnicity (Press 1991).

3. Electronic interactions have both expressive and informational dimensions. The Internet was developed first for defense purposes and then developed for wider usage, was given to the NSF to monitor (the Defense Department has begun a parallel and supersecret dedicated network for defense-based communications), and then sold for public use and economic development (Reingold 1992).

4. *Newsweek* (June 1998) reported that a professional guide dying alone while climbing Mt. Everest, beyond reach of his colleagues in a storm, spoke with his wife twice via cell phone. They discussed names for their unborn child. A climber in the same party had Sherpas carry her cell phone, laptop, and power source to the last base camp.

REFERENCES

Agre, J. 1998. "The Taming of Cyberspace." *TLS,* July 3, p. 3.

Altheide, D. 1996. *An Ecology of Communication.* Hawthorne, NY: Aldine de Gruyter.

Auberbach, E. 1953. *Mimesis.* Princeton, NJ: Princeton University Press.

Benjamin, W., ed. 1969. *Illuminations.* Introduction by Hannah Arendt. New York: Schocken.

Berman, M. 1982. *All That Is Solid Vanishes in Air.* New York: Penguin.

Bogard, W. 1996. *Simulation of Surveillance.* Cambridge: Cambridge University Press.

Cohen, S. 1985. *Visions of Control.* Cambridge: Polity.

DeBord, G. 1990. *Society of the Spectacle.* Cambridge, MA: MIT Press.

Durkheim, E. [1915] 1961. *The Elementary Forms of Religious Life.* New York: Free Press.

Eco, U. 1990. *Limits On Interpretation.* Bloomington: Indiana University Press.

Ewen, S. 1988. *All Consuming Images.* New York: Basic Books.

Fine, G. 1983. *Dungeons and Dragons.* Chicago: University of Chicago Press.

Fiske, John. 1987. *Television Culture.* Boston: Routledge and Kegan Paul.

Foucault, M. 1977. *Discipline and Punish: The Birth of the Prison.* New York: Pantheon.

Garfinkel, H. 1967. *Studies in Ethnomethodology.* Englewood Cliffs, NJ: Prentice-Hall.

Giddens, A. 1990. *The Consequences of Modernity.* Palo Alto, CA: Stanford University Press.

Gladwell, M. 1998. "The Spin Myth." *New Yorker,* July 6, pp. 67–73.

Goffman, E. 1959. *The Presentation of Self in Everyday Life.* New York: Doubleday Anchor.

Goffman, E. 1974. *Frame Analysis.* New York: Basic Books.

Gronbeck, B. 1997. "Tradition and Technology in Local Newscasts." *Sociological Quarterly* 38:361–74.

Hallett, M. and D. Powell. 1995. "Backstage with 'Cops': The Dramaturgical Reification of Police Subculture in American Infotainment." *American Journal of Police* 14(1):101–29.

Herz, J. C. 1995. *Surfing the Internet.* Boston: Back Bay.

Herz, J. C. 1997. *Joystick Nation.* Boston: Little, Brown.

Jay, M. 1993. *Downcast Eyes.* Berkeley: University of California Press.

Kappeler, V., G. Blumberg, and G. Potter. 1993. *The Mythology of Crime and Criminal Justice.* Prospect Heights, IL: Waveland.

Kendall, L. 1998. "Meaning and Identity in Cyberspace" *Symbolic Interaction* 21:129–53.

Lyon, D. 1994. *The Surveillance Society.* Minneapolis: University of Minnesota Press.

Mannheim, K. 1960. *Essays in the Sociology of Knowledge.* London: Routledge and Kegan Paul.

Manning, Peter K. 1996a. "Dramaturgy, Politics, and the Axial Event." *Sociological Quarterly* 37:261–78.

Manning, Peter K. 1996b. "Police and Reflection." *Police Forum* 6:1–5.

Manning, Peter K. 1998. "Media Loops." Pp. 25–39 in *Popular Culture, Crime and Justice,* edited by Donna Hale and Frankie Bailey. Belmont, CA: Wadsworth.

Mead, G. H. 1934. *Mind, Self and Society.* Chicago: University of Chicago Press.

Nadel, S. F. 1953. "Self Control and Social Control." *Social Forces* 31:265–73.

Negroponte, N. 1996. *Becoming Digital.* New York: Viking.

Poster, M., ed. 1990a. *Jean Baudrillard.* Stanford, CA: Stanford University Press.

Poster, M. 1990b. *The Mode of Information.* Chicago: University of Chicago Press.

Press, A. 1991. *Gender and Television.* Philadelphia: University of Pennsylvania Press.

Reingold, H. 1992. *Virtual Communities.* New York: Harper/Collins.

Taylor, L. and B. Mullan. 1986. *Uninvited Guests.* London: Chatto and Windus.

Taylor, R. 1996. "Fear of Crime." National Institute of Justice report.

Thomas, R. 1994. *What Machines Can't Do.* Berkeley: University of California Press.

Turkle, S. 1984. *The Second Self.* New York: Basic Books.

Weick, K. 1995. *Sensemaking in Organizations.* Thousand Oaks, CA: Sage.

Wellman, B. 1997. "The Road to Utopia and Dystopia on the Information Highway." *Contemporary Sociology* 26(4):445–49.

Williams, R. 1974. *Keywords.* Oxford: Oxford University Press.

13

Police Homicide Files as Situated Media Substrates
An Exploratory Essay

NEIL WEBSDALE

INTRODUCTION

General books on policing provide a plethora of details on subjects such as police history, the role of the police in the community, the discretion of police officers, the subcultures officers create and to which they introduce recruits, police corruption, the use of force, and police management and administration.[1] A smaller number of books eschew the formulaic approach of the textbook genre and examine more controversial aspects of law enforcement such as the reproduction of racial inequality,[2] class relations,[3] and patriarchy.[4] Few of the books that eschew the formulaic approach have been as influential as Hall, Critcher, Jefferson, Clarke, and Roberts's *Policing the Crisis: Mugging, the State, and Law and Order* (1978). Hall et al. demonstrate how the social phenomenon of mugging became one vehicle for the amplification of coercive state control in Britain. This amplification occurred during the early 1970s, a period of crisis in British capitalism and race relations. According to certain moral entrepreneurs, mugging and the broader social malaise it evidenced threatened the very fabric of British life. Muggers, ostensibly young black urban youth, became scapegoats or folk devils at the heart of what Hall et al. identify as a moral panic. As a symbol of social malaise the mugger attracted disproportionate amounts of attention from the criminal justice system. The overreaction of the state apparatus to muggers was an integral part of a much broader gearing up of the punitive criminal justice industry. This gearing up obscured deeper-rooted crises in the capitalist state evidenced by rising unemployment, poverty, and despondency. The news media played a central role in the initial construction and later intensification of this panic, thereby encouraging a cultural climate more favorable to coercive state control strategies. This shift from consent to coercion altered the long established "truce" between the ruling and subject class. One of Hall et al.'s original contributions to our understanding of policing is their thoroughgoing analysis of the synergistic relationship between law enforcement and the media portrayal and justification of more coercive social control measures. Without this synergy and the tenuous consent that it helped manufacture, British policing would have had far greater difficulties in managing and mediating the tensions of class and race relations.

In so directing our attention to the ideological linkages and convergences between the representational frames of the news media and emergent criminal justice interest in mugging, Hall et al. (1978) identify an intricate web of nonconspiratorial control initiatives at the heart of modern era government. In this chapter I address one aspect of this mosaic of management strategies, namely the construction of police investigative reports and the relationship between these reporting styles, frames, and boundaries, and broader cultural currents. Books on policing generally neglect these reports or take their significance for granted. Often discussions of police investigations are found in specialized texts devoted to this purpose alone, as if investigation is somehow a rather remote and tangential phenomenon.[5] Likewise, media studies have ignored these investigative files or not appreciated them for what they are: specialized discourses on criminal events that are distributed in a subterranean manner and are read, circulated, used, and reproduced by various social audiences. Criminal justice system personnel, patrol officers, detectives, prosecutors, and court personnel have liberal access to and knowledge of these reports. The news media and the social audiences that consume information about violent crime enjoy only selective access to these rather specialized and subterranean criminal justice substrates. Often detectives will inform media representatives of key facts. These facts are relayed to news media in a number of ways. Local media pick up the tales and sometimes, especially with certain sensational crimes, the bigger media fish enter the fray and a feeding frenzy ensues at a more intense level.

I argue that police investigative reports, as situated media sources, are repositories or factual reservoirs that constitute one of the cultural resources for what other media (e.g., newspapers, television, film, radio, true crime literature) learn about crime. More importantly, I contend that these investigative reports are imbued with an epistemological gestalt that provides other media sources with ways of knowing about crime. In short, crime files are forms of situated media discourse that lie at the heart of the cultural transmission of our understandings of crime. These files follow a microcircuitry, the locus of which is inscribed within the sequelae of criminal justice processes. As arrests, indictments, arraignments, grand juries, trials, convictions, sentences, and incarcerations unfold, other media sources tap into the various disclosures and construct their ritual reports, extensions, and embellishments, thus parlaying the revelations into broader cultural matrices. Given the popular appeal of crime news (Graber 1980), police investigative narratives, and the intricate microcircuits they inhabit, warrant much more careful scrutiny than has hitherto been the case.

SOME EPISTEMOLOGICAL AND METHODOLOGICAL REFLECTIONS

My observations on the thematic continuities in police investigative reports derive from an extensive study of domestic homicides in Florida.[6] I scrutinized three hundred domestic homicide files, which narrate and reconstruct events that originally occurred in 1994.[7] For police and prosecutors each file constitutes a case study of a homicide event. All of the files I examined were from closed cases. Police agencies did not allow me to copy files in cases that had not gone to trial or were pending appeal.

In a sociological sense, each file represents a case study insofar as it is a somewhat bounded body of purposive knowledge amenable to discursive examination. My interest is to identify those discursive qualities of domestic homicide reports and the possible links between these qualities and broader cultural frames concerning law and order. I treat the homicide files as what Stake (1994) calls collective case studies.[8] Domestic homicide reports, like homicide reports in general, are complex documents that defy easy classification. On the one hand they are official records used, among other things, to "accurately" describe killings and to prosecute criminals. However, we should not fall into the trap of seeing them only as official documents with a standardized format. It is tempting to borrow from the distinction made by Lincoln and Guba (1985:277) and see domestic homicide reports as official documents for specialized audiences, thus contrasting them with sources such as personal diaries, letters, and field notes, which have a much more personal feel. However, domestic homicide reports do not fit neatly into a dichotomized appreciation of material culture that conveniently distinguishes between those documents devoted to the personal/subjective (e.g., diaries) and those created out of the white heat of state power (e.g., driving licenses, birth certificates). Domestic homicide reports represent a coalescence of the impersonal, the routine, and the demographic, with personal biographies of pain, bearing witness, accusation, defensiveness, motive, and other etherealities. It is this perhaps unexpected coalescence of the alleged rationality of detection and the condensed minutiae of human experience that makes domestic homicide reports such fertile ground for multiple interpretations of the meaning of crime and order.

I discuss domestic homicide files as discursive instruments designed to uncover the "truth" about homicide. By "truth" I refer specifically to the discovery of the victim and perpetrator, the manner in which the killing occurred, the time and place of the fatal episode, the condition of the bodies, and numerous other minutiae. In the first section, I highlight the detailed interest in bodies (especially dead ones), the concern with time, the photographic depiction of the homicide scene, the taking of statements, and the use of informants. It is these key themes and the overall perspective embedded in the files that lend themselves to other media sources. The construction of messages for consumption by other media sources is carefully managed by police and prosecutors, who have vested interests in closing out the case. In the second section, I note the manner in which some cases are publicized broadly, thereby circulating the representational frames of the investigation far afield. In some higher-profile cases, the police narrative is moved in different directions by the input of various experts. Such input augments and transcends the police investigative narrative but also is somewhat dependent on that narrative. In the final section, I inspect some of the silences, omissions, and parameters involved in investigating homicide, and in offering at least parts of the narrative up for further cultural consumption. I contend that the homicide reports enlighten at the level of individuals and fatal incidents, but fail to address some of the rather obvious patterns embedded in the files as a whole. This style of investigation dovetails nicely with some of the requirements of the legal system. It is also consistent with a dominant value system that celebrates individualism and is overly fascinated with the cult of the individual killer and individual homicides. The "true crime" genre offers living proof of this event-focused appreciation of murder,[9] as do the hugely successful television shows on crime and violence that allow a glimpse of the "seamier sides of life" from the "luxury" of the family living room. In closing, I argue for a much more systematic analysis of police investigative reports as media substrates in their own right.

SELECTED THEMES IN DOMESTIC HOMICIDE
INVESTIGATIVE REPORTS

Investigative reports of domestic homicide differ by the bureaucratic templates imposed by individual police agencies, by the narrative styles of reporting officers, and by the nature of the case itself. The case file narratives of domestic homicides that are more difficult to solve are typically longer and more detailed. At a general level, investigative files tend to follow a formula. This formula depends upon the need to solve cases quickly and produce evidence in accordance with tried and tested routines that generate convictions (see Waegel 1982). In this sense, investigative reports are not unlike other media sources such as newspapers, whose product is influenced partly by routinized production schedules (see Ericson, Baranek, and Chan 1991).

The Detailed Surveillance and Reconstitution of Bodies

In homicide investigations the human body is the center of initial attention. Apart from the usual details of sex, race, age, height, weight, eye color, and hair color, which police record on victims, suspects, and other involved individuals, the body of the deceased undergoes close medical examination. This scrutiny is facilitated by the availability of new technologies including, for example, DNA testing.

Take, for example, the case of Deb Mason, who was murdered by her brother-in-law, Bobby Mason, while her husband, Steve Mason, was out of town.[10] We learn from the report that:

> When detectives arrived at the scene, the victim's body was still warm, but starting to cool. The victim was found lying on her blood-soaked bed with her head to the north, feet to the south. The victim was lying on her stomach with both feet together. Her right arm was bent at a 45 degree angle with her right forearm underneath her chest. Her left arm was resting on her left shoulder. The victim was nude with the exception of a bloody t-shirt. A bloody pillow covered part of the victim's head. The victim's body was turned over by Medical Examiner's Staff and a large laceration was observed on the victim's neck. There also appeared to be other lacerations about the victim's upper torso.

The autopsy report, also contained in the investigative report, provides further information. In particular,

> There were defense wounds on her hands which indicated that the victim may have struggled with her attacker. The victim had a fresh abrasion (tear) in the perineal area and this was indicative of some type of sexual assault.

Marie Riddle was killed by her husband Peter Riddle in a particularly gruesome homicide-suicide. She had feared him for some time and even though she still lived in the same house with Peter, Marie had armed herself. In Marie Riddle's autopsy we find, in numerical order, the gross anatomic diagnoses:

1. Four gunshot wounds.
2. Severe temporary cavity destruction of the heart.
3. Multiple non calcified granulomatous type of lesions to the lung.
4. Status post hysterectomy, remote.
5. Breast implants, bilateral, intact.
6. Multiple old scars.
7. Multiple contusions of the left wrist and forearm.

The postmortem toxicology gives investigators the precise levels of a range of drugs including cannabinoids and antidepressants, found in her urine, blood, and gastric juices. Her medical history, summarized in the report, gives investigators what are deemed to be the essentials: the date of her hysterectomy, details of prior surgeries, number of full-term pregnancies, and her history of depression. The external exam informs that the body "is well tanned and has prominent tanning lines." Each of the four gunshot wounds Marie received is described meticulously. The internal examination informs investigators of the condition of the heart, lungs, spleen, liver, kidneys, neck, GI tract, brain, and lastly the female genitalia. Never in life did anyone likely know as much about Marie's body as we do in her death. Does this level of detail, and comparable levels in other cases, serve any social function? Prosecution? Of whom? Her killer is dead as a result of the homicide-suicide. Indeed, in most domestic homicide cases this detail is infrequently parlayed into a prosecutorial strategy. Dissected as it is, Marie's body has been reconstituted (dare I say resurrected?) for possible social consumption in the numerous microcircuits of knowledge about crime, fear, danger, and death.

Police investigative reports do not simply describe bodies. Rather these reports contain the hallmarks of a selective surveillance that focuses upon some body parts over others, some injuries over others, certain physiological details over others. This alliance between the police and the medical profession provides a rich substrate for other media sources. Newspapers and television engage in similar constructive activities when presented with an array of minutiae and only a limited space to comment upon them. Only minute portions of these extensive details percolate through to other media reports of the homicide. It is the police who play a pivotal role in the dissemination of knowledge from the investigative microcircuit to other circuits of media such as print and television.

In general the media are discouraged from venturing into the crime scene for fear they will somehow "contaminate" it. In the Mason case the positioning of the body never percolated into the newspaper accounts of the killing. However, the "lacerations" became a "slashing" of the neck. We thus need more research on how these linguistic transformations, mediated through certain modes of cultural taste, legal prohibition, and sensationalistic journalism, take place.

Amidst this plethora of facts about the decedent we see the possibility of reconstructing the past with a view to securing a conviction of the guilty party, if alive. The conviction, of course, depends upon combining these facts with many other pieces of information, which when taken together would convince a jury beyond a reasonable doubt of the defendant's guilt. Leave aside for the moment that many of these domestic homicide cases, like most homicide cases in general, were closed by confessions, and that the cases rarely went to jury trial.

The Role of Time

Many social theorists have talked about the changing perceptions of time that attended the rise of modern capitalist societies. E. P. Thompson (1967) demonstrates how the discipline of the clock slowly replaced the rhythm of the seasons as industrial manufacture superseded agricultural production. In the context of punishment, Foucault (1977) demonstrates how precise units of time were built into the attempts to discipline prisoners, and indirectly, modern-era populations. Just as we see a detailed concern with bodies in investigative reports, we also see a deep concern to produce a chronology of events in homicide files. To say we witness a tyranny of time in homicide files is not unreasonable. Take the case of Cynthia Jones, who was killed by William Johnson. In this case the lack of precision is qualified with statements like, "At approximately 0723 hours on 02-18-94 Officer Malcolm responded to 4444 Jackson Avenue." The word "approximately" is employed almost apologetically, as if the officer was not quite sure of the exact minute of his/her arrival. We learn later that "[t]ransport personnel arrived on scene at 1005 hours and the victim was loaded into a transport bag which was sealed by Detective Wonker. The victim was removed from the scene at 1020 hours."

In this case, as in most of the domestic homicide files, different police officers log in and out of the crime scene. The crime scene entry log is also called a "contamination list." All of the officers log in and out of the scene by the minute. The chain of custody for the evidence is measured to the minute. In the Cynthia Jones case, four glass tubes of blood, one glass tube of vitreous fluid, and one glass tube of bile were submitted to toxicology. The receipt of these items is listed in the chain of custody table and timed to the minute. As prime-time TV reminded audiences in the Simpson case, if you cannot account for who held vital evidence and for how long, then the entire prosecution might be undermined.

I will not belabor this discussion of the way time permeates these reports so profoundly. Among many other things, the precise recording of time enables the placement of the suspect at the scene at the time of the killing, the checking of alibis, the tracking of evidence to avoid allegations of tampering, and the supervision of field officers by command personnel. While these are important reasons to use precise time measurements in police homicide investigations, the precise use of time in the reports also acts as a cultural cueing device that other media sources can make use of. In the newspaper report of the Jones killing, the first paragraph reads: "When Palm Bay police responded to a suspicious incident at 7:20 A.M. at 4444 Jackson Avenue they expected to find Cynthia Jones in another altercation with her boyfriend" (*Florida Today*, 19 February 1994, p. 1A).

In the majority of the newspaper and television reports of these domestic homicides, time is a central frame of reference. I contend that this communication of time transcends the mere informational. Rather it allows readers access to the event through a cultural medium (time) with which they are ritually conversant. We might argue that time as cultural cue facilitates the temporal transportation of the audience back into the scene. John Fiske (1995) describes a similar phenomenon with audiences who discriminate between the products of culture industries. He argues that audiences discern between the products of popular culture based in part on the "relevance" of material presented. Importantly he notes: "If the cultural resource does not offer points of pertinence through which the experience of everyday life can be made to resonate with it, then it will not be popular" (ibid.:129).

Homicide investigations and their attendant narratives render crime accessible to both other media circuits and broader audiences in general by providing these "points of pertinence" such as "time," which "resonate" with everyday life. Newspaper reporters and their readership can both identify with time. Creative readerships may consume this seemingly small detail in any number of ways. Some readers may recall what they were doing at the time of the killing; others may ignore it. Put succinctly, because notions of time are inscribed upon police investigations, newspaper reports of homicide, and everyday life, time provides a cultural thread that runs through both media circuits and social audiences alike.

Photographing Domestic Homicide Scenes

Dick Hebdige notes how the use of photography by police departments supplanted the use of more unwieldy techniques such as Bertillon's anthropometric method. Hebdige comments, "By drawing representation closer to reality, photography seemed to make the dream of complete surveillance possible" ([1979] 1997:398). The mug shot is an integral part of the microcircuitry of homicide narratives. These shots are often shared with the media, who pass them on, usually in a very stylized manner, to the public. For example, among the mug shots of perpetrators of domestic homicide in Florida, we rarely find photographs in which perpetrators are smiling. Mug shots are saturated with power and in many ways represent the hegemony of the state over criminals. Likewise we might argue that crime scene photographs embody the power of the living agents of the state over the victims of homicide.[11]

However, crime scene photographs have a much narrower circulation than mug shots, although they may inhabit a number of different microcircuits of knowledge. The photographs taken by police photographers at domestic homicides are not generally made available to other media sources such as newspapers and television. Rather they circulate among criminal justice professionals and others involved in any subsequent investigation and/or prosecution. These photographs are often extremely graphic in their depiction of the deceased and other involved parties. However, the nature of police photography is intimately connected with the use to which the photographs are put. Ideally, photographs of homicide scenes portray the "uncontaminated" scene. In court the investigator attests to the precise correspondence between the photograph of the scene and his/her recollection of the scene before it was disturbed by investigators. Wounds are photographed extensively, as are pools of blood enveloping the deceased. The location of the killing is also usually photographed, contributing to an overall imagery that augments the written narratives. If drugs and/or alcohol are present at the scene, these are photographed, as is any evidence of disruption such as overturned furniture and objects that appear to have been thrown around.

Since the photographs are for consumption within the criminal justice information circuit, their nature is shaped to some extent by the need to secure a conviction. If it can be alleged by the defense that police photographs of the deceased are deliberately "inflammatory," then such a claim may undermine the effectiveness of the depiction in securing a prosecution. In particular, the unnecessary exposure of the sexual organs serves as an example here (see Osterburg and Ward 1992:799). Here we see cultural ideas about taste and what it is appropriate to display, influencing the production, circulation, and consumption of homicide photography. But the influence of broader cultural beliefs of what is appropriate to display does not override the imperatives of police to comprehensively capture crime scenes. There will be times when police cannot avoid views that may later be deemed deliberately inflammatory by the defense. Ultimately police photography works at the interface of a number of sometimes conflicting cultural and subcultural forces. The resulting photographs, their scope, focus, and power, are therefore mediated by a combination of considerations regarding the exigencies of prosecution and common considerations of taste. Under this scheme, the relationship between the sender (police photographer), message (photograph), and receiver (prosecutors, defense attorneys, judges, and juries) is not a linear one. Rather senders and their messages are shaped by the diverse needs and beliefs of receivers, which themselves resonate dialectically with broader cultural tenets. In the case of crime scene photography then, senders, their messages, and the receivers and users of those messages occupy positions of relative autonomy vis-à-vis each other (see also Hall 1993).

In contrast to the photographs in homicide files, newspaper and television photography of the scene is usually more detached from the body and its destruction. Some of the television shows such as "Cops" and "L.A.P.D" get closer to the blood and gore, but still somehow fail to capture the essence of death that emerges in homicide narratives. Perhaps this has something to do with the medium itself. Still photographs have a way of conveying a stark image of dead bodies by freezing them in space and time. Videotape of dead bodies fixes corpses vis-à-vis the crime scene. However those bodies are not frozen in time. Given that death is culturally measured by the suspension/loss of the self/other in time and space, it is perhaps understandable that still photography presents a far more onerous picture of death precisely because it cues into deeply embedded cultural understandings of both temporality and spatiality, and permanence and demise.

Newspaper reports of the three hundred Florida cases typically display recent photographs of the victim or suspect, or capture police and paramedics carrying the dead away from the crime scene. Still others may show shocked and/or mourning relatives/friends/neighbors. But in general the circulation of crime scene photographs is more secretive and guarded, with the police-media liaison officer translating the essence of mutilation into language that media sources like newspapers can either run verbatim, build upon or transform. This more cautious circulation reminds us that the investigative file as a narrative of the homicide event contains elements that are more or less open to other media sources.

The Taking of Statements

Domestic homicide files often contain transcripts from interviews with suspects, witnesses, relatives, friends, workplace colleagues, and others. Some files contain massive amounts of information on the lifestyles of those parties involved in domestic homicides. Just as still photography clicks to life within a cultural climate and fixes bodies and other objects in space and time, the taking of statements allows police to classify, arrange, prioritize, and judge a mosaic of people, events, locations, motives, actions, words, and material objects. Prosecutors feed off of this information and search for inconsistencies, contradictions, and lies. Statements are taken in a very stylized manner. Interviews with suspects are preceded by the issuance of the Miranda warning that anything said by the suspect can and may be used against him/her in court. Suspects are also informed of their right to legal counsel. Police know that if an attorney is made available to a suspect, the attorney will almost always advise the client to remain silent. When suspects relinquish their Miranda rights, the likelihood of police eliciting a confession increases. In a significant number of the domestic homicide cases, suspects gave up their right to have an attorney present at their interrogation.

The flow of narrative deriving from the statements of suspects can also be influenced by the use of polygraph testing. Such testing supposedly determines whether or not suspects are answering questions truthfully. In a number of cases detectives shared the results from polygraphs with suspects. Outcomes of polygraph tests that suggest the suspect was lying about a specific issue occasionally preceded a confession. In such instances, police used polygraph results to imply guilt and elicit confessions or further information about the case.

Statements are taken in isolation to minimize the risk of one person's account "contaminating" that of another. Out of the plethora of accounts, the police and the prosecution must decide where the "truth" lies. There is no postmodernist pontificating about multiple truths at this stage of an investigation. The investigator must decide which statements gel with the other knowledge he/she has of the case and set new directions accordingly. If the homicide investigation drags on, then police will use subsequent interviews with suspects. These interviews may be informed by new evidence such as that derived from DNA testing. The narrative therefore unfolds as different technologies of truth feed into the microcircuit.

The Use of Informants

The police narrative in domestic homicide cases sometimes benefits from information given to the police by informants. Journalists also acquire information in this manner although they employ the more sanitized term "sources" to describe those who provide investigative leads. With both police and newspaper substrates the disclosure of information from informants is guarded. The two cases that follow introduce some of the narrative made possible by informants.

Manual Barcero murdered Milan Arguello just after he had seen his girlfriend, Carmen, kissing Arguello outside Arguello's vehicle. Barcero shot Arguello in the back of the head. Just prior to the killing, Barcero had been driving around Miami in a car with three friends. He happened to see the fateful kissing and apparently remarked to the occupants of the car, "Look at that bitch." He approached Arguello and Carmen with a friend of his known as Freddie, whom Miami police knew as an armed bank robber. Apparently Manuel Barcero had been carrying a gun all evening. The police narrative on this case was richly enhanced by an informant who was a friend of one of the three occupants of the vehicle in which Barcero was riding. Barcero successfully intimidated the occupants, warning them that he had murdered once before and had not been caught for it. He threatened to kill any of them who talked to the police about the murder of Arguello. However, the informant gave police the license plate of the car Barcero was riding in together with details of the ski mask Barcero was wearing as he left the crime scene. This information led police to Barcero, who was subsequently arrested and charged with first-degree murder.

Miami police used an informant to piece together the movements of homicide suspect Kevin Warr during the twenty-four hours prior to the killing of Celia and Janine Parker. Celia had been stabbed numerous times and her daughter Janine was found asphyxiated. The informant in this case was a drug dealer named Mr. Muscle. Mr. Muscle told police that Warr had spent time earlier that day with a prostitute named "Huge Mamma." Warr had given Mr. Muscle a fifty dollar bill to buy narcotics. Mr. Muscle returned to Warr and gave him four rocks of cocaine and thirty dollars change. Warr gave Mr. Muscle one rock for his endeavors. "Huge Mamma" left Warr's room, and according to Mr. Muscle, appeared scared. Mr. Muscle told police that Warr asked him to find another prostitute. The two men then went outside and sat down. Apparently Celia Parker came by and Warr asked her to have sex with him, but she refused. Warr later told Mr. Muscle he was at Celia's apartment in the early hours of the morning using cocaine and drinking with a group of other people. According to Mr. Muscle, Celia caught Warr stealing her money and confronted him. Warr told Mr. Muscle he overreacted and killed Celia and her daughter. Mr. Muscle's information gave police enough evidence to bring in Warr and obtain a confession from him. Consequently Warr was incarcerated, less than twenty-four hours after being released from prison for prior acts of violent crime.

Other media sources did not cover these two homicide narratives in any substantial way. The narrative in the files deriving from the informants remains subterranean. Using "sources" of their own, journalists may well have been able to obtain some of these details. However, it is unlikely that either print or television media could mine the same resources that police departments have at their disposal. For journalists to interview witnesses and family at the scene of a domestic homicide is one thing, for them to regularly penetrate subcultures whose constituent members are intimately connected with violent career criminals, drug dealing, drug use, prostitution, and various other deviantized activities is much less likely. The police narrative, as a situated media substrate, is ideally placed to glean this kind of subterranean information. In particular, given their proximity to the language of the street, detectives are ideally placed to gather information from informants. Detectives use informants carefully and the homicide narrative does not name the tipster or source.[12] Living at the interface of street justice and criminal justice is doubtless a precarious social locus for some "sources." From the narrative in the Warr case, Mr. Muscle does not appear to have been prosecuted for admitting purchasing rocks of cocaine.

If we restrict our definitions of the media to outlets such as newspapers and television, then it is unlikely we will appreciate the full contribution of informants to our knowledge of homicides. However, if we extend our definition of media to include police investigative files, then we can begin to appreciate the confluence of the microcircuitry of the criminal justice system, and the subcultures whose constituents partake in any number of activities including smoking rock cocaine, dealing drugs, armed robbery, prostitution, and murder. Perhaps more than any other investigative practice, the police use of informants highlights the interface between formal policing activities and the media narratives these activities generate and further elaborate, and the subcultures with which police coexist. We need to learn much more about how knowledge from informants becomes part of the homicide narrative, and how minute fragments are guardedly secreted into the newspaper/television arena.

FROM POLICE INVESTIGATIVE SUBSTRATES TO OTHER MEDIA NETWORKS

Dispersion

Sylvia Zakrzewski and her two children, Anna age five, and Edward age seven, were found dead by police in the bathroom of their family home on Monday June 13, 1994. When this triple homicide first hit the local press, details were hard to come by. However, the investigative narrative in the homicide report is clear:

> As I looked into the bathroom I saw three bodies, two of which were slumped over the edge of the bath tub. They appeared to be an adult female, and a small juvenile. I further saw another juvenile laying on its back in the tub. There was a large amount of blood on the floor, and blood spatters on the door. . . . A machete was seen in the bathroom next to the right leg of the juvenile slumped over the tub. This item was covered with blood.

The local media ran stories of the killing. However, the sheriff's department investigating the case "declined to confirm rumors the victims were hacked to death with a machete" and also "stopped short of labeling" the missing husband and natural father as a suspect (*Palm Beach Post,* 16 June 1994, p. 7B). However, within hours of this report appearing, the Okaloosa County sheriff had named Edward Zakrzewski a suspect. The story then takes on much more of a popular appeal as it becomes apparent to both police and other media sources that this is no usual domestic multiple killing where the suspect is already in police custody. Rather Edward Zakrzewski was listed as missing and also AWOL from his job as a Tech Sergeant with the U.S. Air Force. Gradually police secrete other tantalizing details of the case. We learn that on Friday June 10, Edward Zakrzewski withdrew $5,400 from his savings account and line-of-credit. We also learn that Sylvia had asked Edward for a divorce the day before the killing, saying she wanted to return to her native Korea.

When the autopsy report came in it was clear that the three victims died either Friday night (June 10) or early Saturday morning (June 11). Edward failed to show up for work on Monday, June 13, at Eglin Air Force Base. Given that Edward Zakrzewski had withdrawn such a substantial sum of money, that one of the family cars was missing, and that the bodies were not found until Monday afternoon (June 13), police theorized he may well have fled far afield. Consequently a federal warrant for Unlawful Flight to Avoid Prosecution was issued through the Office of the U.S. Attorney for the Northern District of Florida. The FBI then joined the chase.

By July 2, police had still not located Edward Zakrzewski. On that evening information about the case was dispersed nationally through "America's Most Wanted." However, the brief mention the case received on the show was not enough to turn up any leads and Zakrzewski's potential to accrue status as one of America's "most wanted," continued to improve. By October, Zakrzewski was still missing and wanted. On October 14, 1994, "Unsolved Mysteries" ran a segment dealing with the case. The coverage here was much more substantial than that in "America's Most Wanted." One investigator from the Okaloosa County Sheriff's Department made a brief on-camera appearance and was also present at the show's studios in Burbank, California, to take incoming calls from the public. Just prior to the "Unsolved Mysteries" show, the Okaloosa County Sheriff's Department issued a news release saying that although both they and the military had devoted "many hours" to apprehending Zakrzewski, there had been no confirmed sightings or significant leads in the case. The release also noted that the case had now assumed nationwide and international significance.

Within 24 hours of the airing, a man answering Zakrzewski's description and claiming to be Zakrzewski turned himself in to police on the island of Molokai, Hawaii. Zakrzewski, who had apparently been living at the east end of the island under the assumed name of Michael Green, told police he had seen his own photograph on "Unsolved Mysteries," and decided to turn himself in.

The combination of the police investigation and major television network coverage led to Zakrzewski's apprehension. Zakrzewski had seemingly eluded police and cloistered himself away in a remote location. However, the power of media imagery is immense and Zakrzewski himself might have realized this as he saw his own face on television. It was not the long arm of the law that caught Zakrzewski. Rather it was the parlaying of police investigative knowledge into the broader circuitry of media representation that brought the suspect in. In many ways this case, unusual as it is compared with everyday domestic killings, typifies the way police homicide narratives transcend their microcircuitry, and come to inhabit a more general representational terrain that accesses a huge public audience.

From my discussion of the Zakrzewski case, one might be left with the impression that "dispersion" only involves the linear radiation of representational frames about violent crime into a seemingly endless media microcircuitry. These representational frames have at their heart notions that crimes, rather than being socially situated phenomena, stem from the pathology of individuals. However, it is important to stress that dispersion involves more than a one-way spread of representational frames to different media microcircuits. At numerous points, thoughts and theories about crime are refined, transformed, and parlayed into other networks including perhaps the microcircuit from which they originally emanated. Messages about crime can reach social audiences in a style and packaging that seems wholly discordant with the medium from which the case originated. The true crime literature is one case in point. Often writers of true crime base their accounts upon police investigative narratives. The ironic naming of the genre as "true crime" reminds us that there are multiple ways of narrating crime tales and that police versions are one amongst many. Crime fiction may seem on the surface to be more distanced from "real" police narratives than the true crime genre accounts. However, the boundaries between fiction and nonfictive accounts of violent crime are more blurred than initially meets the eye. The notion that fiction and true crime are somehow more distanced from the "reality" of crime accounts embedded in police narratives, is in part a product of the claims-making of criminal justice ideology.

The event-focused, perpetrator-victim gaze of the criminal justice narrative strongly implies that other interpretations are less accurate, secondary, and dependent interpretations of the "truth" of the case. Fictive accounts are presented as just that: embellishments that to varying degrees approximate the "reality." Under this only-one-truth rhetoric about crime, media theorists might be tempted to assume that information leaves the microcircuitry of the police, prosecutors, courts, and juries, and is endlessly dispersed into a proliferation of information circuits. Put differently, there is seen to be a monolithic articulation between criminal justice narratives and other media sources. Such a reductionist appreciation of the relationship between situated substrates such as police investigative narratives and other media sources leaves no room for the cultural continuities between substrates. These cultural continuities transcend (or rather mutually colonize) accounts that pose as truth on the one hand (police, prosecutorial narratives), and fiction on the other (true crime, crime fiction). Take, for example, a recent case involving the novelist Patricia Cornwell. Cornwell's success as an author of crime novels stems in part from her ability to parlay her "real life" experiences working in a medical examiner's office, into her intricate accounts of killing, autopsies, and forensic medicine. At this writing, Cornwell and her publisher MacMillan are being sued by William and Jewel Phelps. The Phelpses claim that Cornwell's 1992 novel, *All That Remains,* is patterned on the 1989 killings of their daughter, Annamaria, and her fiance's brother, Daniel Lauer. The plaintiffs allege that Cornwell used private details from the autopsy reports in her novel. As the case remains open, certain details were never disclosed to the public. Cornwell allegedly had access to these details through her work in the medical examiner's office. Specifically, the plaintiffs point to Cornwell's discussion of the two bodies that were "found positioned arm in arm, face down" (cited in *Arizona Republic,* 6 August 1997, p. B8). If this case goes to civil trial we will once again enter the circus of the courts, juries, and newspaper/television microcircuits. The jury and a much broader social audience will be asked to decide whether, in spite of Cornwell's disclaimer that events in *All That Remains* bear no resemblance to "real events or people," private and police factual data became (inappropriately) public fiction.

This case and others like it serve to remind us that microcircuits feed off and inform each other again and again, and, in a manner that cannot be theorized in a reductionist fashion.[13] In her life experience Cornwell was privy to confidential information and ways of making sense of crime that she may or may not have parlayed into *All That Remains.* However, Cornwell's alleged selective colonization of some of the elements of this case was not a process that occurred in a social vacuum removed from the imperatives of her trade as a writer/grazer of potentially rich sources of crime fiction. Cornwell's alleged gaze was also likely informed by an investigative motif that resonated with what readers deemed to be readable, what publishers saw as marketable, and what Cornwell herself found appealing. In other words, there is no hard and fast separation between the specialized microcircuitry of the files, their epistemological gestalt, and the extractive ethos that the writer/researcher, in this case Cornwell, brings to the file. At still another level, the analytical frames from the medical examiner's report and the homicide files, if used as reference points by Cornwell, first had to find form and voice in the discourse of crime fiction before they were recognized as a potential abuse of the police/medical examiner microcircuitry and a breach of privacy. Put differently, it was their rearticulated form through yet another microcircuit (crime fiction), combined with Cornwell's market position as a best-selling author and Macmillan's deep pockets, that rendered Cornwell's alleged colonization of the privileged information problematic.

My identification of the event-focused, perpetrator-victim gaze of the true crime and crime fiction literature as ideological should not be taken to mean that there is indeed a true and accurate place to stand on the matter of crime. Many academic accounts of crime (not this one of course!) and its portrayal in the media are also socially situated and imbued with all of the clutter and irrelevancy of the ivory tower. The claim that the "scholarly" accounts produced by academics such as criminologists somehow transcend the media fray because they are more systematic, detached, and circumspect is as dubious as the claim that police narratives tell the only truth about crime. Rather it might be more straightforward to acknowledge, as Foucault has done, that the whole "garrulous discourse" of criminology "is of such utility, is needed so urgently and rendered so vital for the working of the system, that it does not even need to seek a theoretical justification for itself, or even simply a coherent framework" (1980:47).

Adding Additional Expertise for New Circuits of Consumption

As situated media sources, homicide files constitute much more than the substrates for newspaper and televisual accounts of crime. As the process of prosecution unfolds, new information is added by the different agencies involved and new files proliferate. Stenographers produce court transcripts, presentence investigation reports are generated, and the microcircuitry expands. There is, of course, far too much here to comment upon in an exploratory essay. Nevertheless, the proliferation of subsequent microcircuits that depend, at least in part, upon the police homicide narrative and its epistemological gestalt remains a much ignored area of media studies. We need to know much more about the manner in which these later narratives build upon parts of the initial police homicide narrative and thus accrete layers of meaning and "truth."

At first glance, the "adding of expertise for consumptive purposes" may seem a rather vague notion. Clearly the homicide files are already characterized by numerous sources of expertise, be it the expertise of investigators, medical examiners, forensic scientists, or informants. Nevertheless, when some of the facts of the homicide begin to be consumed by the public, new information is sometimes added from other specialized knowledge circuits, often the social sciences, in order to edify, to persuade, to argue a point, and/or to (supposedly) aid the public (be it a jury, newspaper audience, court television) in grasping some of the complexities of the case. I will illustrate by discussing the way certain additional forms of expertise were introduced at the stage of broader public consumption of two domestic homicides.

Earl Blanchard shot his wife Merry Blanchard and then killed himself with the same weapon. Merry was killed at a Tampa nursing home where she was a resident. She suffered from Alzheimer's disease. As usual, parts of the police narrative were shared with the press and parts were held back. For example, the suicide note that was signed "mom and dad" is present in the police homicide narrative but the details of it were kept from the press. However, the newspapers brought in an expert on Alzheimer's disease to augment their telling of the homicide-suicide. In the *Tampa Tribune* (2 August 1994, Metro p. 3) we learn from Dr. Donna Cohen that "Ten percent of all Alzheimer's victims live in Florida." Dr. Cohen is reported as saying "she fears this type of murder-suicide will be an 'epidemic' within the next five years." Her reported comments evoke images of a plague of homicide-suicides affecting a state that has a very sizable elderly population and a very large number of people suffering from Alzheimer's disease. The expertise brings a new "point of pertinence" to the homicide tale, thereby providing opportunities for further resonance with readers. Cohen adds that from her own experience, "[E]lderly men are more likely than women to want to end their spouse's suffering this way. Men in their 70s and 80s don't have the support system necessary to deal with this. Many of them were raised in a time when men didn't share their feelings" (ibid.).

Vivian Marshall, executive director of the Tampa Bay Chapter of the Alzheimer's Association is quoted as saying,

> Women caregivers tend to call us early on to find out what kind of services we offer. . . . We generally hear from men when it reaches a crisis point (ibid.).

On January 23, 1994, Kathy Weiand shot and killed her husband Todd during a domestic fight. Todd had prior convictions for disorderly conduct in Wisconsin for striking his first wife. He had also been convicted of striking Kathy in 1992. Kathy said Todd beat her many times and she claimed she acted in self-defense on the night of the killing. Nevertheless the jury convicted her of second-degree murder and she was sentenced to eighteen years in prison. The newspaper and television coverage of this case was extensive. One facet of this coverage is particularly worth noting: the use of experts to argue that Kathy Weiand was suffering from Battered Woman Syndrome when she killed her husband. A number of experts were quoted in the press about the syndrome. Not of all of these experts testified at the trial. One who did testify and whose words were also cited in the press was psychiatrist Michael Maher. Called for the defense, Maher testified that "at the moment she shot her husband through a closed door, Kathleen Weiand believed he was about to kill her" (*St. Petersburg News,* 14 January 1995). This is an important detail because the argument that she was acting in self-defense then becomes possible. Maher, we are told in the *St. Petersburg News,* met with Kathleen Weiand twenty times.

Lenore Walker, author of *The Battered Woman Syndrome* (1984), also testified for the defense and argued that Kathleen Weiand "believed he was going to kill her" (*St. Petersburg News,* 21 January 1995). In her capacity as a clinical and forensic psychologist, Walker interviewed Kathleen Weiand for almost eight hours prior to offering her expert testimony. The testimony also drew upon Walker's reading of police reports of prior domestic problems between the Weiands. Walker informed the court of an "escalating pattern of violence at the hands of her husband, going from pushing and shoving, to slapping her, butting her with his head, slamming her to the floor" (*Tampa Tribune*, 21 January 1995). The *St. Petersburg News* summed up the expert testimony by informing readers that the defense case rested upon a "psychological condition in which women believe they are in a kill-or-be-killed situation" (24 January 1995).

As noted, Walker's testimony was based upon interviews with Kathleen Weiand and prior police reports. Rather than merely passing on Walker's testimony to readers, journalists constructed it meaningfully, thereby mediating between different but interconnected social audiences such as the prosecutorial microcircuit including various police narratives, the jury, and newspaper readers. The press coverage of Walker's expert testimony also aired broader political debates. Prominent among these debates was the question of whether battered women who killed their batterers are individually responsible for their crimes. The newspapers were generally hostile to the cause of Kathleen Weiand and depicted Lenore Walker as a money-grabbing advocate for battered women rather than the objective scientist she claimed to be.[14] It is not my intent to explore whether the press "accurately" conveyed to readers the essence of the expert testimony. Rather I want to point out that the added expertise, especially Lenore Walker's, partially fed off existing police narratives of the homicide. Analyzing and then citing the police narratives enabled Walker to present herself in a more eclectic manner rather than just relying on her interviews with Kathleen Weiand. However, in spite of Walker's resort to police narratives, the jury did not accept "Battered Woman Syndrome" as a defense to murder in the Weiand case. The outcome of the Weiand case reminds us that juries are social audiences. They may be small groups but they consume vast amounts of very specialized information. In some ways one might describe juries as an intense microcosm of newspaper readers in general. Journalists also interpret trials to their readers, although the press and television, except in high-profile cases, rarely have the time to reflect upon the same wealth of details to which juries are typically exposed. The police, juries, journalists, and readers/viewers are all engaged in ongoing negotiations concerning the multiple meanings made manifest in the trials of people like Kathleen Weiand. The police narrative precedes most of the other interpretative microcircuits and to some extent shapes the outcome of later developments. Expert narratives, as we have seen, blend into the emergent overall picture of the homicide event, and just like the narratives upon which they feed, expertise is given, interpreted, accepted, rejected, and perhaps ridiculed.

DISCURSIVE LIMITS AND DOMINANT VALUES

In this exploratory essay I have argued for the recognition of police investigative narratives as situated media sources. The narratives follow a microcircuitry that is guided by the imperative of prosecuting suspects. However, police investigative narratives are also inscribed within broader dominant or preferred cultural understandings of crime, individual guilt, punishment, and justice. These understandings emphasize individual responsibility for the commission of crime rather than the social contexts within which crime occurs and the well-documented social patterns crime follows. The microcircuitry that the police investigative narratives inhabit is at all times underpinned by a constellation of moral-political judgments about offenders, their families, and their acts. Through these files we witness the daily articulation of what Colin Sumner (1990) calls "social censures." According to Sumner, social censures work to "signify, denounce and regulate, not to explain. . . . Their typical consequence is not an adequate account of a social conflict but rather the distinguishing of 'offenders' from 'non-offenders'. . . . They say 'stop,' and are tied to a desire to control, prevent or punish" (ibid.:26–27).

Put differently, the homicide files embody an epistemological gestalt that articulates a form of ideology. This gestalt is continuous with much broader ideological qualities inherent in the criminal justice system. By ideology, I do not refer to deliberate or conspiratorial attempts to mislead the public by, for example, obfuscating the social and political roots of crime. Rather the astructural way of thinking about and explaining crime holds sway over other more structurally informed approaches that implicate the systemic power relations of institutions such as patriarchy, capitalism, and racism. At the center of this immensely successful ideology is "individual responsibility." This notion of individual culpability for crime, to use Jeffrey Reiman's words, "literally acquits the existing social order of any charge of injustice" (1990:124). The language of guilt and punishment fit perfectly with this ideological ethos. Likewise the mapping of crime through the use of crime statistics and the broader language of abstracted empiricism eliminates personal experience and human biography, effectively denying the socially situated dynamics of crime and crime control.

To date there has been little written about the police investigative narrative as a cultural resource or as a situated media substrate. This is rather surprising given the amount of work published on the media representation of crime. We need to learn much more about the synergistic relationship between these police narratives and other cultural forces and media forms. Popular media coverage of crime thrives off the immediate circumstances of the killing, who the suspects are, how they are apprehended, what state the victim's body was found in, and modus operandi. Like the homicide files with which they share a common or similar epistemological frame, popular

discourses on crime pitch their analysis at the level of the individual perpetrator and victim and the acts of violence and killing. Richard Sparks
(1995) notes that television crime dramas evoke powerful social sentiments
such as fear and anxiety. These shows reach large audiences in part by
"fencing in a dominant representation of the city and of its sites and sources
of danger. In so doing they stipulate courses of action and justified responses. They thereby also hedge away the constant possibilities of dissolu-
tion and chaos" (ibid.:61–62). Put simply, at some emotional level these
shows seem to be deeply satisfying and reassuring. We need much more
research on this matter but it is possible, if not likely, that the voyeurism of
viewers fixes the criminal as "outsider," contrasting him or her with the
viewer who resides within the bounds of the "normal" as opposed to the
"deviant." At another level, blaming individuals such as the usual suspects
who constitute the retinue of predictable offenders offered up for popular
consumption, distances viewers from the social order of which we all are
members.

In emphasizing the distinctive character of police homicide narratives, I
run the risk of ignoring the continuities between these narratives and other
situated media sources. My discussion of police narratives implies that other
media sources are dependent upon police narratives for much of their information. At the content level, this is in many cases true. However, we must
not ignore the fact that the censuring gaze of the police narrative is culturally
continuous with the dominant law and order discourse on crime and indeed
both reflects and reproduces that discourse. This continuity transcends content and involves the use of a specialized language of investigation, guilt,
responsibility, accountability, and punishment. Simultaneously, we find
powerful (rhetorical) notions of order and disorder embedded in dominant
and preferred understandings of crime. Concerns with the threat posed to a
"harmonious" social order by pathological individuals pervades the microcircuitry traveled by police narratives and the selective secretion of investigative narratives to broader social audiences. Doubtless audiences have
considerable say in how they construe the selected portions of homicide
narratives that see the full light of day. But within the connotative schema
made available by police narratives, television accounts, newspaper reports,
and fictive versions of criminality, certain broader social patterns are less
readily available to consumers of crime news. An example from the Florida
files serves well here. It is clear that most men who kill intimate female
partners use lethal violence offensively, whereas most women who kill male
partners do so out of a concern for their own and/or their children's safety.
This simple fact about the gendered nature of domestic killing is rarely
percolated out of police narratives by other media sources. It is thus not only
what the police narratives say about domestic homicide that limits subsequent decoding, consumption, and reproduction. In addition, it is what they

do not say, their representational boundaries or frames, that warrant our close attention.

ACKNOWLEDGMENTS

The author would like to thank Jeff Ferrell for his insightful comments on earlier drafts of this manuscript.

NOTES

1. See Walker (1992), Kappeler (1995), Dunham and Alpert (1989), Klockars and Mastrofski (1991), Langworthy and Travis (1994), Wrobleski and Hess (1993), Dantzker (1995), Radelet (1986), and Wallace, Robertson, and Stechler (1995).

2. See Cashmore and McLaughlin (1991) and Centre for Contemporary Cultural Studies (1982).

3. See Harring (1983), Storch (1981), Vogler (1991), and Spitzer (1981).

4. See Hanmer, Radford, and Stanko (1989).

5. See, for example, Osterburg and Ward (1992).

6. This essay discusses domestic homicides. There are many other types of homicides. It is not my contention that the themes I highlight in the domestic homicide files are exactly the same as those in other types of homicide, for example, homicides occurring during drug deals or robberies. However, having read a number of drug- and robbery-related homicide files, it is clear there are strong organizational and thematic continuities between different types of homicides, even if the circumstantial details of the cases are dissimilar.

7. In order to protect the anonymity, privacy, and confidentiality of the people referred to in these case files, I have changed all names and other significant identifiers. Since my interest is in thematic continuities rather the extensive details of individual homicide cases, my approach is entirely appropriate. Where I cite details from individual cases I take special care to disguise identifiers without compromising the illustrative power of the homicide. I only employ real names when the parties have already been publicized through other media sources. Even in these, the more high-profile cases, I refrain from sharing information divulged to police by informants since such sharing may compromise the safety of those informants.

8. For other works that follow a similar mode of inquiry see Kozol (1991) and Gordon (1988).

9. See, for example, Philip Jenkins's (1994) discussion of the true crime literature and serial killing.

10. Names are pseudonyms except in cases where the information is made public record through the press. As mentioned, all cases derive from closed files that were made officially available to me through my research in Florida.

11. For a discussion of the interpretation of photographs and imagery in general, see Harper (1994).

12. For similar observations see Gary Marx (1988).

13. I am grateful to Jeff Ferrell for drawing my attention to the lawsuit against Cornwell and MacMillan.

14. For examples of this depiction, see the article by Debra J. Saunders in the *St. Petersburg News* entitled "Battered Woman 'Expert' behaves true to form" (2 February 1995). In discussing Walker's decision to work for the defense in the O.J. Simpson trial, Saunders notes "Walker told the Los Angeles Times her fee is $200–$400 per hour—which demonstrates that being a this-shrink-for-hire for killers is no small potatoes. . . . Walker calls herself a 'scientist.' This is a joke."

REFERENCES

Cashmore, Ellis and Eugene McLaughlin. 1991. *Out of Order? Policing Black People.* London and New York: Routledge.

Centre for Contemporary Cultural Studies. 1982. *The Empire Strikes Back.* London: Hutchinson.

Cornwell, Patricia. 1992. *All That Remains.* New York: MacMillan.

Dantzker, Mark L. 1995. *Understanding Today's Police.* Englewood Cliffs, NJ: Prentice Hall.

Dunham, Roger and Geoffrey Alpert, eds. 1989. *Critical Issues in Policing: Contemporary Readings.* Prospect Heights, IL: Waveland.

Ericson, R. V., P. M. Baranek, and B. L. Chan. 1991. *Representing Order: Crime, Law and Justice in the News Media.* Buckingham, UK: Open University Press.

Fiske, John. 1995. *Understanding Popular Culture.* London and New York: Routledge.

Foucault, M. 1977. *Discipline and Punish: The Birth of the Prison.* London: Tavistock.

Foucault, M. 1980. *Power/Knowledge: Selected Interviews and Other Writings, 1972–77.* Edited by C. Gordon. New York: Pantheon.

Gordon, Linda. 1988. *Heroes of Their Own Lives: The Politics and History of Family Violence.* New York: Penguin.

Graber, D. 1980. *Crime News and the Public.* New York: Praeger.

Hall, Stuart. 1993. "Encoding, Decoding." Pp. 90–103 in *The Cultural Studies Reader,* edited by Simon During. London and New York: Routledge.

Hall, Stuart, Chas Critcher, Tony Jefferson, John Clarke, and Brian Roberts. 1978. *Policing the Crisis: Mugging, the State, and Law and Order.* London: MacMillan.

Hanmer, J., J. Radford, and E. Stanko, eds. 1989. *Women, Policing, and Male Violence: International Perspectives.* New York: Routledge.

Harper, Douglas. 1994. "On the Authority of the Image: Visual Methods at the Crossroads." Pp. 403–12 in *Handbook of Qualitative Research,* edited by Norman Denzin and Yvonna Lincoln. Thousand Oaks, CA: Sage.

Harring. S. 1983. *Policing a Class Society.* Camden, NJ: Rutgers University Press.

Hebdige, Dick. [1979] 1997. "Subculture: The Meaning of Style." Pp. 130–42 in *The Subcultures Reader,* edited by Ken Gelder and Sarah Thornton. London and New York: Routledge.

Jenkins, Philip. 1994. *Using Murder: The Social Construction of Serial Homicide.* Hawthorne, NY: Aldine de Gruyter.

Kappeler, Victor E. 1995. *The Police and Society: Touchstone Readings.* Prospect Heights, IL: Waveland.

Klockars, C. and S. D. Mastrofski, eds. 1991. *Thinking about Police: Contemporary Readings.* New York: McGraw-Hill.

Kozol, Jonathon. 1991. *Savage Inequalities.* New York: Harper.

Langworthy, Robert H. and Lawrence F. Travis. 1994. *Policing in America: A Balance of Forces.* New York: Macmillan.

Lincoln, Y. S. and E. G. Guba. 1985. *Naturalistic Inquiry.* Beverly Hills, CA: Sage.

Marx, Gary. 1988. *Undercover: Police Surveillance in America.* Berkeley: University of California Press.

Osterburg, James W. and Richard H. Ward. 1992. *Criminal Investigation: A Method for Reconstructing the Past.* Cincinnati, OH: Anderson.

Radelet, Louis A. 1986. *The Police and the Community,* 4th edition. New York: Macmillan.

Reiman, Jeffrey. 1990. *The Rich Get Richer and the Poor Get Prison,* 3rd edition. New York: John Wiley.

Sparks, Richard. 1995. "Entertaining the Crisis: Television and Moral Enterprise." Pp. 49–66 in *Crime and the Media: The Post-Modern Spectacle,* edited by D. Kidd-Hewitt and R. Osborne. London: Pluto.

Spitzer, Steven. 1981. "The Political Economy of Policing." Pp. 314–40 in *Crime and Capitalism,* edited by David Greenberg. Palo Alto, CA: Mayfield.

Stake, Robert E. 1994. "Case Studies." Pp. 236–47 in *Handbook of Qualitative Research,* edited by Norman Denzin and Yvonna Lincoln. Thousand Oaks, CA: Sage.

Storch, Robert D. 1981. "The Plague of Blue Locusts: Police Reform and Popular Resistance in Northern England, 1840–57." Pp. 86–115 in *Crime and Society: Readings in History and Theory,* edited by M. Fitzgerald, G. McLennan, and J. Pawson. London: Routledge and Kegan Paul.

Sumner, Colin S. 1990. "Rethinking Deviance: Towards a Sociology of Censures." In *Censure, Politics and Criminal Justice,* edited by C. S. Sumner. Milton Keynes, UK: Open University Press.

Thompson, E. P. 1967. "Time, Work Discipline and Industrial Capitalism." *Past and Present* 38:56–97.

Vogler, Richard. 1991. *Reading the Riot Act: The Magistracy, the Police and the Army in Civil Disorder.* Milton Keynes, UK: Open University Press.

Waegel, W. B. 1982. "Patterns of Police Investigation of Urban Crimes." *Journal of Police Science and Administration* 10:452–65.

Walker, Lenore. 1984. *The Battered Woman Syndrome.* New York: Springer.

Walker, Samuel. 1992. *The Police in America: An Introduction.* New York: McGraw-Hill.

Wallace, Harvey, Cliff Robertson, and Craig Stechler. 1995. *Fundamentals of Police Administration.* Englewood Cliffs, NJ: Prentice Hall.

Wrobleski, Henry M. and Karen M. Hess. 1993. *Introduction to Law Enforcement and Criminal Justice,* 4th edition. St. Paul, MN: West.

VI

Constructions of Crime and Terrorism

14

Jihad as Terrorism
The Western Media and the Defamation of the Qu'ran

FIDA MOHAMMAD

> Terrorism both creates and confirms the existence of a nearly unbridgeable gulf. It is the expression of a communication failure between those who resort to it and those who are its victims. . . . The terror that terrorism awakens in us is directly proportional to our ignorance of political actors and relations of power. (Wieviorka 1993:ix)

I commence with a definition of terrorism. For me the ready resort to the killing or intimidation of members of a noncombatant population is a terrorist act—whether the perpetrator is an individual, group of individuals, or a state. Anyone who wantonly disregards human rights is also a terrorist. Terrorism is generally utilized as a vague concept, and this very vagueness makes it susceptible to ideological abuse. An exemplar of such ideological abuse may be found in the ways in which the Western media sometimes conflate the Islamic concept of "jihad" with terrorism. Using a case study of the "The Rivera Live Show" (CNBC, 19 April 1995) regarding the Oklahoma City bombing, I provide an example of this ideological abuse.

Jihad is an Arabic word that literally means struggling and striving for excellence. Jihad is a multifaceted struggle for the achievement of good and prevention of evil. In Islam there are the following types of jihad:

- *Jihad-e-bil-Lissan:* Jihad with words; speaking the truth. According to one saying of Mohammad: "To utter a word of truth in the face of a tyrant is a supreme jihad" (that tyrant could also be a Muslim one).
- *Jihad-e-bil-Qalam:* Jihad with a pen; writing the truth against injustice.
- *Jihad-e-bil-Mal:* Jihad with one's property and wealth; spending in the name of God, helping the poor and doing charitable works.
- *Jihad-e-bil-Nafs:* Jihad against one's evil desires.
- *Jihad-e-bil-Saif:* Jihad with the sword, if you are challenged by an outside power.

303

Fighting in Islam is strictly regulated by Islamic moral guidelines. In war a Muslim is prohibited from assaults against noncombatants. The old, the young, women, and priests must not be touched. Even cattle should not be slaughtered. Islam further enjoins one to be magnanimous if one's enemy sues for peace. Muslims sometimes violate these guidelines. Jihad-e-bil-saif can as well be waged against corrupt Muslim rulers: In Islam it is obligatory to resist injustice, whether it is from a Muslim regime or non-Muslim one.

Jihad is never simply a "holy war" waged by fanatics. (When one thinks of holy war, one imagines infidels and crusades.) The expression "holy war" translated into Arabic is *Harb-ul-Muqqadas,* which is meaningless in Islam. To reduce an all-encompassing word like jihad to holy war, as has been done in Western media, is an oversimplification, and that construction of Islam is my focus in this chapter. By Western Media I mean the major American broadcast networks, such as ABC, CBS, NBC, PBS, MSNBC, or CNBC and major newspapers like the *New York Times, Washington Post,* the *Los Angeles Times,* and others.

In the Western media, Islam is often equated with extremism and the Qu'ran is portrayed as a textbook of terrorism. "Fundamentalism," a Christian-specific concept, is often used as the catchphrase to characterize Islam in Western-oriented media materials, but in fact it has no equivalent in Islam. The only fundamental precepts in Islam are contained in the statement of faith, "There is no other deity but God, and Mohammad is the Messenger of God" and the focus on prayer, fasting, charity, and pilgrimage.

I argue that the Western media's coverage of Islam commonly takes the form of what Edward Said (1979) calls "Orientalist discourse." According to Said, Orientalism is a legacy of European colonialism that creates ontological and epistemological distinctions between the West and East. Under the sign of the Orient many highly diverse places are homogenized, and this homogenization presents the West as the dominant pole of an epistemological and ontological opposition. The West treats itself like a universal sovereign subject by labeling those who are different as "the other." This worldview, as it is manifested in the Western media, inscribes its own essentialist rules and regulations on the body of the Orient and Islam (Mutman 1992). Mutman explains this phenomenon:

> With the appearance of rich and influential Arab politicians and sheikhs everywhere, Muslims suddenly became the news. By an adaptation of Orientalist discourse to the crisis, this new enemy "Other" was seen as inversely equal and opposite to "us." Order was opposed to chaos, civilization to backwardness, dynamism and democracy to despotism and stagnation. The only possible way of talking about Islam seemed to be this oppositional or confrontational way. (ibid.:7)

Said, as quoted in Mutman (1992), believes that the essentialist way Islam is articulated in Western discourse confers "immediate and unrestrained meanings." In the Orientalist logic of homogenization, time and space are dissolved. Islam becomes an ahistorical facticity that can be experienced without any mediation. If you want to understand the "universal psyche" of the Muslim, just study a few (preferably notorious and villainous) Muslims. In other words, Muslims are predetermined by their cultural properties. Historical time and space, and any contextually informed analysis, often disappear. Islam is ideologized to the extent that much that originates from the Muslim world is presented as political and uncivil. The electronic media have made Islam a familiar topic in the United States, but at the same time something deeply alien to American ways. As a subset of European and American-constructed Orientalism, Islam is made to confer hegemonic meaning. It is hegemonic not only in the sense that people consent to it, but that it is a signifying force disseminated and reproduced in the mass media (ibid.). In such a discourse the central articulation of Islam will be in binary oppositional terms: us vs. the enemy. Under this scheme the West (we) is juxtaposed against the Orient (they) as follows:[1]

We are:	They are:
rational	irrational
free	unfree
democratic	dictatorial
decent	a threat to decency
civilized	barbarian
law-abiding	outlaw
human	inhuman

BINARY-OPPOSITIONAL POLITICS

The subject doing the "othering" is self-designated as essentially good, just, and superior, while the "other" is cast as essentially evil, unjust, and inferior. This means that American goodness is not something that may be evaluated by looking at what we actually do. We are essentially good— even if we invade other countries like Grenada and Panama, prop up dictators and support death squads. The United States vetoes or ignores United Nations resolutions involving other regions in the world when they are not compatible with its interests, e.g., the Palestine question, on which there are numerous resolutions. But these deviations from international norms do not diminish the U.S.'s inherent "goodness," because they are allegedly done so that goodness will ultimately triumph. That is to say, when "we" triumph, goodness triumphs. For some this perspective is easy to accept because they include themselves among the "us" or the insider group: nothing can reduce "our" moral right. At some level the ends always justify the means.

For a moment try to put yourself in the position of Third World peoples, and in this case Middle Eastern peoples, who are on the receiving end of this inherent American "goodness." How would you feel about having a dictatorship, death squads, and torture chambers, all in the name of democracy and freedom? Why does the United States support undemocratic regimes like those of Saudi Arabia, Kuwait, Egypt, and Jordan, and others elsewhere around the globe? What would words like "democracy" and "freedom" mean to you then? Is it still difficult to understand the incredulity of Third World peoples when then-President Bush tells them that the United States has gone to war against Iraq because the leader of the free world cannot tolerate "naked aggression" and another Hitler? Was not Hitler a European? Was this not the same United States that, under Reagan and Bush, respectively, invaded Grenada and Panama?[2]

John Esposito echoes the same feelings:

> Belief that a clash of worldviews, values, and civilization is leading to an impending confrontation between Islam and the West is reflected in headline articles with ominous titles like these: "Still Fighting the Crusades," "The New Crescent in Crisis: The Global Intifada," "Rising Islam May Overwhelm the West," "The Roots of Muslim Rage," "The Islamic War Against Modernity," and the "Arc of Crisis." While such phrases capture public attention and the popular imagination, they exaggerate and distort the nature of Islam, and the political realities of the Muslim World and its diverse relationship with the West. They also reinforce an astonishing degree of ignorance and cultural stereotyping of Arabs and Islam. For many in the West it is axiomatic that Arabs are nomads or oil sheiks, denizens of the desert and harems, an emotional, combative, and irrational people. Islam is often equated with holy war and hatred, fanaticism and violence, intolerance and oppression of women. (1992:4–5)

The Western media also fail to explore the historical role of imperialism and colonialism in shaping power relations in the postcolonial world. A critique of these power relations reveals that all types of violence do not get labeled terrorism (Perdue 1989). As Perdue notes, "If parties in conflict do not have equal standing, a double standard of terrorism may be expected to emerge" (ibid.:8). Perdue believes that

> the definitions of terrorism that prevail reflect such forces as the influence of office, access to the highly sophisticated and pervasive international media, and the "audience appeal" of common values, stereotypes, and symbols. A presidential address on terrorism will have a vast media audience, many of whom are predisposed to respond favorably to the symbols of office, the

appeals to nationalistic imagery and the attribution of terrorism to ethnic, ideological and religious forces that already carry negative stereotypes. (ibid.:8–9)

We might remember there are over one billion Muslims in the world and that most of them are peaceful people. The Western media tends to homogenize the Muslim world as if it were a monolithic entity with the same ahistorical essence—which is a form of essentialistic argument. This hegemonic construction hides the vast internal diversity inside the Muslim world. "Islam is equated with the Middle East, [while] we tend to forget that the largest Muslim populations are to be found in Asia (Indonesia, Pakistan, Bangladesh, and India)" (Esposito 1992:13). The fact that Islam is professed by so many people and that its adherents stretch from Morocco to Indonesia may generate fear in certain quarters, but that fear is mediated by historical and cultural filters:

> Despite many common theological roots and beliefs, throughout history Muslim and Christian relations have often been overshadowed by conflict—as the armies and missionaries of Islam and Christendom have struggled for power and souls. This confrontation has involved such events as the defeat of the early Byzantine (Eastern Roman) empire by Islam in the 7th century; the fierce Crusades during the 11th and 12th centuries; the expulsion of Moors from Spain and the Inquisition; the Ottoman threat to Europe; European (Christian) colonial expansion and domination in the 18th and 19th centuries; the political and cultural challenge of the superpowers (America and Soviet Union) in the latter of half of the 20th century; the creation of the state of Israel; the competition of Christian and Muslim missionaries for converts in Africa today; and the contemporary re-assertion of Islam in politics. (Esposito 1992:3–4)

Historically, "foreign threats" have been presented as both economic and cultural challenges to the Western world. At various times we see these homogenizing and essentialist forces at work in the form of popular journalism. At first, it was the Native Americans, then the "red peril" of the former Soviet Union, the "yellow peril" of Chinese communism, and now there is an attempt to create the "green peril" of Islam:

> That peril is symbolized by the Middle Eastern Moslem fundamentalist— the "Fundie," to use a term coined by *The Economist*—a Khomeini-like creature, armed with a radical ideology, equipped with nuclear weapons, and intent on launching a violent jihad against Western civilization. (Hadars 1992)

In the words of Douglas E. Streusand: "A new specter is haunting America, one that some Americans consider more sinister than Marxism-Leninism, that specter is Islam" (quoted in Hadars 1992). That fear was reinforced when Islamic parties won national elections in Algeria. The democratic victory of the Islamic political parties in the Algerian electoral process was viewed in the West as a threat to democracy and liberalism. According to Hadars, many Western experts believe that

> the rise of political Islam in North Africa, especially the recent electoral strength of anti-liberal Islamic fundamentalist groups in Algeria; the birth of several independent Moslem republics in Central Asia whose political orientation is unclear; and the regional and international ties fostered by Islamic governments in Iran and Sudan are all producing, as *Washington Post* columnist Jim Hoagland put it, an "urge to identify Islam as an inherently anti-democratic force that is America's new global enemy now that the Cold War is over." (Hadars 1992)

It is ironic that Western powers praised the former socialists in Algeria for using an "iron fist" against Islamic political parties. The military coup in Algeria was considered a lesser evil when compared to the larger evil of the democratic electoral victory of Islamic parties. According to Arnold Beichman,

> If the West does not meet that challenge, a Green Curtain will be drawn across the crescent of instability, and the Middle East and the once Soviet Central Asian republics could become in a few years the cultural and political dependencies of the most expansionist militarized regime in the world today, a regime for which terrorism is a governing norm. (quoted in Hadars 1992)

Amos Perlmutter believes that

> Islamic fundamentalism is an aggressive revolutionary movement as militant and violent as the Bolshevik, Fascist, and Nazi movements of the past. It is "authoritarian, anti-democratic, anti-secular," and cannot be reconciled with the "Christian-secular universe" and its goal is the establishment of a "totalitarian Islamic state." (quoted in Hadars 1992)

Apparently the green peril is now replacing the red menace; it is presented as a cancer that, if not "nipped in the bud," will very soon destroy Western civilization. Thus America, having been defined as the guardian of the West, should foster new alliances while the American people should be prepared for this new and never-ending struggle. Hence a new containment doctrine, surpassing the one imposed as a result of the Truman administration's obsession with the spread of communism, is now to be articulated by the foreign policy elite with its "wise men" and "experts" (ibid.).

Most American policymakers are fascinated by the Islamic threat. According to Hadars, the new peril usually adopts the following logic:

> The creation of a peril usually starts with mysterious "sources" and unnamed officials who leak information, float trial balloons, and warn about the coming

threat. Those sources reflect debates and discussions taking place within government. Their information is then augmented by colorful intelligence reports that finger exotic and conspiratorial terrorists and military advisers. Journalists then search for the named and other villains. The media end up finding corroboration from foreign sources who form an informal coalition with the sources in the U.S. government and help the press uncover further information substantiating the threat coming from the new bad guys. (Hadars 1992)

In order to understand the bad guys, think tanks embark on studies. After the publication of their findings, congressional hearings are held. In the end, a new doctrine is espoused and a new villain is identified. Now with the power of media this new enemy becomes part of popular culture. It is all too tempting to identify another global ideological menace to fill the "threat vacuum" created by the demise of communism (Esposito 1992:4).

"RIVERA LIVE"

With the foregoing as context, I now analyze the Oklahoma City bombing as presented on "Rivera Live," April 19, 1995. While this show may have broken new ground in terms of sensationalism, in many ways it is an ideological exemplar. While I recognize the field of ideology in general as a contested terrain, the "Rivera Live" coverage of the Oklahoma City bombing constitutes a form of ideology that comes close to articulating a false consciousness regarding Islam. We cannot rule out the possibility that the Rivera presentation was also an outright attempt to manipulate the audience. As with most discursive analyses of the media portrayal of crime and deviance, it is difficult, without conducting sophisticated audience studies, to know what effect these messages have on viewers.

I begin by interlacing my analysis with excerpts from a conversation between Rivera and Steve Emerson. Emerson is a self-styled expert on Islam and terrorism, who produced a highly malicious PBS documentary called "Jihad in America." Emerson's ideological perspective emerges soon after Rivera confirms Emerson's nationally recognized expertise:

> Rivera: Let me start off with Steve Emerson, who is often described as the country's foremost journalistic expert on terrorism. He's written four books on international terrorism, and U.S. national security. He reported and produced last year's award-winning documentary "Jihad in America." Steve, does it sound dreadfully familiar to you?
>
> Emerson: Unfortunately the scenes are really reminiscent of the '93 bombing of the World Trade Center and the Omnia bombing in Buenos Aires last

year. . . . Based on circumstantial evidence they [FBI] have, it was Islamic extremists who mounted this attack.

[Emerson takes upon himself a certain poetic license in the interest of terrorist political theater.]

Rivera: You know, Steve, as a parent, I wanted my first reaction—my first reaction was, I wish I could get my hands on them, I would tear their faces off.

Emerson: They want you to respond that way.

[Implying that Muslims have similar violent tendencies perhaps?]

Rivera: I know and the problem is—in the World Trade Center, for example, is not the fact that the people who are on trial and those already convicted come from a disparate bunch of these groups. They have nothing in common other than hatred of the great Satan, the U.S. I mean how can we retaliate? . . . even if we know that it was Hamas[3] and this group and the Hezbollah and whatever.

[This seems to be an attempt to homogenize the Islamic world as well as to falsely unite the Muslim world against their common enemy—the United States.]

Emerson: Well, you have hit the nail on the head. . . . You have these groups that now not only have bases and headquarters in the Middle East, they are headquartered right here in the U.S. We now have the phenomenon that the U.S. has become a haven for many of these groups and many adherents of radical ideology who, you correctly say, hate the U.S. for what it stands for: democracy, secularism, separation of church and state. Those are the institutional freedoms that we cherish and those are the very ones that are despised by the militants.

Here Emerson makes the Orientalist argument, that "they" are the moral and ethical inverse of "us." "Because it does not conform to modern secular presuppositions, to the West's most cherished beliefs and values, Islamic activism is regarded as a dangerous, irrational and countercultural movement" (Esposito 1992:10). "Within a dominant system of values, some positions may be defined as 'extreme' or 'utopian,' and thus are easily ignored rather than fairly debated" (Sederberg 1989:9).

Emerson: Oklahoma City, believe me or not, has been a major center of radical Islamic activity for more than a dozen years.

(Note the implicit ideological alignment between radical Islamic activity and terrorism).

Rivera to Mike Cherkasky ("terrorism expert"):   What do we know of the device itself, is it similar? Does it have the signature of the Middle East?

Mike Cherkasky: Well, certainly similar in that it is a low-tech type of device which is, in fact, what scares all of us. It is low-tech. It could be put together by people who do not have a sophisticated background and it obviously has enormous explosive power.

Here, one implication is that some Muslims are unsophisticated in a technological sense, since they cannot make a rational weapon (such as the U.S. "smart bombs" employed in the war on Iraq, which we all know discriminated between civilians and combatants, and never killed and maimed the innocent!). Unsophisticated Muslims can only make low-tech devices—a position that easily lapses into superficial racism.

> Rivera: Let me go to my colleague, John Gibson, who two years ago was reporting on the Branch Davidian disaster in Waco, Texas. You know, John, I do not believe in coincidence. At first, I thought there was an inevitable connection, because I do not believe in coincidence. Then I started wondering after two of the suspects were described as being Middle Eastern in appearance, was it a coincidence? Or were they so sophisticated they saw to do it on this anniversary to deflect attention from the Middle Eastern sources?

Thus the question: What is "Middle Eastern in appearance"? Rivera looks Middle Eastern to me. The Middle East encompasses a very broad range of people, ranging from blue-eyed, blond, and white to black. Spanish, Greek, and Italian people look Middle Eastern. By making these statements it appears that he is trying to direct the anger of the American people against Muslims in general and Arabs in particular. Ironically, the formerly unsophisticated Muslim bombing suspects suddenly become sophisticated, because Rivera does not want to ignore the possible Waco connections.

> Rivera: I was in Beirut. You know, I was there when they blew up our embassy. I was there when they blew up the French embassy. I was there when they—just after the Marines were slaughtered in a bombing not unlike this one. And it definitely has—the fingerprints of the Middle East on it.

Here Rivera uses the language of criminalization—"fingerprints"—thereby creating evidentiary implications. Rivera is making categorical statements about a situation without any evidence to corroborate his accusation. So it was that the Muslim community was under siege for almost sixty-eight hours after the Oklahoma City bombing. People in Oklahoma City were displaying "Muslim Go Home" placards. "All Arabs are, ex-hypothesis, terrorists or terrorist sympathizers" (Sederberg 1989:30).

REFRAMING THE CASE STUDY: POWER, KNOWLEDGE, AND TERRORISM

Many of the media "experts" on terrorism seem to articulate dominant or preferred social meanings regarding this particular form of deviant behavior.

For example, when Dr. Baruch Goldstein slaughtered Palestinian Muslims on the night of February 25, 1994, as they worshipped in Hebron, the media medicalized his criminal activity. He was characterized as a deranged person. In other words, his mental state was responsible for his criminal activities. Goldstein was thus presented as an aberration among peace-loving Israelis.

When we see the dead bodies of Israelis, Europeans, or North Americans on TV, they come with provocative commentary by the so-called Middle East experts, who simultaneously moonlight as consultants on counterterrorism. The consequence is an intense identification with the victims—as well as the generation of a mob mentality. "This identification contributes to the emotional responses of fear and revulsion associated with terrorism" (Sederberg 1989:23):

> Terrorism for most people is captured more in images than in words. In the West, high-impact media portrayals feature personal and dramatic accounts of victims and their families, with the signature of the terrorist written in blood. (Perdue 1989:2)

Such an emotional identification with victims sometimes distorts events instead of clarifying the situation. Brian Jenkins aptly observes:

> If one group can successfully attach the label terrorist to its opponent, then it has indirectly persuaded others to adopt its moral and political point of view, or at least reject the terrorist's view. Terrorism is what bad guys do. This drawing of boundaries between what is legitimate and what is illegitimate, between the right way to fight and the wrong way to fight, brings high political stakes to the task of definition. (quoted in Sederberg 1989:23)

The sensational language is designed to serve a political agenda. Noam Chomsky and Edward Herman argue:

> The words "terror" and "terrorism" have become semantic tools of the powerful in the Western world. In their dictionary meaning these words refer to "intimidation" by the "systematic use of violence" as a means of both governing and opposing existing governments. But current Western usage has restructured the sense, on purely ideological grounds, to the retail violence of those who oppose the established order. (quoted in Sederberg 1989:23)

Perdue has written in a similar vein:

> The argument again is that the term terrorism unleashes powerful imagery with clear societal and intellectual consequences. Symbolism and allegory are ideological devices that intensify what the Arab social philosopher Ibn

Khaldun termed "Asabiya" or in English—social solidarity: a collective sense of oneness or cohesion among the members of a given social order. (Perdue 1989:9)

Durkheim would later coin the words "collective conscience."

Like the media, American policymakers have too often proved amazingly myopic, "viewing the Muslim world and Islamic movements as a monolith and seeing them solely in terms of extremism and terrorism" (Esposito 1992:6). However, the labels "terrorism" and "extremism" do not emerge in a vacuum. The process of definition is political in nature:

Definition does not involve the discovery of some transcendent ideal; rather, it reflects particular historical eras, intellectual professions, and partisan positions. The definition of terms, like other human actions, reflects the interests of those doing the defining. Those who successfully define the terms of a political debate set the agenda for the community, whether the community is conventionally conceived as the nation-state or, less typically, as the community of inquirers in a particular academic discipline. Definition, therefore, involves the exercise of power. (Sederberg 1989:5)

The imagery of terrorism represents a political use of language that invites a certain level of consensus in a community. As Perdue describes it:

The word terrorism is associated with scenes of outrageous violence such as hostage-taking, aircraft piracy, sabotage, assassination, and indiscriminate bombing and shootings. The victims are routinely described as innocents and noncombatants. And always, those officially labeled as terrorists are said to represent the forces of barbarism who threaten civilization and democratic order. Once the label is official, the term counterterrorism may be used to legitimate extraordinary sanctions directed toward offending parties, sanctions that would otherwise be rejected by many. (1989:ix)

The imagery of terrorism is mediated by means of the nexus between power and knowledge. Power or knowledge in itself is a product of "enduring structures of global dependency in which the forces of order clash with those of change" (ibid.:x). Those in power want to keep the status quo. The modern nation-state is an embodiment of political power, and that formal power is concretely exemplified by its coercive apparatus, including the military, national guard, and police. Given such temporal specificity, it can be expected that definitions of political situations will reflect hegemony in flux. What appears immutable and incontrovertible about the nature of terrorism in one time and place can only be expected to change with the passing of regimes and years. In definitional politics, coercion can compensate for the lack of consent or generate apparent consent out of fear. According to Perdue,

> The state quite frequently enjoys a legitimacy born of political socialization and the power of ideology. Therefore, that which is done in the name of protecting the state, the country, or the leadership may be held up to a different measure. This implies a double standard of terrorism, one for the state and the other for its opponents. (ibid.:x)

Of course, just because social audiences are presented with decontextualized media portrayals of terrorism, we cannot assume a monolithic audience interpretation or suggest that audiences uncritically accept what they consume. Much research remains to be conducted on the ways in which audiences consume, process, and act upon these ideological portrayals of terrorism. Given the diversity of knowledge and political perspectives available to social audiences, we ought not fall into the trap of assuming the passivity of social actors by arguing that they do not critically process shows such as Rivera's airing of the Oklahoma City bombing. Notwithstanding these observations, the disproportionate visibility of Western "truth" tends to render the rest of the world less visible. As we have seen in the Rivera case study, Western media coverage of the bombing does present the political context of the deaths within narrow anti-Islamic parameters. It is also the case that these media outlets are controlled by big business interests that enjoy disproportionate access to the state apparatuses and government sources. Their claim to "universal truth" and "objectivity" is so powerful that other voices are at a distinct disadvantage. In the worst-case scenario, these other voices are often stigmatized with labels such as "propaganda" or "extremism." Indeed, it is often the case that in-groups not only speak for themselves but also enjoy the privilege of speaking for "others."

Terrorism cannot be understood without taking into consideration Western imperialism—with its history of colonialism and cultural hegemony—and the relationships of inequality created by it. Weak political groups often use guerrilla methods in order to compensate for their military disadvantages. Those in power often tactically label such activities as barbaric and terroristic. The terrorism label can ostracize as well as dehumanize a nation or a group. After a successful application of the label in a one-sided way, a group becomes an international pariah. The raison d'être of such movements—their ideology, history, and socioeconomic identities—are dismissed out of hand. "Paradoxically then, the very label of terrorism has of itself assumed a terrifying power" (ibid.:4). Hence, the label of terrorism embodies unequal power relationships. While we often ignore state or state-sponsored terrorism, we ought to critically analyze regime terror as manifested in torture, mass arrests, surveillance, false charges, show trials, and the silencing of critical media.

We ought not forget that not all "terroristic" activities receive equal attention. So-called "terrorist" acts seem more likely to become media constructs if the victims are from the United States or one of its allies. Indeed, when looking at regime terrorism, those regimes that tend to be condemned by the media are those which are the adversaries of the American state. Regime terrorism on the part of friendly states is often either ignored or presented in a benign or "understandable" way. For example, right-wing death squads killed thousands of Salvadorans and few Westerners knew about it until three Catholic nuns from America were raped and murdered. In Afghanistan, the Mujahideen were considered freedom fighters as long as their struggle was compatible with Western global strategic interests of containing the former Soviet Union. However, in Sudan, Algeria, and Iran, Islamists are considered to be terrorists because their political agenda conflicts with Western interests.

American policymakers are worried about the spillover of the Iranian and Sudanese brand of Islamic fundamentalism into Saudi Arabia, Kuwait, and the Persian Gulf countries in general. The problem with this conception of strategic interest is that Saudi Arabia is far more fundamentalist than Iran. The Kingdom of Saudi Arabia is no democratic institution. The collective will of the monarchy (the ruling family) is the law. The Saudi regime uses Islamic rhetoric in order to overcome its legitimation crisis:

> The Saudi regime has been able to stay in power largely because it has had both direct and indirect American military support, most recently during the Gulf War. To paraphrase President Franklin D. Roosevelt, the Saudis are Islamic fundamentalist—but they are our Islamic fundamentalists. (in Hadars 1992)

U.S. policymakers were worried about the independence of Latvia, Lithuania, and Estonia because their citizens were Christian whites of European descent. However, when the massacre in Chechnia started, it was categorized as an "internal affair" of Russia. Why? Because there is a racial and religious double standard. In Egypt, Saudi Arabia, Kuwait, Syria, Iraq, Jordan, and many other Arab countries there are often corrupt and clearly authoritarian rulers, and no democratic institutional mechanism to get rid of them. Islam, in such a situation, becomes an alternative political discourse in which the anger and frustrations of powerless people are articulated. According to analyst Allan Thompson, Islam is now a powerful political force, "not because Arabs in those states want to live in Islamic republics like Iran, but because the existing political order has failed them" (quoted in Hadars 1992). When political options for people are limited, they may resort to political violence.

Many people in those countries see some emancipatory potential in

Islam. Islam offers a sense of identity, fraternity, and cultural values that offset the psychological dislocation and the cultural threat of hegemonic power (Esposito 1992:16). Moreover, neither Islam nor Islamic "fundamentalism" is by its own definition "anti-Western." The anti-American attitudes of Islamic groups and movements in the Middle East are not directed against Christianity or Western civilization per se. They are instead often a reaction to U.S. policies, especially Washington's support for authoritarian regimes and the long history of U.S. military intervention.

Much of the Western media portrayal of Islam is part of a broader hegemonic current. Hegemony refers to a

> process of securing and shaping consent so the power of the dominant classes appears both legitimate and natural. It does not refer to a dominant ideology per se, but a practice, and a set of contested relations which permeates and structures social relations. It is a concept that attempts to capture the complex nature of authority which is both coercive and dependent on the consent of those who are coerced into submission. (Holub 1992:45)

Hegemonic control is both physical and ideological. For Gramsci (1991), hegemony is a "means by which a system of attitudes and beliefs, permeating both popular consciousness and the ideology of elites, reinforce existing social arrangements and convince the dominated classes that the existing order is inevitable" (Grenshaw 1988:1350–51). The media, and its many forms and substrates, serve as vectors of hegemonic discourse. Rivera's coverage of the Oklahoma City bombing serves as one example of such hegemonic force. However, hegemony in the form presented on that program is an unfinished project and always encounters resistance from Muslim communities that resent or reject the terroristic definition of jihad. The Geraldo Rivera case study reveals that jihad and terrorism are mediated by cultural stereotypes, images, and symbolism. Without a comprehensive definition of jihad and terrorism there will be little useful debate about the meaning of either. Instead the discourse will continue to be characterized by essentialist logic, racist invective, and imperialistic posturing, all subject to interpretation and misinterpretation by social audiences.

NOTES

1. I have benefited from personal discussions with Tugrul Ilter on these dichotomies.

2. Here I have borrowed materials and ideas from Tugrul Ilter. He shared this with me in the form of notes.

3. Hamas is a Palestinian Islamic organization.

REFERENCES

Esposito, John L. 1992. *The Islamic Threat, Myth or Reality?* New York: Oxford University Press.

Gramsci, Antonio. 1991. *Prison Notebooks.* New York: Columbia University Press.

Grenshaw, Kimberly Williams. 1988. "Race, Reform, and Retrenchment: Transformation and Legitimization in Antidiscrimination Law." *Harvard Law Review* 101:1331–87.

Hadars, Leon T. 1992. "The 'Green Peril': Creating the Islamic Fundamentalist Threat." *Policy Analysis,* August 27, No. 177. [Leon T. Hadars, a former bureau chief for the *Jerusalem Post,* is an adjunct scholar of the Cato Institute (see http://www.cato.org/pubs/pas/pa-177.html).]

Hoagland, Jim. 1992. "Washington's Algerian Dilemma." *Washington Post,* February 6.

Holub, Renate. 1992. *Antonio Gramsci: Beyond Marxism and Postmodernism.* London. Routledge.

Mutman, Mahmut. 1992. "Pictures from Afar: Shooting the Middle East." In *Inscription,* Vol. 6. Center for Cultural Studies. Santa Cruz: University of California at Santa Cruz.

Perdue, William D. 1989. *Terrorism and the State: A Critique of Domination through Fear.* New York: Praeger.

Said, Edward W. 1979. *Orientalism.* New York. Vintage.

Sederberg, Peter C. 1989. *Terrorist Myths, Illusion, Rhetoric, and Reality.* Englewood Cliffs, NJ: Prentice Hall.

Wieviorka, Michel. 1993. *The Making of Terrorism.* Translated by Gordon White. Chicago: University of Chicago Press.

15

Fighting Terrorism As If Women Mattered
Anti-Abortion Violence as Unconstructed Terrorism

PHILIP JENKINS

Interviewer: What do you recommend that concerned citizens do at this time?

Army of God member: Every Pro-Life person should commit to destroying at least one death camp, or disarming at least one baby killer. The former is a relatively easy task—the latter could be quite difficult to accomplish. The preferred method for the novice would be gasoline and matches. Straight and easy. No tracks. You've kind of got to pour and light and leave real fast because of the flammability factor. Kerosene is great, but a little more traceable, so you would not want to buy it and use it in the same day.

Interviewer: What about explosives?

Army of God member: With time delays, a most wondrous method, and my personal favorite. ("The Army of God" 1996.)

Violent acts against abortion clinics and providers have often been in the headlines over the last decade. One notorious recent incident involved the attack on a Birmingham, Alabama, women's clinic in early 1998, which resulted in the death of a security guard and the maiming of a clinic nurse. Shortly afterwards, the police named a suspect in this attack, who was also wanted for questioning in connection with another clinic bombing the previous year, in Atlanta: the man wanted in these attacks soon found himself on the FBI's celebrated list of the ten most-wanted offenders. Media reports of the Birmingham incident left no doubt that the act was seen as a heinous terrorist crime, and one newspaper showed the scarred and blinded face of the wounded nurse under the powerful caption, "The Face of Terror" (Smith 1998; compare Greenberg 1998). The act was contextualized alongside other threatening political trends on the extreme right, especially the growth of well-armed paramilitary organizations (Archibald, Robinson, and Sanford 1998; Bragg 1998a, 1998b; Reeves 1998). This interpretation seems natural enough given the heinous character of the crime, but it is remarkable how only recently it has become possible to express such a view, i.e., to describe a clinic attack as terrorism.

Though numerous acts of violence have been associated with prolife militancy over the past two decades, including dozens of bomb and arson attacks, it is only since about 1993 that such incidents have generally been described with the damning label of "terrorism." This important omission long protected violent antiabortion groups and individuals from the full weight of official investigation and state sanction.[1] While media and government sources condemned the individual acts, the terminology used fell well short of that normally employed to categorize the most serious forms of organized political violence. Literally thousands of separate acts of politically motivated criminal violence were not constructed as a distinctive social problem urgently demanding an official response, but were seen rather as congeries of isolated and almost random phenomena. For almost twenty years, this particular subset of domestic terrorist violence remained an unconstructed social problem, acknowledged neither by government nor media, and ignored by almost all writers on terrorism and political crime. Not until 1993 was the language of "terrorism" applied, a change that permitted a rapid process of construction and contextualization, both in public discourse and in official policymaking.

The long refusal to employ "terrorist" was striking because in definitional terms, prolife extremism lacked none of the criteria that would characterize this behavior as terrorist. However, the semantic question so crucial to constructing the wider problem has been shaped throughout by political factors, and especially interest-group politics. Throughout the 1980s, the federal agencies that dominated the official interpretation of political violence and criminality were controlled by partisans of the political Right, many of whom sympathized with the goals if not the methods of prolife extremism. The shift toward seeing the violence as terrorism reflects changes in federal perceptions. At its simplest level, the movement toward denouncing antiabortion violence as terroristic was a direct outcome of the 1992 election. This is a clear case study of the subjective and ideological nature of the concept of terrorism, as well as of any responses ostensibly designed to combat the perceived menace.

If indeed prolife extremism merits the name of terrorism, this affects our understanding of political violence in the United States, not least in vastly expanding the amount of recorded political violence in the last two decades, and making even more fatuous the periodically asked question, Can terrorism come to the United States? Moreover, the acts in question appear to form a systematic pattern. While they do not reflect orders from some organizational center, the tactics and chronology of the militant antiabortion campaign closely parallel the actions of other violent groups on the extreme Right, which unquestionably do constitute armed terrorism, and which have been so classified by all relevant law enforcement agencies. These parallels extend to individual actions undertaken by "lone assassins" ostensibly operating free from any organizational context. If this is correct, then antiabortion violence should properly be viewed not merely as terrorism, but as an integral part of the broader pattern of ultraright terrorism that has been so prevalent in the United States since the early 1980s, and that attracted so much public attention after the Oklahoma City bombing of 1995. Even so, sections of the media continue to contextualize antiabortion "protest" quite separately from the "terrorism" of the far Right.

This story illustrates familiar themes in the academic study of how the media approach and interpret crime and deviance, and how they consistently present a narrative that exaggerates the role of relatively powerless offenders, while ignoring or distorting the misdeeds of the powerful and well-connected. The case of prolife violence shows how social constructions of criminality and violence depend on the decisions of agencies of social control, and specifically upon their powers to apply labels and subsequently collect statistics. It also provides a case study of how effectively government agencies can deny or ignore quite blatant endemic public violence and mayhem, with little danger of challenge or contradiction from any outside group or institution. Reactions to prolife violence provide a stark reminder of the dependence of both news organizations and academics on official voices (Sanders and Lyon 1995.) If the aim of journalism is to speak truth to power, then this is one area where the American media have been inexplicably and shamefully silent. And, if anything, the record of academics has been even worse, in that terrorism "experts" have systematically relied on statistics carefully predefined and selected for them by agencies of law enforcement, above all in the federal government.

THE VIOLENCE

There is no serious debate about the reality of the acts under consideration here, nor their frequency (Blanchard 1994; Blanchard and Prewitt 1993; "Abortion," 1995.) Since 1977, antiabortion violence has been traced and catalogued by the National Abortion Federation and other prochoice and feminist groups, whose statistics indicate the extent of extralegal activity. Even so, it should be noted that the figures are minima, and that incidents were less likely to be recorded in the earlier years (see Table 15.1).

Opposition to abortion emerged very shortly after the Supreme Court's *Roe v. Wade* decision of 1973, and a direct action campaign emerged about 1976 (see Risen and Thomas 1998; Solinger, Ginsburg and Anderson 1998; Gorney 1998). The direct action movement reached a new degree of organizational maturity in the mid-1980s, and though the groups then formed were

Table 15.1. Abortion Violence in the United States 1977–1995

	Murder	Attempted Murder	Bombing	Arson	Attempted Bombing/Arson
1977–1983	0	0	8	13	5
1984	0	0	18	6	6
1985	0	0	4	8	10
1986	0	0	2	7	5
1987	0	0	0	4	8
1988	0	0	0	4	3
1989	0	0	2	6	2
1990	0	0	0	4	4
1991	0	2	1	10	1
1992	0	0	1	16	13
1993	1	1	1	9	7
1994	4	8	3	5	4
1995	0	0	0	8	0
Total	5	11	40	100	68

Source: "The Abortion Rights Activist," National Abortion Federation, website maintained by Adam Guasch-Melendez.

not necessarily linked to the ensuing violence, at least some of the militants emerged from their ranks. In 1985, Joseph Scheidler published the influential book *Closed: 99 Ways to Stop Abortion* and his Pro-Life Action League became the most visible activist group until the formation of Operation Rescue in 1986–1987, under Scheidler's influence. These movements used tactics of direct physical confrontation, seeking to close abortion facilities by demonstrations, sit-ins, and invasions.

A violent phase of the antiabortion campaign began in 1977 with an arson attack at a clinic in St. Paul, Minnesota, and a bombing the following year in Cincinnati, Ohio. There were twenty-six incidents and attempts between 1977 and 1983. A firebombing and kidnapping incident in 1982 marked the first appearance of the "Army of God," a name that has since appeared in the context of the most extreme actions, including the recent Birmingham attack (Bragg 1998b; "The Army of God" 1996; U.S. House of Representatives 1987; Stoddard and Norwick 1978). Violence escalated sharply in 1984–1985, when there were at least fifty-two actual and attempted bombings and arsons. On Christmas Day, 1984, two clinics and a doctor's office in Pensacola, Florida, were bombed as "a gift to Jesus on his birthday." The rate of attacks then fell steeply, to revive in 1991. Between 1991 and 1994, seventy-one actual and attempted arsons and bombings were recorded. It was also in these years that the campaign shifted to direct assaults and murders of physicians and clinic staff. The most serious acts recorded in the period 1977–1995 include over two hundred actual and attempted bombings and arsons, in addition to five murders and eleven attempted murders. This list does not include acts of violence and intimidation such as clinic invasions (347), vandalism (596), assault and battery (96), death threats (238), kidnapping (2), burglary (37), and stalking (214). Nor does it include many thousands of disruptive acts using hate mail, phone calls, and bomb threats. Picketing and clinic blockades have led to tens of thousands of arrests.

Several recent incidents illustrate the nature of the violence. In February 1995, for example, at least five clinics in California were struck by deliberately set arson fires in a three-week period: at Ventura, Santa Barbara, San Luis Obispo, Santa Cruz, and San Francisco (Burghardt 1995a). While the acts were not unusual in themselves, they offered unusually clear evidence of a deliberate conspiracy. Moreover, the geographical context appeared to link the actions to an earlier protest campaign by an antiabortion group. In a single month in early 1997, "a doctor at a Baton Rouge, LA., abortion clinic was stabbed; a Planned Parenthood office in Dallas was robbed at gunpoint; a Phoenix clinic was the site of three unsuccessful arson attempts; and a Tulsa, OK., clinic was bombed" (Bragg 1997). This particular sequence culminated in the wrecking of an Atlanta clinic by two powerful bombs. Shortly afterwards, a man attempted unsuccessfully to blow up a clinic in Bakersfield, California, using a truck filled with propane and gasoline ("Man Sentenced" 1998).

In 1993 and 1994, antiabortion protesters carried out their most notorious crimes to date, with the murders of doctors who performed the operations (Risen and Thomas 1998; see Table 15.2).

After years of near-fatal attacks, the watershed came on March 10, 1993, when Dr. David Gunn was shot at a Pensacola, Florida, clinic that had earlier been the scene of repeated protests and violence. The same city provided the venue for another attack on July 29, 1994, when Dr. Paul Britton and a clinic escort were murdered. The assassin in this case was Paul Hill, who had earlier persuaded thirty prolife activists to sign a petition justifying killing abortionists as a form of "defensive action" (Hill 1994). In December 1994, two clinic workers were killed at facilities in Brookline, Massachusetts, by protester John Salvi. Assassinations and murder attempts also occurred in Canada. There were numerous other offenses where a political and antiabortion motive was commonly suspected, though not proven, most strikingly the August 1994 murder of Dr. Wayne Patterson in Alabama.

The violent actions have resulted in numerous arrests, including those of some committed and quite professional militants. In the 1980s, Dennis Malvasi undertook several potentially devastating bomb attacks in the greater

Table 15.2. Major Violent Actions Directed against Abortion Clinics
and Providers

Date	Action
March 10, 1993	Dr. David Gunn murdered by Michael Griffin outside clinic at Pensacola, FL
August 19, 1993	Attempted murder of Dr. George Tiller in Wichita, KS, by Rachelle "Shelley" Shannon
July 29, 1994	Dr. John Britton and volunteer escort James H. Barrett murdered by Paul Hill near The Ladies' Center in Pensacola, FL
November 8, 1994	Abortion provider Dr. Garson Romalis shot and wounded in Vancouver, Canada
December 30, 1994	Two women killed by John Salvi at clinics in Brookline, MA
January 16, 1997	Two bombs destroy an Atlanta building containing an abortion clinic
January 29, 1998	Bomb at abortion clinic in Birmingham, AL, kills an off-duty police officer and severely wounds a clinic nurse

New York City area (Freedman 1987). Army of God "soldier" Michael Bray was convicted of conspiracy in the bombing of ten clinics and facilities in 1984 and 1985, and in 1994 published a tract entitled *A Time to Kill,* justifying antiabortion violence (Naylor 1989). He was also a signatory to Hill's "Defensive Action" petition. From the same organization, Rachelle "Shelley" Shannon earned celebrity for a 1994 murder attempt on a clinic doctor in Wichita, and was also convicted of firebomb and butyric acid attacks on clinics in 1992 and 1993. She had been active in several western states, and had been arrested some thirty-five times for various protests. She had also corresponded with Michael Griffin, assassin of Dr. Gunn. The federal judge at her 1995 trial described her concisely as a terrorist ("Woman Gets Twenty Year Sentence" 1995; Egan 1995b; Hall 1994; compare Johnson 1993).

Though bombings and shootings were disavowed by other antiabortion activists, many stressed that violence was understandable, and perhaps justifiable in view of what was perceived as the annual legal holocaust of babies: in fact, the Army of God is also known to its supporters as the underground wing of the American Holocaust Resistance Movement ("The Army of God" 1996). Within militant prolife circles, the legitimacy of armed violence was discussed widely, to an extent that would have caused serious official concern had it occurred in other political contexts.[2] Extreme prolife views received a wide airing in the best-selling evangelical novel *Gideon's Torch,* cowritten by Chuck Colson (aide to former president Richard Nixon), which describes revolutionary violence against abortion facilities by the so-called Holocaust Resistance: though attacks are not explicitly justified, the prolife pastor imprisoned for inspiring them by his writings is the hero of the novel, and he is even compared to St. Paul (Colson and Vaughn 1995).

ORGANIZED TERRORISM?

At first sight, there is no doubt that we are dealing with quite numerous and active terrorists, and prochoice leaders have suggested that even the apparent "lone nuts" might have been subject to some degree of organization. This is a controversial issue: the broad national right-to-life organizations strictly disavow street activism or violence; the hard-core activists do not possess a "high command," and a federal investigation of a possible national conspiracy in 1995 was inconclusive. In fact, the groups engaged in militant protest are divided among a great many splinter factions including Operation Rescue, the Lambs of Christ, Missionaries to the Preborn, and Rescue America, while the actual assassins and bombers who have been identified never admit participation in organized plots or conspiracies. However, drawing analogies from other organizations engaged in illegality raises the question whether this apparent lack of centralization conceals real structure and direction. At its simplest level, this is suggested by the clear patterns or trajectories of violence nationwide, which developed and faded at very much the same time in widely different parts of the country.[3]

It has long been common for violent activists to carry out their operations under the cover of bogus front groups, partly in order to confuse law enforcement, partly to divert blame for actions that attract significant negative public reaction. This pattern of subterfuge has been common in both Middle Eastern and European terrorism, where false flag activities have been a prominent feature of terrorist campaigns in the last three decades. This type of cover is all the more essential in the legal environment of the United States, where federal laws provide devastating civil and criminal penalties for groups that can be shown to have organized or supported a pattern of illegal acts: among the most fearsome is RICO, the Racketeer Influenced and Criminal Organization law (Greenhouse 1994). The antiabortion movement has often been threatened with such sanctions, and has responded by creating a plethora of small and transient entities to carry out protests.

Investigators from prochoice groups like the Bay Area Coalition for Reproductive Rights (BACORR) argue that the dozens of militant organizations are usually thinly disguised offshoots of a larger network (Burghardt 1995b). While rejecting concepts of an overarching national conspiracy, BACORR argues that within this network can be found a "category of activists who, though related to the public 'rescue' groups, constitute a unique sub-set of cadres whose organizational principles are markedly different: the free-floating agents of terror; the miscellaneous clinic bombers, arsonists, saboteurs, drive-by shooters and assassins." Though not subject to direct control from any central group, these activists are organized in cells in the form of the shepherding groups that have developed in Evangelical and Pentecostal churches in the last two decades (Burghardt 1995d; Diamond 1989). Under the shepherding system, small groups of up to a dozen fundamentalist believers are subject to the guidance of a charismatic group leader, in an authoritarian relationship that ventures far into personal and secular matters.

Evidence of organized prolife terrorism is reinforced by parallels with white supremacist and extreme right movements also active in these years. Prolife violence, like that used by ultraright and racist terror movements, peaked in the years 1984–1985 and 1992–1994. Moreover, both for anti-abortion and racist terror movements, the two eras were marked by a similar change of tactics and strategy. Inspired by texts like William Pierce's novel *The Turner Diaries,* white supremacists began a campaign of terrorist violence in 1983 and 1984, at precisely the point that the campaign against abortion facilities turned to systematic violence and sabotage. Not surprisingly, there was an interchange of ideas between prolifers on the one hand, and the radical Patriot right on the other. Already in the mid-1980s, bomb attacks on abortion clinics were a major emphasis in the guerrilla war planning of the extremist Arizona Patriots (Hall 1986). The post-Oklahoma City exposés of the militia movement have detailed the links to prolife movements, and demonstrated the centrality of abortion in much militia rhetoric (Berlet 1995; Junas 1995; Burghardt 1995c, 1995e).

For the far Right, the evils of abortion are transparent, and the issues involved are very close to those raised by other secular concerns. Shortly after the Oklahoma bombing, one Patriot activist at a convention in Missouri defended the bombing by setting it in the broader context of the "abortion holocaust": "And we will ask *them,* how many babies were killed by abortion today?" ("Militia Enemy List Uncovered" 1995; Jasper 1995). The prolife extremists also share much of the conspiracy theory approach found among the paramilitary Right. Apart from the obligatory attack on the New World Order, both also share tendencies to identify Masonic or Illuminati conspiracies as the roots of present evils. A tract alleging Masonic persecution of Catholics was found on the person of John Salvi following his rampage at two clinics in Brookline, Massachusetts. Both Patriot and prolife movements are in addition influenced by Christian Reconstructionism, which holds that Christians have a right and duty to exercise theocratic authority in the contemporary world, with the detailed application of the moral and criminal laws laid down in the Old Testament. The theory has been especially significant for groups like Operation Rescue (Berlet 1995). Media reports have linked Eric Rudolph, the suspect in the Birmingham clinic bombing, with Christian Identity views (Manuel 1998).

LONE RANGERS

Since the late 1980s, these connections and parallels have become even more evident, as both prolife and white supremacist activists have developed the concept of "leaderless resistance." This shrewd if desperate strategy was a necessary reaction to the numerous arrests and prosecutions of far Right leaders during the mid- and late 1980s. If even the allegedly tightest of cell systems could be penetrated by federal agents, why have a hierarchical structure at all? Why not simply move to a *non*structure, in which individual groups circulate propaganda, manuals, and broad suggestions for activities, which can be taken up or adapted according to need by particular groups or even individuals? To quote rightist Louis Beam, "Utilizing the leaderless resistance concept, all individuals and groups operate independently of each other, and never report to a central headquarters or single leader for direction or instruction. . . . No-one need issue an order to anyone" (Quoted in Burghardt 1995c). The strategy is ideal in that attacks can neither be predicted nor prevented, and that there are no ringleaders who can be prosecuted. The Oklahoma City bombing was presumably the work of one such "autonomous cell" (Hamm 1998).

The issue of individual action is significant here. Each of the militants arrested in antiabortion violence has appeared to be acting at least on the surface as a "lone fanatic," but it might be asked whether coordination is so wholly lacking as it appears. The years in which prolife extremists were beginning to carry out lone murders of abortion providers were precisely the period in which the far Right was exploring notions of leaderless resistance, undertaken by the "Phantom Cell or individual action." This type of individual warfare is amply portrayed in the 1989 novel *Hunter,* by Andrew Mac-Donald (i.e., William Pierce), the author of the *Turner Diaries:* this second book depicts a lone assassin seeking to provoke a racial war by means of individual acts of terrorist violence. Berlet reports a 1994 meeting in Massachusetts in which a prominent organizer of antiabortion protests appeared together with members of the John Birch Society and other far-right pressure groups (Berlet 1995). Among the books on sale on this occasion were militia texts and arms manuals, and copies of *Hunter.* One Army of God militant expresses the concept perfectly: "We desperately need single lone-rangers out there, who will commit to destroy one abortuary before they die" ("The Army of God" 1996.)

For both the far Right and the antiabortion movement, the years between 1992 and 1994 were critical (Dees and Corcoran 1996; Stern 1996; Gibson 1994; Merkl and Weinberg 1993). Rightist outrage at the twin incidents at Ruby Ridge and Waco initiated a new wave of organization and arming, which found its most visible public manifestation in the militia movement. At the same time, the leaderless resistance concept was intensely discussed both in print and on the Internet. The formation of new groups and militias reached a climax in 1994–1995, though this was stemmed somewhat by public horror at the Oklahoma City attack. On the abortion front, 1993 witnessed the critical shift in the nature of violence, with direct assassinations and murder attempts on the doctors themselves. Though ostensibly the work of lone fanatics, these attacks might well be fitted into the broader concept of leaderless resistance, which presupposes a constellation of highly motivated activists or berserkers who receive propaganda but not direct orders from partisan media. When sufficiently galvanized by these sources, or when the movement appears to demand such extreme action, the individuals arise to perform the violence required.

WHY NOT TERRORISM?

Following the clinic bombings of 1984, the Justice Department and the FBI came under intense pressure from liberal political leaders to investigate the antiabortion violence as an aspect of domestic terrorism (U.S. House of Representatives 1986). However, the bureau refused on the explicit grounds that the acts, however reprehensible, constituted criminal rather than terrorist violence, and therefore fell under the jurisdiction of the Bureau of Alcohol, Tobacco and Firearms. In practice, the refusal to recognize the prolife campaign as terrorism meant that for a decade, there was no systematic federal response to the violence, which continued largely unchecked. As the problem was unconstructed, individual crimes were counted and collated not by a federal agency, but by private groups, usually prochoice activists.

In retrospect, the FBI's decision seems astonishing. Leaving aside the apparent links with ultraright groups, the sheer volume and severity of antiabortion violence would seem prima facie to constitute political terrorism. As early as 1988, political scientist David Nice published an important scholarly analysis of the antiabortion bombings, which he contextualized together with other forms of political violence, and that was before the worst upsurges of terrorism and criminality (Nice 1988). However, the application of the terrorist label has proved controversial. That the term is pejorative rather than "objective" is indicated by the fact that no so-called "terrorist" group either foreign or domestic acknowledges that title, and prefers some other terminology: they are instead soldiers, partisans, guerrillas, the resistance. One prolife militant has published what is described as *A Guerrilla Strategy for a Pro-Life America* (Crutcher 1992). The cliché justly holds that "one person's terrorist is another person's freedom fighter," or indeed, "defender of life."

In contrast to other countries, the United States has no legal definition of terrorism; thus no prisoner has ever been accused or tried on the simple offense of terrorism. Laws ostensibly designed to combat the behavior have generally focused on certain specific actions, such as bomb-making, arms offenses, and hostage taking. Individual agencies have therefore enjoyed considerable latitude in applying this evocative term. The standard FBI definition presents terrorism as "the unlawful use of force or violence against persons or property to intimidate or coerce a government, the civilian population, or any segment thereof, in furtherance of political or social goals" (Smith 1994:18). The problems here are manifold, for example, in setting all governments on a moral par, so that an act of resistance against the most savage dictatorship is treated as indistinguishable from that against a liberal democracy, while "unlawful" could mean an act contrary to any statutes, however repressive. The definition makes no allowance for justified resistance, and in fact uses terrorism as a blanket term for any act of political violence that the U.S. government happens to stigmatize.

During the 1980s, the imposition of sanctions against "terrorists" of various kinds led to years of intense controversy among academics and policy specialists about whether this label could properly be applied to those engaged in a paramilitary struggle against an oppressive regime. The two cases most frequently mentioned were the IRA and the South African ANC, both of which commanded broad sympathy in North America. The focus of the definition has subsequently shifted from the armed nature of the violence to its indiscriminate character, and the U.S. government now tends to accept the State Department view of terrorism as premeditated, politically motivated violence directed against noncombatant targets. Even this delineation is flexible, and on other occasions, the definition is expanded to include factors like the following: the acts must be clandestine or surreptitious in nature; they are random in their choice of victims; they are intended to create an overwhelming sense of fear; and they should be undertaken by a nonstate or subnational group. Other violent actions that do not fall within these categories might be variously classified as acts of war or resistance, of partisan or guerrilla conflict, of subversion or sabotage.

Antiabortion terrorism would seem to fit either the State Department or the FBI definitions perfectly. In the California arson fires, for example, or the murders of Drs. Gunn and Britton, the actions were premeditated, politically motivated violence directed against targets that by common consensus would be noncombatant. Moreover, the arson fires at least were clandestine or surreptitious in nature, and a primary goal was to create an overwhelming sense of fear among providers and supporters of abortion, virtually to provide general deterrence by the threat of privately administered capital punishment. While prolife extremists would argue that the doctors and clinics targeted are "combatants" in the sense of being engaged in killing, and must be prevented by whatever means are necessary, no government or court would currently accept such a perspective.

In the face of so much evidence to the contrary, the FBI's refusal to acknowledge prolife terrorism depended on two factors, both of which seem, to say the least, tenuous. One was the apparent lack of structure, direction, or organization in the attacks, so that incidents appeared to be the work of numerous lone individuals, rather than any concerted conspiracy. As we have seen, this perception depended on a limited and highly traditional notion of how terrorist campaigns were and should be directed, assuming the necessity for some kind of highly organized general staff or command center. Related to this was the question of the *political* character of the antiabortion crimes. The political motivation might seem self-evident, in that the violence resulted from protests against the operation of a law that the activists profoundly wished to change. However, the FBI was influenced by the argument that these acts represented protests by angry individuals rather than deliberate political action, and moreover did not seek to change national policy in a manner that would denote behavior as "political." It was social protest, rather than political—though interestingly, the FBI's own criteria for terrorism specified violence "in furtherance of political *or social* goals" (emphasis added). The unwillingness to see clinic bombers as terrorists was all the more surprising in view of the obvious parallels and linkages to the ongoing neo-Nazi campaign, which during 1984–1985 represented the agency's prime domestic priority.

The FBI reached its position by the most specious and improbable arguments, which egregiously contradicted their own definitions and policies, to say nothing of common sense. In reality, it is difficult to avoid the conclusion that the bureau's aversion to focusing on the topic was chiefly partisan and political, and above all reflected a fear of alienating the broad right-wing political constituency that supported the goals of the antiabortion movement. The Reagan administration elected in 1980 was strongly prolife: the president himself declared a National Sanctity of Life Day, and used audio links to address huge prolife rallies in Washington D.C. It was wildly improbable that only a few months after Reagan's stunning electoral victory in November 1984, his administration might have extended the terrorist label to a section of the prolife movement, especially when the embarrassing consequences of such an action might have resulted in the investigation of large sections of the mainstream movement. There is thus no need to postulate any kind of official conspiracy or connivance to explain the official underplaying of terrorism, which arose predictably out of the political alignments of the day.

POLICY IMPLICATIONS

For whatever constellation of reasons, antiabortion violence did not receive the FBI's imprimatur as authentic terrorism, and this decision had far-reaching social and legal consequences. The decision was particularly critical in the legal arena, where such a definition would have opened the potential for a whole new panoply of official sanctions, which would have in turn affected the whole prolife movement rather than only the extremists.

Prior to the 1970s, the FBI enjoyed enormous latitude, formal and otherwise, to decide which political groups might legitimately be investigated, bugged, and penetrated by agents, a pattern that led to widespread abuses. Following a series of Watergate-era scandals, Congress introduced severe limitations on the powers of this and other federal agencies, with the goal of preventing the intimidation of organizations that merely opposed or criticized official policies, or even the actions of a particular party or administration. There were, however, due exceptions where imminent violence might be prevented, and the Reagan administration refined these rules so that a clear warning of a terrorist act or campaign would bring a suspect group within the proper domain of federal investigation. Wiretapping and surveillance would become far easier in such cases, and it would be possible to investigate the group by means of infiltrators and defectors. Proof of organized terrorist activity would also expose the network involved to action under civil and criminal RICO laws, under which property could be seized prior to trial, and heavy fines and lengthy prison terms imposed. In summary, the "terrorist" label would summon forth the same range of powers that caused the decimation of traditional organized crime groups since the early 1980s, and that led to the uprooting of the right-wing terrorist band known as the Order during 1984 and 1985.

In practical terms, federal definition of conduct as "terrorist" means a far more proactive (rather than reactive) stance in the face of a given campaign, a stance that virtually all observers view as the only potentially successfully strategy. Decades of experience have suggested that terrorist groups tend to operate in certain ways, and need certain facilities that if properly observed and investigated can provide rich opportunities for security forces. Often, groups exist simultaneously both above and below ground: a mass party or pressure group provides a cover for illegal underground operations, as well as channeling money for clandestine operations, and providing potential recruits. It is thus essential to observe the legal arm of a movement as a way of identifying the armed illegals.

Let us for example imagine a number of attacks on the embassies and facilities of a particular nation in the United States, and messages to the media that have linked these attacks to the grievances of a dissident party or ethnic group. A reactive stance might consist of improving security at these installations, and perhaps for any diplomats or business people connected with them, followed by intense criminal investigation to determine the individuals or groups directly responsible for given acts. This would, however, be immensely labor-intensive and time-consuming, and would make no progress whatever in rooting out the terrorist factions responsible. A proactive position would rather involve identifying the public or above-ground organizations associated with the suspected dissidents. These would be subject to surveillance with a view to compiling a network analysis to see if links to violent groups might be identified, or even chains of command and communication between the legal and the clandestine arms of the movement. A similar endeavor might also take the form of tracing individuals within the broader movement who have given signs of sympathy for violent action, for example, by writing articles or signing petitions to this effect, or by campaigning on behalf of imprisoned militants. Crucially, infiltrators would have to be placed inside the terrorist organization, initially by making contact through the above ground party. Effective counterterrorism must be proactive, interventionist, and firmly based on the widespread collection and collation of intelligence, and these are all strategies that can only be achieved legally once the crucial designation of "terrorism" has been affixed to the movement in question. Ideally, authorities could gain such a stranglehold on the group's potential operations that it would be induced to cease its campaign.

The investigative scheme outlined here would currently be absolutely illegal in the context of the antiabortion movement, but once the terrorist label had been applied, restraints would be removed accordingly. If it was agreed that the shooting of doctors constituted organized terrorism, then detailed investigation and surveillance could begin in earnest, beginning with the signatories to petitions advocating violence or murder, and the memberships of all groups involved with such documents. Networking would be pursued wherever leads suggested, which in the case of the prolife movement would assuredly mean through the fundamentalist churches and underground religious networks, and perhaps sections of the organized religious Right that was so critical to the Republican electoral effort in these years. In reality, however, the lack of a terrorist definition prevents a proactive response of the sort that would alone be effective against such a threat. The FBI's failure to respond did not only mean that investigators were deprived of the assistance of one agency; rather it implied the absence of all those tactics that are the core of any policy of prevention and eradication.

To understand the potential scope and implications of a proactive antiterrorist investigation, we need only consider other events in progress at precisely the time that the FBI was refusing to regard a series of bombings as evidence of an organized terrorist campaign (Gelbspan 1991). In the early 1980s, the FBI desperately wished to investigate the quite legal and pacific movement against U.S. intervention in Central America, an investigation that could not be pursued unless a "terrorist connection" could be established, however implausibly. With minimal difficulty, informers were found to assert that Central American solidarity groups were, in fact, covers for terrorist plots and assassination schemes, and these claims provided the rationale for a vast campaign of bugging, infiltration, and dirty tricks, much of which was directed against churches, religious communities, and individual church workers. Though such actions were controversial in terms of violating constitutional guarantees of freedom of religion, the argument was that the actions were essential to prevent the outbreak of violence, even though no criminal or terrorist act had been committed. In this instance, the mere suggestion that such events could potentially occur was sufficient to invoke law enforcement agencies engaging in quite intrusive behavior. There is a stark contrast to the antiabortion situation, in which armed attacks were commonplace by mid-1980s. The inescapable conclusion is that the terrorist label was applied too generously when dealing with opponents of government policy, but with astonishing parsimony in the case of political friends and sympathizers.

UNCONSTRUCTED TERRORISM

The consequences of the FBI's attitude have reached far beyond the realm of law and policing, and have ensured that antiabortion violence has been essentially invisible in the mass media and in scholarly sources. This is striking, as the extreme wing of the prolife movement would deserve to be listed among the most active of domestic American terrorist groups, whether this is assessed in terms of the frequency of incidents, the number of fatalities, or the extent of property damage inflicted. In terms of endurance, moreover, the extremist prolife campaign has been one of the hardiest of such movements, quite comparable to other more celebrated insurgencies like that of militant Puerto Rican nationalists, or domestic neo-Nazis.

In terms of scholarship, most published works on terrorist activity in the United States do not even discuss antiabortion violence, still less contextualize it together with other forms of acknowledged terrorism. For example, the pages of the prestigious journal *Terrorism* have included articles on virtually every violent and secessionist movement around the world, but very little on the abortion theme; and the issue does not even rate an index entry in standard works like Brent L. Smith's otherwise compendious *Terrorism in America* (1994). The abortion issue receives sparse if any coverage in most of the major works on terrorism from these years (Smith 1994; compare O'Sullivan 1986; Wilkinson 1986; Livingstone and Arnold 1986; Merkl 1986; Laqueur 1987; Poland 1988; Stohl 1988; Wardlaw 1989; Livingstone 1990; Vetter and Perlstein 1991; Crenshaw 1995). In one commonly used college textbook on terrorism, the issue receives a page and a half out of nearly three hundred pages—relatively generous compared with most of the literature! (White 1991:179–80). The reasons for this systematic omission are straightforward, in that most academic sources tend to rely on official categories and designations to define the scope of their study, so that when the FBI made its *ex cathedra* pronouncement that abortion violence was not terrorism, the topic was thereby excluded. With the FBI deciding not to cover the topic, the agency could provide no convenient speakers, experts, or statistics to use on news shows to discuss and contextualize new acts of violence. Without such resources, prolife violence attracted little academic interest, and offered no attraction for the army of "true crime" authors who normally flock to sensationalistic subjects. We have no such true crime studies of the murders of abortion providers, no case studies of the most notorious bombers and arsonists. The omission of this sort of crime from the scholarly and professional literature is a stark demonstration of the thorough reliance such works normally place on federal sources and information.

Though it is difficult to illustrate a negative, prolife violence was also largely absent from the mass media throughout the years of its sharpest intensity. In general, the topic of terrorism has often been addressed in movies, TV movies, and dramatic series, with Middle Eastern militants a common feature of popular fiction. Groups closer to home have nearly always been treated with somewhat greater sensitivity for fear of offending domestic constituencies, and character portrayals have usually been more subtle than in the depictions of evil Muslim fundamentalists or Palestinians. Nevertheless, domestic terrorist groups have featured in films and television dramas, often in works involving major stars and directors. The fascist Right was the subject of films like *Talk Radio* and *Betrayed,* the violent Left of the film *Running on Empty,* while the Puerto Rican situation has also featured sporadically. On television, neo-Nazi, white supremacist, and militia groups have appeared increasingly as themes since the sudden spotlight cast on such groups by the Oklahoma City bombing. In contrast, abortion in general has always proved a very delicate theme, and the media have been reluctant to approach antiabortion protest in general, and still less the violent extremes. Only in 1993–1994 did the issue emerge, and then chiefly in stand-up comedy shows mocking the hypocrisy of "prolife" advocates who supported the assassins of abortion workers. When antiabortion violence eventually appeared in television movies, as late as 1996, such a portrayal was still too daring for the networks: the films *If These Walls Could Talk* and *Critical Choices* were both broadcast on pay cable channels, respectively, HBO and Showtime (James 1996).

Why did the antiabortion theme not attract the same media fascination as other forms of terrorism? Certainly it was not for lack of intrinsic interest, and one can easily construct the sort of fictional themes that might have been employed. Imagine for example the obvious film that could have been made about a determined female investigator rooting out a network of fanatical clinic bombers and assassins, and in so doing uncovering highly placed sympathizers for the terrorists within her own organization, perhaps among her superiors at the FBI or the Justice Department. One would have thought the subject overwhelmingly attractive, offering as it does the adaptation of familiar genres such as the antiterrorist film, the lone investigator, and the conspiracy story. The hypothetical film would also present a superb opportunity for a strong female lead, and could have been expected to have enormous demographic appeal to younger women. Of course, there never was such a feminist *Mississippi Burning*, and the issue has been as absent from cinema screens as from TV movies. If only for the basest financial motives, one would have thought that filmmakers would have been attracted to such conflicts.

The lack of attention is far more than a historical curiosity, because the media serve such a critical role in constructing an issue for public consumption, and thereby in establishing both public and official priorities for responding to it. Some degree of interpretation is inevitable: if the media are to report on any question, they must attempt to give it some meaning, to place it in a frame of reference that will be familiar to the assumed audience. To quote Stuart Hall et al., "If the world is not to be represented as a jumble of random and chaotic events, then they must be identified (i.e. named, defined, related to other events known to the audience), and assigned to a social context (i.e. placed within a frame of meanings familiar to the audience). This process—identification and contextualization—is one of the most important through which events are 'made to mean' by the media" (Hall, Critcher, Jefferson, Clarke, and Roberts 1978:54). If, however, the abortion violence issue is simply absent, while other forms of terrorism receive intense attention, the message is clearly that this form of violence either does not exist or has no real significance. In turn, this lack ensures that there is no public pressure on elected and appointed officials, no cry for a "war on terror" in this particular form; and no rewards for the bureaucratic agencies that achieve success in such a struggle. Throughout the 1980s, the phenomenon remained unconstructed, and thus did not exist as a social problem.

Conversely, the absence of federal sanction leaves the issue as the preserve of prochoice, feminist, and liberal groups, who are alone left to make the point that the behavior in question is authentic terrorism. In this context, the fact of expressing concern about anticlinic violence, or even using the word "terrorism," is perceived as making a partisan political statement. A filmmaker who addressed the issue from this standpoint would thus be denounced by the prolife movement for "extremism" and "hysteria" in the prochoice cause, and the studio or network in question would certainly attract commercial boycotts, and possibly political sanctions. The FBI's stance of magisterial "objectivity" effectively delegitimated any potential movement to expose and counter prolife violence.

CONSTRUCTING TERRORISM 1993–1995

Official attitudes to clinic violence began to change during 1991, following Operation Rescue's mass blockades, which sought to close abortion facilities in Wichita, Kansas, and other areas ("Wichita's Long Hot Summer" 1991). These actions entered the national political arena following the refusal of federal authorities to defend the clinics, apparently aligning the Republican administration not only with the prolife cause, but with its militant direct-action wing. The 1992 elections brought to office the first Democratic president in twelve years, and one moreover supported by liberal and feminist groups. In the aftermath of Wichita, the Clinton administration took seriously the demands of prochoice advocates for federal measures to defend clinics, while prolife militants were discouraged and outraged. In his first month in office in 1993, Clinton lifted several federal restrictions on abortion policy imposed during the Reagan and Bush administrations. The change of regime may well have encouraged the desperation that erupted in the new tactical direction of the extremist movement, and specifically the decision to employ personal violence against abortion providers. Furthermore, the blockade movement had peaked after the 1991 Wichita operation, and subsequent campaigns in 1992 were embarrassing failures.

The crescendo of violence in 1993 and 1994 brought demands for these acts to be counted as terrorism and to be treated with appropriate seriousness. Such calls had been frequently heard in the prochoice and feminist press for years, but now each major attack called forth a chorus of support in the mainstream media, and the murders of doctors and clinic workers were especially influential ("Anti-Abortion Acts" 1992). The volume of coverage, as measured by electronic databases such as *Newspaper Abstracts* and *Periodical Abstracts,* now increased dramatically. *Newspaper Abstracts* offered 208 entries under "abortion violence" for the years 1989–1995, only sixteen of which appeared in the three years 1989–1991. The murder of Dr. David Gunn in March 1993 caused a dramatic upsurge of coverage, as did the Britton shooting in July 1994. Over half the total, 120 items, appeared between the Britton murder and the end of 1995. The changed climate appears to be a direct response to the new attitude of the federal government, and the consequent change in tone of statements from federal law enforcement. However, the relationship between governmental definitions of terrorism and media products regarding antiabortion violence cannot be simply reduced to a linear causal model. For example, the definitional imperatives apparently emanating from the Clinton administration were continuous with the claims-making activities of diverse groups that fed the formal polity at a number of levels. These claims-making activities were not distinct from media sources but were at times an articulation of those forces. If any model is appropriate in terms of understanding the relationship between governmental definitional initiatives and the media portrayal of antiabortion violence as terrorism, that model would have to acknowledge the synergistic reciprocal relationship between government and media or the shifting ideological homologies between those two seemingly distinct entities. This does not mean that at certain pivotal moments the motive force behind definitional drives does not tend to emanate primarily from either the government or the media.

The terminology applied by the media also changed. In the databases, before 1992 the word "terrorism" was very rarely found in conjunction with the words "abortion," "antiabortion," or "prolife," although specific arson and bomb attacks were very widely reported.[4] From 1992 onwards, however, the conjunction "prolife terrorism" becomes quite frequent, with about twenty-five entries between 1992 and 1995, most occurring immediately after one of the best-known attacks. The shooting of Dr. Gunn caused a particular media outcry, and the *Atlanta Constitution* typically asserted that "Christian terrorists" were incited by the extravagant vocabulary of the prolife leadership (Teepen 1993; Karten 1993; Barringer 1993). The timing of events was particularly important here, in that the first Pensacola shooting occurred only two weeks after the World Trade Center bombing, as a result of which the media had regularly been denouncing terrorism and religious fanaticism on American soil. Late February had also marked the beginning of the Branch Davidian siege in Waco, Texas, an event that culminated in April with the massacre of seventy-five people. This affair further drew attention to the apocalyptic views and fanatical behavior of the Christian ultra-Right, and its penchant for armed violence.

This far graver perspective influenced the deliberations of a House Judiciary subcommittee, which was then considering measures to protect clinics, and which was told by the son of the murdered doctor that "these anti-choice groups, I can't refer to them as pro-life anymore, are using terrorist tactics" (Orman 1993; U.S. House of Representatives 1993; Corbin 1993). In addition, the American Medical Association used the attacks to draw attention to violence against doctors both from prolife extremists and animal rights activists (Gravois 1993). Though religious Right leaders like Chuck Colson and Ralph Reed naturally rejected the "terrorist" label and complained that Christians were being unjustly pilloried as fanatics, the image of prolife terrorism appeared widely in the media, and endured over the following months. An editorial in the *Denver Post* asserted, "Shooting of abortion doctor was terrorism, not just assault," while *the Atlanta Constitution* warned of "Domestic Terrorists at Work." ("'Pro-life' Terrorism" 1993; "Shooting of Abortion Doctor Was Terrorism, Not Just Assault" 1993; Abcarian 1993; "Domestic Terrorists at Work" 1993). The Britton attack in July 1994 was equally influential in promoting the concept of the violent prolife activist as not merely a terrorist but also a "fanatic," a word commonly used previously in the context of Middle Eastern violence and Muslim fundamentalism ("When Extremism Becomes Terrorism" 1994; Risen 1994; O'Connell 1994; Hedges 1994). The radically changed tone of press coverage was suggested by a spate of headlines associating antiabortion violence with terms like "terrorist" and "fanatic," and with the state of war in which clinics now found themselves.

An increasingly hostile media atmosphere culminated following the Brookline attacks that December. These attacks were explicitly described as "domestic terrorism" by President Clinton (Puga 1994a, 1994b; "Pro-Life Terrorism: A How-to" 1995). The days following the Brookline shootings were marked by the starkest media condemnations yet of antiabortion violence (Goodman 1994; "Vigilance and Violence at Abortion Clinics" 1995; Abcarian 1995). Headlines variously proclaimed: "Clinic Killings Another Form of Terrorism" (*Boston Globe*), "Abortion Clinic Killers: Terrorists, Not Saviors" (*USA Today*), and "Pro-Choice Forces Urge War on 'Organized Terrorism'" (*Houston Post*) (Shea 1995; "Abortion Clinic Killers" 1995; Freelander 1995; Swarr 1995). An article in the *Houston Chronicle* was typically entitled "Call Them As They Are: Anti-Abortion Terrorists" (Pike 1995:C11; Wicklund 1995; Parshall 1995). This grim vision was further reflected in cartoons depicting those who attacked abortion facilities and providers as savage fanatics. In the *Washington Post,* Herb Block depicted an antiabortion fanatic declaring, "They should lock up those foreign nuts that are told what to do by some other god," and the cartoonist returned to these themes on several occasions during 1994 and 1995 (Block 1994, 1995a, 1995b). This perception was reflected in some of the media reaction to the Oklahoma City bombing, and specifically the new attention that it attracted to the violent actions of the political extreme Right ("Taking the Measure of Terrorism" 1995). The fact that this incident seemed designed to avenge the Waco massacre further suggested linkages between the violence of secular and religious extremists. Meanwhile, arguments about the political and gender-based nature of clinic violence were reinforced by the growing influence of feminist views in the shaping of federal crime policy. Nineteen ninety-four was the year of the sweeping Violence Against Women Act, which radically reformulated official responses to crimes like stalking and domestic violence.

In the face of such rapidly changing attitudes, the federal government came under heavy pressure to use its power to deter further prolife attacks, both to offer immediate protection to the clinics, and to provide longer-term security. In the immediate aftermath of the Pensacola killings, federal marshals were dispatched to protect clinics across the country in August 1994, while the Justice Department made the critical decision in July 1994 to create a task force to investigate any organized national campaign or conspiracy in the violence ("Federal Marshals Have Been Sent" 1994; Sharp 1994). Though the task force established by Attorney General Reno found no such evidence, the mere reporting of its activities served to focus media attention on prolife violence as a systematic threat, and potentially a form of organized terrorism (Egan 1995a; Johnson 1994). Also critical was the new Federal Access to Clinics legislation, which was credited with suppressing the worst of the street disruptions that had hitherto been permitted in anti-abortion protests (Navarro 1996; Pear 1996; U.S. Senate 1995).

The reduction of street violence may have contributed to the decline in outright terrorism, in that unstable individuals now found less in the way of blatant stimuli encouraging direct violence against clinics and providers. The changed environment was epitomized by prolife militant Andrew Burnett, a friend of militant Shelley Shannon. Interviewed in 1995, he complained, "The pro-life movement has changed radically. Funds are down. People are discouraged. They call us terrorists. But those who have chosen violence have made a big bang." We note that the simple fact of being named as terrorists is listed as one of the major elements in the discrediting of the militant campaign (cited in Egan 1995b).

Between early 1993 and early 1995, antiabortion violence came to be constructed as a significant social problem. In explaining the remarkably rapid transition in attitudes, one obvious factor was that the nature of the behavior in question had changed quite radically in degree, in that while scattered arsons could be played down in the press or treated as isolated incidents, a campaign of assassination obviously demanded a major official response. It now became difficult for the FBI and other agencies to ignore the violence, especially when the new administration clearly shared feminist and liberal perceptions of the nature and scale of the threat. With administration sanction, the media could now turn its full attention to the violence, and portray it as at least parallel to other forms of terrorism that attracted public concern in these years. In fact, these linkages were so powerful that the question is less why the problem came to be constructed in this way in the mid-1990s, than why it had not been so regarded a decade earlier.

REAL POLITICS AND REAL TERRORISM

During the 1992 election campaign, abortion providers made the grim joke that the only way that they could obtain government protection from assault would be to paint American flags on the walls of their buildings, so that attackers could at least be prosecuted for desecrating the national symbol. The humorous observation raises a serious point, about why politicians and official agencies so long failed to accord due seriousness to an authentic terrorist threat, rather than to such symbolic issues as flag protection. If a group of Middle Eastern or Muslim orientation had carried out assaults against life and property on American soil on a scale far smaller than prolife extremists, official agencies would have made its suppression an absolute priority, and Congress would have passed whatever draconian legislation might have been perceived necessary for this purpose.

In the case of prolife extremism, two critical factors permitted the official refusal to accept the diagnosis of terrorism. One was the identity of the perpetrators, whose affiliations were with groups and ideologies that retained official favor, and the other was the nature of the real and potential victims, who were seen as representing women's causes. It is tempting, but simplistic to suggest a mere imbalance of power here, in that the perpetrators represented groups with far more power and access to authority than did the victims. According to classic conflict theory, the more powerful group exercised the ability to grant or withhold a label of severe deviance according to its own interests (Sanders and Lyon 1995).

However, the real problem was more fundamental, in that the conflict not only concerned the appropriate targets for the imposition of state power, but the appropriate limits of that power. Gender played a vital role in this ideological division. For women's groups, it was natural to insist that the state should intervene forcefully to protect the exercise of a constitutional right, but the conservative administrations of the 1980s largely denied that such enforcement fell within the legitimate scope of state operations. However much this flouted common sense and consistency, antiabortion violence of whatever scale was not until 1993 recognized as a political problem, as it was directed against one segment of the population, namely women. As such, it was only "social" in nature and therefore beneath the dignity of federal intervention. We are reminded of the old argument that violence and rape in the domestic context did not constitute "real" crime, as these acts were a private domestic transaction in which legal authorities should not interfere.

The modern American experience with terrorism provides rich ammunition to support the feminist argument that matters of grave concern to women are not currently regarded as appropriate for serious political discourse, and in fact do not merit a political label at all. This was the attitude that for many years led to women being appointed to government office in departments responsible for matters such as health and welfare, family and children, where they could fulfill what was virtually an extended domestic role. Confined to the realm of the "merely social," women's issues were not to intrude on the pressing concerns of the state and its proper functions, such as war and peace, law and order, and national security. In this view, the merely personal is emphatically not political. The official depiction of abortion violence as a women's issue, or still more damning, a feminist issue, meant that the problem was framed as a conflict between two groups of zealots, in which the state could and should play no role. The administrations in power between 1981 and 1993 largely shared the view of the antiabortion movement that the staff and patients in an abortion clinic were participating in a morally tainted activity, and could not be regarded as fully innocent victims even if attacks occurred. From such a perspective, conservative administrations felt that treating a "women's issue" like clinic violence under the grave label of terrorism would be frivolous, and a diversion of resources badly needed in the struggle against "real" terrorism. Changing attitudes to prolife terrorism thus symbolize and encapsulate crucial changes in popular views of the appropriate scope and function of politics, and the place of women in the polity. For a grim decade, violence was allowed to flourish precisely because women's concerns were not believed to matter. A proper response could only be formulated once this form of ideological exclusion had been confronted and removed.

NOTES

1. The term "prolife" is the one generally employed by members of the movement itself, though it is highly value-laden in implying that opponents or nonmembers oppose life, or are even "prodeath." For convenience, the term "prolife" will here be employed without quotation marks, though this should not be taken to suggest the author's acceptance of these implications. I am aware of the consequent absurdity involved in using terms such as "prolife killings."

2. From a large literature, see, for example, Risen and Thomas (1998), Solinger et al. (1998), Gorney (1998), Manegold (1995:26), Vrazo (1995), Kerrison (1994),

Lewin (1994), Hunter (1994), Rimer (1993), Hertz (1991), Condit (1990), Faux (1990), Terry (1988).

3. Examples include the bombing wave of 1984, the upsurge of arson between 1991 and 1993, and most sensationally, the emergence of assassination as a tactic in 1993–1994.

4. For the tone of earlier coverage, see for example Cleninden (1985).

REFERENCES

Abcarian, Robin. 1993. "A War of Attrition against Abortion." *Los Angeles Times,* October 20.

Abcarian, Robin. 1995. "Where Does Free Speech End, Terrorism Begin?" *Los Angeles Times,* January 4.

"Abortion." 1995. *MS Magazine,* special feature, May–June, pp. 42–66.

"Abortion Clinic Killers Terrorists, Not Saviors." 1995. *USA Today,* editorial, January 3.

"Anti-Abortion Acts a Form of Terrorism, Court Is Told." 1992. *Chicago Tribune,* February 20, p. 2C.

Archibald, John, Carol Robinson, and Peggy Sanford. 1998. "Officer Dies, Nurse Hurt in Abortion Clinic Blast." *Birmingham News,* January 30.

"The Army of God Overview." 1996. *The Abortion Rights Activist,* National Abortion Federation, WWW site maintained by Adam Guasch-Melendez. http://www.cais.com/agm/main/aoginter.htm

Barringer, Felicity. 1993. "Slaying Is a Call to Arms for Abortion Clinics." *New York Times,* March 12.

Berlet, Chip. 1995. "Armed Militias, Right Wing Populism, and Scapegoating." *Political Research Associates,* April 24. http://burn.ucsd.edu/archives/ats-1/1995.May/0027.html.

Blanchard, Dallas A. 1994. *The Anti-Abortion Movement and the Rise of the Religious Right.* New York: Twayne.

Blanchard, Dallas A. and Terry J. Prewitt. 1993. *Religious Violence and Abortion.* Gainesville: University Press of Florida.

Block, Herb. 1994. "Shooting Doctors? Bombing Clinics? How Could People Think of Doing Such Things?" Cartoon, *Washington Post,* August 3, p. A16.

Block, Herb. 1995a. "They Should Lock Up Those Foreign Nuts That Are Told What to Do by Some Other God." Cartoon, *Washington Post,* January 19.

Block, Herb. 1995b. "Greetings, Brother." Cartoon, *Washington Post,* July 19.

Bragg, Rick. 1997. "Abortion Clinic Hit By Two Bombs." *New York Times,* January 17.

Bragg, Rick. 1998a. "Bomb Kills Policeman at Alabama Abortion Clinic." *New York Times,* January 30.

Bragg, Rick. 1998b. "Group Tied to Two Bombings Says It Set Off Clinic Blast." *New York Times,* February 3.

Burghardt, Tom. 1995a. "Anti-Abortion Terror Escalates in California: Four Women's Clinics Attacked in February." Bay Area Coalition for Our Reproductive Rights. http://www.webcom.com/pinknoiz/right/bacorr6.html.

Burghardt, Tom. 1995b. "Dialectics of Terror: Anti-Abortion Direct Action." Bay Area Coalition for Our Reproductive Rights. http://www.webcom.com/pinknoiz/right/terror1.html.

Burghardt, Tom. 1995c. "Leaderless Resistance and the Oklahoma City Bombing." Bay Area Coalition for Our Reproductive Rights. http://nwcitizen.com/public-good/reports/leadless.htm.

Burghardt, Tom. 1995d. "Church Cells." Bay Area Coalition for Our Reproductive Rights. http://www.webcom.com/pinknoiz/right/churchcells.html.

Burghardt, Tom. 1995e. "Neo-Nazis Salute the Anti-Abortion Zealots." *Covert Action Quarterly* (Spring):52.

Cleninden, Dudley. 1985. "Abortion Clinic Bombings Have Caused Disruption for Many." *New York Times,* January 23.

Colson, Chuck and Ellen Vaughn. 1995. *Gideon's Torch.* Dallas: Word.

Condit, Celeste Mishelle. 1990. *Decoding Abortion Rhetoric.* Urbana: University of Illinois Press.

Corbin, Beth. 1993. "Florida Physician Murdered by Clinic Terrorist." *National NOW Times* (April):1.

Crenshaw, Martha, ed. 1995. *Terrorism in Context.* University Park: Pennsylvania State University Press.

Crutcher, Mark. 1992. *Firestorm: A Guerrilla Strategy for a Pro-Life America.* Lewisville, TX: Life Dynamics.

Dees, Morris, and James Corcoran. 1996. *Gathering Storm.* New York: Harper-Collins.

Diamond, Sara. 1989. *Spiritual Warfare.* Boston: South End.

"Domestic Terrorists at Work." 1993. *Atlanta Constitution,* editorial, October 4.

Egan, Timothy. 1995a. "Seeking a National Conspiracy. Abortion Task Force Is Set Back." *New York Times,* June 18.

Egan, Timothy. 1995b. "Shooter Falls Silent about Anti-Abortion Terrorism." *Tacoma News Tribune,* June 18.

Faux, Marian. 1990. *Crusaders.* New York: Carol.

"Federal Marshals Have Been Sent." 1994. *Wall Street Journal,* August 2.

Freedman, Samuel G. 1987. "Abortion Bombings Suspect: A Portrait of Piety and Rage." *New York Times,* May 7.

Freelander, Douglas. 1995. "Pro-Choice Forces Urge War on 'Organized Terrorism.'" *Houston Post,* January 4.

Gelbspan, Ross. 1991. *Break-Ins, Death Threats, and the FBI.* Boston: South End.

Gibson, James William. 1994. *Warrior Dreams.* New York: Hill and Wang.

Goodman, Ellen. 1994. "Danger Closes In on Us." *Boston Globe,* December 31.

Gorney, Cynthia. 1998. *Articles of Faith.* New York: Simon & Schuster.

Gravois, John. 1993. "AMA-Led Coalition Seeking Protection from 'Terrorism.'" *Houston Post,* March 17.

Greenberg, Mary Lou. 1998. "The Fire This Time: When Pro-Life Means Death." *On The Issues* (Summer):24ff.

Greenhouse, Linda. 1994. "Court Rules Abortion Clinics Can Use Rackets Law to Sue." *New York Times,* January 25.

Hall, Andy. 1986. "Secret War Patriots Have Loose Ties to Rightists Nationwide." *Arizona Republic,* December 21.

Hall, Mimi. 1994. "Indictments Tie Oregon Woman to Clinic Attacks." *USA Today,* October 25.

Hall, Stuart, Chas Critcher, Tony Jefferson, John Clarke, and Brian Roberts. 1978. *Policing the Crisis: Mugging, the State, and Law and Order.* London: Macmillan.

Hamm, Mark. 1998. *Apocalypse in Oklahoma.* Boston: Northeastern University Press.

Hedges, Stephen J. 1994. "Abortion: Who's behind the violence?" *U.S. News & World Report,* November 14, pp. 50–67.

Hertz, Sue. 1991. *Caught in the Crossfire.* New York: Prentice Hall.

Hill, Paul. 1994. "Should We Defend Born and Unborn Children With Force?" http://www.webcom.com/pinknoiz/right/knowenemy.html.

Hunter, James Davison. 1994. *Before the Shooting Begins.* New York: Free Press.

James, Caryn. 1996. "Choices and No Choices in the Abortion Wars." *New York Times,* December 18.

Jasper, William F. 1995. "The Rise of Citizen Militias." *New American,* February 6, p.1

Johnson, David. 1994. "No Link Found to Connect Abortion Clinic Violence." *New York Times,* December 31, p. A9.

Johnson, Dirk. 1993. "Abortions, Bibles and Bullets." *New York Times,* August 28.

Junas, Daniel. 1995 "The Rise of Citizen Militias: Angry White Guys with Guns." *Covert Action Quarterly* (Spring).

Karten, Howard A. 1993. "A Disdain for Political Theology." *Wall Street Journal,* April 15.

Kerrison, Ray. 1994. "The Real Abortion Violence Is inside Clinics." *Human Life Review* 20(Winter):108–9.

Laqueur, Walter. 1987. *The Age of Terrorism.* Boston: Little Brown.

Lewin, Tamar. 1994. "A Cause Worth Killing For?" *New York Times,* July 30.

Livingstone, Neil C. 1990. *The Cult of Counter-Terrorism.* Lexington, MA: Lexington.

Livingstone, Neil C. and T. E. Arnold, eds. 1986. *Fighting Back.* Lexington, MA: D.C. Heath.

Manegold, Catherine S. 1995. "Anti-Abortion Groups Disavow New Killings." *New York Times,* January 1.

"Man Sentenced for Attempt to Bomb Abortion Clinic." 1998. *Los Angeles Times,* February 10.

Manuel, Marlon. 1998. "Clinic Blast Witness May Have Shared Group's Views." *Atlanta Constitution,* February 5.

Merkl, Peter, ed. 1986. *Political Violence and Terror.* Berkeley: University of California Press.

Merkl, Peter H. and Leonard Weinberg 1993. *Encounters with the Contemporary Radical Right.* Boulder, CO: Westview.

"Militia Enemy List Uncovered." 1995. Institute for First Amendment Studies. http://www.bodypolitic.org/mag/back/art/O5Oipg25.htm.

Navarro, Mireya. 1996. "Abortion Clinics Report Drop in Harassment." *New York Times,* April 4.

Naylor, Janet. 1989. "Bomber of Clinics Won't Halt Opposition." *Washington Times,* July 4.

Nice, David C. 1988. "Abortion Clinic Bombings as Political Violence." *American Journal of Political Science* 32:178–95.

O'Connell. Lorraine. 1994. "Fanatics Differ from the Rest of Us in Absoluteness of Their Thinking." *Atlanta Journal Constitution,* August 7.

Orman, Neil. 1993. "Slain Doctor's Son Accuses Abortion Foes." *Houston Chronicle,* April 2.

O'Sullivan, Noel, ed. 1986. *Terrorism, Ideology and Revolution.* Boulder, CO: Westview.

Parshall, Gerald. 1995. "Abortion: Violence Begets Violence," *U.S.News & World Report,* January 9, p. 10.

Pear, Robert. 1996. "Protests at Abortion Clinics Have Fallen, and New Law Is Credited." *New York Times,* September 24, p. A18.

Pierce, William. 1980. *The Turner Diaries,* 2nd edition. Arlington, VA: National Vanguard.

Pierce, William. 1989. *Hunter.* Hillsboro, VA: National Vanguard.

Pike, Otis. 1995. "Call Them as They Are: Anti-Abortion Terrorists." *Houston Chronicle,* January 4.

Poland, James M. 1988. *Understanding Terrorism.* Englewood Cliffs, NJ: Prentice Hall.

"'Pro-Life' Terrorism." 1993. *Progressive,* December 10.

"Pro-Life Terrorism: A How-to." 1995. *Harper's,* January, pp. 19–22.

Puga, Ana. 1994a. "'Newcomers' Preach Violence." *Boston Globe,* October 30.

Puga, Ana. 1994b. "Pressed, More Providers Halting Their Practices." *Boston Globe,* November 1.

Reeves, Jay. 1998. "1 Killed in Abortion Clinic Bombing." *Birmingham News,* January 29.

Rimer, Sara. 1993. "Abortion Foes Boot Camp Ponders Doctor's Death." *New York Times,* March 18.

Risen, James. 1994. "Shooting Suspect Has Advocated Clinic Violence." *Los Angeles Times,* July 30.

Risen, James and Judy Thomas. 1998. *Wrath of Angels.* New York: Basic Books.

Sanders, Clinton R. and Eleanor Lyon. 1995. "Repetitive Retribution." Pp. 25–44 in *Cultural Criminology,* edited by Jeff Ferrell and Clinton R. Sanders. Boston: Northeastern University Press.

Scheidler, Joseph M. 1985. *Closed: 99 Ways to Stop Abortion.* San Francisco: Ignatius.

Sharp, Deborah. 1994. "Abortion Foes Speak Up to Reject Attacks." *USA Today,* August 1.

Shea, Lois. 1995. "Clinic Killings Another Form of Terrorism." *Boston Globe,* January 8.

"Shooting of Abortion Doctor Was Terrorism, Not Just Assault." 1993. *Denver Post,* editorial, August 25.

Smith, Brent L. 1994. *Terrorism in America.* Albany: SUNY Press

Smith, Gita M. 1998. "The Face of Terror." *Atlanta Constitution,* March 3.

Solinger, Rickie, Faye Ginsburg and Patricia Anderson, eds. 1998. *Abortion Wars.* Berkeley: University of California Press.

Stern, Kenneth S. 1996. *A Force upon The Plain.* New York: Simon & Schuster.

Stoddard, Thomas B. and Kenneth P. Norwick. 1978. *Denying the Right to Choose.* New York: American Civil Liberties Union's Campaign for Choice.

Stohl, Michael, ed. 1988. *The Politics of Terrorism,* 3rd edition. New York: Dekker.

Swarr, Amanda. 1995. "Terrorism and Murder." *Off Our Backs,* May.

"Taking the Measure of Terrorism." 1995. *St. Louis Post-Dispatch,* editorial, May 14.

Teepen, Tom. 1993. "First Amendment Doesn't Protect Abortion Terrorism." *Atlanta Constitution,* March 16.

Terry, Randall. 1988. *Operation Rescue.* Springdale, PA: Whitaker House.

U.S. House of Representatives. 1987. Abortion Clinic Violence: Oversight Hearings before the Subcommittee on Civil and Constitutional Rights of the Committee on the Judiciary, House of Representatives, 99th Congress, first and second sessions, March 6, 12, April 3, 1985; and December 17, 1986. Washington, DC: GPO.

U.S. House of Representatives. 1993. Abortion Clinic Violence. Hearings before the Subcommittee on Crime and Criminal Justice of the Committee on the Judiciary, House of Representatives, 103rd Congress, first session, April 1, June 10, 1993. Washington, DC: GPO.

U.S. Senate. 1995. Violence at Women's Health Clinics. Hearing before a subcommittee of the Committee on Appropriations, U.S. Senate, 104th Congress, first session, special hearing. Washington, DC: GPO

Vetter, Harold and Gary R. Perlstein. 1991. *Perspectives on Terrorism.* Monterey, CA: Brooks-Cole/Wadsworth.

"Vigilance and Violence at Abortion Clinics." 1995. *St. Louis Post-Dispatch,* editorial, January 4.

Vrazo, Fawn. 1995. "Abortion Fight's Lethal Side." *Philadelphia Inquirer,* January 8.

Wardlaw, Grant. 1989. *Political Terrorism,* 2nd rev. edition. Cambridge: Cambridge University Press.

"When Extremism Becomes Terrorism." 1994. *Los Angeles Times,* editorial, July 30.

White, Jonathan R. 1991. *Terrorism.* Monterey, CA: Brooks-Cole/Wadsworth.

"Wichita's Long Hot Summer." 1991. *Christianity Today,* September 16, pp. 44–46.

Wicklund, Susan. 1995. "An Abortion Doctor's Diary of Terror." *Glamour* 93(4):282ff.

Wilkinson, Paul. 1986. *Terrorism and the Liberal State.* New York: New York University Press

"Woman Gets Twenty Year Sentence in Attacks on Abortion Clinics." 1995. *New York Times,* September 9.

VII

Conclusions and Prospects

16

Taking the Trouble
Concluding Remarks and Future Directions

NEIL WEBSDALE and JEFF FERRELL

INTRODUCTION

In this final chapter, we examine the key themes that emerge from the collection and take the trouble to point out future lines of fruitful inquiry suggested by contributors. Given that a number of contributors identified the social significance of discursive lacunae in the cultural construction of crime, deviance, and control, we highlight, in addition, the broad areas that *Making Trouble* fails to fully confront, explore, or develop. Our aim in doing so is not to engage in self-flagellation because we have not been exhaustive, or captured the "whole truth." Indeed, *Making Trouble* has continually argued that studies of crime, deviance, and control are historically and culturally contingent social products. As such they articulate socially situated arguments rather than incontestable master narratives. Thus *Making Trouble* is itself a cultural product, which, like other cultural products, is imbued with its own will-to-truth, its own inclusions and exclusions, and its own claims-making tactics.

Making Trouble especially highlights the manner in which various control initiatives are embedded in intersecting *microcircuits of knowledge* regarding crime, deviance, and the societal reaction to these phenomena. These intersecting microcircuits often feed each other or blend into one another. On other occasions the factual flow, contextual explanations, and epistemological resonances between circuits are impeded or blocked by what we might call *circuit breaks*. In addition, the collection demonstrates the multimediated nature of the social world and the complex articulation between knowledge and power, expressed through the language of cultural reproduction, ideological currents, and hegemonic forces. Contributors also identify a number of cultural metaphors, which among other things, provide the symbolic and linguistic connective tissue to assist with the demonization of certain groups and individuals. Other contributors identify the importance of *cultural silences*. By cultural silences we refer to the sociohistorical inattention to phenomena that appear to warrant a deviant label or, indeed, later come to attract such an attribution. We distinguish between three components of cultural silences: constructive silences, contextual silences, and factual silences. Further contributors emphasize the value of seeing social life from the perspectives, social circumstances, and biographies of social actors who engage in trouble, confront trouble, become the targets of trouble, or come to be constructed as trouble. Put differently, because trouble is made into flesh and given social meanings, it is important when exploring those meanings to resort, wherever possible, to an ethnographic appreciation of multimediated processes and those who are subject to these power-knowledge relations. Finally, contributors not only point out the mediated power of labels but they also identify the character of those power relations, tracing them to the operation of systemic axes of oppression such as capitalism, patriarchy, and racism.

As an exploratory exercise, *Making Trouble* leaves a trail of issues unaddressed, a number of acknowledged omissions, and, paradoxically, its own minefield of unintended silences and gaps. We in turn leave it to readers to discover silences of which we are not aware and silences that emerge as the discourse on mediated images of crime, deviance, and control unfolds. Among those silences or undeveloped topics of which we are aware, three are discussed here: the role of the social audience; bodies and meaning; and the historical construction of crime, deviance, and control issues.

THE MICROCIRCUITRY OF KNOWLEDGE ABOUT CRIME, DEVIANCE, AND CONTROL

One of the hallmarks of the Modern Era is the appearance of the constitutive political subject as the object of specialized bodies of knowledge. Criminals became the objects of the knowledge of penology, criminology, sociology, and psychiatry. The sovereign power of the monarch to punish, mark, mutilate, and kill has been slowly but surely replaced with what Foucault (1977) calls disciplinary power, the aim of which was to train bodies, reform them, and render them useful. Surveillance increased dramatically as new normalizing judgments emerged about what it was to be law abiding, psychologically sound, physically healthy, and sexually normal. In short, the power to manage Modern Era populations depended in large part upon the inculcation of subjectivities that were cognizant of what it was to be "normal" in everyday life and labor.

Contributors to *Making Trouble* acknowledge these numerous links between knowledge, power, and the social construction of crime, deviance, and control. For example, Manning highlights how the increasing presence of technologies like computers, cameras, and television screens have profound implications for social control. In the arenas of medicine, the workplace, and law enforcement, increased surveillance capabilities intensify the possibilities for new and tighter disciplinary mechanisms. In addition to discussing the role of film, newspapers, crime fiction, television, academic research, and computer technology, we have identified some *hitherto unrecognized media substrates*. Ferrell's analysis of freight train graffiti reminds us that part of the political subversiveness and lyricism of graffiti writing is its geocultural mobility. Like many illegal activities, graffiti writing is performed in a subterranean, some might say "furtive" manner. Under the light of day, tags and pieces surface as large as life, bumming a ride with the rhythm of the railroads. Like freight train graffiti, the communicative rhythm of police homicide files is crafted in confined subcultural space, namely that of criminal justice and particularly law enforcement subcultures. Arguing for the recognition of these files as media substrates, Websdale identifies the complex way these files circulate, inform, and blend with other fact patterns, contextualized explanations, and epistemic frameworks evident in other media substrates such as television, the press, and fictional accounts of crime. Using the term "dispersion" to describe this movement of information and ways of knowing about crime, Websdale stresses that dispersion is not a simple linear process of radiation. Rather information and epistemic frames circulate and loop back into other circuits. Websdale's point is homologous to Manning's observation that media loops continually relay information and ideas back and forth between creators and audiences, generating a swirl of knowing (Manning 1998). Thus, social actors reading police homicide files do not just engage that medium and material with an interpretive schema that sits on their shoulders. Rather, to use Ferrell's (1997) term, criminological *verstehen* develops out of a social actor's resort to and organic enmeshment in cultural matrices regarding crime, criminals, and control issues that permeate widely and inform other areas of social life simultaneously.

A number of contributors further emphasize the constructive circuitry regarding crime, deviance, and control as a means of reproducing long-established cultural matrices. For example, Meyer's chapter discusses the way traditional stories reinforce notions of right and wrong. The cultural conduit for traditional stories is the human voice and the oral history tradition. These voices are subject to the sands of time and are altered in accordance with contemporary power relations. Indeed, Meyer cites examples of how some stories are adapted to fit prevailing political climates. These traditional stories therefore capture and embody something of the core values of human interaction. Although her position echoes some of Durkheim's (1964) observations about traditional primitive societies and the manner in which a high degree of social solidarity translates into low levels of deviance, it is important to note that Durkheim well recognized the importance of value pluralism. Traditional stories may reinforce commonly shared meanings but these cultural stockpiles, with their attendant silos of symbolism, remain socially situated and culturally contested.

Blending Circuits

Just as knowledge about crime and deviance circulate in traditional or established channels, the flow of ideas and understandings is often joined by information and epistemic frameworks from other circuits. Howe illustrates the manner in which knowledge of violence against women crystallized into newspaper discourse. This discursive articulation was imbued with a sensationalism that Howe identifies as a form of "selective amnesia," in that such coverage was not new or original. In addition, the series entitled "The War Against Women" was shot through with ideas and information from mainstream patriarchal discourse that either minimized violence against women, rationalized it, or limited its political electricity by engaging in "strategies of recuperation." Likewise, Websdale's analysis of the predator discourse captures the way epistemic channels, contextual explanations, and factual material from the fields of law, psychiatry, and popular understandings of dangerous individuals coalesce in newspapers, television, and true crime outlets. In Howe's and Websdale's chapters, we see a common feature of blended circuits of media discourse, namely, accretion that is selective and strongly shaped by hegemonic forces. While Howe and Websdale identify the selective colonization and subsequent representation of knowledge regarding violence against women and children, Chesney-Lind notes how certain academics credit newspapers for "piquing" their interest in the increasing involvement of females in violent street crime. As with Howe's and Websdale's analyses, Chesney-Lind points to the failure of newspaper, television, and academic coverage to contextualize female violence against the power relations of gender. According to the press, television, and academic rubber-stampers, women are increasingly violent because they are increasingly liberated, not because they are subject to the oppressive intersecting forces of racism, patriarchy, and capitalism. In both Howe's and Chesney-Lind's analysis, mainstream media portrayals blend information back and forth between various microcircuits of knowledge. These microcircuits anastomose with dominant or preferred value systems, in turn constructing ontological and epistemological channels for making sense of trouble.

Circuit Breaks

A number of contributors also point to the disruption of knowledge-power circuits under different historical and political conditions. Webszdale's chapter on police homicide files shows how the police and prosecutorial arm of the state closes off files to the public, allowing only guarded access to a variety of media sources until after a conviction has been secured or until the case is otherwise disposed of. This closing off of information is linked to the criminal justice system's practical function of prosecuting criminals and assigning individual culpability.

In a somewhat different manner, as Jenkins shows, the failure of the government and FBI to label antiabortion violence as terrorism ensured that much of this violence remained subterranean and virtually invisible in the mass media and scholarly outlets. Here we see the flow of knowledge being impeded by a failure to construct such knowledge on the part of formal agencies of social control. Thus the FBI provided no experts or speakers to address the topic of antiabortion violence, as, for example, they had done in the case of serial killers (Jenkins 1994). Academics who rely on official definitions to delineate their projects had little or nothing on which to graze. Without the expertise discourse, the media were left without sources and statistics, and true crime writers, who usually feed off sensational crime, produced little or nothing on antiabortion violence.

KNOWLEDGE-POWER RELATIONS

A number of contributors to *Making Trouble* identify the way in which media products are continuous with various ideologies of oppression. These ideologies do not always trace a clear path back to systemic power relations regarding class, gender, race/ethnicity, and youth. Rather, contributors typically point to the complex articulation between media products and the various intersections of these power relations. This concern to highlight these various intersections is informed by a critical appreciation that ideology is not a simple matter of false consciousness, legitimation, or manipulation. Rather, contributors note the contested nature of knowledge-power relations in which social audiences perceptively consume and negotiate multimediated messages.

Leaving aside the fact that media messages are subject to various interpretations, some contributors point to the internally contradictory currents within particular media microcircuits. For example, Leblanc's analysis of the so called "punk uprisings" in Montreal in the summer of 1996 identifies the way different voices in a single media outlet can, especially with the passage of time and the use of different primary sources of information, both legitimate and criticize authorities. She convincingly shows how *La Presse*'s coverage of these disturbances at times adopted a view sympathetic to punks and at odds with the mainstream law and order discourse. Although

La Presse's earlier coverage relied upon official sources such as police, city councilors, and local store owners, later accounts constituted examples of "reporting as ethnography" and drew on punks themselves, who told a very different story. This shifting melange of interpretations reminds us that the relationship between knowledge and power, or ideology and the reproduction of social advantage, is highly complex.

In his exploration of crime genre films, Cavender investigates the manner in which films from different time periods "traffic in ideology." Just as Leblanc reminds readers that media interpretations can change during the relatively short coverage of an event, Cavender highlights the ways portrayals of hegemonic masculinity are historically contingent, reflecting as they do the gender issues of their time. The films he discusses constitute silos of symbolism for "doing masculinity." At the same time these films circulate ideologies about crime, reinforcing one of the central ethics of the detective, namely, the pursuit of criminals. In fact, the quest of the detective is a means of articulating hegemonic masculinity, thereby providing important links between ways of knowing about crime and ways of becoming a man. Cavender stresses that hegemonic masculinity is a process and as such is continuously reproduced and negotiated. This is a far cry from the notion of ideology as false consciousness, legitimation, or manipulation. Nevertheless, Cavender's analysis is steeped in the important recognition that circuits of knowledge regarding gender are saturated with power.

Two contributors especially emphasize the links between media products and race/ethnic relations. Using a case study of Geraldo Rivera's television coverage of the Oklahoma City bombing, Mohammed identifies the ways in which cultural stereotypes about generic Muslims or Middle Easterners resulted in a highly skewed analysis of this terrorist act. In this contribution the notion of ideology comes closer to concepts of false consciousness or manipulation, and is rather reminiscent of Marx's earlier work on religion as an opiate of the people (Marx and Engels 1985). For Mohammed, the skewed portrayal and analysis of this bombing are continuous with what Edward Said (1979) has called "Orientalist discourse." As such, the phenomenon of terrorism cannot be understood without first contextualizing it against the power relations of imperialism.

Murji's analysis of the construction and representation of yardies highlights the manner in which culturalist arguments have, in some quarters, replaced biological explanations of racial inferiority. Like Middle Eastern terrorists, yardies were constructed as particularly threatening groups of violent criminals who typified the extreme fringe of pathological black culture in Britain. Here the lightning rod of representation is clearly traceable to discourses on race, the nation, "alien invasion," and fears of contagion and pollution that recur in racist ideology. However, in a manner similar to Leblanc's analysis of punks, Murji also concludes by pointing out that an inquiry carried out for chief police officers in Britain admitted that previous reports demonizing yardies were greatly exaggerated. His conclusion reminds us once again that the discursive construction of threat, criminality, danger, and deviance is not monolithic in either form or substance, but complex and at times contradictory.

If contributors like Leblanc, Cavender, Mohammed, and Murji have variously dealt with issues of youth, gender, and race/ethnicity, Chesney-Lind's exploration of the media fascination with female violence references the intersection of these power relations. Drawing upon a number of different media substrates, Chesney-Lind shows how concerns about alleged increases in female violence are infused with gender, racial, and age stereotyping. Thus for Chesney-Lind, our understanding of the ideological imperatives of the various media outlets depends upon appreciating the intersection of these axes of oppression.

CULTURAL METAPHORS

Making Trouble demonstrates how crime, deviance, and control exist as socially and culturally constructed phenomena, rather than as random events in the "natural" world. The social meaning of crime and deviance does not simply arise out of the laws, norms, and values that demonize, stigmatize, taint, or otherwise label certain actions, words, or deeds vis-à-vis others. Troublesome individuals are not simply a product of a codification process that reflects, for example, the parameters of tolerance of the majority of the population in a democracy. Rather, "trouble" is constantly made and remade through the *everyday metaphors* that render some acts more heinous than others and some behaviors more worthy of social control than others. The establishment, refinement, and elaboration of these cultural boundaries bears a complex relationship to laws and norms. Cultural metaphors mediate this relationship by providing a series of signifying mechanisms to sharpen the focus on trouble; make danger into flesh; flag unacceptable defiance; demonize, stigmatize, or taint derailed individuals; and recommend gentle or draconian controls. The metaphors for making and confronting trouble are forged and realized at the very boundaries they appear to maintain. These are the boundaries between socially situated notions such as good and evil, pure and impure, right and wrong, acceptable and unacceptable, and desirable and undesirable. These boundaries have social origins traceable to the multitude and variety of groups that employ them, eulogize them, resist them, and reject them. As new "outsiders" appear, the tried and tested metaphoric devices gather like storm clouds. The metaphors may be expressed through different words, material

objects, styles of dress, and bodily markings. However, their links to systemic power relations, which are profound, and their binary logic, saturated
with essentialism, are unmistakable hallmarks.

Just as we observed networks and circuits of media products, and the
manner in which these circuits were both informed by and infused with
political energy, contributors note the way cultural metaphors congeal vividly
where power is systemically deployed. Thus race, ethnicity, class, and gender
relations are rich sites for the condensation of cultural metaphors. Chesney-
Lind shows how the media depict certain "girls in the hood" as the dispensers
of "quite graphic" violence. She notes the dramatic shots of young women with
"large tattoos on their stomachs," "youths . . . making gang signs," "young
women selling dope," while young women stand around talking about being
violent. All of this occurs against the backdrop of covered corpses apparently
killed in drive-by shootings. These and other metaphors regarding the seeming
propensity of young women, particularly young black women, for violence,
are explained, implicitly or explicitly, in terms of women's liberation. This
contextual frame of women's liberation and growing involvement in public
sphere activities clearly links the elaboration of cultural metaphors to the
power relations of gender. In particular, the "liberation" metaphor is highly
evocative, suggesting that liberation provides a license to kill.

Sometimes metaphors appear in dyads. For example, in Websdale's discussion of "predators" we see the evil of the predator juxtaposed against the
innocence of children. Here the animalistic regression takes us back to the
wild, where biological forces reign in a world of the hunter and the hunted.
In dyadic combination, metaphors assume more potency as they play off
each other in an amplifying spiral of intensity. These spirals are accompanied by, reinforced by, and hot wired into a labyrinth of other socially
situated meanings and broader belief systems. In the predator discourse the
evil of the stranger sex offender is continuous with a generalized fear of
strangers and the great unknown. Perhaps the strongest examples of these
binary bifurcations in cultural metaphors are seen in the work of Mohammed and Murji. Both talk of the way Orientalist discourse uses "race
thinking" to demarcate groups of people who are on the one hand moral (the
essentialized Westerner) and on the other exotic, decadent, and tending
toward the uncivilized and dirty. All of these metaphors (exotic, decadent,
uncivilized, and dirty) apply to a group of people who reside outside the
bounds of normal, self-restrained (Western) decency. These outliers are thus
more likely to be prone toward terrorism. As Mohammed points out, the
early discussions of the Oklahoma City bombing used language such as the
"fingerprints of the Middle East," which as Mohammed argues, implies a
strong connection between a unitary and essentialized Middle East, criminality (accessed through the fingerprints metaphor), and terrorism. As part of
the discourse on yardies, Murji identifies "invasion" metaphors that connote

a sense that Britain is being overrun by alien forces. This language parallels the metaphors used in moral panics about drugs "flooding" into Britain. Underlying these metaphors is a sense of ritual pollution and a fear of contagion that permeates other discourse on race. These invasion metaphors depict young black Jamaican males as "yardies," or individuals who stand at the intersection of a number of particularly dense socially stigmatizing forces. Here the conflation of race, crime, violence, crack use, and guns spells social danger of the most acute kind. For example, yardies allegedly exhibit aggression, sexual promiscuity, and conspicuous consumption in the form of fast cars and showy jewelry. Thus clusters of stigmatizing cultural metaphors do not congregate at random. As Murji notes, the congealed evil of the yardie is further intensified by juxtaposing it alongside something idyllic and unsullied. For example, Murji's discussion of the yardie invasion of the neat apple and peach orchards in West Virginia illustrates how metaphors of contamination emerge more powerfully when set against metaphors of idyllicism and tranquillity.

Leblanc identifies the startling juxtaposition of metaphors used to describe on the one hand vilified punks as public fauna, "noisome, bothersome beasts, pigeons without wings, squirrels without charm," and on the other, the green patches of urban cultural space that punks sought to colonize. Here we see the language of sanctified cultural space in urban areas recalling those long lost days of the rural idyll, alongside talk of the unkempt who would violate or destroy those remaining traces of better (preurban) days. As with the yardies and the neat apple and peach orchards in West Virginia, the punks were a source of ritual pollution that symbolized much more than the contamination of mere physical space. Rather the potential contamination struck at the core of an idealized set of values about the perceived virtues of (contested) cultural space.

CULTURAL SILENCES

If the threat posed by Middle Eastern terrorists has been "overconstructed," then it is equally clear from Jenkins that some forms of deviance remain "unconstructed." Unconstructed deviance leaves cultural silences about issues. Since sociologists and criminologists identify these issues as unconstructed, we might say that unconstructed deviance has certain "latent" qualities that have the potential to be worked up to the status of a social problem. Unconstructed deviance of the kind Jenkins identifies is obviously not indiscoverable. However, its social elaboration is partially contingent upon the character of the deviance, the homologies between that unconstructed deviance and other similar yet socially recognized forms of deviance, and shifting societal and epistemic power relations. As Jenkins so eloquently notes, the numerous bombings of abortion clinics shared many of the characteristics of other violent and destructive behavior labeled as "terrorism." However, these bombing campaigns were not socially defined as terrorism until after the 1992 election. The failure to construct is a potent reminder that it is not the nature of violent or deviant acts per se that ensures legal sanction or, more significantly, a place in the annals of history, but rather the social definition of those acts. As Jenkins shows, these social definitions, or lack thereof, are traceable to political processes. In the case of abortion clinic bombings, these processes include changes in the party political makeup of the polity and shifts in broader sets of power relations, particularly in the arena of gender. Thus the addition of abortion clinic bombings to the annals of terrorism reminds us that history, like trouble, is made out of the power-knowledge disputes of the present, as opposed to emerging sublime out of the ashes of an inevitable past.

In addition to "constructive silences," contributors also note other cultural silences that do not amount to a failure to construct a particular phenomenon, but nevertheless place limits on the way phenomena are presented for public consumption. A number of contributors identified "contextual silences," or astructural appreciations of seemingly discrete or episodic deviant or criminal phenomena. For example, Chesney-Lind draws attention to media discourses that fail to contextualize the violence committed by prostitutes or sex workers against the structure of patriarchy. Similarly, Websdale's analysis of the predator discourse shows how the predator law fails to frame the violence of stranger sex offenders against the power relations of gender. At still another level, Leblanc points to "factual silences" that pervade media discourses on punks. She observes, "Perhaps more interesting than what La Presse reported was what it omitted." She notes, for example, one newspaper article that documented protesters' arrests, but failed to inform readers how many of those arrested were punks.

ETHNOGRAPHIC ORIENTATIONS

The notion of cultural silences suggests the importance of not relying on either official statistics or the media coverage and embellishment of those statistics to map the locus of social problems. In the case of unconstructed terrorism, as Jenkins shows, the fact that the bombing of abortion clinics was not officially recognized as terrorism, did not mean the behavior was not seen by many social actors as terroristic. Immersing oneself in the social milieu and situated media of those one is studying, rather than relying on second- and thirdhand mediated accounts and representations of social activity, is more likely to provide the perspective needed to identify the collective and intersubjective nature of meaning and to enable researchers to identify "constructive," "contextual," and "factual silences" in media discourses regarding deviance, crime, and control. Ferrell's ethnographic work on freight train graffiti offers a case in point. He commences with the question, "How is a researcher to interrogate the meaning of an image, to avoid simply assuming or imposing a facile understanding of it, when the producer of that image remains unavailable for interrogation?" He answers with an ethnography of images that identifies freight train graffiti as having a "remarkable consistency of style across locations" and the "same shared codes of subcultural meaning" as other hip hop graffiti. This kind of ethnographic immersion, informed by Ferrell's own weltanschauung, effectively inverts and subverts more traditional mediated images of freight train graffiti, replacing them with a subcultural politics of ritualized resistance.

Several contributors point to the manner in which mediated images themselves can arise out of what we might call a "journalistic *verstehen*." Kooistra and Mahoney highlight the philosophy of James Bennett, editor of the *New York Herald,* that "an editor must always be with the people—think with them, feel with them." Likewise Leblanc, in highlighting the complex, ironic, and contradictory currents in newspaper coverage of punks, notes the way journalist Charles Grandmont, "became both an ethnographer of and apologist for the local punk scene." For Leblanc, this kind of reporting constitutes one sort of ethnography.

In recommending ethnography as a means of fleshing out situated meanings and circuits of mediated knowledge, we are not suggesting that there exists a supreme point of pure ethnographic reflection that truly captures the one essence of social action and social life. Rather, our point is that media circuits regarding crime, deviance, and control involve a continuous flux of contested epistemic frames, contextual arguments, and factual information that defy the categorical elucidation of one overarching truth, and thus invite a multiplicity of cross-checks and critiques.

PROBLEMATIZING TAKEN-FOR-GRANTED CATEGORIES

The postmodernist challenge to modernist sociology, criminology, and media studies questions the efficacy of certain taken-for-granted analytical concepts. Foucault's immense contribution not only problematized the efficacy of the constitutive political subject of the modern era; it situated that seeming efficacy amidst a plethora of regulatory mechanisms, not least of which was the claim that rational democracies were liberating for citizens

(Foucault 1977). Since the human subject became the object of an increasingly specialized and detailed body of knowledge (the human sciences), notions such as "experience," "reflection," "the self," and "agency" were called into question. True to its name, *Making Trouble* contains examples of the way taken-for-granted analytical concepts have been challenged. For example, Howe openly admits to rejecting "essentialized notions of women and men," and questions why she should even "bother with a newspaper series that takes for granted fixed gender categories?" Manning's contribution raises important questions about the sanctity of the "self." He notes that Mead (1934) theorized the self as a social construct. According to Mead, social actors behave and see themselves partially as a consequence of the way others see and react to them. Social life is not fixed but rather subject to continual negotiation and renegotiation. In articulating these observations about the shifting negotiations of everyday social life into the sociological perspective known as symbolic interactionism, Blumer notes that social actors "have the same common task of constructing their acts by interpreting and defining the acts of each other" (1969:67). However, as Manning shows, with the evolution of numerous forms of visual representation the self is endlessly displaced into a hall of mirrors that represent multimediated versions of other distant selves. The reference points for the self have changed and are increasingly mediated in ways that constitute new forms of social interaction and social control. As Manning points out, "modern reflection seems notoriously elusive, resembling more a revolving set of mirrors than a matter of perspectival representation."

If seemingly axiomatic categories like "woman and man," "self," and "reflection" are problematic for contributors, we must also note one of the key themes of the collection: the dangers of binary analytical categories, particularly in the arenas of race and gender constructions. Our sense that the binary birfurcation of analytical categories is inherently problematic is consistent with the observations of contributors that knowledge flows in microcircuits, that power permeates and is exercised in Foucauldian fashion (Foucault 1980). This recognition of power as diffuse and exercisable at multiple levels contrasts with more traditional sociological approaches, which tend to see power as a property, stressing the way in which certain individuals or groups hold power at the expense of others (see Weber 1974:180).

ISSUES YET TO BE DEVELOPED

The Social Audience

Like other social actors, the contributors to this volume are part of a social audience that produces and consumes images of crime, deviance, and control. However, mapping the manner in which the social audience consumes, processes, and reproduces such images and meanings remains difficult. *Making Trouble* does not significantly add to our understanding of the relationship between the manufacture of microcircuits of knowledge about crime, deviance, and control, and the consumptive/interpretive understandings generated by social audiences. What contributors *have* made clear is that there is no easy separation between media messages regarding crime, deviance, and control and the interpretive activities of the social audience. As Kooistra and Mahoney note, Joseph Pulitzer's newspaper (*New York World*) was strongly influenced in both physical style and linguistic content by the characteristics of the readership. Howe points to another set of assumptions that cloud the boundaries between media source and social audience. Borrowing from Hall, Critcher, Jefferson, Clarke, and Roberts's (1978) language, she points out how reporters assume they are "taking the public voice." However, this voice is not the voice of just any audience. Rather, the assumed audience and the newspaper discourse are both keyed into the imperatives of "masculinist criminological positivism." In a similar manner, Websdale's study of the use of police homicide files reveals the continuities between the epistemological gestalt of the files, criminal justice ideologies, and socially preferred or dominant understandings of crime and justice. What permeates all these circuits is the notion that crime is caused by pathological individuals rather than enduring social conditions. However, without directly asking and participating with people in regard to their perceptions of what they see, hear, read, and process, we are at a distinct disadvantage in developing a finely nuanced understanding of their intersubjective systems of meaning regarding crime.

Bodies and Meaning

We noted earlier that one of the hallmarks of the Modern Era involved a shift away from punishing, brutalizing, mutilating, and destroying the body, toward rendering the body more docile and useful (Foucault 1977). These observations mean that the body remains a profoundly important substrate for the inscription of socially situated meanings regarding crime, deviance, and control. A number of contributors allude to this profound importance. For example, Leblanc recognizes the manner in which the styles of punks convey certain meanings. Murji alludes to the ways in which the demeanor of yardies is colonized by others as a means of status enhancement, including the emulation of Jamaican accents by Nigerian and Ghanian drug dealers. Websdale elucidates the manner in which the body and its injuries and various markings become the site of a rich tapestry of postmortem meanings, themselves linked to the epistemological gestalt of homicide files.

Similarly the body is often a repository of injuries and mutilations that themselves provide rich epistemic frameworks for the elaboration of marginalized meaning. Thus contributors to *Making Trouble* suggest that further exploration into the relationship between bodies and the social meanings of crime, deviance, and control is required.

Cultural Criminology, Society, and History

In the introductory chapter, we pointed out that cultural criminology investigates the numerous links between contemporary cultural life and crime. This observation does not mean that cultural criminology ignores the role of societal factors in the construction of deviance, crime, and control. Indeed, it is clear from the work of contributors that exploring the multimediated representation of crime, deviance, and control necessitates constant reference to the inextricable links between culture and society. Similarly, the emphasis on contemporary cultural issues does not mean that cultural criminology is closed to a more historically informed analysis of crime, culture, and society. Indeed, some of the works often cited as examples of cultural criminology draw part of their power from their resort to history. Hall et al.'s (1978) analysis of the panic regarding mugging in 1972 in England debunked the argument that mugging constituted a new form of terror by pointing out that similar kinds of crimes (e.g., garroting) had been common in London and Manchester in 1862–1863.

Other works on the history of crime weave an elaborate cultural embroidery regarding the relationship between crime, culture, and society, producing insightful analyses of social control mechanisms (Hay, Linebaugh, Rule, Thompson, and Winslow 1975; Hobsbawm 1965; Hobsbawm and Rude 1985; Pearson 1983; Rude 1964; Thompson 1975). Thompson's (1975) beautiful exploration of the origins of the draconian Black Act of 1723 examines newly created offenses for activities such as hunting, wounding, or stealing red or fallow deer, and poaching hares or fish. If offenders committed these deeds while in disguise the crime was punishable by death. After the passage of the Black Act the number of capital offenses enlarged to include killing or maiming cattle, cutting down certain trees, setting fire to houses or haystacks, maliciously shooting at people, or sending anonymous letters demanding money or venison. Thompson contextualizes this growing number of capital offenses against shifting historical conditions, including the loss of traditional rights to land, the rise of new economic activities, and the articulation of popular cultural discontent. These criminal activities of men with blacked-out faces thus became part of a broad form of cultural protest and renegotiation. Thompson identifies the rule of law at the center of a nexus of cultural shifts. He notes:

The rhetoric and rules of a society are something a great deal more than sham. In the same moment they may modify, in profound ways, the behavior of the powerful, and mystify the powerless. They may disguise the true realities of power, but, at the same time, they may curb that power and check its intrusions. And it is often from within that very rhetoric that a radical critique of the practice of the society is developed. (1975:265)

Work such as Thompson's cultural history of crime sheds important light on social control processes akin to those in contemporary culture. We might well draw parallels between Thompson's appreciation of the complex rule of law and contributors' work regarding the relationship between media and crime. For example, Leblanc's point that *La Presse* adopted contradictory positions on punks challenges notions of a monolithic authoritarian media voice that simply reproduces the status quo. These kinds of parallels are to be expected if, as we argued earlier, the history of crime is not merely produced by bygone events, but is rather constructed by the knowledge-power machinations of the present. Indeed, cultural criminology incorporates this kind of rich historical analysis as part of its own intellectual heritage. The British cultural Marxist tradition, of which E. P. Thompson's work (1975) is but one example, shares similar theoretical influences to those in Hall et al.'s (1978) analysis of mugging. Both draw upon Gramscian themes that celebrate culture as a contested historical terrain and crime as a problematic rather than taken-for-granted phenomenon. In documenting the many contested and intersecting circuits of contemporary meaning regarding crime, deviance, and control, *Making Trouble* acknowledges the importance of social and cultural history, as documented in the work of Thompson (1975) and others. As the contributions by Meyer, Kooistra and Mahoney, Cavender and others remind us, the complex dynamics of making trouble always exist before and beyond the immediacy of the moment.

REFERENCES

Blumer, H. 1969. *Symbolic Interactionism.* Englewood Cliffs, NJ: Prentice Hall.

Durkheim, E. 1964. *The Division of Labor in Society.* New York: Free Press.

Ferrell, Jeff. 1997. "Criminological Verstehen: Inside the Immediacy of Crime." *Justice Quarterly* 14:3–23.

Foucault, M. 1977. *Discipline and Punish: The Birth of the Prison.* London: Tavistock.

Foucault, M. 1980. *Power/Knowledge: Selected Interviews and Other Writings, 1972–77.* Edited by C. Gordon. New York: Pantheon.

Hall, Stuart, Chas Critcher, Tony Jefferson, John Clarke, and Brian Roberts. 1978. *Policing the Crisis: Mugging, the State, and Law and Order.* London: MacMillan.

Hay, Douglas, Peter Linebaugh, John G. Rule, E. P. Thompson, and Cal Winslow. 1975. *Albion's Fatal Tree: Crime and Society in Eighteenth-Century England.* New York: Pantheon.

Hobsbawm, Eric J. 1965. *Primitive Rebels: Studies in Archaic Forms of Social Movement in the 19th and 20th Centuries.* New York: Norton.

Hobsbawm, Eric J. and George Rude. 1985. *Captain Swing.* Harmondsworth: Penguin.

Jenkins, Philip. 1994. *Using Murder: The Social Construction of Serial Homicide.* Hawthorne, NY: Aldine de Gruyter.

Manning, Peter. 1998. "Media Loops." Pp. 25–39 in *Popular Culture, Crime and Justice,* edited by Donna Hale and Frankie Bailey. Belmont, CA: West/ Wadsworth.

Marx, Karl and Frederick Engels. 1985. "On Religion." Reprinted in *Religion and Ideology,* edited by R. Bocock and K. Thompson. England: Penguin, Harmondsworth.

Mead, G. H. 1934. *Mind, Self and Society.* Chicago: University of Chicago Press.

Pearson, Geoffrey. 1983. *Hooligan: A History of Respectable Fears.* London: MacMillan.

Rude, George. 1964. *The Crowd in History.* New York: Wiley.

Said, Edward W. 1979. *Orientalism.* New York: Vintage.

Thompson, E. P. 1975. *Whigs and Hunters.* Manchester: Manchester University Press.

Weber, M. 1974. *From Max Weber: Essays in Sociology.* Edited by H. H. Gerth and C. Wright Mills. London and Boston: Routledge & Kegan Paul.

Biographical Sketches of the Contributors

Gray Cavender is a Professor in the School of Justice Studies, Arizona State University. His teaching and research interests include media and crime. He is the author of *Parole: A Critical Analysis* (Kennikat Press, 1982) and coauthor of *Corporate Crime under Attack: The Ford Pinto Case and Beyond* (Anderson, 1987). He is coeditor (with Mark Fishman) of a book on reality crime television, *Entertaining Crime* (Aldine de Gruyter, 1998).

Meda Chesney-Lind, Ph.D., is Professor of Women's Studies at the University of Hawaii at Manoa. She has served as vice president of the American Society of Criminology and president of the Western Society of Criminology. Nationally recognized for her work on women and crime, her books include *Girls, Delinquency and Juvenile Justice* 2nd edition (West/Wadsworth, 1998), which was awarded the American Society of Criminology's Michael J. Hindelang Award for the Outstanding Contribution to Criminology, 1992; and *The Female Offender: Girls, Women and Crime* (Sage, 1998). She is currently at work on an edited collection entitled *Girls and Gangs in America* to be published by Lakeview Press. She was named a fellow of the American Society of Criminology in 1996, and has also received the Donald Cressey Award from the National Council on Crime and Delinquency; the Paul Tappan Award for outstanding contributions to the field of criminology, from the Western Society and Criminology; and the University of Hawaii Board of Regent's Medal for Excellence in Research.

Ceres U. Duskin is a doctoral student in Clinical Psychology at the California Institute of Integral Studies in San Francisco. She received a B.A. in sociology in 1994 at the University of California at Santa Cruz, where she was a teaching assistant for the Sociology of Law. She also studied at the University of Glasgow, Scotland, where she worked in the city-funded Intermediate Treatment Unit for at-risk youth. Prior to enrolling in graduate school she worked for two years with severely emotionally disturbed adolescents at True to Life Children's Services, a group home in Sebastopol, California.

Jeff Ferrell is Professor of Criminal Justice at Northern Arizona University. He is the author of *Crimes of Style: Urban Graffiti and the Politics of*

Criminality (Garland, 1993; Northeastern University Press, 1996); editor, with Clinton R. Sanders, of *Cultural Criminology* (Northeastern University Press, 1995), the finalist for the American Society of Criminology's 1996 Michael J. Hindelang Award for Most Outstanding Contribution to Criminology; and editor, with Mark S. Hamm, of *Ethnography at the Edge: Crime, Deviance, and Field Research* (Northeastern University Press, 1998). He is the recipient of the 1998 Critical Criminologist of the Year Award, presented by the Critical Criminology Division of the American Society of Criminology.

Adrian Howe is Senior Lecturer in Law and Legal Studies at La Trobe University, Australia. She has published widely in the fields of criminology, feminist legal theory, feminist politics, and history. Her book *Punish and Critique: Towards a Feminist Analysis of Penalty* (Routledge, 1994) was published in the Carol Smart and Maureen Cain Sociology of Law Series in the United Kingdom. She also edited the book *Sexed Crime in the News* (Federation Press, Sydney, 1998). Ongoing research interests center around poststructuralist approaches to law and crime.

Philip Jenkins is Distinguished Professor of History and Religious Studies at Penn State University. His recent publications include *Pedophiles and Priests: Anatomy of a Social Crisis* (Oxford University Press, 1996); *Hoods and Shirts: The Extreme Right in Pennsylvania c. 1925–1950* (University of North Carolina Press, 1997); and *Moral Panic: Changing Concepts of the Child Molester in Modern America* (Yale University Press, 1998).

Paul Kooistra is Associate Professor of Sociology at Furman University. He has published articles in the areas of criminology, the sociology of sports, and media. He is the author of *Criminals as Heroes* (Bowling Green State University Press, 1989), which examines how organizational needs of media and politicians shape images of criminality. He is currently researching how local news present images of race and crime.

Lauraine Leblanc received her Ph.D. in Women's Studies from Emory University in 1997. She is the author of *Pretty in Punk: Girls' Gender Resistance in a Boys' Subculture* (Rutgers University Press, forthcoming). She currently lives in Montréal with her dog, Lucky 7. Lauraine Leblanc can be reached via e-mail at spikeyrat@juno.com.

John S. Mahoney, Jr. is a Professor of Sociology at Virginia Commonwealth University. His areas of interest are collective behavior, media, minorities, and work organizations. He currently directs an off-campus education program for a major U.S. corporation.

Peter Manning is a Professor in the School of Criminal Justice at Michigan State University.

Jon'a Meyer is an Assistant Professor of Criminal Justice in the Department of Sociology at Rutgers University, Camden. She received her Ph.D. in Social Ecology at the University of California-Irvine. She has published on many aspects of criminal justice, including sentencing, criminal courts, Native American legal systems, prison industry and reform, community-oriented policing, and computer crime. She is the coauthor of *Doing Justice in the People's Court: Sentencing by Municipal Court Judges* (State University of New York Press, 1997) and the author of *Inaccuracies in Children's Testimony: Memory Suggestibility or Obedience to Authority?* (Haworth Press, 1997).

Fida Mohammad was born and raised in the North West Frontier Province of Pakistan. He is an Assistant Professor of Sociology at Eastern New Mexico University. His research interests include torture and human rights; death as an aesthetic experience; and comparative criminal justice. Among other courses he teaches introductory criminal justice, juvenile delinquency, criminological theory, and interrogation.

Karim Murji is Senior Lecturer in Sociology and Social Policy at Roehampton Institute, London. He received his Ph.D. from the University of Surrey. He is the author of *Policing Drugs* (Ashgate, 1998) and coauthor of *Traffickers: Drug Markets and Law Enforcement* (Routledge, 1992) and *Drug Prevention* (ISDD, 1992). Articles include works on policing and racial attacks, closed-circuit television and crime prevention, managerialism and organizational reform of the police, drugs, media and moral panics, and police narratives. Recent publications appear in the journal *Policing and Society* as well as the edited books *Policing Futures* (Macmillan, 1997), *The Control of Drugs and Drug Users* (Harwood, 1998), and *Drugs: Controls, Cultures and Everyday Life* (Sage, 1998). He is a member of the editorial board of *Critical Social Policy*.

Craig Reinarman is Professor of Sociology and Adjunct Faculty in Legal Studies at the University of California, Santa Cruz. He has served on the board of directors of the College on Problems of Drug Dependence and as a consultant to the World Health Organization's Programme on Substance Abuse. Dr. Reinarman is the author of *American States of Mind* (Yale University Press, 1987), coauthor of *Cocaine Changes* (Temple University Press, 1991), and coauthor of *Crack In America: Demon Drugs and Social Justice* (University of California Press, 1997). He has published numerous articles on drug use, law, and policy in such journals as *Theory and Society, The*

British Journal of Addiction, The International Journal of Drug Policy, Addiction Research, and *Contemporary Drug Problems.*

Neil Websdale received his Ph.D. from the University of London in 1991 and is currently Associate Professor of Criminal Justice at Northern Arizona University in Flagstaff. He has published work on the history of policing, violence against women, the state response to domestic violence, and the media portrayal of intimate partner and stranger violence. He has completed two books: *Rural Woman Battering and the Justice System: An Ethnography* (Sage, 1998), which won the Academy of Criminal Justice Sciences Outstanding Book Award for 1999 and *Understanding Domestic Homicide* (Northeastern University Press, 1999). He is currently working on a book manuscript concerning the killing of children in families, due to be published by Northeastern University Press in 2000.

Index